MW01194720

American Heretics

American Heretics

Religious Adversaries of Liberal Order

Jerome E. Copulsky

Yale

UNIVERSITY PRESS

NEW HAVEN AND LONDON

Yale University Press books may be purchased in quantity
for educational, business, or promotional use. For information, please
email sales.press@yale.edu (U.S. office) or
sales@yaleup.co.uk (U.K. office).

Set in PS Fournier Std Petit type by IDS Infotech, Ltd.
Printed in the United States of America.

Library of Congress Control Number: 2024932003
ISBN 978-0-300-24130-3 (hardcover : alk. paper)

A catalogue record for this book is available from the British Library.

This paper meets the requirements of ANSI/NISO Z39.48-1992
(Permanence of Paper).

10 9 8 7 6 5 4 3 2 1

In loving memory of my father
Dr. Robert H. Copulsky

À côté de chaque religion se trouve une opinion politique qui, par affinité, lui est jointe.

Laissez l'esprit humain suivre sa tendance, et il réglera d'une manière uniforme la société politique et la cité divine; il cherchera, si j'ose le dire, à *harmoniser* la terre avec le ciel.

(Alongside each religion is found a political opinion that is joined to it by affinity.

Allow the human spirit to follow its tendency, and it will regulate in a uniform way political society and the divine city; it will seek, if I dare say so, to *harmonize* earth with heaven.)

Alexis de Tocqueville, *De la Démocratie en Amérique*

Contents

Introduction

"When I arrived in the United States, it was the religious aspect of the country that first struck my eyes," recounted Alexis de Tocqueville in *Democracy in America*, his celebrated analysis of the political institutions of the United States and the ethos of its people. "As I prolonged my journey, I noticed the great political consequences that flowed from these new facts." Having spent nine months touring the young republic, studying its political institutions, and conversing with its citizens, Tocqueville came to perceive a happy compatibility, indeed synergy, between American Christianity and the political values and institutions of the young nation. Whereas in his native France "the spirit of religion and the spirit of liberty march almost always in opposite directions," in 1830s America the young nobleman found them to be "intimately joined the one to the other: They reigned together over the same soil."[1]

Christianity, Tocqueville believed, had made all people equal before God; democracy would make them so in society. From the time of the first English settlements in North America, "politics and religion found themselves in accord, and they have not ceased to be so since." The Puritans brought and planted their "democratic and republican" Christianity in New England; later, Catholic immigrants from Ireland came to "form the most republican and most democratic class that exists in the United States." Surveying the scene, the French commentator concluded that "you can say that in the United States not a single religious doctrine shows itself hostile to democratic and republican institutions."[2]

Indeed, Tocqueville powerfully argued that the American churches played a vital role in the maintenance of democratic society and its social and political institutions. They did so by helping shape and cultivate the people's mores, those habits of the heart that are crucial for social cohesion, teaching them "the art of being free." While he did not deny the manifold differences in styles of worship that prevailed among America's churches, Tocqueville found that such diversity did not pose a threat to the republic. The nation's many sects "all agree on the duties of men toward one and other" and "preach the same morality in the name of God." All agreed on the social utility of religion: religion served to mitigate the pernicious tendencies toward individualism, atomization, and materialism; turned minds from the desire for and enjoyment of worldly goods to obligations to others; and regulated individuals' taste for well-being, curbed their ambitions, and provided hope to endure the challenges of this life. He went so far as to suggest that it was less important for society that all its citizens profess the "true religion" than that "they profess a religion." Americans universally "believe it necessary for maintaining republican institutions," Tocqueville noted, so much so that religion ought well to be regarded as "the first of their political institutions."[3]

This was so even as the churches existed apart from the institutions of government. Tocqueville recounted that the clergymen of various faiths he consulted during his travels "all attributed the peaceful dominion that religion exercises in their country principally to the complete separation of Church and State." They kept aloof from politics and party intrigues, neither running for office nor accepting public appointments. In part, Tocqueville suggested American ministers were, in the main, simply following the teachings of Christianity. ("The Gospel," he wrote, "speaks only of the general relationships of men with God and with each other. Beyond that, it teaches nothing and requires no belief in anything.") The refusal of the churches to ally with the transient authorities or get bound up with the give-and-take and ambitions and rivalries of political life, he believed, served to enhance the reputation of their ministers and the vitality and durability of religion in American society. This was a lesson for those in Europe, where the ongoing conflict between the forces of religion and the forces of democracy was the unfortunate but understandable consequence of the long history of "Christianity allow[ing] itself to be intimately united with the powers of the earth." As those powers were crumbling, the churches were in danger of becoming buried beneath the wreckage.[4]

Tocqueville no doubt overstated his case, oversimplifying the relationship between religion and government and overestimating the moral consensus in the young nation. But he noticed something true and profound about the relationship of religion and the American political project. Many Americans had

come to believe that there was some deep correspondence between their religion and the nation's growing democracy. The Old World entanglements of
church and state had been left behind; the religious pluralism of the nation was
secured by a regime of religious liberty. In short, in the young republic, many
Americans (or, more precisely, many white Americans) shared the principles of
liberty and equality and the conviction that legitimate political power originated with the people. And they also saw the benefits of the constitutional
arrangement of the separation of church and state. Since then, many have
agreed with Tocqueville's assessment that there has been an "intimate union" of
Christianity and American political ideals, if not institutions of government.

But not all have.

Such confidence in the complementarity of the Christian religion and the
American political project has never been universal. From the outset, the American project was contested by religious voices who believed that democratic
values were not an expression of Christian teaching but were rather false and
dangerous; that religion should not be separated from the state but ought to
guide political life; and that the protection, indeed celebration, of religious
liberty was a violation of divine dictates. They accordingly sought to re-form
and re-found the nation so that its institutions would conform to divine
wisdom, to bring into being a harmonious and well-ordered state. They believed
in the intimate union of politics and religion. And they demonstrated that
America hadn't solved the church-state problem.

Given such deviations from the nation's founding principles, religious
pluralism, and church-state settlement, we might well think of these men as
theological-political adversaries of the American order. American heretics, if
you will.

Heresy, to appeal to the authority of the *Oxford English Dictionary*, may be
defined as "theological or religious opinion or doctrine maintained in opposition, or held to be contrary, to the 'catholic' or orthodox doctrine of the Christian Church, or, by extension, to that of any church, creed, or religious system,
considered as orthodox"; and, by extension, "opinion or doctrine in philosophy,
politics, science, art, etc., at variance with those generally accepted as authoritative." The concept of heresy is, of course, relational—it is a term deployed by
a group to mark out its boundaries, define its foes, and police deviance within
its ranks. Simply put, "heretics" are those who hold beliefs that the "orthodox"
in power consider false or in error. (As John Locke, in one of the foundational

documents of liberalism, gamely observed, "Every Church is Orthodox to it self; to others Erroneous or Heretical.")[5]

Here we are concerned with America's theological-political "heretics." I use the term loosely and a bit playfully, against a background of religious pluralism and liberty, but also with serious intent—as a way of registering the fundamentally religious nature of their dissents and highlighting the irony that they did so while claiming to be upholding Christian orthodoxy. While most American Christians have regarded the Founding to be compatible with their religious beliefs and practices (and, indeed, celebrate the "American creed" as articulated in its founding documents), these heretics considered it from their theological perspectives and found it deeply flawed, even faithless.

Those beholden to a vision of cosmic order and the social hierarchy it legitimated were hostile to the modern principles of liberty and equality that they feared would sow confusion and chaos. They rejected the "self-evident" truths of natural equality and unalienable rights and the political theory that emerged from them (namely that legitimate government was established by social contract, based on and maintained by the consent of the governed to preserve those rights). Such claims, they believed, were rather based on false-hoods about human nature and the origin and purpose of government.

Others bewailed the failure of the Constitution to acknowledge the Deity and provide a theological sanction for the new order. They looked upon the nation's congenital and ever-increasing religious diversity as regrettable—a source of instability, dissension, and disorder. By excluding a religious test for federal office, the Constitution made it possible for atheists and infidels to govern, and by prohibiting Congress from making laws establishing a national church or interfering with free exercise of religion, it safeguarded and even encouraged religious pluralism (that is to say, the propagation of infidelity). The Constitution's separation of politics from religion undermined the place of religion within the commonwealth.

Others disdained the country's ethic of individualism and the disregard for traditional order and the social leveling and moral loosening it was bringing into effect. The seemingly inexorable advance of democracy in America was not the plan of Providence but the consequence of the arrogant rebellion of sinful human beings.

Think of this book as a heresiography ("a description of, or treatise on, heresy or heresies"—again, sayeth the *OED*). Each chapter closely explores a particular episode of American "heresy," providing an intellectual portrait of the thinkers who propounded it, their critique of the American political order (as they understood it), and their account of the regime that ought to be constructed in its stead.

These thinkers were engaged in the practice of what is known as "political theology." Theological ideas—about God, creation and the world, and the nature and destiny of human beings—shaped the way in which the origin, purpose, and legitimacy of the political community was to be understood. To be sure, such visions also reflected the all-too-human interests, privileges, and prejudices of their envisioners, who desired to uphold their power or to attain it in the first place. Most were clergymen; others were laypeople—journalists, scholars, and activists. Their objections to American liberalism, democracy, pluralism, secularism, or some combination thereof were preached in sermons and delivered at conferences and published in pamphlets, periodicals, and dense scholarly tomes. These theological-political dissenters ought not to be simply dismissed as marginal, oddball malcontents. Some may have been lonely prophets, but others occupied positions of considerable prestige and power. They all were deeply learned. In their writings, they tapped into deep wells of thought from their respective theological traditions—Anglican, Reformed, and Roman Catholic; their work reflects the tensions and conflicts within those traditions themselves on the problem of politics and how the American order was to be understood and engaged.

Those theological commitments yielded different accounts of the origins of the nation's theological-political error. Some inveighed against the "false principles" of the Declaration of Independence or against a Constitution that failed to acknowledge divine authority over the nation. Others discovered the roots of the problem earlier—in the Enlightenment's break from traditional authority, or in the Reformation's revolt against the Roman Catholic Church and the subsequent fracturing of Europe's religious unity, or in the anthropological turn of Renaissance humanism, or in the nominalists' break with scholasticism. They differed, too, in what they envisioned the proper theological-political order to be, and how the United States might yet be transformed into it. Anglican Loyalists hoped to maintain and expand the established church; Reformed Presbyterians prayed and eventually lobbied for a constitutional amendment that would acknowledge the nation's dependence on God and transform the United States into an explicitly Christian republic; Southern proslavery theologians called for secession from the Union to preserve and expand an aristocratic republicanism premised on the natural inequality of the races; Catholic traditionalists looked back to the confessional state advocated by the nineteenth-century papacy; Christian Reconstructionists looked further back to the ancient Israelite commonwealth as a model for a future theocratic republic; and contemporary postliberals anticipate the reassertion of religious traditionalism or nationalism to rescue a nation from the seductions of so-called cultural Marxism and the demands of the "woke" and replace a decadent and decaying liberal democratic regime.

For all, religion was a concern of the state and politics was fundamentally theological; the only legitimate government would be one that acknowledged the true faith, was governed by the righteous, protected the church, cultivated morality, and directed its subjects to their common—and the highest—good.

That there are so many ways to imagine a Christian commonwealth illuminates the ambiguity and paradoxes of the Christian revelation regarding the origin, nature, and purpose of the this-worldly political community, together with its responsibilities to the church and the church's responsibilities to it. What did this new covenant established by the advent, crucifixion, and resurrection of Christ—this inbreaking of the kingdom of God, a universal communion that transcended the human loyalties of family, tribe, and nation—entail for life here and now in this world prior to its fulfillment?

Many answers have been proposed. Christianity could seem to counsel a disinterest in this-worldly governance: Did not Jesus himself proclaim that his kingdom was not of this world and that one ought to render to Caesar what is Caesar's and to God what is God's? Did not the apostle Paul preach submission to existing authorities? It was no doubt prudent for members of a small, despised sect in the Roman Empire to wait patiently and peacefully for the eschaton they believed imminent. But then a Christian empire itself came to be, and Christian thinkers had to contend with the realities, complexities, and paradoxes of Christian power, and the tensions and conflicts between the spiritual and the political realms, between the church and the state.

And so, over the ensuing centuries, Christian thinkers theorized the relationship of the "city of God" to the "city of man," described the responsibilities of the two swords of spiritual power and temporal power, and mapped out the jurisdictions of church and state. They demanded obedience to magistrates and inspired rebellion against earthly tyrants, and preached liberty and equality and hierarchy and servitude. Some argued that civil government was necessary to restrain evil; others that the sinfulness of human beings meant that the civil power they might abusively wield needed to be held in check. Reformers inspired their followers to construct biblical commonwealths on the model of ancient Israel. Radical proponents of religious liberty vowed to build walls of separation to protect the garden of religion from the wilderness of temporal power. Messianic enthusiasts endeavored to hasten the coming of the millennium through revolutionary action or encouraged their followers to shun a world so corrupted by sin and patiently (or impatiently) await Christ's triumphant return. For some, to be a Christian in this world means always to be a pilgrim sojourning in a strange land. The church is a counter-society; there can be no truly Christian commonwealth. For others, to be a Christian requires incarnating the faith in the political order, restructuring all human institutions according to revealed truth, working to establish the kingdom of God in the here and now.

The various views on the relationship of church and state expounded in this book were all quite at odds with the common attitude expressed by the clergymen Alexis de Tocqueville conversed with during his journey. Our consideration of theological-political dissent against America is necessarily selective; given the nation's variegated religious landscape, one could well travel in a number of directions. In planning this expedition, I've opted for depth over breadth, limiting our visits to those operating within the Christian tradition and focused on challenging the very foundations of the American political order. We will bypass, then, those many religious communities (such as the Old Order Amish or ultra-Orthodox Jews) that have been determined to preserve their traditional ways or to pursue utopian experiments in separatist enclaves, as well as millenarian sects (such as the Jehovah's Witnesses) who have inveighed against the United States as a new Babylon or Rome while expecting the imminent advent of a radically new order that would sweep away the very problems that politics attempts to manage. These separatists struggled to maintain the purity of their ways of life from the various and sundry pressures and temptations of America, from time to time appealing to the religious-liberty protections of the Constitution to do so or to ward off government encroachment. Though they tried to keep their distance from the United States in space and time, they nevertheless settled and sojourned within its liberal frame.[6]

The American heretics and heresies explored in this book complicate the way in which the debate regarding the relationship of religion and politics is usually conducted in the United States. Those engaged in these more familiar debates tend to find themselves arrayed in two broad camps—those who believe that American democracy requires more religion in public life and those who want there to be less. Each camp has its view of the role of religion in public life, defends it as the traditional American one, and furnishes a creation myth about the Founding and the Founders to support its position. Those in the first camp—we can call them religionists—contend that Christianity influenced the political ideas and institutions of republican government and should continue to be acknowledged and promoted in the public square and inform policy and governance. Some argue that the Founders were Christian or had been shaped by Christianity, that in their work they had drawn deeply from the Protestant (or Christian or Judeo-Christian) tradition and devised a government that, while not establishing a national church, nevertheless assumed a Christian people and a commonly shared Christian morality. Others assert that Protestant (in particular, Calvinist) theology was a key, if not explicitly acknowledged, source of American constitutional values and architecture. (A Roman Catholic flank submits the case that American constitutionalism emerged from the medieval natural law tradition.) And a fringe within those ranks goes so far as to proclaim that the nation was founded as a Christian republic (theologizing the founding documents to make them seem more amenable to the cause and baptizing the Founders as pious believers), a nation chosen by God, a new Israel, guided by the steady hand of Providence.[7]

If the United States was indeed established as a Christian nation, then the Supreme Court's mid-twentieth-century decisions on the separation of church and state were a betrayal of the national inheritance and a departure from long-standing practices, inaugurating a time of cultural decadence, moral decline, and social disorder. A reaffirmation of the nation's biblical heritage, a restoration of the Founders' original vision and constitutional plan, would help heal the nation of its ills, vanquish its domestic enemies, and make America righteous again.

Those in the second camp—let's call them separationists—maintain that the realms of government and religion ought to be kept distinct. They, too, call upon the authority of the Founders. The signatories of the Declaration of Independence invoked "Nature's God" and the "Creator," appealed to the "Supreme Judge of the world," and proclaimed their "firm reliance on the protection of divine Providence," language that could encourage orthodox Christians but which came out of the lexicon of rationalist deists, and the document's argument for the colonies' right to dissolve political ties with Great Britain and institute new government rested on Enlightenment notions of natural rights and the social contract that provided the basis for legitimate government. In their view, the delegates at Philadelphia set out to establish a secular state (even if it had been only imperfectly realized until the middle of the twentieth century). They came up with a "godless" Constitution; the government it created was an entirely human and this-worldly affair. In their *novus ordo seclorum*, there was to be no "established" church nor appeals to the Creator and his providential order (even if they generally believed that Providence had favored their undertakings). The Framers had wisely erected a wall between church and state, protecting the institutions of civil government and the citizens' sacred rights of conscience from fanatical or unscrupulous ecclesiastics. Federal officers were unhampered by religious tests, and the nation's many churches unfettered by government oversight, influence, and money. Americans would be free to believe in and worship God as they see fit, but not to impose their beliefs and practices on others using the mechanisms of the state. American democracy would depend on maintaining this distinction. One might say that the Constitution envisioned a federal government that was neutral, though not hostile, with respect to religion and that would govern a religious—and religiously diverse—people. The Supreme Court's church-state jurisprudence endorsing legal secularism was a deeper realization, not a betrayal, of the ideals and values of the Founding.[8]

These disagreements are at the bottom of ongoing controversaries over such issues as prayer and Bible reading in public schools, public funding for religious institutions, and religious symbols on public property, and they shape concerns and disputes over commercial activities, immigration, foreign policy, marriage, reproductive freedom, and what it means to be a citizen.

It's worth noting, however, that there are some significant grounds of agreement among both parties. Both read the same founding documents, and each invokes the statements of the Founders themselves to determine what kind of state the United States was meant to be or ought to become. They appeal to the Declaration of Independence as a statement of fundamental political values and to the Constitution as the charter of government. They generally agree that constitutional democracy is a legitimate, even favored form of government and that the Framers of the Constitution were correct both in declining to establish a national church and in guaranteeing the religious liberty of the nation's citizens (even if they have very different understandings about what the Establishment Clause really prohibits and what religious liberty actually entails). The Founding was perhaps not perfect, but on the whole it was very good. They would agree the Founders did not intend to establish a "theocracy" in America. Some of the religionists might regard the Puritans of New England as the nation's forefathers, but they don't tend to look back to the holy commonwealths of the seventeenth century as models for contemporary government. And of those who believe that the Founders set out to erect a secular state, only the most militant dream of eradicating all religious expression from the public sphere. To be sure, there are advocates of a Christian America who try to smuggle in elements of Christian supremacy (by saying that religious liberty protected by the First Amendment pertained only to Protestants, for example), but the very fact that they appeal to the constitutional order demonstrates that they find it necessary to argue within its terms. And we might also say that when we go beyond the quarrel about the church-state relationship, there is a broad, if perhaps not terribly deep, agreement on the fundamentals of the American order and the procedures of liberal democracy. In short, the quarrel is over how we understand the Founding, not about the legitimacy of the Founding itself.[9]

The thinkers discussed in the pages that follow comprise another broad camp in the debate over religion and politics in America. They concurred with the believers in a Christian nation that America ought to be so and with the secularists that it was not. Despite their manifold differences in theology, interpretation of Scripture, diagnosis of the nation's ills, and proscriptions for the future, they were all engaged in a deep critique of American liberalism, democracy, pluralism, and secularism. They challenged, in some manner or other, the very foundations of the American project and its church-state settlement. In doing so, they demonstrated that the fundamental theological-political questions that Tocqueville believed Americans had solved or cast off still endured. They endure still.

When the Founders of the United States inaugurated their political project, they also launched an ongoing public argument—always passionate, sometimes heated, occasionally violent—about the country's animating ideals and how they would be actualized, the continuing relationship of religion to politics, and the purpose and destiny of the nation itself. The spiritual detractors we will encounter in these pages were important participants in this argument, indeed often at the center of the nation's most acute controversies and conflicts. By arguing against a politics they believed to be unmoored from the transcendent and proclaiming that the nation needed to be placed under divine governance, they challenged the various ways in which Americans tried to articulate a shared religious basis for the liberal democratic order, whether by appeals to an "unofficial pan-Protestant establishment," Judeo-Christian "biblical faith," "natural law," or "civil religion." The reverberations of many of their ideas can still be felt today. By heeding their complaints against American political values and the constitutional order, pondering their alternative visions of political community, and appreciating how their challenges have helped sculpt the contours of the nation's politics and law, we can reconsider the dispute between those who insist that America was founded as a "Christian nation" and those who maintain that the Founders intended the country to be a "secular republic." And in engaging these heresies, we can, I hope, better appreciate the virtues as well as the limitations, fragilities, and possible futures of the liberal democratic constitutional order that has slowly and not without struggle come to be in the United States.

CHAPTER ONE

Those Licentious Principles of the Times

The Loyalist Churchmen

"When mens Principles are wrong, their Practices will seldom be right." Such was the pronouncement of Church of England divine and exiled president of King's College Myles Cooper near the conclusion of a fast day sermon preached at the University of Oxford on Friday, December 13, 1776. "When they suppose those Powers to be derived solely from the People, which are 'ordained of GOD,' and their heads are filled with idea of Original Compacts which never existed, and which are always explained so as to answer their present Occasions; no wonder that they confound the duties of Rulers and Subjects, and are perpetually prompted to dictate where it is their Business to obey. When once they conceive the Governed to be superior to the Governors, and that they may set up their pretended Natural Rights in Opposition to the positive Laws of the State; they will naturally proceed to 'despise dominion, and speak evil of dignities,' and to open a door for Anarchy, 'Confusion, and every evil work,' to enter."[1] The civil war raging across the ocean was fundamentally a battle over principles, a contest between two visions of the origins and purpose of government and its relationship to the divine order. In the eyes of Cooper, as in those of other High Church clergy committed to episcopacy and monarchy, the American action was not justified resistance to British tyranny, the assertion of their natural rights against illegitimate dictates of the state, or a mere political squabble over British policy. It was a rebellion against God and his established order.[2]

Cooper knew of anarchy and confusion all too personally. The Oxford-educated clergyman arrived in America in 1762 and a year later was appointed president of the King's College in New York City (founded in 1754). He entertained grand hopes for the institution, aiming to secure a royal charter to transform the fledgling college into a great American university with faculties of law, medicine, and theology—an Oxford for the New World. By cultivating deep learning, religious piety, and political conservatism, such an educational institution would promote order and harmony, countering the corrosive values of individualism and religious enthusiasm.³ Alas, events had rendered such aspirations moot. The previous May, a mob had driven Cooper from his college lodgings, his escape rumored to have been assisted by King's College student Alexander Hamilton. He found refuge on a British naval vessel in New York Harbor and soon thereafter set sail for his native England, where he spent the remainder of his days.⁴

The purpose of Cooper's fast day oration was to call his "Sinful Nation" to a "general Repentance, Reformation, and Amendment," and to beseech God "to put a speedy End to that *enormous* wickedness,—to that wanton and barbarous REBELLION." But he also endeavored to assign "the Causes of the present Rebellion in America." This required some explanation, for Britain had been a nation much blessed, "a pattern to the WORLD, of every religious, moral, and political Accomplishment." "Our RELIGION," Cooper noted, "is that of the GOSPEL OF CHRIST." "By the Reformation, it has been restored to its original Perfection; and of Course has recovered its original Quality of being profitable—'for doctrine, for reproof, for correction, and instruction in Righteousness.'" Further, the nation enjoyed good government: "Our CIVIL Constitution, which is fair and beautiful in Theory, is admirably fitted for the Regulation of an orderly, if not for the Restraint of an unruly people."⁵ The two spheres worked in tandem, two sides of the body politic: religion disclosed a cosmic order in which governments were ordained by divine wisdom and beneficence and all creatures great to small were set in their proper place of wealth, privilege, and power, with their assigned roles to perform; a grand tapestry of duty and obedience in which children submitted to their parents and servants their masters, subjects honored their king, colonies were subservient to their motherland—a Great Chain of Being. All was held together by the church—the national communion—which sanctified the political order and, in turn, received the government's support and protection. The monarch, the supreme head of the church and God's vicegerent, was the living symbol of this arrangement, binding together in his person and sovereign authority the spiritual and temporal realms. Church and state, episcopacy and monarchy (and, following the settlement of 1688–1689, Parliament), were mutually reinforcing institutions.[6]

This theological-political vision was manifested in the Book of Common Prayer, the official liturgy of the Church of England and its most influential religious production, first assembled in 1539 by Thomas Cranmer, archbishop of Canterbury. Prayers for the king and the royal family accentuated the association between the church and the sovereign. Later editions added commemorative services for the anniversaries of the execution of Charles I and the restoration under Charles II. And commitment to this political theology was impressed on clergymen by the oaths they took, upon ordination to the diaconate and repeated at ordination to priesthood, to the king's supremacy and to perform the liturgy without alteration. The High Church clergy accordingly instructed their flock to revere this divinely instituted order and to be content with their providentially assigned stations.

"WITH these advantages, internal and external, religious and political," Cooper said, "we ought to be the most thankful people upon the earth; the most virtuous, and the most happy." Yet the nation had strayed. And for "Kingdoms and States" the administration of Providence doles out rewards and punishments in the here and now. War was an instrument of chastisement, and civil war was "one of the severest scourges of Heaven." That the colonies revolted "on pretenses most frivolous, and with insolence the most provoking," illuminated the "unquestionable marks of the indignation of Heaven." Thus, the present difficulties were to be understood "as a Punishment for the sins of This Nation, for our Immoralities and Corruptions,—our ingratitude to Heaven and our neglect of religion." Cooper pointed to Britain's wallowing in luxury and vice, the usual corruptions of a commercial society. But he observed, too, that the nation bore guilt "perhaps partly for our neglecting to provide property for the Support of it in our PROVINCES and PLANTATIONS," for the Church of England was not as solidly planted in the colonies as it ought to have been. That failure, he suggested, was the root of the present troubles.[7]

Even so, British authorities, political and ecclesiastical, had long understood the impossibility of imposing a homogeneous Anglican establishment on its imperial holdings. And so the American colonies came to contain a patchwork of religious establishments and jurisdictions where no church was established. Religious diversity existed within the context of this ecclesiastical pluralism. The patchwork of different religious regimes undercut the fundamental idea of establishment as a bond between theological and political order, something that the High Church clergymen well understood and deeply lamented. In their eyes, rather than protecting and promoting the true church, in the interests of maintaining and expanding its empire, the British state was protecting and promoting its religious competition.[8]

Yet, by the eve of the American Revolution, the Church of England had grown to be the second-largest denomination in the colonies. Some three hundred clergy, many of them missionaries sent by the Society for the Propagation of the Gospel in Foreign Parts (SPG), served more than four hundred congregations nestled throughout the thirteen colonies. In Virginia, Maryland, the Carolinas, and Georgia, the church was established and enjoyed official recognition, public support through taxes, and particular privileges and immunities. The nature and extent of government support and the church's authority varied considerably from colony to colony on account of its stage of development and particular religious complexion. In all these places, colonial establishments were necessarily of a derivative nature, and far from the ideal that would require a religiously homogeneous society. Particularly in the Restoration colonies, the economic demands and strategic realities of the British colonial project took precedence over considerations of religious uniformity. Immigrants were needed to populate the domains. Liberty of conscience was a crucial concession to Quakers, Presbyterians, Baptists, Lutherans, Huguenots, and Jews considering the journey across the Atlantic to settle in the New World.[9]

Outside the southern colonies, only in the four lower counties of New York (New York, Westchester, Queens, and Richmond) did the Church of England enjoy official recognition and preferential status, although the 1693 Ministry Act had only authorized the payment of salaries for "good and sufficient Protestant ministers."[10] No formal church-state relationship pertained in the rest of the colony, nor in the other middle colonies of Pennsylvania, Delaware, and New Jersey, where Presbyterians, Quakers, German and Swedish Lutherans, Moravians, Mennonites, Dutch Calvinists, French Huguenots, and Sephardic Jews, among many others, had settled. And then there was New England, where, with the exception of the religious sanctuary of Rhode Island, Congregationalism was firmly established and anti-Anglicanism deeply rooted.

To the clergymen sent by the SPG, those colonies were a vast mission field. Many of those who joined the Venerable Society, as the SPG was sometimes called, were of the "High Church" disposition, committed to the traditional liturgy and vestments; the superiority of the clergy over the laity; and episcopacy, monarchy, and establishmentarianism. Their idealism and moral seriousness provided them the strength to endure many hardships; supervision and financial support from the SPG ensured their orthodoxy and conformity. The missionaries set out to the colonies to preach their gospel to the native "heathen" and to enslaved persons, but they were also charged with instructing "the principals of true religion" in those places where the church had not yet been established. They preached their gospel to Huguenots, Swedish and Dutch Reformed, and German Lutherans. They also dreamed of bringing New England's dissenting populace back into the fold. For its members, the church stood as a symbol of British authority and prestige. For its detractors, it was an expression of British imperial power, an ever-looming threat to religious liberty.[11]

The very presence of the Church of England in their midst and the tenacious proselyting of the SPG missionaries was menacing to those whose forebears had left their homes to live and worship according to their own lights and establish their own holy commonwealths in the New World. Their fears were not unwarranted. There was that scandalous affair of 1722, when a group of graduates at the two-decades-old Yale College sat in the library filled with theological tracts sent over by the Society for Promoting Christian Knowledge and literally read themselves into the Church of England. The example of those "Yale Apostates"—whose number included such notables as Timothy Cutler, Samuel Johnson, and Samuel Seabury—revealed the allure of the Church of England even in the very heart of Congregationalist New Haven.[12] That appeal seemed only to increase over the subsequent decades. Defections increased in consequence of George Whitefield's revivals and the "Great Awakening" of 1739–1745 as the outbursts of enthusiasm and appeals to conscience and the challenges to tradition and hierarchy rent Congregationalists and Presbyterians into warring camps of New Lights and Old Lights and New Sides and Old Sides, weakening the cohesion of their churches and the authority of their clergy. By contrast, the Churchmen among them appeared to be paragons of order and stability.

And yet, despite these strengths, something fundamental was missing. Episcopacy was a "salient feature" of the Church of England, the only legitimate form of church governance, resting on the assertion of apostolic succession, an uninterrupted chain of authority that reached from the very first followers of Jesus to the present bishops.[13] Bishops were necessary for the supervision of clergy, the convening ecclesiastical courts, the management of complex pastoral challenges, the performance of confirmation, the ordination of priests, and the consecration of bishops. They also performed civil functions, such as the issuing of marriage licenses and the probation of wills. But a resident bishop had not been placed to preside over the colonial church.

American parishes operated under the distant authority of the bishop of London. The civil duties bishops performed in England were taken on by the government, and vestries composed of laymen managed the affairs of each parish. The ordination and licensing of an American-born would-be clergyman required an expensive and arduous six-thousand-mile journey to England and back, and many who undertook the voyage perished from accident or disease. The absence of a resident bishop was the American church's most serious deficiency, inhibiting its growth, stability, and coherence. From the beginning of the eighteenth century, in the 1710s, 1750s, and early 1760s, High Church clergymen in the colonies lobbied their superiors in England to remedy the situation. Time and again, Dissenters in the colonies made known their opposition, and the ecclesiastical and political authorities failed to accede to the requests.[14]

In October 1766 a group of nineteen High Church clergymen convened under the leadership of Thomas Bradbury Chandler in Elizabeth Town, New Jersey, to renew the effort. Sensitive to public opinion, especially after the tumultuous reaction to the Stamp Act, they deliberated over a scheme that would allow for the settlement of a bishop while tempering colonial anxieties. Chandler had been raised a Congregationalist before converting to the Church of England while studying at Yale, and he was particularly zealous about the need for a colonial bishop. But he understood that the American situation would require some modification of tradition. In a pamphlet, he proposed "a purely spiritual episcopate" in which *"the Bishops to be sent to America, shall have no Authority, but purely of a Spiritual and Ecclesiastical Nature, such as is derived altogether from the Church and not from the State."* The authority of such a bishop, he noted, *"shall operate only upon the Clergy of the Church, and not upon the Laity nor Dissenters of any Denomination."* This would be a departure from the tradition of English establishment where bishops were officials of the state and sat in the House of Lords but a reasonable concession to the realities of the American situation. Or so it seemed to them.[15]

Theological, political, and practical arguments were advanced to support the proposal and to answer the objections to episcopacy made by its opponents. The Churchmen even appealed to the rhetoric of religious liberty. If New England Congregationalists had their standing orders and Presbyterians their synods, and the Roman Catholic Church was able to retain its bishop in Quebec, surely the Church of England—the national church (indeed, the "true Religion")!—ought to have the right to complete its ecclesiastical structure in the colonies.[16] At the same time, they described the political benefits for Britain that even a "primitive bishop" without official state functions would bestow: deepening the church's roots in the colonies, strengthening loyalty to the Crown and Parliament, and serving as a bulwark against the gathering forces of political enthusiasm. "Episcopacy and monarchy are, in their Frame and Constitution, best suited to each other. Episcopacy can never thrive in a Republican Government, nor Republican Principles in an Episcopal Church," Chandler maintained. This was not a sentence that would assuage the feelings of Americans inclining toward republicanism or those who suspected that the plan for a "purely spiritual episcopate" was merely the opening gambit for a thoroughgoing establishment of the Church of England in the colonies and further Anglicization of American society.[17]

So it was not a surprise that the proposal served to inflame long-simmering fears of an Anglican ecclesiastical-political conspiracy, setting off a literary skirmish that played out in newspapers and pamphlets through 1770. Opponents published the *American Whig* in New York and the *Centinel* in Philadelphia; the clergymen Thomas Bradbury Chandler, Myles Cooper, Charles Inglis, and Samuel Seabury Jr. responded with their *Whip for the American Whig* coming out of New York. Chandler penned two further pamphlets in support of his appeal in 1769 and 1771.[18]

The acquiescence of the Congregationalists and Presbyterians and Baptists to the proposal to settle a bishop of the Church of England in America was not to be expected. But the plan also failed to win the support of many Anglicans, especially in the southern colonies where the church had long been established, the clergy and laity worrying that a resident bishop would disturb local practices and self-governance. In the end, the ecclesiastical and political authorities in England were simply unwilling to entertain any plan for settling a bishop in the American colonies and stir up an already volatile situation. The controversy nevertheless stoked long-standing tensions that would contribute, along with those grievances regarding British rule, to the movement toward rebellion.[19]

Despite the hundreds of churches built, the more than six hundred missionaries dispatched to the colonies by the Society for the Propagation of the Gospel, and the thousands of books printed and sent across the Atlantic by the Society for Promoting Christian Knowledge, the Church of England had been unable to establish its institutional authority firmly throughout the American colonies.[20] By failing to support the parishes in the colonies in a proper fashion, the Church of England had allowed the Dissenter population, predisposed by false religion to republican disorder, to take root, flourish, and spread their "wild, visionary, enthusiastic Notions, with regard to Society," thereby setting the stage for the rebellion, Myles Cooper contended, elucidating the nation's guilt.[21] In a similar fashion, Thomas Bradbury Chandler noted that "many of the first setters imported with them an aversion to the *regal* part of our Constitution, and were through-paced *Republicans*." They "stiffly Maintained, and zealously endeavored to propagate their own antimonarchial principles; and those principles have been handed down by an uninterrupted succession, from father to son, and from generation to generation, to the present day." That planting was now bearing its bitter fruit, as "the confusions of the present time" provided a "favorable opportunity, for putting their design in execution." He likened "these rebellious Republicans" to those who joined Sheba's revolt against King David; they were "hair-brained fanaticks, as mad and distracted as the ANABAPTISTS *of* MUNSTER."[22]

That religious dissent and political disobedience were bound together could explain the gap between the trifling nature of the colonists' grievances and their bearers' vehemence against the mother country. "The Colonists were not in a state of Oppression; nor could they be made to *believe* that they were," Cooper argued. "Grievances indeed were pretended; and a List of them was publicly exhibited: But of these, some were evidently no grievances at all; and if any of them were really deemed to be so they were much more counterbalanced by peculiar Advantages." The origins of the conflict lay deeper than their objections to British tax and trade policy, the punishment of Boston, or the toleration of Catholics under the Quebec Act. And Cooper detected this in the political prejudices of some of the American colonists: "That Many of the Colonists were of Republican Principles, and had a hereditary disaffection to the English constitution: who wished for an opportunity, and endeavored to create one, of becoming independent on the parent Kingdom." Such men had allowed themselves to be taken advantage of by "ambitious and needy Adventurers," encouraged by the enactment and then repeal of the Stamp Act. Further, "religion" was being deployed as a weapon against the rightful political order. "Religion itself, or rather the Appearance of it, humbly ministered as a handmaid to Faction and Sedition. And it is well known, that solemn Prayers, public

Fastings, and pathetic Sermons, were some of the most effectual means that were employed to invigorate the Rebellion." It was no surprise, then, that a great many colonists were duped by these malignant actors ("the artful Conductors, in imitation of the Father of deceit and rebellion") into taking up arms against their lawful sovereign. "SUCH arts," Cooper exclaimed, "would almost 'deceive the Elect'; and it is no wonder that they prevailed with the ignorant, the prejudiced and unprincipled, to join with the crafty, the profligate and desperate, in executing the measures of their aspiring Demagogues."[23] He commended those who remained loyal, "who have been induced by no Menaces or Persecutions, to bow the knee to the BAAL of INDEPENDENCY, or to swerve at all from the duties of Allegiance," taking particular note of "the Greater Part of the Members of the Church of England, and, in Several of the colonies, all its Clergy, without Exception."[24]

As the crisis began to heat up, those Church of England veterans of the bishop controversy turned to apply their labors to the Loyalist propaganda effort.[25] Entering the contest for public opinion in the months surrounding the convening of the First Continental Congress, they composed some of the most influential, and notorious, pro-British pamphlets. These focused principally on the political, economic, and social aspects of the quarrel. They were published anonymously, their authors masking their clerical roles, both because they believed their position as Church of England ministers would have hindered their attempts to shape public opinion and out of real concern for their personal safety.[26] Most prominent among them were Samuel Seabury Jr.'s series of four *Letters from a Westchester Farmer* (the first of which inspired an ambitious seventeen-year-old student at King's College named Alexander Hamilton to enter the public foray with his first political work; a promised fifth never appeared); Thomas Bradbury Chandler's *The American Querist* (1774), *A Friendly Address to All Reasonable Americans* (1774), and *What Think Ye of Congress Now?* (1775); *A Letter from a Virginian* (1774), attributed to Jonathan Boucher; and *The True Interest of America Impartially Stated* (1776), the Irish-born assistant minister at Trinity Church in New York City Charles Inglis's rebuttal of Thomas Paine's incendiary bestseller *Common Sense*.

"*I find no* Common Sense *in this pamphlet, but much* uncommon *phrenzy,*" Inglis, writing as "an American," roared in its preface. "*The principles of government laid down in it, are not only false, but too absurd to have ever entered the head of a crazy politician before. Even Hobbes would blush to own the author as a disciple.*"

He unites the violence and rage of a republican, with all the enthusiasm and folly of a fanatic." Inglis denounced the author of *Common Sense* as "an avowed, violent Republican, utterly adverse and unfriendly to the English constitution" driven by "malice and antipathy to monarchial government," mocking the aspiration to overturn "the wisdom of ages" in favor of his "Utopian" system. Inglis disputed Paine's contention that "society is produced by our wants, and government by our wickedness," proposing instead that human beings are born into society, that governments emerge to serve its ends and cannot do so "but by subordination, order and the regulation of laws." Government, therefore, "is agreeable to the will of the Deity—that it has its origin in the nature and state of man—that in framing governments by mutual compact, men act according to the law of their nature, and dictates of reason, which thus point out the only effectual way to attain happiness and avoid evil." The republican had not only attacked Britain's venerable and balanced constitution but went so far as to declare that monarchy itself was a heathen institution that the Israelites had wrongfully imitated, daring to employ Holy Writ to make his case. Such "perversion of scripture" raised the Churchman's ire, and he spent several pages dismantling such impetuousness. Paine had contended that the Bible was anti-monarchal (submitting the Israelites' rejection of theocracy in 1 Samuel 8 and 12 as evidence); Inglis countered with Deuteronomy 17:14–20, the cluster of laws regulating the powers of the king, as well as a list of proof texts from both the Old and New Testaments that comprised "the Scripture Doctrine of monarchy." "I must therefore renounce my bible, if I believe this republican," he concluded. Not that many Americans would have noticed, as the entire first printing of the pamphlet was destroyed by a mob.[27]

While acknowledging the sincerity of many colonial grievances, the clerical pamphleteers took as axiomatic the goodness of the British constitutional order and its legitimate authority over the American colonies and the unlawfulness of the committees and assemblies that were springing up. They expressed alarm over the "republican schemes" being deliberated and the violence they feared would be unleashed if the colonies resisted British authorities. Counseling prudence and restraint, they explained the advantages of working within time-honored constitutional channels and encouraged reconciliation, admonished against "independency," and darkly prophesied the disorder and violence that would ensue should the colonies attempt to sever the bonds with the mother country. "Whenever the fatal period shall arrive, in which the American colonies shall become independent of Great-Britain," Seabury wrote in his second *Letter* of November 1774, "a horrid scene of war and bloodshed will immediately commence. . . . There will be no supreme power to interpose; but the sword and bayonet must decide the dispute." The powerful British military, he believed, would ultimately prevail, but in the improbable event that the rebellion did indeed succeed, Seabury dreaded even greater disorder. "But horrid indeed would be the consequence of our success!" he warned. "We should presently turn our arms on one another, province against province, and destruction and carnage would desolate the land. Probably it would cost the blood of a great part of the inhabitants to determine, what kind of government we should have—whether a Monarchy or a Republic. Another effusion of blood would be necessary to fix a Monarch, or to establish the common wealth."[28]

From his study of British history and his own experiences in New England, Chandler had concluded that challenges to the authority of the church inevitably brought about a weakening of civil order.[29] He took care to detail the baleful consequences for religious liberty should the colonies come under the domination of "the madmen of *New-England* in their scheme of an *Independent Republic.*" If their rebellion succeeded, "there would be no peace in the colonies, till we all submitted to the republican zealots and bigots of *New-England.*" He foresaw a dark future of persecution for all those Quakers and Baptists, members of German and Dutch churches, as well as "the moderate part" of the Presbyterians and Congregationalists. If you think that the "demagogues of New-England have been thus intolerant," consider well how they will behave when no longer subordinate to the British! "As soon therefore, as people of this stamp come to be in possession of an established authority . . . the dire effects of their persecuting, and intolerant spirit will be dismally felt by all that shall have courage to *dissent.*" He chastised those joining the calls for rebellion as "absurdly acting against their own interest and honour, and contributing to prepare yokes for their own necks."[30]

But Chandler concentrated his indignation on his coreligionists who were supporting the rebellious cause. "It is amazing," he marveled, "that any of you should be so blind to your own interests, and such apostates from common sense, as to countenance and cooperate with a plan of proceedings, which, if it succeeds, will at once distress and disgrace you." He went on: "You are endeavouring to provide arms for your enemies, and to put power into the hands of those who will use it against you. You are setting up a sort of people for your masters, whose principles you despise, and who were always fond of subduing by the iron of oppression, all those, whose principles or sentiments were different from their own. Their inveterate enmity to the Church of *England*, has polluted the annals of the *British* history. . . . Their descendants, who inherit their principles, are the very persons that will govern you, if the projected revolution should take place." If the fanatical New Englanders were to come to power, "you then, who are members of the Church of England, must renounce your principles relating both to religion and government, or you can expect no quarter under the administration of such intemperate zealots. You must cease to be Churchmen, or become victims of their intolerance." But it wasn't only that Anglicans were failing to consider the consequences of their political commitments. For Chandler, turning against the king was a betrayal of the church's teachings. "Indeed it must be confessed, and I am sorry to say, that many of you appear already to have renounced one half of your principles; or you could not proceed, as you do, in direct opposition to the established rules and doctrines of the Church," he wrote, spelling out the connection between religious commitment and submission to political authority in detail:

> The principles of submission and obedience to lawful authority are as inseparable from *a sound, genuine member* of the Church of *England,* as any religious principles whatever. The Church has always been famed and respected for its *loyalty*, and its regard to order and government. Its annals have been never stained with the history of plots and conspiracies, treasons and rebellions. Its members are instructed in their duty to government, by Three *Homilies* on *Obedience*, and six against *Rebellion*, which are so many standing lessons to secure their fidelity. They are also taught to pray in the Litany, that the Almighty would preserve them, "from all sedition, privy conspiracy and rebellion." And more than one solemn office is provided, for the annual commemoration of former deliverances from the power of those, whether *Papists* or *Protestants,* "who turn religion into rebellion, and faith into faction." But if you regard none of these things, you are untoward, undutiful, and degenerate sons of the Church, and she will be ashamed to own you for her children.

Submission to the king and his government flowed from the duty of obedience to God and his commandments; this was enjoined by Scripture and taught by the church and reinforced by the lessons of English history. To bow down before the "Baal of independency" was akin to apostasy.[31]

As Chandler's pamphlet suggests, support for Britain among the colonial Anglicans was far from universal. As the dispute intensified, Church of England clergy and laity took the range of available political positions, some adjusting their allegiances as the conflict carried on. Among them could be found the most prominent Loyalists and the most illustrious Patriots. Several of the most vocal supporters of the Crown emerged from the ranks of its clergy, particularly in middle colonies. Some two-thirds of the fifty-five signers of the Declaration of Independence were Church of England laymen, as were Patriot leaders such as George Washington, Thomas Jefferson, and Patrick Henry.[32] Unlike the clergy, they were not bound by oaths to the king.[33]

Such explicitly religious arguments for obedience to the king were at the center of the sermons the Anglican critics of colonial resistance delivered to their congregations and, once the war came, to soldiers in the field. The sources are limited; only a few of their sermons enjoyed publication. Jonathan Boucher later wrote that "the press was shut to every publication of the kind."[34] The extant materials, however, provide a clear view of the Loyalist clergy's position on the conflict and of the political theory and theology that lay behind it. That political theology was rooted in Scripture, relying on a cluster of texts from the New Testament—Jesus's instruction to "render unto Caesar what is Caesar's" (Mark 12:13–17, Matthew 22:15–22, Luke 20:20–26), Paul's counsel to "be subject unto the higher powers" (Romans 13:1–7), and Peter's command to "fear God, honor the king" (1 Peter 2:17). From such scriptural warrants, the High Church divines proclaimed the Christian duty to obey the sovereign under which God's providence had placed them. Human beings are not born free and equal in a state of nature but are born in sin and into society, consigned by Providence to their stations in this life. Government is not formed by individuals freely entering into a compact to protect their rights but ordained by God. Men have no right of resistance to its authority; they are bound instead by the duty, disclosed by revelation as well as reason, to respect its officers and obey its dictates. The divines complemented this teaching with appeals to human reason and experience and an analysis of the nature of human society and the origin and purpose of government. They perceived the providential design of Britain's imperial glory and its current woes, and championed the admirable qualities of the British constitution and the many virtues of George III. And they drew parallels between the current conflict and the English Civil War of the previous century. (It's worth noting that the king and his supporters regarded the conflict as a "Presbyterian Rebellion.") In their eyes, the American conflict was a continuation of that older dispute about the nature of government and the duties owed to the sovereign, the relationship between a religious establish-ment and political stability, dissent and disorder.[35]

During his December 1776 sermon, Myles Cooper called on his audience at Oxford "to be particularly guarded against those licentious Principles of the Times, which in their natural Tendency are subversive of Government; which have more immediately contributed to bring on the calamity we now deplore."[36] Already in 1773, the English-born divine Jonathan Boucher had been cautioning his parishioners about the false and dangerous ideas regarding government that were not only found in treatises of political theory but also circulating in popular periodicals and pronounced in sermons, confounding American minds and exacerbating tensions with Britain.[37] Boucher, then rector of Queen Anne's in Prince George's Country, Maryland, spoke of "the degeneracy of modern times," a "corruption of principles," and a "destruction of foundations" through "the inculcating a general persuasion that government is neither sacred nor inviolable." Subjects of government were rather duty-bound to defend those foundations. "The doctrine of *obedience for conscience sake* is," he told his flock, "the great *corner-stone* of all good government; which, whenever any *builder* of constitutions shall be so unwise as to *refuse*, or, not refusing, shall afterwards suffer to be destroyed, what can he expect but that the whole fabric should be overturned." Only upon such a foundation could "a superstructure of greatness and happiness" be erected.[38] Chandler similarly warned that "the bands of society would be dissolved, the harmony of the world confounded, and the order of nature subverted, if reverence, respect, and obedience, might be refused to those whom the constitution has vested with the highest authority."[39] Order required subordination. Government demanded obedience.

As obedience taught by religion served as the foundation of civil govern-ment, Boucher feared its being disrespected and maligned. "I sincerely believe that the low estimation in which this fundamental principle is held is the great evil of our age," effecting the deterioration of the manners of the community and relations between parents and children, employers and the employed. Society was crumbling into decay. Such disregard of religion explained, too, the attacks on the Church of England. "The great doctrine of the liturgy and of the homilies of our Church, as well as of the Laws of the Land, we are now, alas, intemperately hastening with the most deplorable ignorance to *destroy!* and at the same time encouraging a novel experiment in the world; an experiment by which it is proposed to keep society together, or, in other words, to build up a Constitution without any *foundations*." Boucher preached against such "a loose notion respecting government": the belief coming into vogue that "all government is the mere creature of the people, and may therefore be tampered with, altered, new-modelled, set up or pulled down, just as tumultuous crowds (who on such occasions are always so forward to call themselves *the people*) may happen in some giddy moments of over-heated ardour to determine"; the opinion that "government is a combination among a few to oppress the many"; and the false principle of equality—the same pernicious doctrine, he noted, that had inspired the rebellion of Korah, Dathan, and Abiram against Moses.[40]

That danger soon became evident. On July 20, 1775, the day the Second Continental Congress had set for "publick humiliation, fasting and prayer," some two hundred armed men surrounded Queen Anne's Parish, Maryland, to prevent Boucher from preaching. When he set to enter the church—"with my sermon in one hand and a loaded pistol in the other," as Boucher later recounted the episode—a Patriot friend tried to restrain him, informing the clergyman that some in the crowd had been given orders to shoot him the moment he reached the pulpit. Boucher was undeterred but was pulled away by "well-wishers"; a disturbance in the church ensued, as a good number in attendance "insisted I was right in claiming and using my own pulpit." The angry mob surrounded Boucher, who was able to escape the fracas by grabbing the collar of its leader, holding his pistol at his head, and "assuring him that if any violence was offered to me I would instantly blow his brains out, as I most certainly would have done." The following Sunday, Boucher returned to the church, took to his pulpit, and, with a pair of loaded pistols set on the cushion before him, preached his sermon "On Civil Liberty, Passive Obedience, and Non-Resistance." It could well be described as the epitome of the Loyalist theological-political argument.[41]

Boucher's oration was a rejoinder to one recently given by another Church of England clergyman, Jacob Duché, the charismatic thirty-eight-year-old rector of Christ Church and St. Peter's in Philadelphia. A member of a prominent family in the city and a man of evangelical sensibilities, Duché had been called on September 7, 1774, to officiate at the First Continental Congress. After reading from the Book of Common Prayer and Psalm 35, he uttered an extemporaneous prayer, well received by the audience. The following July, he delivered two patriotic sermons, the first, *The Duty of Standing Fast in Our Spiritual and Temporal Liberties*, before the First Battalion of Militia of the City and Liberties, and the second a fast day sermon, *The American Vine*, to his church. Both were published and distributed in the colonies and beyond.[42]

The Duty of Standing Fast seemed to provide a religious warrant for the Patriot endeavor. Duché opened with ecumenical prayer (which included an entreaty for King George III), then took up his text: "Stand fast, therefore, in the Liberty wherewith Christ has made us free" (Galatians 5:1). Paul, Duché informed the soldiers assembled before him, was speaking of two distinct types of liberty: spiritual and temporal. Spiritual liberty, he said, "is nothing less than such a release from the arbitrary power of sin, and such an enlargement of the soul by the efficacy of divine grace, and such a total surrender of the will and affections, to the influence and guidance of the divine Spirit." But the apostle was also concerned with civil liberty, that which concerns "our well-being here," "as much a gift of GOD in CHRIST JESUS," and to which those soldiers were enjoined also "to stand fast."[43]

Duché briefly sketched out an account of the social contract theory that underlay his appeal to civil liberty. "It must have been this WISDOM OF THE FATHER, who first taught man, by SOCIAL COMPACT, to secure to himself the possession of those necessaries and comforts, which are so dear and valuable to his natural life," Duché suggested. "And though no particular mode of government is pointed out to us in his holy gospel, yet the benevolent spirit of that gospel is directly opposed to every other form, such as has the common good of mankind for its end and aim." And he went on to state that "our best writers, moral and political, as well as Clergy and Laity, have asserted, that true government can have no other foundation than COMMON CONSENT." It followed, then, that "all Rulers are in fact the Servants of the Public." And so, "whenever this divine order is inverted, whenever these Rulers abuse their sacred trust, by unrighteous attempts to injure, oppress, and enslave those very persons, from whom alone, under God, their power is derived, does not reason, does not scripture, call upon the Man, the Citizen, the Christian of such a community to *'stand fast in that Liberty wherewith Christ* (in their very birth, as well as by succeeding appointments of his Providence) *hath made them free?' "*[44]

Such was the clergyman's potentially revolutionary conclusion. Duché waved away the well-known scriptural injunction "to submit to every ordinance of man for the Lord's sake" (1 Peter 2:13), countering that "surely a submission to the unrighteous ordinances of unrighteous men, cannot be *'for the Lord's sake.' "* "Possessed of these principles," he remarked, "I trust it will be no difficult matter to satisfy your consciences with respect to the righteousness of the cause in which you are now engaged." While still claiming to "venerate the Parent Land," denying "any pretentions to, or even desire of, independency," and recalling his profession of "an inviolable loyalty to the person, power, and dignity of our SOVEREIGN," Duché cautioned, "If, notwithstanding all this, BRITAIN or rather some degenerate sons of BRITAIN, and enemies to our common liberty, still persist in embracing a DELUSION, and believing a LIE—if the sword is still unsheathed against us, and SUBMIT OR PERISH is the sanguinary decree—why then——" And here the minister's words came to a halt, Duché refraining from describing "the tragic scene of fraternal slaughter" he so dreaded would come to pass. Instead, turning back to address his audience in its "military capacity," he offered words of encouragement to "stand fast," in faith and dependence on Jesus Christ, in unanimity, with courage and magnanimity, constancy and perseverance, and instructed them to "coolly and deliberately wait for those events which are in the Providence, and depend upon him alone for strength and expedients suited to your necessities." And, again, to " 'stand fast' as the Guardians of LIBERTY."[45]

Boucher's response to Duché's call to *stand fast* was rather for Americans *to be quiet, and to sit still.* His sermon could be read as the summation of the High Church position on the growing conflict, an attempt to effect "the restraining [of] the body of the people from taking any active part" in the Patriot cause.[46] Duché's argument, Boucher said, was "of a pernicious and dangerous tendency, (and the more so, perhaps, from it's [*sic*] being delivered in the form of a sermon,)" and he promised that his reply would furnish "an antidote to the poison which has been so industriously dispersed among you."[47] He began his counterargument by pointing out that the Philadelphian had based his discourse on a misinterpretation of Scripture and a false understanding of the origin and ends of government. Eager to find a scriptural warrant for rebellion, Duché had grossly abused the text, reading into Paul's words a political meaning that simply was not there and which contradicted the actual testimony of Scripture concerning the Christian's duty of obedience. "The passage cannot, without infinite perversion and torture, be made to refer to any other kind of liberty; much less to that liberty of which every man now talks, though few understand it." The "flowery panegyrics on liberty" that Americans have come to hear "are the productions of ancient heathens and modern patriots: nothing of the kind is to be met with in the Bible, nor in the Statute Book. The word *liberty*, as meaning civil liberty, does not, I believe, occur in all the Scriptures." The liberty Scripture proclaims, rather, "is wholly of the spiritual or religious kind," freedom from the power of sin and from Jewish ordinances and Gentile superstition.[48] Scripture instructs Christians of their duty of "*honoring*

and obeying the king, and all that are put in authority under him," nowhere sanctioning rebellion against the temporal authority under which one has been
providentially placed.[49] "The doctrines of the Gospel," he continued, "make no
manner of alteration in the nature or form of Civil Government; but enforce
afresh, upon all Christians, that obedience which is due to the respective Constitutions of every nation in which they happen to live. Be the supreme power
lodged in one or in many, be the kind of government established in any country
absolute or limited, this is not the concern of the Gospel." Christ and his apostles had called for "submission to *the higher powers*"; it is therefore evident that
"when Christians are disobedient to human authorities, they are also disobedient to God." Scripture could not be legitimately deployed to justify rebellion.
Further, civil liberty "consists in a subserviency to law."[50] "The only rational idea
of civil liberty, or (which is the same thing) of a legitimate and good government," Boucher declared elsewhere, "is, when the great body of the people are
trained and led habitually to submit to and acquiesce in some fixed and steady
principles of conduct."[51]

Having thus reproached Duché for mishandling the Bible, Boucher
turned to the deeper issue—those "loose and dangerous" opinions on government that were animating the present unrest. Most of his lengthy discourse he
dedicated to demonstrating the erroneousness of the theory that legitimate
government came about by means of a "social contract" agreed on by free and
equal individuals to escape from the inconveniencies of "the state of nature."

The theory of a social contract rested on the assertion of the natural
equality of human beings. For Boucher, the claim that "the whole human race
is born equal; and that no man is naturally inferior, or, in any respect, subjected
to another; and that he can be made subject to another only by his own consent"
was empirically false as well as unbiblical. "Man differs from man in everything
that can be supposed to lead to supremacy and subjection, *as one star differs
from another star in glory*." God had intended human beings to be social creatures, but in their fallen state, human society requires government to maintain
peace and stability, and government itself depends on fixed distinctions of
rank. And the very appeal to natural equality destabilized a government based
on consent: "If (according to the idea of the advocates of this chimerical scheme
of equality) no man could rightfully be compelled to come in and be a member
even of a government to be formed by a regular compact, but by his own individual consent; it clearly follows, from the same principles, that neither could
he rightfully be made or compelled to submit to the ordinances of any

government already formed, to which he has not individually or actually consented. On the principle of equality, neither his parents, nor even the vote of a majority of the society, (however virtuously and honourably that vote might be obtained,) can have any such authority over any man. Neither can it be maintained that acquiescence implies consent; because acquiescence may have been extorted from impotence or incapacity." And, even if one did explicitly consent at some point, one would still retain the right to withdraw that consent if one ever saw fit. Just imagine the volatility that would ensue if such a scheme were ever attempted to be put into place: "Governments, though always forming, would never be completely formed: for, the majority to-day, might be the minority tomorrow; and, of course, that which is now fixed would soon be unfixed." John Locke had said that by entering into the compact each individual agreed to submit to the decree of the majority, but he conceded that the members of the compact nevertheless retained a right to resistance against the very government they had agreed to establish. Boucher further noted that "there is no record that any such government ever was so formed. If there had, it must have carried the seeds of it's [sic] decay in it's very constitution." Government by consent would defeat the fundamental purpose of government, which is to maintain the social order: "Such a system . . . can produce only perpetual dissentions and contests, and bring back mankind to a supposed state of nature."[52]

Boucher worked through the social contract thought experiment, exposing its flaws and contradictions. Was it possible to believe that an assembly of presumably equal individuals would freely choose to submit themselves to the rule of another? Did not granting the right of another to exercise power over oneself demonstrate that human beings do, in fact, hold that some are superior to others, thus belying the fanciful notion of natural equality? He reflected, "The supposition that a large concourse of people, in a rude and imperfect state of society, or even a majority of them, should thus rationally and unanimously concur to subject themselves to various restrictions, many of them irksome and unpleasant, and all of them contrary to all of their former habits, is to suppose them possessed of more wisdom and virtue than multitudes in any instance in real life have ever shewn." Moreover, as governments finally possess the terrible power over life and death, was it credible that an individual would transfer to another the power over his own life (a right, Boucher maintained, "that he does not himself possess")? No, Boucher announced; such a right could only come from God.[53]

Boucher concluded that the social contract theory was nothing but a "Utopian fiction," first dreamed up by the Scholastics and then taken up by Calvinists and now sadly even adopted by some within the Church of England. What was the attraction of this notion of government? It flatters our pride and legitimates our baser desires. "Mankind have listened, and continue to listen to it with a predilection and partiality, just as they do to various other exceptional notions, which are unfavorable to true religion and sound morals; merely from imagining, that if such doctrines be true, they shall no longer be subjected to sundry restraints, which, however wholesome and proper, are too often unpalatable to our corrupt natures. What we wish to be true, we easily persuade ourselves is true," the minister observed.[54]

Having so detailed the implausibility of the social contract theory, Boucher called on his listeners to turn away from such vain imaginings and back to revelation.[55] "Of all the theories respecting the origin of government with which the world has ever been either puzzled, amused, or instructed," Boucher explained, "that of the Scriptures alone is accompanied by no insuperable difficulties." And what Scripture teaches is that government originated from and was ordained by God. "It was not to be expected from an all-wise and all-merciful Creator, that, having formed creatures capable of order and rule, he should turn them loose into the world under the guidance only of their own unruly wills; that, like so many wild beasts, they might tear and worry one another in their mad contests for preeminence." Human nature had become corrupted at the fall, "but as men were clearly formed for society, and to dwell together, which yet they cannot do without the restraints of law, or, in other words, without government, it is fair to infer that government was also the original intention of God, who never decrees the end, without also decreeing the means." Echoing the arguments laid out in the previous century by Sir Robert Filmer in *Patriarcha* (arguments that Locke himself had aimed to dismantle in his *First Treatise on Government*), Boucher described the patriarchal origin of civil government. "As soon as there were some to be governed," he explained, "there were also some to govern: and the first man, by virtue of that paternal claim, on which all subsequent governments have been founded, was first invested with the power of government. . . . The first father was the first king: and if (according to the rule just laid down) the law may be inferred from the practice, it was thus that all government originated; and monarchy is it's [sic] most ancient form." The idea that the patriarchal family provides the pattern for political authority and the duty to honor and obey government "has not only the most and best authority of history, as far as history goes, to support it; but … it is also by far the most natural, most consistent, and most rational idea," and "always has prevailed, and still does prevail" among both enlightened and unenlightened peoples. This teaching has the benefit of being "equally an argument against the domineering claims of despotism, and the fantastic notion of a compact."[56]

As government is ordained by God, it follows that we are "commanded to *be subject to the higher powers:* and this subjection is said to be enjoined, not for our sakes only, but also *for the Lord's sake.*" Countering Duché's contention that magistrates ought to be regarded as creatures of and therefore servants of the people, Boucher proclaimed

> the uniform doctrine of the Scriptures, that it is under the deputation and authority of God alone that *kings reign and princes decree justice.* Kings and princes (which are only other words for supreme magistrates) were doubtless created and appointed, not so much for their own sakes, as for the sake of the people committed to their charge: yet they are not, therefore, the creatures of the people. So far from deriving their authority from any supposed consent or suffrage of men, they receive their commission from Heaven; they receive it from God, the source and original of all power. However obsolete, therefore, either the sentiment or the language may now be deemed, it is with the most perfect propriety that the supreme magistrate, whether consisting of one or many, and whether denominated an emperor, a king, an archon, a dictator, a consul, or a senate, is to be regarded and venerated as the vicegerent of God.[57]

The duty to submit to authority that the apostles had enjoined was also instructed by Christ himself. Boucher insisted that "everything our blessed Lord either said or did, pointedly tended to discourage the disturbing of a settled government. Hence it is fair to infer the judgment of Jesus Christ to have been, that the most essential duty of subjects with respect to government was (in the phraseology of a prophet) *to be quiet, and to sit still.*" The Jews expected their Messiah would be a temporal prince who would "restore to Israel the supremacy, of which the Romans had deprived it … and, having subdued the rest of the world, make Jerusalem the seat of a universal monarchy." Jesus belied these expectations. Indeed, "in no instance whatever did our Saviour give greater offence to his countrymen than he did by not gratifying them in their expectations of a temporal deliverance." He believed the Jews should not be distracted by dreams of political revolution and the world should have "no precedent to which revolutionists might appeal."[58]

In the closing pages, Boucher addressed the Anglo-American crisis directly. He had engaged in this long discussion regarding "the divine origin and authority of government" in order to refute the "contrary opinion" and the "dangerous inferences" that Duché's sermon had disseminated: "Government being assumed to be a mere human ordinance, it is thence inferred, that 'rulers are the servants of the public:' and, if they be, no doubt it necessarily follows, that they may (in the coarse phrase of the times) be *cashiered* or continued in pay, be reverenced or resisted, according to the mere whim or caprice of those over whom they are appointed to rule. Hence the author of this sermon also takes occasion to enter his protest against 'passive obedience and non-resistance.' " It was Boucher's purpose to obviate this supposed "right of resistance"—which Locke had conceded and had "incessantly been delivered from the pulpit, and inculcated by statesmen"—by setting forth "the dictate of religion" and "the doctrine of the established Church." On the contrary, government *requires* submission; to resist government is to destroy its power and invite chaos.[59]

Yet Boucher had to answer those critics who attacked conservative Anglicans for appearing to encourage submission to tyranny. He thus took pains to demonstrate that Christianity did not demand absolute acquiesce to unjust human power.[60] While Jesus's injunction to render to Caesar the things that are Caesar's suggests that "unless we are good Subjects, we cannot be good Christians," nevertheless "our paramount duty is to God, to whom we are to render *the things that are God's*." Where a conflict appears between our duties, a Christian is required to observe the ordinances of God. A government cannot coerce someone to act contrary to the laws of God, "because everyman is under a prior and superior obligation to *obey God in all things*." In such a case of "incompatible demands of duty," one is to undertake "passive obedience": while one refuses to disobey God by performing the action that violates one's conscience, one willfully submits to any civil penalties for which one may be liable for disobeying men. Such a stance of "passive obedience" is a far cry from "unlimited obedience" to government, but it also does not express a positive right of resistance.[61]

By counseling resistance to British authority, those such as Duché were in the end sanctioning resistance "clearly and literally against *authority*."[62] And here Boucher turned from his clerical opponent to challenge the Continental Congress itself, citing the "extraordinary sentiments" of its recent declaration. "Can men who exercise their reason believe," Congress had asked, "that the Divine Author of our existence intended a part of the human race to hold an absolute property in, and an unbounded power over, others marked out by his infinite wisdom and goodness as the objects of a legal domination never rightfully resistible, how-ever severe and oppressive?"[63] This statement, Boucher said, would justify resistance not only to the existing British authority over the American colonies but to political authority as such; it was "a denial of that just supremacy which 'the Divine Author of our existence' has beyond all question given to 'one part of the human race' to hold over another. Without some paramount and irresistible power, there can be no government."[64] If Americans were to release themselves from the authority of the king and Parliament, they would find themselves in submission to some other power, constituted differently, but no less absolute and possibly more terrible. Boucher scoffed at the notion that the colonies were being oppressed by the British government "on account of an insignificant duty on tea." "Is it the part of an *understanding people*, of loyal subjects, or of good Christians," he asked, "instantly to resist and rebel for a cause so trivial?"[65] Should they feel so terribly oppressed and aggrieved, the colonists ought to take their petitions and remonstrations to the proper constitutional channels. And if their grievances, once brought to the attention of the authorities, were to fall on deaf ears and to go without redress or resolution, what then?

Confident in the wisdom and benevolence of the British authorities, Boucher did not expect matters would come to that. But if the Americans failed to convince Parliament of the justness of their complaint, Boucher simply shrugged, saying, "I wish and advise you to act the part of reasonable men, and of Christians." And what would that entail? "Patiently suffering."[66]

This was, in the end, a broader statement about the proper stance of the Christian toward this fallen world. Christianity teaches that the world is not perfect and that it is not within our all-too-human power to perfect it. We are to reconcile ourselves to life's many inconveniences and difficulties rather than take up "projects of redress," which may instead cause even greater pains and miseries to fall on ourselves and others. Do not seek perfection on this side of eternity, Boucher counseled. For "what is the whole history of human life, public or private, but a series of disappointments?" Learn to endure patiently through them, to submit as their Master and his disciples had submitted. "Those persons are as little acquainted with general history, as they are with the particular doctrines of Christianity, who represent such submission as abject and servile."[67]

Jonathan Boucher concluded his discourse "On Civil Liberty" with the instruc-tion of 1 Peter 2:13–17: "*fear God: honour the King*," a text to which Myles

Cooper had appealed toward the end of his fast day sermon.[68] Those same verses also served as the text for the pair of sermons delivered by Samuel Seabury Jr. and Charles Inglis in the midst of the war.[69] Inglis noted at the outset of his oration that St. Peter "connects the respectful Honour and Obedience we owe to our Sovereign, with that filial, reverential Fear which is due to our Creator; not only because they are characteristic of a real Christian, and should be inseparable; but because our Welfare, Peace and Happiness, temporal and eternal, depend on the Discharge of them." As these were "Duties which God hath thus united and joined together, no Man should ever presume to put asunder," he said, alluding to Jesus's ban on divorce (Matthew 19:6).[70]

Both clergymen placed the apostle's exhortation in historical context, noting the "immediate Occasion of the strong Expressions used by St. PETER and St. PAUL, when they speak of the Authority of civil Government, and that of the Submission which we owe to it": the vulnerable state of the nascent Christian community regarded and reviled by Roman authorities as a Jewish sect. The Jews' political pretentions were a source of ongoing tension between them and Roman authorities. "Whatever Governor they were under, they were always turbulent, factious and rebellious," Seabury remarked. "They were the *chosen,* the *peculiar People* of God, and expected that God would give them the Empire of the World, and, under the Messiah, make them the Lords of the Earth. The Prevalence of this Temper excited them to perpetual Insurrections and Rebellions, and finally drew upon them the Vengeance of the Romans, which put a Period to their Nation and City."[71] Inglis suggested that "their general Conduct raised the Aversion of Mankind against them. They were persecuting and uncharitable towards others; whilst rent by the bitterest Animosities among themselves. They were seditious also, frequently raising Insurrections, dissolving the Obligations between the Prince and the Subject, and making Religion the Cloak of Disloyalty." Considered from the historical point of view, the apostles' counsel of submission to the government reflected their assessment of the situation, the vulnerability of their flock to anti-Jewish animus. Inglis said that "there was a Necessity, that the Apostle should exhort Christians to distinguish themselves by those Virtues which were opposite to the Vices so frequently practiced by the Jews—to convince the World that they were different People, guided by different Principles; that so their Lives might bear the strictest Scrutiny, and turn the Detraction of their Enemies into Praise."[72] Similarly, Seabury claimed, "IT became, therefore, necessary from political as well as religious Motives, to discountenance and discourage every Sentiment that was unfriendly to Order and good Government, that no unjust Suspicions might lie against the Christian Religion upon that Account."[73]

The apostles' instruction to submit to the government was to be regarded not just as pragmatic and contingent advice but as a religious duty, incumbent on all Christians as a general rule, irrespective of the nature of the regime or the personal character of the sovereign. "Christians were to distinguish themselves from others, and manifest the native Excellence and Spirit of their Religion. The Honor of Christ, and the Success of the Gospel, depended on its Professors observing this Line of Conduct—I may affirm, that they also greatly depend on it even now," Inglis said.[74] The contrary principle "must necessarily and daily fill the World with Confusion and Disorder."[75] He derided those Christians who failed to regard this duty as binding upon them. "How then can any who call themselves Christians disregard this commandment; or think that Conscience is not concerned in obeying it?"[76] In another sermon, Inglis inveighed against such misuse of religion by the revolutionaries: "LET enthusiastic Republicans belie Heaven, if they will, by claiming its Sanction to Schemes which have Falshood [sic], Rebellion and Usurpation for their Basis—turning Faith into Faction and the Gospel of Peace, into an Engine of War and Sedition. We dare not thus prevaricate, or trifle with the living God; or handle his Word deceitfully."[77]

The duty of obedience was also imparted by human reason and could be demonstrated from practical experience. Human beings are social creatures. They are born into society, upon which they depend for their very survival and temporal happiness. And society relies on government, the authority of rulers and their civil power to maintain order and security, restrain the passions of the strong, and protect the weak. "Here then, at least, the Commands of God, and the Reason and Nature of Things coincide," Seabury avowed.[78] Inglis observed that government "is the Band which unites the Interests of Individuals; it secures to them their respective Rights, and preserves from them Injuries; it is the Source of numberless Blessings, which are interrupted, or wholly vanish, the Moment it is disturbed. In a Word, whatever Portion of Happiness is allotted by Providence to the Children of Men, is attainable only through the Means of Government."[79] He added that "as our benevolent Creator undoubtedly willed the Happiness of his Creatures, he must have willed the Means also without which that Happiness could not be obtained. Hence, Government in general should be resolved into the Divine Will. It is 'the Ordinance of God, ordained by him' to minister to our Good."[80]

Now, as the purpose of government is to protect individuals and preserve society, reason and common sense may appear to counsel that if a government is wicked or is failing in its duty to protect the weak from the strong, it may be considered illegitimate and those suffering under its yoke possess the right to rebel. But are human beings truly competent to judge whether the ruler is truly bad? "Shall we," Seabury asked, "give the Reigns to Passion and Whim and Caprice, and break through all the Bonds of Society, because *they* whom God's Providence hath placed over us have failed in *their* Duty?" To suffer under a bad or even a wicked ruler would be preferable to the disorder ushered in by rebellion. "It would be to dissolve all the Ties of Government," Seabury stated, "and introduce Anarchy, and Oppression, and Confusion, because some of the Officers of the Government had behaved amiss." The likely consequences of rebellion were no doubt much worse than whatever injustices were currently being borne. And he reminded the soldiers that "it was to these Emperors and Magistrates,— even to *Nero* and *Caligula*—that the Apostles commanded Honor and Respect, at all Times; and when ever it could be done consistently with Obedience to God, Duty and Submission."[81] Similarly, Inglis contended that "this was to be a general Rule for all Christians. The personal Character of the Magistrate was not to interfere with the Civil Duty of the Subject: Even when bad, it did not dissolve the Obligation of the latter—were the contrary principle admitted, it must necessarily and daily fill the World with Confusion and Disorder. The Christian therefore, is here injoined to honour the Person who is vested with legal Authority, and whom the Providence of God hath placed over him."[82]

The heart of the matter was that the duty to obey the government and to honor its magistrates flowed from one's fear of God and respect for his commandments. "WHILST you honour the King, fear God also. These Duties should be inseparable. The one naturally rises out of the other," Inglis announced.[83] Seabury explained that "our Duty to obey our Rulers and Governors arises from our Duty to obey God."

> He has commanded us to obey Magistrates; to honor all Men according to their Degree in Authority. If we fear God we shall obey his Command from a Principle of Duty to him.—Civil Government is the Institution and Ordinance of God:—He hath ordained the Powers that are:—He hath committed to them the Sword of Justice, i.e. the right and Power of Punishment:—He hath told us, That if we resist this Power, we resist his Ordinance; and that if we do resist, we shall receive to ourselves

Damnation: He himself will punish us for it. The Fear of God, there-
fore, binds all the Duties which we owe to civil Government upon the
Conscience; and will make us obey all the lawful Commands of those
who have the Rule over us, for the Lord's Sake, lest, by resisting his
Ordinance, we bring his Judgments upon us in this World, and eternal
Condemnation in the World to Come.[84]

While the British constitution vested authority in the king and Parliament, it was
the monarch who symbolized the supreme authority of the state and the bond of
the spiritual and political orders: "Considered in a *religious* View, He is the *Vicegerent* of God, to whom He hath committed his Sword of Justice, and his Right and
Power to govern the British Empire. Considered in a *political* View, He is *the Power,
the Glory, the Majesty of the whole People*; and therefore, considered in either View,
*the highest Honor and Respect, that are due to any Mortal, are due to him, from every
Individual who inhabits those extensive Territories that are Subject to his Command.*"[85]

Given these considerations, the American rebellion could only be
regarded in a devastating light. "How great must be their Crime, how atrocious
their Wickedness, who, in Contempt of every Obligation, have excited, and still
support and carry on, the present Rebellion against the legal Government of
the British Empire to which they belonged!" Seabury declared, "—breaking
through all the Bonds of civil Society, effacing the Principles of Morality from
among Men, treading under Foot the Dictates of Humanity and the Rights of
their Fellow Subjects, subverting the most mild and equitable System of Laws,
introducing the most horrid Oppression and Tyranny, and filling the Country
with Confusion, Rapine, Destruction, Slaughter and Blood!" The unwarranted
rebellion, driven by "*Impiety, Ingratitude* and *Falshood*," was a betrayal of that
loving parent who had so tenderly planted and protected and nurtured those
colonies and had resulted in broken families, imprisonment of friends, destruction of property, and banishment.[86] The rebels, Inglis remarked in his sermon to
those same soldiers, are "our infatuated Adversaries" striving to replace the
British constitution ("formed by the Wisdom of Ages, and . . . the Admiration
and Envy of Mankind") with "a motly Fabric, composed partly of the discordant
Shreds of Heathen Republics, and perfectly adapted to popular Tyranny!"[87]

In his December 1776 sermon at Oxford, Myles Cooper lamented that the Loyalist
clergy "from the Beginning, have been the objects of Republican Rage, and fanatic
malignity." He hinted at the insults and worse they were enduring on account of

their convictions ("were this a proper time and place for the narrative, I could unfold such scenes of Persecution and Cruelty, as would excite the Indignation and Horror of every Soul in this Assembly") before providing a brief sketch of what they faced— "hunted like so many Beasts of Prey, by their inhuman Tormentors."[88] Around the same time, Samuel Seabury wrote to inform the SPG of the troubles he and other Loyalist clergy faced following the states' declaration of independence. (He had already suffered much abuse on account of his activities. Back in 1775, he was abducted from his home by the Sons of Liberty and taken to New Haven, where for six weeks he was held captive as they attempted in vain to extract a confession of his authorship of the notorious A. W. Farmer's pamphlets).[89] The New York Provincial Assembly, he wrote, had "published an edict, making it death to aid, abet, support, assist, or comfort the king, or any of his forces, servants, or friends." Until this time Seabury had kept his church open, but with the arrival of about fifty armed men in his neighborhood, he was compelled to reassess. "I was now in a critical situation. If I prayed for the king the least I could expect was to be sent into New England; probably something worse, as no clergyman on the continent was so obnoxious to them. If I went to church and omitted praying for the king, it would not only be a breach of my duty, but in some degree countenancing their rebellion, and supporting that independency which they had declared." Seabury chose, as he put it, "the least culpable course," deciding to stay away from his church until such a time as he "could pray for the king, and do my duty according to the rubric and canons."[90] That time was not soon coming. In early September, Seabury took flight from his Westchester home and climbed aboard a British ship of war in Long Island Sound. For the duration of hostilities, he served His Majesty's cause as a physician and chaplain and by turning out pro-British articles for the New York press.

As the Anglo-American crisis progressed, Patriot authorities announced fast days and enacted test oaths and laws prohibiting public support for the king and Parliament. For Church of England clergymen, these measures ushered in a time of religious persecution. To recite the prayers for the king or refuse to pray for the new Congress and recognize days of fasting and humiliation meant risking hefty fines (of one hundred pounds, in some cases—a year's salary) or worse. Political sentiments expressed from the pulpit, in print, even in informal conversation, and the failure to open churches on fast days or read the Declaration of Independence, could lead to harassment by the mob or punishment by the state. Clergy reported public insults, mob attacks, fines, property seizure, house arrest, and imprisonment. Churches were vandalized or commandeered for military use. (In a somewhat comical example, William Clark of

Massachusetts complained of being held captive at an inn and forced to gaze on a portrait of Oliver Cromwell for forty-five minutes.)[91] Charles Inglis informed the SPG secretary in London that "the Declaration increased the embarrassment of the Clergy. To officiate publickly, and not pray for the King and Royal Family according to the Liturgy, was against their Duty and Oath, as well as Dictates of their Consciences; and yet to use the Prayers for the King and Royal Family, would have drawn inevitable Destruction on them."[92] Jonathan Boucher later reflected that "many of them were called upon to give such proofs of fortitude in *suffering for righteousness sake,* as would not have discredited primitive martyrs."[93]

At the same time, Anglican clergy struggled to balance the keeping of their oath against the obligations to their parishioners and the demands of the new de facto sovereign. In New England and outside British lines in the Middle Colonies, Loyalist Church of England clergy chose to close their doors rather than cooperate with the new governments' mandates. In the fall of 1776, an SPG minister reported that most of the churches in Pennsylvania, New York, New Jersey, and Connecticut had been shuttered. Others fled their parishes, either to New York City, which remained under British control, or to England or British colonies in Canada or the Caribbean. For those who chose to stay put in the rebellious colonies, withdrawal from the public square appeared to be the most prudent course of action.[94]

By the end of 1778, the Connecticut clergy decided to seek out a compromise on the liturgy that would allow them to reopen their churches. Samuel Seabury wrote to Thomas Bradbury Chandler, then in exile in England, to inquire if the bishop of London would allow them to conduct the public service with the omission of the state prayers. In his reply, which arrived in early 1779, Chandler recommended that they do "as they shall judge best for the Interest of the Church," so long as no prayers to Congress were added to the liturgy.[95] In a later letter, Chandler reported that the SPG and the bishop of London would "under the present situation of affairs" permit the American clergy to omit the prayers for the king so long as those for Congress were not offered in their place. "The *Canons* of the Church must for the present, give way to the CANNON of Congress," he conceded.[96] That dispatch was dated December 3, 1781. But by then the issue was mostly moot. Though the fighting would continue for another year, it had become clear to the Churchmen that George III was no longer the sovereign of those united states.

Back in 1774, Jonathan Boucher preached, "Lawful government is the greatest blessing that mankind enjoy, and the very life and soul of society; without which, men must live together rather like wolves and tigers, than like rational creatures. To resist and to rebel against a lawful government, is to oppose *the ordinance of God*, and to injure or destroy institutions most essential to human happiness. He, therefore, who can hope that God, *who is a God of order and not of confusion*, will give his blessings to such attempts, does neither more nor less than expect that he will act in contraction to his most glorious attributes, and cease to be the friend and father of mankind."[97] Myles Cooper envisioned in late 1776 "the complete and speedy re-establishment of order, harmony, and good government, in a miserably distracted country."[98] In his sermon to the British troops, Charles Inglis remarked that "if Truth and Loyalty, if just Government and human Happiness, are pleasing and agreeable to his Will—and that they are so, we have the express Declarations of his own unerring Word—If this, I say, be the Case, we may humbly and confidently trust that the just Ruler of the Universe favours our Cause—that it hath HIS Approbation who is a God of Order."[99]

The Loyalist clergy believed that if its people feared God and honored the king, Providence would continue to favor Britain's undertakings. In the end, however, it appeared that it was the Patriot's God of Liberty that emerged triumphant.[100] "The general part I took in the last contest was the result of principle and conscience; to their dictates I honestly adhered, and conceived I was thereby promoting the best interests and welfare of America," Inglis confided toward the end of the war. "But the views of Divine Providence, respecting this Country, were different; and it is my indispensable duty to acquiesce in the decisions of Providence."[101] In November 1783, he resigned his position and set sail with evacuating troops to Nova Scotia, where he joined some forty thousand other refugees; in 1787 he was appointed that colony's first bishop, the Church of England's first in North America. Thomas Bradbury Chandler had first been offered the position, but he declined on account of bad health. After the conclusion of the war, he returned to his congregation in Elizabeth Town. Myles Cooper remained in Edinburgh. A number of his former King's College students—Alexander Hamilton, John Jay, Gouverneur Morris—took their place as political architects of the new nation.

The American Revolution devastated the Church of England in the former colonies. The old church establishments were quickly dismantled; over the course of the war, the ranks of its clergy were cut by half on account of emigration or death; the SPG withdrew its support. Educational institutions such as King's College in New

York and the University of Pennsylvania shook themselves free from their Anglican origins. The Methodists, who had emerged as a pietist evangelical movement within the Church of England, broke off to form a separate denomination in 1784. In Virginia that same year, Patrick Henry proposed a general assessment bill that, claiming that "the general diffusion of Christian knowledge hath a natural tendency to correct the morals of men, restrain their vices, and preserve the peace of society," would have levied taxes for the Episcopalian and other churches to support religious teachers, setting up a kind of "multiple establishment" in the state. James Madison set to work to defeat the measure, quickly drafting and publishing his "Memorial and Remonstrance against Religious Assessments," and mobilizing Baptists and others against the purported assault on religious liberty. In 1786, sectarian and enlightened joined together to pass Thomas Jefferson's Act for Establishing Religious Freedom, which ushered in an entirely new regime of church-state relations in the state. From then on, no religious institution would enjoy official recognition, privileges, or financial support from the government. (That legislation later informed the language of the religion clauses of the First Amendment.) Jefferson later wrote that the measure "meant to comprehend, within the mantle of it's [sic] protection, the Jew and the Gentile, the Christian and Mahometan, the Hindoo and infidel of every denomination." Elsewhere, the tyranny of New England fanatics that Churchmen such as John Bradbury Chandler feared would be the consequence of a Patriot victory did not come to pass. The New England Standing Orders remained so for a while longer in Connecticut, New Hampshire, and Massachusetts, but even in those states the "dissenting" denominations—Presbyterians, Baptists, Quakers, and Episcopalians—obtained greater religious liberties. In time, those establishments, too, would be dismantled. Connecticut's 1818 constitution abolished the vestiges of its establishment; New Hampshire followed suit a year later. In 1833, amid ongoing legal squabbles between Congregationalists and Unitarians over church property, Massachusetts amended its constitution, removing the provisions that had granted privileges to the old parishes.[102]

Acquiescing to the decree of Providence, the former Church of England clergy took to the process of reorganizing their church, convening a series of conventions to make alterations in church governance and the liturgy and to unite the state churches and High and Low factions (which held divergent views on ecclesiastical governance and liturgical reform) into a single governing body. It was simple enough to make those changes in the Book of Common Prayer necessary to "render it consistent with the American revolution and the Constitutions of the respective States."[103] Coming to agreement on other liturgical and structural matters proved more challenging and threatened the possibility of a merger of the states' episcopal churches.

Particularly fraught was the question of the episcopate and what it would look like under the new political dispensation where the traditional ties between church and state no longer pertained. The Connecticut clergy wasted no time in setting out a plan to obtain a bishop. In a secret meeting conducted in the spring of 1783, the leaders of the Connecticut Episcopalians concluded that a bishop was required to lead the reorganization of the church; in a follow-up meeting, they settled on Samuel Seabury Jr., then busy assisting the evacuation of Loyalist refugees from New York to Nova Scotia, as their candidate. Seabury accepted the assignment and set sail across the Atlantic, arriving in England in June. He had hoped to obtain consecration from the English bishops, but after an eighteen-month wait the English bishops refused Seabury's application (in part because the consecration service contained a loyalty oath to the monarch, but also because there was no established diocese in Connecticut and the application did not have the sanction of the state government).[104] Not to be deterred, Seabury then journeyed to Scotland, where in November 1784 he was consecrated by nonjuring bishops in Aberdeen. Seabury returned to the United States in June 1785 to take up his post. There was some irony—and no little controversy—that the first Anglican bishop in America was a High Churchman and former Loyalist planted in Congregationalist New England.

For Episcopalians of a more latitudinarian and democratic mindset, this was not an especially auspicious development. But in 1787, Patriot William White, the rector of Christ Church in Pennsylvania, and Samuel Provoost, rector of Trinity Church in New York City, were consecrated in England, with the participation of the archbishop of Canterbury (Parliament having enacted legislation permitting the English bishops to consecrate American candidates a year earlier). White had been Jacob Duché's assistant and then successor at Christ Church and St. Peters; Duché, who had advised him on the reorganization of church governance and served as an intermediary between the American clergy and English hierarchy, attended his consecration.[105]

When the General Convention of the Protestant Episcopal Church in the United States of America met in 1789, its delegates adopted a constitution, a set of canons, and a revised Book of Common Prayer and settled on a purely spiritual episcopacy. The laity would participate in the election of delegates who would choose episcopal candidates, bringing the principles of representative government into ecclesiastical policy. And so the Episcopalians, having undergone their own "ecclesiastic revolution," settled into their place as members of one of the nation's increasing number of religious denominations.[106]

This accommodation is powerfully represented by the Cathedral Church of St. Peter and St. Paul, the seat of the presiding bishop of the Episcopal Church and the bishop of the Diocese of Washington, a place better known as Washington National Cathedral. From the massive neo-Gothic structure of Indiana limestone, the world's sixth-largest cathedral, one may gaze down from its heights on that other, more famous, hill across town where the city's quadrants meet, the people's elected political representatives discuss and debate, bills become laws, and the distinguished justices of the Supreme Court hear the cases brought before them, deliberate over their merits, and arrive at their decisions. In the report accompanying their designs for the structure, George F. Bodley and Henry Vaughan, the architects initially commissioned for the project, noted that "the site is a remarkably fine one, very commanding and beautiful. The Cathedral will be a conspicuous object from the Capitol and other parts of the city. When complete, with its surrounding buildings, it will be 'as a city set on a hill.' "[107]

In stonework and stained-glass windows National Cathedral powerfully communicates an intertwined narrative: the Christian story, from creation to redemption, alongside the story of America, its founding, growth, triumphs and tragedies, saints and martyrs. In doing so, the space expresses the conviction that America's democracy is a gift of God to be celebrated and protected. That blending of the spiritual, national, and political becomes manifest the moment one steps into the building. The flags of the states, in the order of their entrance into the Union, hang along the nave. Peer down in the narthex and you see their seals emblazoned on the floor, surrounding the Great Seal of the United States and the District of Columbia. In the corner on your left stands a seven-foot marble statue of George Washington, depicted not as a general or president but, tricorne in hand, as a humble churchgoer. (His orthodoxy might be called into question by the three Masonic symbols carved into the wall behind him.) Walking from the first president to the right, you approach a bronze statue of Abraham Lincoln, words from his farewell address at the Springfield railroad station calling on "the assistance of the Divine Being," as the president-elect prepared for his dangerous journey to the White House, are engraved in the wall beside him. Up above, beginning with the great West Rose window depicting creation, from west to east the clerestory stained glass, the highest level of windows of the building, intertwine episodes of the history of ancient Israel and the story of the American republic. Topping these are windows bearing tiny images of the Supreme Court Building, the White House, and the US Capitol, representations of the three branches of the United States government; below are inscribed the words of the opening sentence of the Constitution. On the ground level, other windows depict significant personages and events in American history. A series that runs along the north transept features the emergence and practice of American governance, centered on the figures of Thomas Jefferson and James Madison, situated below a figure of Christ. On the left lancet, Jefferson is framed by images representing what he considered his most important accomplishments: the Declaration of Independence, the Virginia Statute for Religious Freedom, and the founding of the University of Virginia. Madison's window depicts the framing of the Constitution and has images of a swearing-in of a president and a meeting of the Supreme Court. The "American Statesmen" window replaced one that had depicted Jesus counseling the people to "give unto Caesar" and to "give unto God."[108]

In time, its iconography came to reflect the nation's dynamic pluralism. Figures of eminent Americans—Helen Keller (who lies buried in the crypt), Eleanor Roosevelt, Rosa Parks, Dr. Martin Luther King Jr., and most recently Elie Wiesel—as well as noteworthy religious leaders from around the world (such as Dietrich Bonhoeffer, Pope John XXIII, Archbishop Óscar Romero, and Mother Teresa) are set throughout the Cathedral's walls, a panoply of unofficial saints. The nearly two hundred kneelers in St. John's Chapel are embroidered with the names of renowned Americans (and some foreign dignitaries, such as Winston Churchill), religious figures (including such prominent Dissenters as John Winthrop, Increase Mather, and Roger Williams, the fierce advocate of separation of church and state, and the Congregationalist theologian and revivalist Jonathan Edwards) and Founding Fathers, presidents and politicians, military heroes and civic leaders, novelists and poets, artists and explorers, inventors and visionaries. All could be incorporated in the Cathedral's capacious and eclectic celebration of the nation's ever-expanding spiritual family. And those in the know might seek out a few objects representing the American church's first bishop, Samuel Seabury Jr.: a carved stone of "sailing ships" commemorating his journey to Scotland for consecration; a niche statue in the nave, south transept vestibule, south wall above portal doors and another on the canopy of the Presiding Bishop's Stall; a stained-glass window celebrating his work on the revision of the American prayer book.

On July 7, 1776, Jacob Duché, after deliberating with the vestry of Christ Church and St. Peter's, stood at his pulpit and recited the liturgy without the royal prayers. The following day, he received a letter from John Hancock informing him that "the Congress has been induced, from a consideration of your piety, as well as your uniform and zealous attachment to the rights of America, to appoint you as their Chaplain." Duché accepted the position.[109] When he took up his assignment as the first chaplain of Congress on July 9, the clergyman opened the meeting with a prayer similar to the one he delivered to the First Continental Congress nearly two years earlier. But he did not last long in that position. He resigned from the post on October 17, citing ill health and the need to attend to his church duties. The Sunday following the British occupation of Philadelphia on September 26, 1777, Duché officiated at Christ Church, reinstating the royal prayers. He was nevertheless arrested by British forces as he left his church, and held overnight. On October 8, he dispatched a letter to Washington expressing his disenchantment with the revolution and entreating the general to persuade Congress to rescind the declaration of independency, cease hostilities, and negotiate a settlement. Duché tried to explain his own actions that seemingly supported the Patriot endeavor, his agreement with the vestry to omit the royal prayers and keep his church open, his rash decision to accept the appointment as chaplain, and the influential sermon he dedicated to Washington back in July of 1775 ("My sermon speaks for itself & utterly disclaims the idea of independency").[110] Washington dismissed the clergyman's petition as a "ridiculous—illiberal performance" and turned the letter over to Congress.[111] As news of his political apostasy leaked out, the once celebrated clergyman was condemned a traitor to the revolution. On December 9, Duché informed his vestry that he planned to travel to England to explain his actions to the bishop of London. Three days later, the preacher of *Stand Fast* sailed into exile. Duché did not relinquish hope of one day returning to his native city. After the war, he inquired about the possibility of repatriation, even penning a letter to Washington begging his pardon and requesting his assistance. It would not be until 1793, after Pennsylvania's laws excluding political refugees were repealed, that Congress's first chaplain set foot again in his Philadelphia and in the nation his words had helped inspire.[112]

Not long after delivering his oration "On Civil Liberty," Jonathan Boucher was ejected from his position as rector of Queen Anne's. In the autumn of 1775, he set sail to his native England, where he took up the post of vicar of Epsom in the county of Surrey. In 1797, deeply troubled by the French Revolution, the "acknowledged and most distinguished offspring"[113] of the American rebellion, and the turmoil it unleashed, he assembled some of the sermons on "political subjects" he had delivered in America into a volume titled *A View of the Causes and Consequences of the American Revolution* and dedicated to his former friend turned political adversary, not "the General of a Conventional Army" but "the late dignified President of the United States," whom he called "a friend of rational and sober freedom." "The loose principles of the times are still to be regarded as the *one great cause* of the American revolt," he wrote in a long preface composed for its publication.[114] "*How* much it was the fashion, at the period in question, for people of all ranks to speculate, philosophize, and project Utopian schemes of reformation; which, as it was conducted in America, led, as regularly as ever any cause produces its corresponding effect, first, to the demolition of the Church, as that, in its turn, no less certainly led to the over-turning of the State."[115] Boucher placed the blame for the conflict squarely on that "spirit of Republicanism," which had beget the English Civil War (of which, "in all it's leading features, whether considered in it's origin, it's conduct, or it's end, it was but a counterpart") and which the Puritans had carried over and transplanted in America.[116] That spirit had even infected some of his fellow Anglican clergy in Virginia and Maryland, who, "unmindful of their own princi-ples, became rebels," "were exposed, like the rest of mankind, to the influence of those opinions of the times, which, like a torrent, swept away all cool and sober thought, and all sedateness of judgment, in men of all ranks and orders, in one mad phrensy of ambition." The recent revolution in France was "that yet more awful lesson which the world has been taught by that more fatal exemplifica-tion of the effects of false principles."[117]

Boucher reflected sourly upon the doings of that breakaway republic across the Atlantic. He did not prophesize a happy future for the new nation. "Ever since they have become a distinct people, their Government has been unsettled, agitated, and sometimes even on the brink of revolution." "All they have in their history, that is either ancient or venerable, they have in common with the nation which they have renounced." The Americans, he contended, "have none of those hereditary attachments to country, which are the strong ligatures of government; nor any of that constitutional devotion to institutions of long standing, which nothing but long habits can form; for the want of which no new institutions, however wise and salutary, have any compensations to offer." "And it is just that they who contributed most to bring this great evil of revolution into credit should most feel it's bitter effects, so it is highly probable," Boucher predicted, "that the people of the States will have the most reason to lament their success. They set out on principles incompatible with stability;

and of course it is natural to suppose that their people, following the example of their founders, will always be prone to revolt and rebellion. With the seed of almost every political evil that can be named, and perhaps, most of all, that of tyranny, thickly sown in their Constitutions, it is hardly possible that they should be either easily or well governed; and by being ill governed, they are sure to become an unworthy people—and if unworthy, it is still more certain that they must and will be unhappy." As a hedge against the coming disorder, the aging clergyman proposed that the new country forge a grand alliance with Great Britain—a "federal union" of "two distinct, and completely independent States" but "with some considerable degree of community in government."[118]

In his dedication, Boucher took notice of Washington's statement in his Farewell Address that "the only firm supports of political prosperity are religion and morality." "Those best friends of mankind," Boucher mused, "who, amidst all the din and uproar of Utopian reforms, persist to think that the affairs of this world can never be well administered by men trained to disregard the God who made it, must ever thank you for this decided protest against the fundamental maxim of modern revolutionists, that religion is no concern of the State." But being a concern of the United States would not entail the establishment of religion.[119]

CHAPTER TWO

We Cannot Yield Obedience, for Conscience Sake

The Covenanters

It was probably not a surprise to astute political observers of the time that the document that emerged out of the Philadelphia Convention in September 1787 did not include among its provisions a formal connection between church and state—a national establishment of religion. The extant notes of the proceedings suggest the drafters were completely unconcerned with the matter. Perhaps that team of political architects deemed it prudent to pass over controversial issues that might disrupt the project of erecting a national government, delineating its differing branches of authority, and carefully enunciating and balancing their powers. Religious pluralism made the establishment of any one church untenable; federalism provided a principle by which to leave such matters to the jurisdiction of the states. Whatever state establishments might remain, there would be no established church of the United States.[1]

But the proposed Constitution included what appeared to some as a startling and potentially dangerous innovation on church-state relations. Article VI, Section 3's prohibition of any religious test "as a Qualification to any Office or public Trust" was a positive measure. Adopted by the convention without much debate, the measure represented a departure from prevailing practice and suggested that their Constitution and the government it would establish did not rest on Christian principles or depend upon (publicly professed) Christian officials.

And then there was the text's utter silence regarding the Deity. Unlike the Declaration of Independence, the Constitution made no appeal to "the Laws of Nature and Nature's God," the rights-endowing Creator, "the Supreme Judge of the world," or "a firm reliance on the protection of divine Providence." Unlike the Articles of Confederation that it would replace, the Constitution made no mention of "the Great Governor of the World." The document that emerged from the Philadelphia convention appeared to be, in the words of later scholars, "a godless constitution."[2]

A number of explanations for this departure from traditional practice acknowledging God and his authority have been advanced by commentators: the omission could be for prudential reasons, to avoid controversies over religion, or on account of the Framers' commitment to the doctrine of delegated powers or the principle of federalism; or, in accordance with their Enlightenment rationalism, they intended to design by means of human wisdom a state that derived its authority from "We the People" and directed to "establish Justice, insure domestic Tranquility, provide for the common defence, promote the general Welfare, and secure the Blessings of Liberty to ourselves and our Posterity." Over such a constitution a divine imprimatur was not only unnecessary but unseasonable. When asked why the document had failed to recognize God or the Christian religion, Alexander Hamilton, one of its principal architects, is said to have replied, "I declare we forgot it."[3]

The "godlessness" of the Constitution did not go unnoticed and was seized on by its critics. During the course of the debates over its ratification in the states, Anti-Federalists disparaged the document's "cold indifference to religion," decried its failure to acknowledge God and to recognize the religious foundations upon which the state depended, and warned of its pernicious effect on a populace on whose virtue republican liberty depended.[4] Some opponents feared that the prohibition of a religious test would allow all manner of infidels— Catholics, Quakers, Jews, deists, Muhammadans, and pagans—to obtain public office. Indeed, it allowed the possibility that an infidel might be elected chief magistrate! And it was alleged that the instrument was the work of a deistic conspiracy to undermine Christianity in the new republic. Then again, some worried that the Constitution did not go far enough in safeguarding the rights of conscience and religious liberties of Americans from the interference of the national government, concerns that would be addressed with what became the religion clauses of the First Amendment.[5]

Such anxieties about the dangerous potentialities of a constitution that ignored the role of religion as the foundation of civil institutions did not vanish following its ratification and after the government it established came into being. "Many pious people wish the name of the supreme Being had been introduced Somewhere in the new constitution," Dr. Benjamin Rush informed Vice President John Adams in a June 1789 letter. "Perhaps an acknowledgement may be made of his Goodness or of his providence in the proposed amendments."[6] In October of that year, a collection of Presbyterian ministers and elders wrote to President George Washington to register their disappointment that "some explicit acknowledgement of the *only true God and Jesus Christ, whom he hath sent*" had not been inserted in the document, even as they conceded that "this defect has been amply remedied, in the face of all the world, by the piety and devotion" of Washington's official acts. The new chief executive replied, "I am persuaded, you permit me to observe, that the path of true piety is so plain as to require little political attention. To this consideration we ought to ascribe the absence of any regulation, respecting religion, from the Magna-Charta of our country."[7] In a 1793 sermon, the Presbyterian reverend John Mitchell Mason of New York lamented the lack of gratitude to the Deity who delivered the nation from its adversaries and blessed it with prosperity and peace. "One would imagine that no occasion of making a pointed and public acknowledgment of the divine benignity, could have presented itself so obviously, as the framing an instrument of government which, in the nature of things, must be closely allied to our happiness or our ruin. And yet, that very constitution which the singular goodness of God enabled us to establish, does not so much as recognize *his being!*" Indeed, "from the constitution of the United States, it is impossible to ascertain *what* God we worship; or whether we own a God *at all.*" And Mason darkly warned, "Should the citizens of American be as irreligious as her Constitution, we will have reason to tremble, lest the Governor of the universe, who will not be treated with indignity by a people any more than by individuals, overturn from its foundations the fabric we have been rearing, and crush us to atoms in the wreck."[8] A few years later, in the midst of the heated election contest of 1800, Mason worried that his worst fears were being realized. The defective Constitution would make it possible for such a man as the "infidel Mr. Jefferson" to be elected president. "The federal Constitution," he complained, "*makes no acknowledgement of that God* who gave us our national existence, and saved us from anarchy and internal war." If the people so chose an infidel as their chief executive, Mason continued, "you will sanction that neglect, you will declare, by a solemn national act, that there is no more religion in your collective character, than in your written constitution:

you will put a national indignity upon the God of your mercies; and provoke him, it may be, to send over your land that deluge of judgments which his forbearance has hitherto suspended."[9] Despite such warnings, Jefferson emerged triumphant, and most American denominations found themselves able to grow in spite of (or perhaps on account of) the nation's "irreligious" foundations— memorably described by the "infidel" president as "a wall of separation between Church & State."[10]

In 1803, a little book appeared with the title *The Two Sons of Oil; or, The Faithful for Witness Magistracy and Ministry upon a Scriptural Basis.* Its author, a young minister named Samuel B. Wylie, announced in the preface his intention to advocate for the principles of the Reformation; although no longer fashionable, they are "the doctrine of the Bible, and the cause of Christ." The first part of the book was a rather technical presentation of "the two great ordinances of Magistracy and Ministry," or the state and the church, how they relate to one another, and the duties one owes to civil government, when morally constituted. But then the author turned to expound the reasons the members of his church, the Reformed Presbyterians, "cannot yield obedience, for conscience sake, to the present civil authority in North America." That present authority, he argued, was an infidel regime, on account of the federal constitution's failure to acknowledge God and Christ and establish a Christian government.[11] As the government was illegitimate, members of the church were forbidden to bestow their consent through participation, whether by holding public office, voting, or even serving on juries. We might think of them as conscientious objectors—keeping their distance from the government until such a time as the nation came to repent of its original sin, submit to divine authority, and establish a godly regime.[12]

The Reformed Presbytery of the United States of North America had been constituted in Philadelphia in 1798, but its roots lay back in the theological-political struggles of the seventeenth century and in the radical Presbyterian dissenters from the Church of Scotland in the eighteenth. Like other Presbyterians, its members adhered to the Westminster Confession of Faith. But they remained committed to two other theological-political documents: the Scottish National Covenant of 1638 and the Solemn League and Covenants of 1643. Responding to the attempt to impose English liturgical reforms and ecclesiastical practices on the Scottish Kirk, the Scottish National Covenant united the Scots under the banner of Presbyterianism, its signatories swearing to the purity of their religion against any innovations. The Solemn League and Covenants of 1643 pledged Scotland's military to the side of the English Parliament for religious unity—the establishment of a Presbyterian empire in England, Scotland, and Ireland, and then beyond. The Covenanters deemed these promises not mere human compacts but covenants entered into with God, still binding even as dreams of a Presbyterian empire collapsed with the restoration of the monarchy under Charles II in 1660. Those who refused to accept the settlement of the Glorious Revolution of 1688, which placed a Protestant on the British throne and reestablished the Church of Scotland under his rule, swore to separate themselves from an uncovenanted state.[13]

The Reformed Presbytery was organized in Scotland in 1743. Those who came to America carried with them across the Atlantic their idiosyncratic theological-political commitments and religious practices of closed communion and psalm singing, settling in the hinterlands of Pennsylvania, New York, what would later become Vermont, and the Carolina backcountry. When the Revolutionary War erupted, many were enthusiastic patriots engaging in "godly resistance" against a tyrannical British monarchy and its corrupt church-state arrangement.[14] The coming to be of the new nation provided an opportunity for the Covenanters and other dissenting Scotch Presbyterian churches to reconsider whether those old covenants were still binding and reconcile their political theologies to the new order and with one another. In 1777, members of the Associate Presbytery (also known as the Seceders) and the Reformed Presbytery entered into discussions over the possibility of a union of their churches. What stood in the way was their difference of opinion over the source of civil government as an ordinance of God and the necessity of a Christian magistrate. Government was instituted by God the Creator for all humanity, the law of nature known independently of Scripture setting down the principles of civil government, said the Seceders; in contrast, the Covenanters maintained that the proximate source of legitimate government was Christ the mediator and therefore concluded that the state and its magistrates needed to acknowledge him as the source of civil authority. Following years of negotiations, in 1782 the Associate Reformed Synod was formed under compromise language that largely reflected the Seceder position on the origin of civil authority. Magistrates ought to be guided by Scripture, but a religious test other than an oath to fidelity was not necessary. Most of the Seceders and Covenanters went along with the union, but there were some holdouts, so the Associate Reformed Church came on the scene as yet another American denomination. When the General Assembly of the Presbyterian Church attempted to bring the various American Calvinist denominations into its fold in 1785, all the fringe sects declined to join on account of their particular theological-political commitments regarding civil government.[15]

For some time, the Reformed Presbyterians remnant who refused to enter the Associate Reformed Church lacked ministers and an organization, maintaining themselves as a lay movement while petitioning authorities across the ocean for assistance. They soon found that they had another theological-political problem to be concerned about: the infidelity of the new nation. This was noted by James McKinney in a pamphlet he wrote for the church in South Carolina in 1795, calling for "A Day of Public Fasting." Forced to flee Ireland on account of a sermon deemed treasonable by British authorities, McKinney escaped to America in 1793. Upon his arrival, he traveled around the country preaching to Covenanter communities. McKinney inveighed against what he saw as a corrupt nation swelling with ignorance, unbelief, and wickedness, lamented his former brethren who "wearied of the cross," and called on his audiences "to mourn at the lax and wicked notions that a great part of this nation entertains upon the article of civil government, namely: that it is utterly resolvable into the corrupt will of unprincipled and ungodly men, without any regard to the moral law, than which, perhaps, a more wicked doctrine has never been broached among Adam's miserable posterity." The nation, he contended, had squandered the opportunity "of setting up a good moral civil constitution." Indeed, they would protect all manner of abominable heresies, permitting them to propagate wildly within their borders.[16] McKinney had transposed the Covenanter complaint into a new key. Uncovenanted Britain wasn't their problem; uncovenanted America was. As a later historian of the church put it, "While the colonists had a right and just reason to declare their independence of Great Britain in 1776, they had not a right nor a just reason for declaring their independence of the God of battles in 1789. The Declaration of Independence was right, but the Constitution of the United States was wrong." With his brother-in-law William Gibson, another refugee from Ireland, and without authorization from Scottish or Irish church authorities, McKinney established the new Reformed Presbytery in America. It was thus in the face of a godless Constitution that the American Covenanters fashioned themselves as a religious movement of political dissent.[17]

The Two Sons of Oil was the first comprehensive elucidation of the American Covenanter's political theology and its application toward the Constitution and government of United States. A historian of the denomination later called Wylie's treatise "the best presentation of the position of the Covenanter Church that has been written."[18] It was also the most influential and notorious. Its title was taken from Zechariah's vision of "the two anointed ones" (in Hebrew, *the sons of oil*) in the Temple (Zechariah 4:14), which Wylie interpreted as representing the institutions of magistracy and ministry—that is, civil and ecclesiastical power, state and church. His exposition of political theology followed. God, "the Supreme Governor of the Universe," the Being from which all powers of lower creatures are derived, delegates power to Christ in his role as "Mediator." Though both institutions of church and state were committed to Christ's control, "they differ in their immediate origin." Civil power "flows immediately from God Creator, as the Governor of the universe" and was committed to the Mediator "by donation of the Father"; ecclesiastical power "flows immediately from Christ, as Mediator." Wylie rejected the view that civil government was a necessary concession to the debased state of humanity on account of the fall. Government, rather, "existed previously to the fall, and would necessarily have existed, even had we never revolted against God; though, no doubt, in that case, it would not have been clothed in some of its present modifications. Man's subjection to the moral government of his Maker would have then been similar to that of beings of a more dignified order." The hierarchal order suggested by "the denominations of Archangels, Thrones, Dominions, Principalities, and Powers" was proof of the preexistence of civil order.[19]

The two branches of magistracy and ministry are thus two aspects of the divinely ordained government, differing in their immediate origin and their objects, forms, ends, effects, subjects, and jurisdictions. Magistracy respects "things external," the "outward man" as "members of the commonwealth, and subjects of the realm"; ministry "things spiritual," considering "men as members of the mystical body of Jesus." The functionaries of magisterial power "exercise dominion, as the vicegerents of God"; the aim of civil power is to maintain the temporal security and civil liberty of the commonwealth and for all persons residing within its realm. Though civil power may be vested in different constitutional forms, it must remain in conformity with the moral law (as delineated in the Decalogue). The functionaries of ecclesiastical power serve "as stewards of the manifold mysteries of the spiritual kingdom"; its end is "the conviction, conversion, and edification of the souls of men"; it is vested by Christ to a consistory of presbyters, and its jurisdiction extends "only to those professed members of the mystical body of Jesus Christ." While operating on human souls, ecclesiastical power indirectly assists the welfare of the commonwealth as "the benign influences of the religion of Jesus, upon the human heart, may be highly advantageous to national prosperity."[20]

Though wielding no authority over ecclesiastical matters, civil government is nonetheless commissioned to promote and protect the true church. Magistrates are commanded to serve as defenders of the true faith and consequently are granted the authority "to remove all external impediments to the true religion and worship of God, whether they be persons or things; such as persecution, profaneness, heresy, idolatry, and their abettors," "to promote purity, unity, and reformation, in the church," "to support the laws of God, by their secular authority, as keepers of both tables of the law, enjoining and commanding all to observe the same under such civil pains as may be calculated to effect their performance," and "to exercise a compulsory and punitive power about things religious." Wylie cited Isaiah 49:23 ("Kings shall be thy nursing fathers, and their queens thy nursing mothers"), a proof text frequently deployed by Protestants to demonstrate that civil authority is tasked with promoting the "correct" form of worship and stamping out "incorrect" ones (in this case, "unbiblical" practices that the Reformed Presbyterian Church regarded as "idolatry").[21] To do so, those magistrates needed to be men capable of a clear profession of (Reformed) Christianity. "For a Christian people to appoint a Deist to govern them, to say nothing of its repugnancy to the divine law, is even shameful," Wylie wrote. "Is it to be expected that the man, who is not a brother in the profession of the religion of Jesus, but an obstinate Infidel, will make his administration bend to the interests of Immanuel, whose existence he denies, whose religion he mocks, and whose kingdom he believes to be fictitious?"[22]

Insofar as magistracy and ministry were separate institutions wielding authority over distinct jurisdictions, this entailed a technical "separation" of church and state. But it was not a separation of religion from government as such, as the institutions functioned in coordination with one another, each "bound to take the moral law, as the unerring standard of all their administrations" and aiming at the same end, "the glory of God."[23]

Wylie enumerated the duties the people owed to civil government when "legally" or "morally constituted," citing the usual New Testament proof texts—Romans 13, 1 Peter 2, and 1 Timothy 2. To these responsibilities he adjoined the people's obligation to support and defend such a state from its enemies. "Have we any right, then, to be stigmatized as antigovernment men?" Wylie asked. "If anti should at all be used, it should immediately precede the word immoral, and then it is completely applicable. We always have been, and intend uniformly to continue, anti-immoral-government men."[24]

The United States, however, was not such a morally and legally constituted government. The federal constitution had failed to erect a Christian magistracy and support the ministry. (In Wylie's judgment, most state constitutions fared no better.) The minister enumerated nine reasons to explain why Reformed Presbyterians "cannot yield obedience, for conscience sake, to the present civil authority in North America." He complained first about the failure of the Framers of the US Constitution to recognize the authority of God and the ultimate purpose of civil government:

> The federal constitution, or instrument of national union, does not even recognise the existence of God, the King of nations. In these civil deeds, though the immediate end may be the happiness of the commonwealth, yet the ultimate end, as well in this as in every other thing we do, should be the glory of God. Ought not men, in the formation of their deeds, to consider their responsibility to the moral Governor, and this obligation to acknowledge his authority? . . . Did not the framers of this instrument act, not only as if there had been no divine revelation for the supreme standard of their conduct; but also as if there had been no God? . . . Every official act of the governor of a province must have some specific stamp of his dependence upon the authority which appointed him; and shall a nation act as if independent of the God of the universe, and expect to be guiltless?

Second, the majority of the state constitutions "contain positive immorality"; that is, they protect the "rights of conscience that sanction every blasphemy, which a depraved heard may believe to be true." Such a recognition of rights of conscience, Wylie wrote, "is insulting to the Majesty of Heaven, and repugnant to the express letter of God's Word." It is a "rejection of the divine law, as revealed in Scripture," and "an obstinate drawing back to heathenism." And, as the state constitutions "necessarily bind to the support of the federal, as the bond of national existence," they all partake in its immorality. Third, constitutional protections of the religious liberty and rights of conscience in the end amounted to the very *establishment* of infidelity. "The government gives a legal security and establishment to gross heresy, blasphemy and idolatry, under the notion of liberty of conscience." To worship in a way other than indicated by God's law would be to defy the divine will and would be a criminal offence.

Insofar as these constitutions recognize a right "to worship God whatever way a man may think most proper," Wylie asked, "Does not this amount to an establishment of religion?" There could be no neutrality in the matter; either the state protected and promoted the true religion or it permitted all manner of idolatries. The so-called right of conscience, he averred, was simply a government-sanctioned permission to sin. "The dispute, then, will not turn upon the point, whether religion should be civilly established? (we take it for granted that Americans think so, seeing that they have done it,) but it is concerning what religion ought to be civilly established and protected. Whether the religion of Jesus alone, should be countenanced by civil authority? Or every blasphemous, heretical, and idolatrous abomination which the subtle malignity of the old serpent, and a heart deceitful above all things, and desperately wicked, can frame and devise, should be put on an equal footing therewith? The former we contend for, the latter we reject. The latter, however, is the plain doctrine of the constitution." By allowing false religions to exist "upon equal footing," the Constitution is "friendly to the enemies of Jesus." Wylie further objected—and this was his fourth point—that civil officers are made to swear to support these immoral provisions. Indeed, "this obligation to support gross heresy, &tc., is not confined to officers under the constitution. It extends to all who swear allegiance to it, and thus incorporate with the national society upon the footing of this bond of union." By their allegiance to the Constitution, all citizens are obliged to license false religion.[25]

Fifth, Wylie noted that the federal and state constitutions "make no provision for the interest of true religion," an "indifference to the religion of Jesus, which is contrary to the law of nature ... and contrary to the word of God."[26] Sixth, the United States was currently "in a state of national rebellion against God" by refusing to accept divine law, "a written transcript of his will, ... superior to any thing which would have ever been discovered by the mere light of nature," as the supreme law of the land, and was also "aiding and assisting his enemies, by supporting those who are at war with the Almighty"—that is, by protecting "idolatry, and all manner of anti-christian delusion."[27] The seventh problem was the Constitution's prohibition of a religious test for holding public office. "Deists, and even atheists, may be chief magistrates," Wylie lamented. And he further introduced as evidence of the nation's godlessness the Treaty of Tripoli of 1797, which "disclaimed the religion of Jesus and cast away the cords of the Lord's anointed" by announcing that "the government of the United States of America is not, in any sense, founded on the Christian religion."[28]

Wylie's eighth reason for not yielding obedience was the institution of slavery. The Covenanters had long been an antislavery church (it was a position going back to Samuel Rutherford and likely informed by their ancestors' experiences of forced expatriation and bond servitude in the New World).[29] In 1800, the Reformed Presbytery disallowed a slaveholder from being in communion with the church. Wylie himself had traveled along with James McKinney to South Carolina in November of that year to enforce the church's position. Alexander McLeod published *Negro Slavery Unjustifiable* in 1802, the first of many such sermons from Covenanter pastors.[30] Although Wylie did not undertake an extended refutation of slavery in *Two Sons of Oil* (he simply asserted that the institution violated Jesus's precept that "whatsoever ye would that men should do unto you, do ye even to them; this is the law and the prophets" [Matthew 7:12]), he powerfully indicted the nation for its hypocrisy.

> Strange it is, indeed, that in a land of such boasted liberty, such horrid inhumanity should be tolerated! It is contrary to the Declaration of Independence, and most of the state constitutions, which justly declare, "that all men are created free and equal, and that Liberty is one of the invaluable rights with which their Creator has endowed them." Is it not strangely inconsistent, that the constitution, the paramount law of the land, should declare all men to be free, and the laws pretended to be constitutional, doom a certain portion of them to hopeless bondage, and subject them to the wanton barbarity of savage and inhuman masters, who, in many instances, treat their brutes with more tenderness?[31]

Finally, Wylie declared that Reformed Presbyterians were obligated to reject what was opposed to the moral law of God. "This obligation necessarily flows from our relation to God, as the Moral Governor." They therefore could not accept a government that protected "heresy, idolatry, and every thing contrary to sound doctrine, and the power of godliness."[32]

And yet, despite all these objections, Wylie acknowledged that "we consider the American government, with all its evils, the best now existing in the Christian world; and, if we know the sentiments of our own souls upon this subject, desire nothing more than its reformation, happiness and prosperity; though we feel bound by our duty to God, to testify against all its immoralities." Nevertheless, he pronounced that members of the church could not "homologate" (that is, associate) with the regime until such time as these defects were corrected and the constitution conformed to their own particular theological principles. Until such time, the faithful remnant was to remain aloof from the state.[33]

Wylie elucidated the proper conduct toward such an uncovenanted government: the testimony of "political dissent." Reformed Presbyterians had the "duty to mourn before God over all the prevailing abominations"; "to pray for their reformation with earnestness at a throne of grace"; "to use every lawful endeavour to promote reformation, such as rational arguments, and decent remonstrances." Wylie also counseled his flock "to do no act which may justly be considered an homologation of their illegitimate authority." This meant that church members were prohibited from taking an oath of allegiance to the Constitution. They were not to participate in elections; they were forbidden to vote—even for candidates who pledged to amend the Constitution so to correct its defects, as that would entail having those people make an oath on the immoral Constitution on their behalf ("for between the elector and the elected there is a representative oneness. . . . Whatever, therefore, we cannot do ourselves on account of its immorality, we ought not to employ others to perform"). They could not accept any official position, serve on juries, or join state militias. They were, however, "to do every thing commanded, which is in itself rightful and lawful," insofar as the moral law requires such things be done, or church members "may be compelled to do them by physical force." And Wylie conceded that they had no practical means to avoid the payment of taxes, even as he likened this to extortion; "I may give away part of my property, to save the remainder, though the man who demands it has no other right than physical force, or a power of compelling obedience."[34]

One doesn't hear a call to rebellion or justification for violence in the young pastor's treatise, despite the aspersions later cast by some of its detractors. Wylie simply instructed his followers to distance themselves from the government and wait for the nation to repent and correct its defective Constitution. He did not, however, believe that his coreligionists could help correct the instrument through normal political means, for that would require associating with the government. Instead, he counseled the loyal remnant instead "to wait patiently, under these disadvantages, till the Lord be pleased to bring back again the captivity of Zion." Hopefully, other Americans would one day soon come to recognize their government's infidelities and take upon themselves the task of laboring to mend the Constitution and usher in a truly Christian republic. In the meantime, while life in political exile in an infidel United States might be inconvenient, the faithful ought, "like Moses, to prefer affliction to the treasures of Egypt." They should strive to live "peaceable and regular lives" and, in doing so, "to oppose all riotous and seditious practices, which may arise to injure the peace and prosperity of the land wherein we live—to comply with the common order of society, in all things in themselves lawful—to live as citizens of the world, and not incorporate ourselves with the national society, in any of their political movements; looking up for the day of our redemption, when God's appointed time for favouring Zion shall come."[35]

All those New Testament verses entreating obedience to civil authority Wylie did not regard as controverting his testimony of political dissent. In his preemptive replies to anticipated objections, the minister insisted that the Bible's teaching of obedience to civil authority only pertained when that authority was rightly constituted. The "powers" referred to in Romans 13 and 1 Peter 2:13 were "the moral and preceptive kind." Humans were, of course, not required to submit to the mere "physical" power of, say, the devil or a beast of prey. Wylie dismissed what he called "the justly exploded doctrine of passive obedience and non-resistance." Indeed, he turned the tables against his patriotic critics: if that were a genuine objection to his teaching, "the people of these states, who justly and valiantly resisted the wicked domination of the British tyrant, would have thereby rendered themselves obnoxious to damnation!!!" And Christ's commandment to render tribute to Caesar did not, in Wylie's view, entail an acknowledgment of the legitimacy of the emperor's civil authority. Such tribute "may be given to the worst of tyrants, if not demanded as a *tessera* of loyalty."[36] "We lament that we cannot join with you in your national capacity," Wylie announced to Americans vexed by his thinking. "The fault is not ours, but your own. Much as we love you, and much as we prefer your government, comparatively, yet we cannot fully incorporate with you, lest we should sin against God, and be found unfaithful to him who is the King of nations. As witnesses for the Lord Jesus Christ, we are also bound to testify against every immorality in the constitutions of the land in which we dwell."[37]

This obligation of "political dissent" was incorporated into the denomination's official *Declaration and Testimony*, developed under the guidance of Alexander McLeod and adopted in May 1806. The section "Of Civil Government" stated, "It is the will of God, revealed by the constitution of human nature, and more clearly in the sacred scriptures, that his rational creatures, living together in one part of the world, and connected by a common interest, and by common duties, should enter into a civil association, for the better preservation of peace and order, in subserviency to godliness and honesty." Believers were enjoined to obedience to lawful commands for conscience' sake, but at the same time were not to regard a power "which authorizes false religion" as "approved of, or sanctioned by God," nor ought such a power "be esteemed or supported by man as a moral institution." In non-Christian countries (that is, those where Christians do not constitute the majority) they may submit to the authority of the ruler, but in Christian ones they were to reject the position that "the magistrate . . . has nothing to do with the Christian religion, nor the minister a right to examine the policy of nations, and teach civil duties." In the following section, "Of the Right of Dissent from a Constitution of Civil Government," Reformed Presbyterians were informed of their duty "to conform to the common regulations of society in things lawful; but to profess allegiance to no constitution of government which is in hostility to the kingdom of Christ, the head of the church, and the prince of the kings of the earth." While the community "approve[d] of some of the leading features of the Constitution of the Government in the United States" (such as its ability to preserve liberty and protect persons and property), they still regarded it as laced with immorality and impiety:

> There are moral evils essential to the constitution of the United States, which render it necessary to refuse allegiance to the whole system. In this remarkable system there is no acknowledgment of the being or authority of God—there is no acknowledgment of the Christian religion, or professed submission to the kingdom of Messiah. It gives support to the enemies of the Redeemer, and admits to its honours and emoluments Jews, Mahometans, deists, and atheists—It establishes that system of robbery, by which men are held in slavery, despoiled of liberty, and property, and protection. It violates the principles of representation, by bestowing upon the domestic tyrant who holds hundreds of his fellow creatures in bondage, an influence in making laws for freemen proportioned to the number of his own slaves. This constitution is, notwithstanding its numerous excellencies, in many instances inconsistent, oppressive, and impious.[38]

The document reaffirmed the Reform Presbyterian Church's "constant Testimony against these evils." "Much as they loved liberty, they loved religion more. Anxious as they were for the good of the country, they were more anxious for the prosperity of Zion. Their opposition, however, has been the opposition of reason and of piety. The weapons of their warfare are arguments and prayer," the text testified.[39]

In 1808, William Findley, congressman from Pennsylvania and veteran of the Revolutionary War, was informed about a dangerous book circulating among his state's Presbyterians. A "very respectable and intelligent neighbor" told him that, during an argument with some folks who had been disparaging the government of the United States, one boasted that "if they should kill him that instant, we had no law to punish murder, &c." The ruffian had based his claim on the authority of a book titled *The Two Sons of Oil.* Not long after this conversation with his neighbor, Findley received a letter from a government official regarding a similar exchange.[40]

Findley had first heard about the book back in 1803, having come across newspaper advertisements promoting what he took to be simply another scholarly commentary on the prophecy of Zechariah. His interest now piqued, Findley set out to procure a copy of the offending volume. He was horrified by what he read. "I found that the half of the mischief which it was calculated to promote, had not been told me," he wrote; "that it not only grossly misrepresented the government and laws of the United States in general, but more particularly that of Pennsylvania. The encouragement given to people so disposed, to kill their neighbors with expectation of impunity, and for slaves to kill their masters, are but a few, out of numerous instances, of the insidious slanders which his book contains. If teaching to resist the ordinance of legitimate civil government to refuse to obey the magistrates, for conscience sake, from whom they receive and claim protection; if despising dominion, speaking evil of dignities, and stirring up sedition, are contrary, not only to the moral law, but also to the precepts of the gospel, the Sons of Oil is certainly so." Fearing its poison was spreading, Findley took it upon himself to compose a repudiation of its nefarious doctrine. "It was a duty," he realized, "to endeavor to prevent the delusion from taking such deep root as to draw many into its vortex, and disturb the peace of society, to preserve which, civil government was instituted, with divine approbation among men." Despite his advanced age and many other commitments, Findley recognized that he was the man for the job, having both the theological and political bona fides to undertake the effort. He had himself been "educated by the old dissenters" in Northern Ireland, had been a clerk and an elder in the Reformed Presbytery in Pennsylvania, and had participated in the discussions between the Covenanters and the Seceders that brought about the Associate Reformed Church. Further, Findley had been deeply involved in the revolutionary cause and the process of "making or ratifying" the constitutions of Pennsylvania and the United States; he had been a prominent

Anti-Federalist, had served many terms as a member of the state General Assembly, and then as a legislator in Congress. He had heard James McKinney preach and even had the opportunity to speak with him. "I found he spoke too freely about what he did not understand, not having opportunity to be informed," Findley reflected. Given this background, Findley understood he was uniquely qualified to come to the defense of his state, his nation, and their instruments and institutions of governance against Wylie's seditious slanders.[41]

In his long and digressive *Observations* (Findley's 366 pages of text in the original edition—and this was a revision of Findley's first draft, which "was too extensive for the design"[42]—was several times longer than the offending book), Findley took on Wylie's misinterpretation of Scripture and the multitude of his theological errors. In his call for a theocracy, the author of *Two Sons of Oil* agreed with "the Mahometans [that is, Muslims] in the method of propagating and enforcing religion, by the sword of the magistrate," as well as with "the other apostate Christian church, viz. of Rome." But the theocracy based on the law of Moses, Findley alleged, was instituted solely for the Israelites and for a particular place and time. Civil government is distinct from the kingdom of Christ. Though instituted by men, it is founded on "the moral law of nature" inscribed on their hearts, which "consists of the eternal and immutable principles of justice as they existed in the nature and relation of things, antecedent to any positive precept," and compels men to form governments for their own protection, to be an ordinance of God and thereby entitled to "obedience for conscience sake."[43]

Wylie, Findley claimed, had also misrepresented the federal constitution and the political union it created.[44] "Did he seriously expect that a federal government must also have a federal religion, and a federal creed?" Findley asked, as it was "the result of the union of different sovereign states, not for internal purposes, but as a bond of union for general defence, and foreign relations." Congress simply did not have power over the internal concerns of the states, which included matters of religion. Nevertheless, he noted that federal officers were required to swear an oath (to God), a provision that effectively excluded atheists from occupying such positions. He noted too that both houses of Congress employed ministers to open their sessions with prayer. "I leave it to the author himself to explain how he came to assert that that federal government *did not acknowledge the being of a God, the king of nations*."[45]

Findley also called attention to Wylie's inconsistency in contending that the Mosaic law remained binding yet condemning the practice of slavery. He then asserted that "no nation in the world ever made such exertions to abolish slavery, as the United States has done." Findley also warned of the perilous consequences of Wylie's view: "On the author's principles, it is the duty of slaves to assassinate their masters, and to take away their own lives also, in preference to living in slavery. This is not the opinion of Moses and the patriarchs, nor of the apostles of Christ." (Findley was referring to Wylie's remark that, despite what Scripture says about the matter, slavery is "impolitic and dangerous." "By what tie is he bound to spare my life, seeing I rob him of that which is dearer than life itself, and without which life is miserable?" he asked.)[46] He concluded that Wylie "practically disowns all the civil governments that are, or ever were in the world." Indeed, by his own principles Wylie could have "*homologated* the peculiar government of Israel. . . . There never has been a civil government in the world, which the author, on his declared principles, could have acknowledged as a moral or legitimate government, or even whose lawful commands ought to have been obeyed."[47]

That a seasoned politician like Congressman Findley took the time to record and publish his "observations" on Wylie's treatise suggests that, despite its small numbers, he regarded the denomination as a grave threat to the republic. Wylie's church was "a new sect of religious adventurers come to avail themselves of the christian liberty secured and protected in the United States, agreeably to the moral law, spying out our liberty that we have from Christ, in order to make themselves conspicuous"; it was "not founded on the authority of Christ." Findley went so far as to insinuate that those who slander the Constitution, preach religious persecution, and sow sedition ought not to be tolerated by the civil government.[48]

Yet Findley need not have agonized so deeply about the pernicious influence of *The Two Sons of Oil* and the potential dangers of the testimony of political dissent to civil peace and the commonweal. Soon after his *Observations* was published, the United States found itself embroiled in what came to be called the War of 1812. And the outbreak of hostilities put Reformed Presbyterians who had refused to take the oath of nationalization and thus remained resident aliens (and technically subjects of the enemy nation) in a more perilous position that Findley's riposte could ever have.

The conflict weighed heavily upon the minds of members of the Reformed Presbyterian Synod when they met in Pittsburgh in August 1812. In an effort to demonstrate their patriotism—despite their political dissent—the Synod prepared a statement to Congress explaining the church's position on the war and the Constitution, and hammered out a formula that could allow its members to demonstrate their loyalty to the United States and their willingness to fight in its defense without having to take an oath of allegiance to the Constitution itself: "I, A. B., do solemnly declare in the name of the Most High God, the searcher of hearts, that I abjure all foreign allegiance whatsoever, and hold that these states and the United States are and ought to be sovereign and independent of all other nations and governments and that I will promote the best interests of this empire, maintain its independence, preserve its peace and support the integrity of the union to the best of my power." A historian of the church later noted, "As no immoral oath was required of them, the Reformed Presbyterians were hearty supporters of the nation's rights and cheerfully bore arms in defense of the country." Robert Baird, the eminent chronicler of American religion, concurred. "During the late war with Great Britain, no portion of the citizens were more forward in defence of the country than Reformed Presbyterians," he acknowledged approvingly in his description of the denomination.[49]

The notable opposition to the war by Federalist ministers provided another opportunity for the Reformed Presbyterians to display their patriotic bona fides and explain their theological-political convictions. In a series of sermons (first published in January 1815; a second edition appeared in March of that same year), the Reverend Alexander McLeod took up the task, explicating the morality and providential nature of the conflict. In the second of these discourses, "The Moral Character of the Two Belligerents," McLeod compared the infidel American republic to covenant-breaking Great Britain. In the course of the matter, he expounded on the Covenanter criticisms of the American Constitution—its failure to acknowledge God and its violation of human liberty through its authorization of slavery. Regarding the first problem, McLeod conceded that "it is not to be expected that specific provision should be made for the interests of religion in particular congregations"; nevertheless, "no association of men for moral purposes can be justified in an entire neglect of the Sovereign of the world." He suggested that the nation's founders and statesmen had been overly influenced by the abuse of religion for political ends in the Old World and by writers "friendly to the cause of civil liberty" but whose principles led to "a disrespect for religion itself." They were right to overthrow the old Church of England establishments; they went to "the opposite extreme," however, by "withholding a recognition of the Lord and his Anointed from the grand charter of the nation." Slavery in America, McLeod argued, both violated the biblical prohibition of manstealing (Exodus 21:16) and was unfaithful to those self-evident maxims proclaimed in the Declaration of Independence.

While the United States had ended the Atlantic slave trade in 1808, the Constitution regrettably permitted the perpetuation of the institution and provided the slaveholding states an outsized influence in Congress. (McLeod later took part in the organization of the American Colonization Society in 1816.)[50]

Despite "the irreligion of the general constitution of our government," McLeod insisted that "the Church of God is, in this country, upon a better footing, as it respects the national power, than in any other country on earth," as elected representatives cannot interfere with the church and with the spiritual concerns of citizens. Americans enjoyed religious liberty, notwithstanding "the infidelity of the national compact." (Unlike Wylie, McLeod regarded the Constitution's protection of religious liberty as a commendable trait.) By contrast, the British system was "a *despotic usurpation—A superstitious combination of civil and ecclesiastical power—A branch of the grand antichristian apostacy—Erastian in its constitution and administration—*and *Cruel in its policy.*" McLeod spent nearly forty pages describing these offenses, concluding that while both American and British constitutions were found wanting, "the difference, in point of immorality, between them is great. There is scarcely any comparison." The current war was divine chastisement for America's transgressions, it was true, but if one should "suppose an intelligent man elevated to some spot in space, above the world, whence, without partiality to either of the belligerents, he could take a survey of both, and mark the contest between them—He would, upon principles of humanity, wish success" to the United States, the more innocent of the two clashing parties. Despite its flaws, the US Constitution rightly enshrined the principle of representation, the basis of lawful power. "REPRESENTATIVE DEMOCRACY IS AN ORDINANCE OF GOD," McLeod announced.[51]

Throughout the course of that conflict, the Reformed Presbyterians worked to strike a balance between their patriotic feelings and the demands of their testimony of political dissent; over time, some of the old guard came to reassess their traditional teaching and to consider the possibility of conciliation. At the same time, recalcitrant hard-liners were renewing the lament against the infidelities of the United States. And one even dared to proclaim the testimony of political dissent directly in the halls of power.

The notorious episode involved a sermon delivered by the Reverend James Renwick Willson before the New York State Legislature in 1831. The American-born preacher, founder and editor of *Evangelical Witness* (1822–1826) and the short-lived *Christian Statesman* (1826), and later the *Albany*

Quarterly (1832–1834), had already established himself as a commanding voice within his denomination. A nineteenth-century historian of the Reformed Presbyterians remembered him as "the most powerful preacher the Covenanter Church in America has ever produced, and in intellectual grasp, classical scholarship, and pulpit eloquence, ranked among the first preachers of the country. . . . He was an American patriot, at the same time a consistent and ardent covenanting protestant against the evils of the country, and the infidelity of the Constitution of the United States."[52]

Willson's sermon, in due course published as a pamphlet, was titled *Prince Messiah's Claims to Dominion Over All Governments and the Disregard of His Authority by the United States in the Federal Constitution*. The first part was a fairly straightforward restatement of Covenanter political theology: the "ordinance of magistracy" originates from the Father and is given over to the mediatorial administration of Christ, who is head of both the church and the state. Therefore, "*nations are bound in the constitutions of their governments, to recognize formally the authority of the Mediator as their King.*" All individuals within a nation have the duty to obey Christ, and the collective body must acknowledge him in its constitutions. Representatives are to legislate according to his law and are not to allow his enemies to hold public office; civil authorities are to be "nursing fathers" to the church. Thus, "to permit atheists, deists, Jews, pagans, profane men, heretics, such as the blasphemers of Messiah's Godhead, and papists, who are gross idolaters, to occupy places of honor and power, as legislators, judges, &c. is to offer a direct insult to the holy Jesus," Willson said.[53]

All of this was fairly boilerplate Covenanter language, and the sermon would have likely been forgotten if Willson had just ended it there. But he was just getting started. In the sermon's second part, "An Examination of the Constitution and Government of the United States, Relative to Messiah's Claims," the pastor turned prophetic, audaciously casting judgment upon the nation's ungodly Founders and what they had wrought. "On this side of the Atlantic, the people have established, by their representatives, a federal constitution, have relapsed into the ancient temper of the nations—adulation of the form of government, which they organized. This is self-adulation. The political machinery has wrought tolerably well, for nearly fifty years, as far as relates to the mere personal liberty of the whites, the security of property, the increase of wealth, and the encouragement of enterprise." Willson acknowledged the prosperity enjoyed by the United States, but this was to be attributed to the Deity. "That by the blessing of God, the condition of our country is much better than that of any other nations in Christendom, must be admitted by all who are tolerably acquainted with the condition of the old world." However, despite, or on account of, the nation's material prosperity, "the morals of the people grow worse." And like an Old Testament prophet, Willson darkly warned the sinful nation of a future reckoning. Look back and reflect on what happened to the Hebrew commonwealth in the latter reign of Solomon, Babylonia when conquered by Persia, Rome during the time of Cicero and Theodosius. "Their prosperity was their ruin; because, being vicious, they abused their blessings." An immoral constitution inevitably leads to "a desecration of public morals, which must result in national calamity." And that was exactly what was happening in the United States.[14]

Willson accordingly embarked on a thoroughgoing critique of the Constitution and the moral character of its administration. He rejected outright the federalist explanation of the failure to acknowledge God, put forth by William Findley and others, that the Constitution was like a "business-transaction" or treaty between states. Under such a theory, Willson said, one could argue that the kings of the twelve tribes of Israel were not bound to acknowledge God as a nation. To do so would, of course, be ridiculous. "The claims of *the Lord of all*, cannot be set aside by subtle distinctions of state rights, and national jurisdiction. The United States are in the dominion of the King of kings, whom they have nationally dishonored in both theory and practice." In any event, he insisted that the instrument formed "a true and proper civil magistracy," "a firm national government" to replace the old alliance of states established by the Articles of Confederacy.[15]

Willson went on to catalogue the various sins of the American constitutional order: the prohibition of a religious test permits "Atheists, Deists, Jews, and profane men, of the most abandoned manners" to hold federal office; the law of God is not recognized by it;[16] the "King of Kings and Lord of Lords" is not acknowledged (indeed, such an homage to Christ would have prevented the participation of such noted infidels as Benjamin Franklin and James Madison in the Constitutional Convention and would have introduced a religious test); the First Amendment prevents the government to advance the Christian religion (thus violating the biblical instruction that "Kings shall be thy nursing fathers, and their Queens thy nursing mothers"); there is neither acknowledgment of nor any statement of national subjection to Almighty God, the Creator ("It was a deliberate deed, whereby God was rejected; and in the true atheistical spirit of the whole instrument, and of course, done with intent to declare national independence of the Lord of hosts. . . . When the country was plainly in peril, and the arm of Jehovah perceived to be necessary for our defence, then the God of creation was acknowledged. But when he had conducted our armies to victory, and set our country free from the oppression of foreign despotism— then with a blackness of ingratitude, and an atheistical impiety, his name was erased from the fundamental law of the empire").[57] Moreover, the Constitution sanctions the immoral practice of slavery (by "a circumlocution, as if a figure of speech would conceal that iniquity for which conscience was chiding them, when the article was penned and ratified"), another affront to "the Messiah who came to proclaim liberty to the captives." By means of its system of apportioning representatives, the Constitution makes the holding of Africans in bondage "one of the pillars of the government upon which the fabric of American freedom is made to rest; thus committing the two fold evil of making slavery essential to the constitution, and of violating the holy and benign doctrine of representation, which is the palladium of religious and social liberty." Such an evil had been sustained by later congressional acts such as the Missouri Compromise, federal control over the territories, the slave laws of the District of Columbia, the application of these laws by the judiciary, and the use of federal troops in suppressing slave insurrections in North Carolina and Virginia. He concluded this invective calling attention to Jefferson's own condemnation of slavery in his *Notes on the State of Virginia*.[58]

Willson proceeded to recount the "practical results" that the Constitution had begotten and "over which every true disciple of Christ, and Christian patriot, will mourn." He considered first the consequences of the prohibition of a religious test for federal office. "Ungodly men have occupied, and do now occupy, many of the official stations, in the government," he alleged. "The clause of the constitution, barring all moral qualifications, has not been a dead letter. There have been seven Presidents of the United States—and each of them it may be said, as Jehovah says of the kings of Israel, after the revolt of the ten tribes, 'He did that which was evil in the sight of the Lord.' " He then expounded the sundry infidelities of nearly every one of them. He did not pull his punches.[59]

Willson hadn't been entranced by the hagiographic myths that had been cultivated about the figure of the revolutionary general and first president.[60] While George Washington was "raised up, in the providence of God, like Cyrus of Persia," he turned out like the rich young man in the gospel who, unwilling to relinquish his possessions, turned away from Jesus. "There is no satisfactory evidence that Washington was a professor of the Christian religion, or even a speculative believer in its divinity, before he retired from public life," Willson glumly reported. "In no state paper, in no private letter, in no conversation, is he known to have declared himself a believer in the Holy Scriptures, as the word of God." It got worse. "Rousseau, an avowed infidel, has said more in honor of Christ, than is known to have been uttered by Washington." The pastor denounced Washington's profane and immoral behavior—his attendance at balls and cardplaying, his failure to observe the Sabbath and refusal of the Sacrament of the Supper, his ownership of slaves. Washington had served as president of the convention "that voted the name of the living God out of the Constitution. . . . The conviction forces itself upon us, that that act of national impiety, was done with the approbation of Washington." His death was "much more like a Heathen Philosopher's, than like that of a Saint of God." According to Jefferson, he was a deist. "To be ashamed of Christ, which no one can reasonably doubt he was, is infidel. He did not set an example of godliness, before the nation, over which, in the Providence of God, he was made President." His cabinet picks, such as the disreputably unchaste Hamilton (who was killed in a duel) and Jefferson ("an avowed infidel, who mocked at every thing sacred" and was "notoriously addicted to immorality"), clearly demonstrate that Washington was not God fearing. Indeed, "the practical piety of the Bible . . . *had she been introduced to the inmates of Washington's Palace,* would have been derided as a fanatic." While John Adams had once acknowledged the Redeemer in a public document (in a fast proclamation), the pastor caustically disparaged him as a Unitarian. Jefferson was subject to sharper derision; his *Notes on Virginia* exposed him as "an enemy of revealed religion, and a virulent foe to the Church of God." Had the American people known the extent of Jefferson's infidelity, he would never have been elected president. Though Madison had been reared by godly parents and had studied theology with Dr. John Witherspoon at Princeton, he later came under the nefarious sway of Jefferson, "who probably made him a deist." Willson dismissed his successor with a single sentence: "Mr. Monroe lived and died like a second-rate Athenian Philosopher." He passed over John Quincy Adams and the incumbent Andrew Jackson with little comment (though he did pause to report that friends of the latter had affirmed that the president, well known for swearing and dueling, had "repented and reformed" and was therefore fit for the office. In this, Jackson compared favorably to that unrepentant gambler Senator Henry Clay).[61]

Willson did not trouble himself to explain the ways in which such ungodly men had failed leading the nation, nor did he have anything particular to say about the immoral policies pursued by any of their administrations. He did allege that America's wicked presidents had allowed for various heresies to take root and spread throughout the nation. He specifically pointed to the baleful influence of Adams and Jefferson, blaming the former for the spread of Unitarianism in New England and the latter for the persistence of deism in the South, heresies that denied the divinity of Christ. He likened the "Socinian President" Adams to the biblical Jeroboam who set up idolatrous altars at Dan and Beth El, and he said that "the demoralizing influence of slavery in the south, paved the way for the spread of Deism from the palace, by Mr. Jefferson."[62]

And so, the Christian denominations became infected with heresy as the people "adopted more convenient creeds, for the purpose of flattering the depravity of human nature, and of paying court to the ungodly great." And in time the morals of the nation's citizens had become ever more corrupt; drunkenness, profane swearing, the violation of the Sabbath were all too prevalent. The federal government profaned the Sabbath by opening the post offices for the delivery of mail. Public officers took solemn oaths "to support the immoralities embodied in the United States, and other [state] constitutions"; "thousands commit this sin without a moment's reflection." Before those elected representatives, Willson pronounced, "Let all the fearers of the Lord, all who love to honor the Lord Jehovah and his holy law—all who honor and adore Prince Messiah, reflect on the fearful fact, that nearly all the men who enter on the discharge of their official functions, are qualified for those public offices, by swearing an oath that involves what is contrary to the law of God, the rights of man, and the honor and glory of Him who is King of kings and Lord of lords."[63] His litany of charges went on: juries upheld slavery; the promulgation of idolatries had sanction of the law; the government persecuted the faithful. In short, the nation was going to hell in a handbasket, sadly the all-too-predictable consequence of its defective constitution.

One of those "ungodly men" Willson inveighed against was none other than a Jewish representative from New York City named Mordecai Myers who had supported a motion to dispense with the practice of opening the daily session with prayer. "This was in character," the pastor sneered, "as all the chaplains pray in the name of Jesus of Nazareth, whom his fathers crucified, and whom he rejects as an imposter. Yet, for a Jew to oppose prayer, as offered up in the legislature of a Christian country, was an act of discourtesy to the Christian people whom he represents, that we would scarcely have expected from a gentlemen of the bar, who has been called 'a learned and honorable Israelite.' "[64]

In response to Willson's discourtesy, one of Myers's colleagues, David Moulton of Oneida County, sponsored a resolution to remove the pastor from the list of clergymen permitted to lead the opening prayer for having "wantonly assailed the good name of the revered Washington, and insulted the memory of the Illustrious Jefferson ... [and] by the publishing of an odious pamphlet purporting to be a religious essay, he has unnecessarily endeavored to detract from the fair fame of many of the benefactors of our country." For two days the legislature deliberated the matter, while out in the street Willson was spat on, his effigy burned in front of the State House, his pamphlets tossed into a bonfire. A mob had even resolved to burn down his house—with the offending pastor still in it. (Willson was rescued from this fate by friends who got wind of the plot and swiftly escorted him out of town.) *Prince Messiah's Claims to Dominion* continued to be condemned in the New York and New England press; one publication attacked Willson's "religio politico sermon" as "a blasphemous perversion and misapprehension of scripture" and "a production worthy of proscriptions and exclusions of a dark and bigot age, and a fit auxiliary in the promotion of a political combination as profligate as any that disgraces the annals of history."[65] The New York State Assembly passed Mr. Moulton's resolution by a 95 to 2 vote, and Rev. Willson's name was stripped from the list of Albany clergy invited to offer prayers before the body.[66]

Given all the tumult surrounding Willson's presentation, it should be mentioned that the pamphlet closed on a surprisingly hopeful note. "The sins of the nation are, indeed, aggravated, but the Divine goodness has not been withdrawn from us," he wrote. The United States could well take its place as a shining light to the world. "In this commonwealth, the exercise of government, by the representatives of the people, has given security to liberty and prosperity; and has been productive of great national prosperity.... The example of these states is exhibited, in God's providence, to the whole world, that the friends of liberty and man, may be animated to perseverance." He remained confident that Christ "will not abandon our land for its many sins, and that he will dispense to us pardon, though he will take vengeance on our sinful deeds." Such optimism rested on Willson's abiding faith in the virtue of the American people who "were not so bad as a few practical atheists, into whose hands the management of the national affairs fell, immediately after the revolution." Despite the prohibition of Article VI, Section 3, the people, it seemed, had unofficially adopted a test of moral qualifications for office: recalling the election of 1800, he suggested that the people would have never voted for Jefferson had they known his genuine religious views; more recently, many had objected to John Quincy Adams becoming president on account of him being a Unitarian. Willson also regarded the formation of the Anti-Masonic Party as an expression of the people's moral sense. And he was encouraged, too, by the diffusion of the Bible throughout the land, which "teaches the claims of Messiah, the Prince," and would inspire repentance for national sins and spark moral reform. "The public mind," he predicted, "will soon become so enlightened by the Word and Spirit of the Lord, that the atheist and the deist shall be no longer able to sustain their power, which is as much supported by moral darkness, as the thrones of tyrants are, by the ignorance of their subjects." At the same time as he presented his throughgoing critique of America, Willson discerned a nation turning back to its God. The people still had the capacity and perhaps the will for self-correction and could overcome the corruption of the elites.[67]

Yet even as James R. Willson's incendiary *Prince Messiah's Claims to Dominion* was rolling off the press, some of the old guard Reformed Presbyterian ministers, such as Alexander McLeod and Samuel B. Wylie, the very men who had developed the church's distinctive testimony of political dissent, had come to relax their position on the government of the United States. They accordingly sought to adjust the teaching of the church to their new appreciation of the virtues of the state and to permit Reformed Presbyterians to exercise the franchise and serve on juries. Hard-liners such as Willson regarded any such adjustment as a renunciation of fundamental religious commitments, an abandonment of their Covenanter heritage, and a succumbing to the temptations of America. A rift was coming.[68]

In 1828, the Reformed Presbyterians appointed a committee on civil relations to study the issue. The committee, chaired by Willson, submitted a report upholding the traditional position. The report did not settle the controversy. In 1831, the Reformed Presbyterian Synod agreed to allow members to conduct "Free Discussions" over its testimony in the denomination's organ, the *American Christian Expositor*. But free discussion was not going to settle the issue. A new committee, this one chaired by Samuel B. Wylie, appointed to the issue presented a "Pastoral Address" on the question of civil relations to the Eastern Subordinate Synod in April 1832. While recognizing the diversity of opinion among Reformed Presbyterians on "the practical application of the religious sentiments we have espoused, to the free and liberal republican institutions, of this happy and highly favored, empire," the committee declared that "it is susceptible of demonstration, that since the commencement of Christianity, no government on earth has had a fairer claim to recognition as the ordinance of God, than that of the United States." The document was adopted, but only after a motion requiring that the above and other controversial passages be expunged passed by a single vote. The redacted text was then published in the *American Christian Expositor*.[69]

In response, the Wylie faction resolved to publish the entire address as it had been originally reported out by the committee. The man who had composed the classic treatise spelling out the reasons why the Covenanters could not homologate with an infidel government now contended that its Constitution contained nothing that was *"positively* immoral" and that continued political dissent against it was unwarranted. He extolled the document: "The recognition of natural rights, the protection of person, property and religion, guaranteed by these institutions of the land, and the provision for self-regeneration contained in the instruments themselves, must command the respect and admiration of every sensible, unprejudiced man. Indeed, it is a matter of astonishment to find them so good." He conceded "the obnoxious feature" of slavery but felt that it was "rapidly softening in its unsightly aspect." Further, he denied that slavery was endorsed by the Constitution itself; the federal compact "curbed the growing evil, and prepared the way for its complete extinction," even if it could not abolish it outright.[70]

"Various illiberal attempts," the document complained in an appendix, "have been made, to stamp as the ordinance of the devil, the best government on earth, and of all governments existing, possessing the fairest claim to be designated as the ordinance of God." This was, of course, a reference to Willson's notorious sermon. A note to the published document engaged it further: "[The subscribers to this document] thus *publicly disclaim all responsibility* for the obnoxious sentiments contained in the publication above referred to, and express their unqualified reprobation of the inconsistent, partial and erroneous statements with which it is replete. The *mental alienation* under which its author labors, divests him of all personal responsibility. And as this has now become notorious, there is little danger that the *ravings of insanity* will be mistaken for the expressions of truth and holiness." The text defended Washington's reputation from Willson's calumniations. "The charge of infidelity against Washington is false"; if Willson believed this to be true, it was nevertheless imprudent for a minister "to consign into the hands of infidels, a distinguished individual whom common fame had always denominated a professing Christian"; and, even if it were true, that would not support his argument that the Constitution itself was infidel, as Washington's private behavior did not void his "just and legal authority." Five pages of extracts of testimony followed to demonstrate that Washington was indeed a good and pious Christian in his public activities and private life.[71]

Around the same time as *The Original Draft of a Pastoral Address* was published, there appeared Gilbert McMaster's *Moral Character of Civil Government*, which spelled out in greater detail what came to be known (following the terminology of earlier Presbyterian squabbles) as the "New Light" position. McMaster upheld the fundamentals of the Covenanter political theology—civil government as an ordinance of God, the distinction of civil and ecclesiastical jurisdictions, the need for nations to submit to Christ—and he endorsed the denomination's preference for "well regulated representative Democracy" to forms such as oligarchy or monarchy, "or any modification of these, such as we find in the British empire." The question he raised was whether the existing American government was "good enough" for a Covenanter to associate with. In McMaster's estimation, it was. "Our own United States, more than half a century since, furnished the world with an august exemplification of the principle which we vindicate. The spirit of revolution, now so extensively abroad among the nations, is the voice of God, speaking through outraged humanity, in favour of my position. In this respect the maxim is true, *vox populi vox Dei, the voice of the people is the voice of God.*"[72]

The United States Constitution was not perfect, McMaster admitted. But no human institution could be expected to be so. "Mere defects in high and ultimate moral attainments, if fundamental attributes be in conformity with, and in nothing contrary to, moral principle, will not render illegitimate a constitution of government," he proposed. The question was whether a state "embracing no immoral principle, and imposing no immoral act; but resting, by common consent, its constitution upon the principle of universal equity, in affording protection to persons, reputation, liberty, property, and the pursuits of virtue and happiness," one "supposed to possess, substantially, all the fundamental principles of government, for the attainment of its more immediate and proper ends; and only to be defective in the recognition of things, in themselves, indeed, important, but incidental to the institution, and not radically belonging to it," ought to be "confounded with one based on immorality, and maintained by unrighteousness." While defective, the Constitution was not to be outright rejected as illegitimate. As one was not required "to approve of an unsound principle, or to perpetuate either an abuse or a defect," and indeed, has the ability to give testimony against them, McMaster maintained that a Christian could associate with the state.[73]

McMaster rested this conclusion on his assessment of "the moral estimate of the civil institutions of the United States" and the state governments he found to be adequately Christian. In the case of his home state of New York, for instance, he noted that its constitution had indeed acknowledged God, secured freedom of worship, and abolished slavery; the law protected the sanctity of the Sabbath and punished blasphemy; its courts did not accept the testimony of infidels; and its legislature employed Christian chaplains and paid them out of the public purse. Other states (New Jersey, Vermont, North Carolina, Maryland, Pennsylvania) had constitutions with similar provisions that satisfactorily demonstrated their Christian character. What appeared to be the great omission of the federal constitution—its failure to acknowledge God and Christ—could thus be excused when one considered how the federal and state governments complement one another. McMaster adopted the same argument Findley had used against Wylie's *Two Sons of Oil.* The Constitution set up a *federal* union—"a compact of sovereign states"—rather than a *national* or *consolidated* government. The federal government was authorized limited powers within its own sphere (in arbitrating the relations between the states and with foreign nations), while leaving to the states "all those residuary *powers,* upon which the governments may draw for the public advantage." It was left to those state governments to care for the interests of the morals and religion of their citizens and to promote the common good. Considered from this perspective, it was not surprising that the "Federal Union presents but few features of God's ordinance of civil magistracy." "The whole mystery of this is explained," he wrote, "by bringing the Federal government into union with each of the state governments. Then you have a complete system. The state supplies what the federal wants, and the federal makes up the deficiencies of the government of the state. . . . Bring the two together to make a whole, and you have before you the system of government to which the citizen is pledged." Problem solved.[74]

Further, McMaster looked over the Constitution of the United States and the actions of the federal government and perceived that Christianity was indeed recognized, albeit imperfectly, in text and in practice. The Declaration of Independence, "a deed that lies deeply at the foundation of all our political institutions," acknowledged God and his providence; the Constitution implicitly recognized the sanctity of the Sabbath; oaths of office positively affirmed the functionary's belief in God; the First Amendment protected the free exercise of worship; the houses of the legislature employ chaplains; the Chief Executive has proclaimed days of fasting and thanksgiving. Rather than being godless, when closely considered the Constitution is "distinguished by many religious characteristics." He was not troubled by the lack of a religious test for federal office, and the loss of state support for the church was counterbalanced by the "freedom from either the reproach of *persecution*, or the profanity of an *authoritative toleration*." And, as the Constitution contained within itself the means for its own improvement by amendment, whatever original flaws it had might well in time be remedied by the citizenry.

On the question of slavery, McMaster insisted that the federal government had not authorized the slave trade (which the Constitution had ended in 1808), was not really a party to the crime, and lacked the power to rectify or outlaw the institution in the states. (He noted, too, that while slavery was an evil, the Bible had not called for it to be abolished but provided laws for its regulation.) McMaster hoped for the eventual eradication of slavery in the United States but did not regard immediate and universal emancipation of the enslaved as feasible. "A combination of means, physical and moral, are now in powerful operation to remove this evil from the land; and perhaps as soon as could be reasonably expected, or, for the final good of the slaves, desired," he wrote, but cautioned against more radical actions. "Patient perseverance in the application of sound principles for the removal of evils incorporated with the habits of society is found exemplified both by prophets and apostles. A more violent course is unwarranted." Nor did he think former slaves of African descent would be able to assimilate into white American society; it would be better, he averred, for them to be resettled in some other region.[75]

On the whole, then, McMaster found that the United States enjoyed a Constitution "in which, though imperfect, no immoral principle is embraced, nor immoral act enjoined; and under which a condition of society has arisen that is the admiration of patriots, and a model to the nations."[76] Though its roots lay in the church's wrestling with its awkward theological-political position during the War of 1812, his apologetic was a significant departure from the traditional Covenanter testimony. (In a subsequent text, McMaster questioned whether the church's leadership in the early 1800s had the authority "to settle, for coming generations, the complicated question of civil relations in the United States," and then he alleged that "they did not attempt it, except for themselves individually; certainly they never meant to do so for the Church.")[77]

His recommendation was to heed the adage of not allowing the perfect to be the enemy of the good. Covenanters ought not to stand aloof from the government, but "let it be our business to point out to our fellow men the course of active duty, indicate the defects that exist, the improvements that may be made, the facilities afforded for improvement, and to press the motives for their application. . . . It behooves the friend of sound moral order to do more than to fold his arms, and stand as a looker on. Let the weight of his moral worth be felt in well direct action." Indeed, McMaster appeared downright sanguine about the moral character of the United States and its positive inspiration to the nations of the world on the cusp of momentous political—and spiritual—change.[78]

The hard-liners remained unmoved, rejecting what the New Light faction believed was a deeper understanding of the government as just a failure of conviction. "Those readers whose minds are already made up on this subject, and anxious to act on the decision, and have been waiting only till they could obtain a pretext for so great a practical change as the view of civil government here advocated necessarily leads to, among reformed Presbyterians, will hail these letters, not only as an apology, but as a vindication of their opinions on civil government," wrote the "Old Light" David Scott. He later called McMaster's work "a bold, yet cunning attack on the principles and position of the Church. . . . Dogmatic in statement, sophistical in its reasoning, and unscrupulous in its pretensions; this publication was by far the most dangerous weapon that had yet been wielded against the testimony of the Church."[79] Another pamphlet contrasted extracts from Samuel B. Wylie's *Two Sons of Oil* with the *Original Draft.* "The Doctor has evidently lowered, in great degree, the standard by which he once thought civil government should be tested," it crowed. "The government of the United States is as liable *now* to all the objections stated in the 'Sons of Oil,' as it was when these objections were offered as reasons, why we could not fully incorporate with the national society. . . . Rebellion is chargeable upon the nation, in 1832, in as high degree as in 1803."[80]

Yet the members of the New Light faction had come to believe that the America in which they dwelled was indeed a Christian nation, even if their fellow citizens did not share their peculiar theology and austere style of worship. "It is a principle which is well understood, at least in our own country, that subordinate to the Supreme legislator, all power is inherent in the people, and all free governments are founded on their authority." As the people were Christian, so too was the government they established. The First Amendment's Free Exercise Clause could thus be recognized as a manifestation of the people's religiosity: "Here, the present and continued existence of religion in the country is taken for granted; it is supposed that it will be exercised; and that its exercise will be of advantage to the community. Thus the constitution recognizes the existence and utility of religion. It *presupposes* the existence of religion, and leaves it where it was before that instrument was formed, and where it now is, in the hearts and habits of a Christian people." Christianity was and continued to be "the religion of the country." The convictions of the people will emanate in the state. If the body politic is good, so will be its civil institutions. A Christian people would not elect heretics or infidels to public office. And the emergence of so many benevolent institutions, Bible and missionary societies, and Sabbath schools and the diffusion of biblical knowledge throughout the country, they believed, illuminated that the United States was indeed a "Christian nation," de facto if not yet de jure. They had come to appreciate—and to endorse—the country's unofficial pan-Protestant establishment. The US Constitution's failure to explicitly mention God was not dispositive; after all, "there are entire books in the Bible, in which the name of God is not found, but this does not destroy their divine authenticity."[81]

The publication of Wylie's *Original Draft* initiated a sequence of libel charges and excommunications that eventually led to the schism of the Reformed Presbyterians. At the General Synod meeting in Philadelphia in August 1883, the hard-liner Old Lights walked out to form their own group. Their Synod of the Reformed Presbyterian Church remained committed to the testimony of political dissent as the distinguishing characteristic of the true church and their station as a faithful remnant. They would accept no constitution as an ordinance of God that did not enshrine their political theology among its provisions.[82]

CHAPTER THREE

An Excrescence on the Tree of Our Liberty

The Proslavery Theologians

On June 13, 1861, the day President Jefferson Davis assigned for the first Confederate "day of fasting and prayer," Benjamin Morgan Palmer, minister of the First Presbyterian Church in New Orleans and one of the most renowned spokespersons for the Southern cause, delivered a discourse titled *National Responsibility before God*. His purpose that day was to provide to the infant nation an accounting of the people's failings and point ahead to its glorious destiny to fulfill God's will on earth.

Palmer opened his jeremiad likening the young Confederacy to ancient Israel. The eleven secessionist states had "sought to go forth in peace from the house of political bondage," but "our modern Pharoah" with a hardened heart refused to let them go, and so they implored God for deliverance. And as the Hebrew tribes rededicated themselves to the covenant after crossing the Jordan (Joshua 8:30–35), "not less grand and awful is this scene to-day," Palmer announced, "when an infant nation strikes its covenant with the God of Heaven." "Confessing the sins of our fathers with our own, and imploring the divine guidance through all our fortunes, the people of these Confederate States proclaim this day, 'the Lord our God will we serve, and his voice will we obey.' " Such an act of public contrition was necessary as the nation was not "a dead abstraction, signifying only the aggregation of individuals," but "an incorporated society, and possessing a unity of life resembling the individuality of a single being"—with a distinct character, moral responsibility, and providential mission. And as nations receive divine judgment in temporal sanctions, chastisements in history, the punishment for the sins of one generation set on later ones, the minister called on his fellow Southerners to recognize and lament their national sins—those "being committed by the people in their public association and in their corporate existence"—and those of their forebears.[1]

Palmer then went through his catalogue of the nation's sins. The first of those transgressions was that of the Constitution of 1787, which had forged the Union from which they had recently separated. "*We bewail*," Palmer said, "*the fatal error of our Fathers in not making a clear recognition of God at the outset of the nation's career.*" Though they were a "most religious people," when they "undertook to establish an independent government, there was a total ignoring of the divine claims and of all allegiance to the divine supremacy." How, Palmer wondered, had those who had earlier pledged "with a firm reliance on the protection of divine Providence" in "that great instrument by which the several States were linked together in a common nationality, and which was at once the public charter and the paramount law of the land," come just a few years later to ignore the existence of the Deity and the nation's responsibilities to him? "This omission was a fearful one; and it is not surprising that He who proclaims his jealousy of his own glory, would let the blow which has shattered *that* nation." Fault was to be cast not on the people who were "predominantly christian" but on the nation's leaders who had been "largely tinctured with the free-thinking and infidel spirit which swept like a pestilence over Europe in the seventeenth and eighteenth centuries, and which brought at last its bitter fruits in the horrors of the French Revolution." Palmer surmised that the omission was also owing to "the jealousy entertained of any union between Church and State, at a time when the novel, grand and successful experiment was first tried of an entire separation between the two." But whatever may have been the cause of the Framers' omission, "the certain fact is that the American nation stood up before the world a helpless orphan, and entered upon its career without a God." The preacher conceded that, though its Constitution was indeed godless, the nation itself had not entirely neglected its duties. "Through almost a century of unparalleled prosperity, this error has been but partially retrieved; as the religious spirit of the people has silently compelled the appointment by executive authority, of days of public thanksgiving and prayer." Nevertheless, Palmer lamented, "to this day, in the great national act of incorporation there is no bond which connects the old American nation with the Providence and Government of Jehovah."[2]

That appalling omission had now been corrected. "We, the people of the Confederate States, each State acting in its sovereign and independent character, in order to form a permanent federal government, establish justice, insure domestic tranquility, and secure the blessings of liberty to ourselves and our posterity invoking the favor and guidance of Almighty God do ordain and establish this Constitution for the Confederate States of America," read the preamble of the new nation's charter. With those words—unveiled on February 8 and adopted on March 11, 1861—the Confederacy announced itself to a candid world as a godly and righteous nation.[3]

"Thanks be unto God ... for the grace given our own Confederacy, in receding from this perilous atheism!" The Confederacy was in Palmer's eyes both a restoration of a purer American past (as he imagined those early English settlements) and the dawning of a new dispensation. "When my mind first rested upon the Constitution adopted by the Confederate Congress, and I read in the first lines of our organic and fundamental law a clear, solemn, official recognition of Almighty God, my heart swelled with unutterable emotions of gratitude and joy," he reflected. "It was the return of the prodigal to the bosom of his father, of the poor exile who has long pined in some distant and bleak Siberia after the associations of his childhood's home. At length, the nation has a God: Alleluia." Palmer lavished praise on the instrument: the states of the Confederacy were "called upon to ratify the covenant, and set up the memorial stone"; it was "no ordinary State Paper, filled with cold and starched commonplaces," but "a religious unction pervades every clause and line"; the document "summons us to 'recognize our dependence upon God,' to 'humble ourselves under the dispensations of divine providence,' to 'acknowledge his goodness' and 'supplicate his merciful protection.'" His encomium went on in this manner for a page. "This is truly a Christian patriot's prayer," he proclaimed. "It breathes no malignant revenge; but calls the nation to nestle beneath the wings of Almighty power and love" and that "upon this central truth—that 'God is and that He is the rewarder of them that diligently seek him'—all of us can stand. Hebrew or Christian, Protestant or Catholic—all can subscribe this ultimate truth." And he prayed, "May God keep this nation under the power of those religious convictions, which to-day moves the hearts of our people as they were never moved before!" With this instrument, the states of the Confederacy had atoned for the sin of the Fathers of the Union and had forged a new covenant with its God.[4]

But was that preambular phrase "invoking the favor and guidance of Almighty God" enough to announce the Confederacy as an explicitly *Christian* union? For Reverend Palmer's teacher, the distinguished theologian James Henley Thornwell, the Confederacy's acknowledgment was a welcome advance but in the end insufficient. Widely regarded as the leading Presbyterian divine in the South, Thornwell had served as president of South Carolina College and was the founder and editor of the *Southern Presbyterian Review* and editor of the *Southern Quarterly Review*. His disciples dubbed him "the Calhoun of the Church." In a paper submitted to the First General Assembly of the newly organized Southern Presbyterian Church in December 1861, he worried that the Confederate Constitution "still labours under one capital defect. It is not distinctively Christian."[5]

Thornwell had come to believe that the failure of the US Constitution to recognize divine sovereignty had inexorably led to the sectional crisis. "The Constitution of the United States was an attempt to realize the notion of popular freedom, without the checks of aristocracy and a throne, and without the alliance of a national Church," he stated. "The conception was a noble one, but the execution was not commensurate with the design. The fundamental error of our fathers was, that they accepted a partial for a complete statement of the truth." While they rightly regarded government as originating from the will of the people, that governments are the people's servants and not their masters, they had "failed to apprehend the Divine side—that all just government is the ordinance of God, and that magistrates are His ministers who must answer to Him for the execution of their trust."[6]

In Thornwell's thinking, this failure was to blame for the breakdown of constitutional safeguards and the rise of unchecked democracy that had culminated in the secessional crisis. Without an acknowledgment of God's sovereignty to keep the ambitions of fallen human beings in check, the calm and careful deliberation of republican government had been displaced by the rule of the mob. "The consequence of this failure, and of exclusive attention to a single aspect of the case," he wrote, "was to invest the people with a species of supremacy as insulting to God as it was injurious to them. They became a law unto themselves; there was nothing beyond them to check or control their caprices or their pleasure. All were accountable to them; they were accountable to none. This was certainly to make the people a God; and if it was not explicitly expressed that they could do no wrong, it was certainly implied that there was no tribunal to take cognizance of their acts." Built on so unsound a foundation, the declension was preordained, the United States set on the path toward what Thornwell regarded as "the worst of all possible forms of government—a democratic absolutism" ("a godless monster," he called such a regime in another sermon). In the spiritual vacuum left by the omission, "the will of majorities must become the supreme law, if the voice of the people is to be regarded as the voice of God; if they are, in fact, the only God whom rulers are bound to obey."[7]

In their invocation of divine favor and direction, the drafters of the Confederate Constitution had rightly determined not to repeat that error. Yet Thornwell was unsatisfied with the language they settled on. A new constitution presented the opportunity to demonstrate the coming to be of a genuine Christian republic by properly articulating the relationship of the nation to its God. "We venture respectfully to suggest, it is not enough for a State which enjoys the light of Divine revelation to acknowledge in general terms the supremacy of God," Thornwell stated; "it must also acknowledge the supremacy of His Son, whom He hath appointed heir of all things, by whom also He made the worlds. To Jesus Christ all power in heaven and earth is committed. To Him every knee shall bow, and every tongue confess. He is the Ruler of the nations, the King of kings, and Lord of lords." And the state ought also to recognize the Scriptures as the word of God "and regulate its own conduct and legislation in conformity with their teachings."[8]

This was, Thornwell was careful to say, neither a call for the establishment of a national church nor a demand that the state interfere with the individual's freedom of religion. The church and the state were distinct entities, each with jurisdiction over a different province of life: "They differ in their origin, their nature, their ends, their prerogatives, their powers and their sanctions. They cannot be mixed or confounded without injury to both." The assignment of the state is to realize the idea of justice on the earth; the church is to preach the gospel. Accordingly, the political magistrate has no jurisdiction over matters of religion, and the clergy, as they expound the Word of God in their pulpits, ought not to interfere in political affairs.[9]

Yet the state was not to be regarded as a purely secular institution, independent of any relation to religion or its divine author. The Framers of the US Constitution had erred when, in their zeal to avoid the establishment of any particular denomination, they confused the idea of a state with an established national church—a *union* of church and state—with "the religion of the State ... embodied in its Constitution, as the concrete form of its organic life." They mistakenly endorsed the complete *separation* of religion and the state, and in doing so "they virtually expelled Jehovah from the government of the country, and left the State an irresponsible corporation, or responsible only to the immediate corporators. They made it a moral person, and yet not accountable to the Source of all law."[10]

What, then, did Thornwell mean by "the religion of the State"? As Thornwell put it in a fast day sermon preached on November 21, 1860, the state "must be impressed with a profound sense of His all-pervading providence, and of its responsibility to Him as the moral ruler of the world." A state that did not regard itself as an ordinance of God and an institute of heaven and as accountable to the Source of law would fail to secure the obedience of its subjects and thereby be unable to fulfill its role to promote justice. The state's "earthly sanctions," "its rewards and punishments, are insufficient for the punishments of vice or the encouragement of virtue, unless they connect themselves with the higher sanctions which religion discloses." Any state, whether Christian or pagan, needed to proclaim a religion "or it would cease to be a government of men."[11] The state, then, is no mere expression of human will, but of "will regulated and measured by those eternal principles of right which stamp it at the same time as the creature and institute of God." "The will of God, as revealed in the Scriptures, is not a positive Constitution for the State; in that relation it stands only to the Church. It is rather a negative check upon its power."[12] And such acknowledgment of the sovereignty of God and his revealed law over the state and its citizens is even more crucial in the case of a confederated government, a treaty of parties bound together in "plighted faith." Indeed, it was the very breach of faith by the Northern states, their disregard for those agreed-upon constitutional provisions of 1787, that Thornwell blamed for the crisis that had befallen the people.[13]

Now, as a moral agent the state could not commit to religion as such or to all religions as true, for "the sanctions of its laws must have a centre of unity somewhere." In the case of the new Confederacy, its Constitution was obliged to acknowledge the religion of its citizens. "We are a Christian people, and a Christian Commonwealth," he said, speaking of his native South Carolina. "As on the one hand we are not Jews, Infidels or Turks, so on the other we are not Presbyterians, Baptists, Episcopalians, or Methodists." This "Christianity, without distinction of sects"—Protestant, it should be observed—"is the fountain of our national life," and the Bible is "the great moral charter by which our laws must be measured, and the Incarnate Redeemer as the Judge to whom we are responsible." The "inward principle" of religion, cultivated by the church but going well beyond the sphere of worship, touches on all human relations and pervades all social institutions, shaping a Christian citizenry and their Christian representatives who would legislate in accordance with the teachings of the

Bible. In such a state, "the service of the commonwealth becomes an act of piety to God."[14]

Thornwell did not insist, however, that the officers of a Christian common-wealth needed to be professing believers themselves. In contrast to those who had feared that the US Constitution's prohibition of a religious test might permit Jews and other infidels to serve as federal officeholders, in a remarkable display of broad-mindedness, he went so far as to suggest that even the chief magistrate of a Christian Confederacy could well be a Jew, "provided he would come under the obligation to do nothing in the office inconsistent with the Christian religion. . . . All that he would do would be to acknowledge it as the religion of the State, and to bind himself that he will sanction no legislation that sets aside its authority." There may have also been a prudential element to this concession; at the time of the December General Assembly meeting, the secretary of war happened to be the Jewish Judah P. Benjamin. (Benjamin had served as attorney general of the Confederate government; a few months later, he was appointed secretary of state.)[15]

Secession heralded the possibility of establishing a radically new regime. "We long to see," concluded the former Unionist, who had in the past professed his confidence in the destiny of the United States, "what the world has never yet beheld, a truly Christian Republic, and we humbly hope that God has reserved it for the people of these Confederate States to realize the grand and glorious idea." But the South Carolinian divine also warned that "our republic will perish like the Pagan republics of Greece and Rome, unless we baptize it into the name of Christ." To ensure it would be set on its proper course, Thornwell asked his fellow Southern Presbyterian divines to petition the Congress of the Confederate States of America in Richmond to amend the Constitution "so as to express the precise relations which the Government of these States ought to sustain to the religion of Jesus Christ." He suggested amending the following words to the section on religious freedom (Article 1, Section 9.12): "Nevertheless we, the people of these Confederate States, distinctly acknowledge our responsibility to God, and the supremacy of His Son, Jesus Christ, as King of kings and Lord of lords; and hereby ordain that no law shall be passed by the Congress of these Confederate States inconsistent with the will of God, as revealed in the Holy Scriptures."[16]

Support for the proposal at the General Assembly was robust but not unanimous. Lacking the time for proper deliberation of the question, Thorn-well agreed to withdraw the paper and bring the matter up at a later meeting. (The measure was never approved by the Assembly; Thornwell's document was, however, published posthumously in an issue of the *Southern Presbyterian Review,* the journal he had founded and edited.)[17] By 1863, Benjamin M. Palmer had come around to his former teacher's view. "Thanks be to God for the grace given to our rulers in receding from the perilous atheism of our forefathers! and the heart of this christian people throbbed with unutterable joy, when at length the nation as such found its God, and wrought the recognition of his being and providence into its organic and fundamental law," he told the legislature of Georgia on another Day of Fasting, Humiliation and Prayer. "But, my Hearers, the whole truth has not yet been acknowledged even by us." And then Palmer proceeded to inform his audience of their young nation's continuing sin:

> This national confession fails to define whether the God whom we invoke be Jehovah Jove or Lord,—whether the God of the Pantheist, the Pagan, the Christian, or the Deist. It does not cover the mighty truth that the king, whose footsteps are seen in all the grand march of history, is God in Christ—ruling the world by the double right of creation and redemption, by the Father's grant and by the purchase of his own blood. Certain it is, no government will ever prove stable which denies the authority of this "blessed and only Potentate, the king of kings and Lord of Lords." The lessons of the past are lost upon us, if we fail to discover in the revolutions of Earth the voice of him who says, "I will overturn, overturn, overturn it, and it shall be no more, until He come whose right it is, and I will give it him." It is ours to take this young nation as it passes through its baptism of blood, and to seal its loyalty to Christ at the altar of God.[18]

While the framers of the Confederate Constitution may have fallen short of acknowledging the new nation as a distinctly Christian commonwealth, they did ensure that it explicitly enshrined and protected what Thornwell and Palmer believed God and the Bible sanctioned—their institution of "negro slavery." Unlike those men who had gathered in Philadelphia in 1787, they felt no scruples about explicitly mentioning slavery some ten times in their instrument of governance. It was an explicitly proslavery document, the blueprint for an aristocratic republic premised on the natural inequality of the human beings. The "religion of the state," as Thornwell put it, was proslavery Christianity, and behind its proslavery Constitution was a proslavery theology that had been constructed and preached by the Southern theologians and clergymen.[19] Well before the drafting of the Confederate Constitution, before the first states seceded from the Union, the theological defenders of that peculiar institution were dreaming up a comprehensive social vision of a Christian social order, what one scholar has called the "Metaphysical Confederacy."[20]

Perhaps no institution did more to provide moral and intellectual legitimation for slavery, readied the slave states for secession, and sustained its white population through the long war that followed than the Southern church.[21] The emergence of the abolitionist movement in the 1830s pushed the issue of slavery into the center of national debate, and the religious and moral condemnations of slavery that its members advanced compelled the development of a distinctive proslavery theology in the South. By the mid-1840s, the quarrel had brought about the division of the nation's largest denominations, the Methodists and Baptists, into Northern and Southern churches. (The Presbyterians split into an Old and a New School back in 1837, not directly over the slavery question but due to a controversy over theological anthropology; twenty years later, the Southerners in the New School broke off to form a sectional church.)[22]

The early battles between pro- and antislavery forces were fought over the Bible. The proslavery ministers constructed their position on what they believed to be unassailable foundations. Careful study of both the Old and New Testaments, they said, would fail to provide evidence that the ownership of human beings was indeed sinful. Indeed, they pointed to a number of texts that could even be read to provide divine sanction to the "relation" of masters and slaves, tracing Scripture's tacit acceptance and explicit endorsement of the institution from the time of the patriarchs through the apostles. Abraham, Isaac, and Jacob kept slaves in their households; the Israelites were commanded to take those they conquered into bondage (Deuteronomy 20:10–16); and the law of Moses provided detailed instruction regarding the proper acquisition, treatment, compensation for injury, and manumission of Hebrew slaves (Leviticus 25:44–46 and Exodus 21, for example; that the same chapter in Exodus included a law against man-stealing and capital punishment for its violation did not appear to trouble proslavery advocates much). Moving on to the New Testament, they noted that Jesus said nothing about the subject, even as he denounced a variety of sins and abrogated other aspects of the Mosaic law. Nor did the apostles condemn the institution of slavery or slave owners. In the hands of proslavery apologists, even the Golden Rule could be construed to serve proslavery purposes.[23]

This argument from Scripture, however, presented a problem for those who wished to uphold slavery but to limit the enslaved to people of African descent. Most were unwilling to go along with George Fitzhugh's conclusion that if slavery was a positive good, it ought well to be extended to the poor of all races.[24] As Scripture taught that all human beings were descendants of Adam and Noah, of one blood and fellow children of God ("It is publick testimony to our faith, that the Negro is of one blood with ourselves—that he has sinned as we have, and that he has an equal interest with us in the great redemption. . . . We are not ashamed to call him our brother," Thornwell announced),[25] many proslavery theologians rejected the "scientific" polygenist theories in vogue that imagined multiple human origins, with the various races possessing different moral, intellectual, and physical attributes and capacities. But those divines' recognition of shared humanity and common sinfulness from Adamic descent did not bring them to a recognition of human equality. And to justify their commitment to the inequality of the races, a fanciful take on the story of the curse of Ham (Genesis 9:18–27) or that of Cain (Genesis 4) provided a useful warrant. Those who found this bit of scriptural interpretation to be straining the plain meaning of the text too far could always appeal to the inscrutable workings of Providence that had stationed the enslaved under their masters' benevolent care.[26]

For opponents of American slavery, for whom the evil of the institution was self-evident, the scriptural defense represented a stubborn clinging to a purportedly proslavery letter while overlooking its liberationist and humanitarian spirit. Some antislavery commentators conceded that the texts of the Bible did appear to allow a certain type of human bondage but stressed that the racial chattel slavery practiced in the South was not analogous to the Israelite or Greco-Roman arrangements. Dependent on a patient explication of the text and a presentation of the particular social and economic practices of ancient Israel and classical Rome, these nuanced arguments faced difficulties finding a receptive hearing by an audience reared on the plain meaning of Scripture.[27] The Reformed Presbyterians had also developed a literal antislavery reading of Scripture, but in the cacophony remained a largely unheeded voice. (When the prominent New School Presbyterian Albert Barnes published the second edition of his antislavery book *The Church and Slavery*, he added a prefatory note apologizing for his ignorance of the testimony and actions of the Reformed Presbyterian Church; he also included extracts from their antislavery writings and a description of the sect taken from Robert Baird's *Religion in America* in an appendix. He did not make mention of the denomination's biblical argument of the issue.)[28]

Given the prestige accorded to the literal word of the Bible in the Southern antebellum America, the proslavery argument appeared orthodox and common-sensical. Proslavery ministers dismissed the scriptural arguments of their anti-slavery opponents, which they criticized as being based on the subjective authority of the human conscience over the unerring Word of God, theologi-cally suspect if not outright heretical. As Scripture did not clearly say that slavery was sinful, those who insisted that it was were defying God's own revela-tion. The difficulty wasn't lost on some of the more radical abolitionists such as William Lloyd Garrison and Gerrit Smith, who conceded that if the Bible did indeed sanction slavery, then the Bible was simply wrong.[29]

With their literal "common sense" reading of the Bible at hand, and with arguments marshaled from theology and moral philosophy, the religious advo-cates of proslavery set about to sanctify the institution and the social and economic order of the planter class.[30] In innumerable sermons, tracts, and arti-cles in denomination periodicals and learned journals, religious scholars, minis-ters, and church officials celebrated slavery as a providentially ordained social institution for the betterment of all people. In the development and propaga-tion of proslavery ideology, the theologians and preachers were joined by a slew of secular intellectuals who advanced arguments from history, political economy, moral philosophy, jurisprudence, and the new science of sociology. (Given the prestige accorded to religion, social theorists such as Thomas Roderick Dew, president of the College of William and Mary, and the agriculturalist Edmund Ruffin appealed to Scripture and Christian doctrine in making their case.)[31] Such works portrayed the South as a traditional and virtuous Christian society, one that valued personal relationships over abstract institutions, its organic social stratification and attendant inequalities reinforced by aristocratic values, an ethos of chivalry, and orthodox piety.

Slavery was not just an aspect of this social theory; it was its very founda-tion. Slavery sanctified by God, a social order based on the inequality of human beings born in sin and servitude without consent determined by Providence, was the cornerstone of their America. The republican liberty of Southern whites depended on such an arrangement. They therefore rejected the ideas of Locke and Jefferson, the infidel doctrines of natural equality and unalienable rights that had animated the American Revolution and now fueled the abolitionist movement.[32]

The fundamentals of this "slaveholding ethic," as it was christened, were by and large shared across the evangelical denominations in the South. Thus sanctified, the institution of slavery was recognized and celebrated as a benefit to both master and slave and the very basis for the ordering of modern Christian society, and preachers concerned themselves with how it ought to be run in accordance with Christian religious teachings and ethics.[33]

The well-educated Presbyterian Southern divines stood at the vanguard of the development and dissemination of proslavery theology.[34] And of those men, it was the estimable James Henley Thornwell who emerged as the most famous and formidable voice. His sermon "The Rights and the Duties of Masters," originally preached at a dedication of a church "erected for the religious instruction of the Negros" in Charleston, wove together the scriptural warrant for slavery, a moral defense of the master-slave relationship (the slaveholding ethic of social relations), the religious mission to slaves, a justification in terms of providential theology, and the contention that the Christian South stood as a bulwark against religious infidelity, economic conflict, and social disorder—that is, against the materialistic and heretical North. Published and distributed widely, "The Rights and the Duties of Masters" may well be regarded as a précis of the proslavery worldview.[35]

Taking as his text Colossians 4:1, in which Paul exhorted, "Masters, give unto your Servants that which is just and equal; knowing that ye also have a master in Heaven," Thornwell contrasted the Christian benevolence of the slaveholder against the so-called philanthropy of the opponents of slavery. The fundamental issue was "not the narrow question of abolitionism or of slavery—not simply whether we shall emancipate our negroes or not; the real question is the relations of man to society—of States to the individual, and of the individual to States; a question as broad as the interests of the human race."[36]

Thornwell broached the condemnations of antislavery moral philosophers only to dismiss their concerns entirely. The moralists, he argued, were simply confused about the true nature of the institution, inaccurately defining slavery as "the property of man in man," the conversion of a person into the instrument of another—a mere "thing." Thornwell argued that slavery was rather "a relation of man to man—a form of civil society, of which persons are the only elements, and not a relation of man to things." Slavery Thornwell defined as "the obligation to labour for another, determined by the Providence of God, independently of the provisions of a contract" (that is, without consent). As the free worker exchanges his labor for monetary payment, the enslaved voluntarily obeys his master, the difference in the latter case being that the service rendered is in consequence of the master's command rather than a mutually agreed-upon contract. Thus conceived, the master has the right to his slave's labor but not to his slave's very being. Providence had placed the African in his master's hands. In return for his service, it was the master's duty to provide for the necessities of his life and, crucially for the minister, the care of his soul. This was not, as the abolitionists wrongfully charged, the unjust possession of a person's body over his will but a moral relationship between rational, responsible agents, determined by Providence, shaped by Christian religion, for their mutual benefit. It is not hard to perceive the difficulties in this argument, which simply defined away the injustices, violence, and horrors of the slave system, but Thornwell did not appear to be much troubled by its deficiencies.[37]

True slavery, Thornwell went on to explain, was "slavery to sin." And true freedom was the freedom one gained in Christ. But this was, in the end, a freedom not of this world. It was not the freedom to choose one's own direction in life, for whom to labor and at what hour. "It is *the* freedom," rather, "which God approves; which Jesus bought by his blood, and the Holy Spirit effectually seals by His grace; the liberty wherewith Christ has made us free. ... It is a freedom which the *truth* of God brings with it—a freedom enjoyed by the martyr at the stake, a slave in his chains, a prisoner in his dungeon, as well as the king upon his throne." Thornwell thus arrived at an astonishing conclusion: "To obey under the influence of these motives, is to be slaves no longer. This is a *free* service—a service which God accepts as the loyal homage of the soul— and which proclaims them to be the Lord's freed-men, while they honor their masters on earth. Such slavery might be their glory—might fit them for their thrones in the kingdom of God." The slave could be truly free in Christ. And it was the duty of the master to provide the religious instruction so that he or she might be so liberated.[38]

Those who regarded slavery as a fundamental violation of human rights, Thornwell insisted, ignored "the real scope and purpose of the Gospel, in its relation to the present interests of man." The South's peculiar institution was a legitimate but, as every human institution administered by sinful men, an imperfect one. "Slavery is a part of the curse which sin has introduced into the world," he conceded, "and stands in the same general relations to Christianity as poverty, sickness, disease or death." The regrettable social evils that arose from its practice were not essential but contingent and did not detract from the benevolence of the institution itself. Nevertheless, the purpose of the gospel is not to reform this world, to transform it into an earthly paradise. The philanthropists "picture themselves imaginary models of a perfect commonwealth; they judge good and evil by the standard of such idea schemes; they condemn whatever comes short of their conceptions, without reference to the circumstances, which, after all, may make it relatively good," but they fail to realize that human progress is not directed by human design. "It can be affirmed of no form of government, and of no condition in society, that it is absolutely the best or the worse; in the inscrutable Providence of God, it is no doubt arranged that the circumstances of individuals, and the social and political institutions of communities, are, upon the whole, those which are best adapted to the degree of their moral progress." One must regard what might appear to one's eyes as an unjust institution from the perspective of eternity, Thornwell counseled. For now, "slavery may be a good, or so to speak more accurately, a condition, though founded in a curse, from which the Providence of God extracts a blessing. We are not to judge of the institutions of the present, by the standard of the future life—we are not to confound the absolute and relative." Abuses do of course regrettably occur (as they do and must in all human institutions in a world disordered by sin) and must be duly censured, but the imperfection of the institution does not justify its abolishment. Proslavery theologians accordingly called for the amelioration of such abuses and for providing religious instruction of slaves and protecting marriage relations among them.[39]

The Christian institution of slavery, then, was "not destructive of the essential rights of humanity" but rather the means for the enslaved person's heavenly salvation: "It is one of the schools in which immortal spirits are trained for their final destiny." The church regards slaves (as all human beings) as sinners in need of salvation, not as persons desiring of mere liberty; the duty of the teacher of the gospel "is not to civilize them—not to change their social condition—not to exalt them into citizens or freemen—it is to save them."[40] Born "pagan savages," they had been providentially brought to the plantations of the New World; it was their masters' responsibility to restrain them and teach them to be "civilized Christians." Some ministers suggested that, in time, an enslaved person may become capable of enjoying liberty in the here and now. However, they feared that, if emancipated too soon, the insufficiently Christianized might well revert to heathenism.

The religious mission to the slaves would have the added benefit of fostering their obedience and docility. "Christian knowledge," Thornwell informed his audience, "inculcates contentment with our lot; and, in bringing us before the tremendous realities of eternity, renders us comparatively indifferent to those passions and prejudices, from which all real danger to the social economy springs." While it was the Christian duty of masters to provide such instruction, in doing so they would "be consolidating the elements of your social fabric, so firmly and compactly, that it shall defy the storms of fanaticism, while the spectacle you will exhibit of union, sympathy and confidence, among the different orders of the community, will be a standing refutation of all their accusations against us." Religion, indeed, was helpfully the opiate of the slave, and of the slaveholder's conscience.[41]

The slaveholding ethic was a component of the Southern clergy's broader conception of the social order. Proslavery theologians rejected Enlightenment notions of natural equality and rights. Human beings were, in their view, social creatures by nature, the individual born bound up in a thick network of dependencies from which a hierarchal order providentially emerged. In such an order, the slave had rights, Thornwell acknowledged, "all the rights which belong essentially to humanity," but this did not mean that he was entitled to "the rights of the citizen," to be a "free member of the commonwealth." Political rights were not essential to one's humanity but contingent on one's place and role in society; "they do not spring from humanity simply considered," he noted, "for then they would belong to women and children—but from humanity in such and such relations."[42] Slavery was an aspect of the divinely ordained institution of patriarchy—the authority of fathers over their children and husbands over their wives, and the reciprocal duties and obligations that these relationships involved and from which bond society organically developed. (Unlike their white sons, the enslaved Black would not age out of his master's authority.)

The proslavery theologians enhanced this work with a cluster of economic, sociological, and political contentions that had been developed by their secular counterparts. They weighted the virtues of the political economy of the plantation favorably against the abstract and inhumane mechanisms of modern industrial capitalism in the North and in Western Europe. Converting capital into labor had resolved their tragic contradictions, uniting the interests of both. In their view, the peculiar institution thus fostered a more Christian and humane form of social and economic organization than which pertained in the free labor system. Contrasted with the shallow individualism and crass materialism of the North, the corrosive marketplace values that dissolve all human bonds and foment social unrest, revolution, and disorder, the Southern slave system bestowed social and economic stability, forestalling pauperism and agrarian revolt. Called by his religious duties to be responsible for the cradle-to-grave care of his slaves' bodies and the religious instruction for their souls, the Christian slaveholder would become a more righteous master than the factory owner intent on squeezing as much profit from his workers as possible. The great classical civilizations of the past, they recalled, had been based on slavery. Under the benevolent supervision of their ministry, slavery was destined not only to remain the socioeconomic system of the South but to spread beyond it in the future.

Those so-called philanthropists (in the eyes of proslavery theologians, "philanthropy" was simply the disguise infidelity wore) had failed to comprehend the nature and thus the beneficence of the system; speaking of "the speculative rights of man," they aimed, Thornwell announced, at "the utter ruin of this vast imperial Republick . . . to be achieved as a trophy to the progress of human development." The debate was not just over the legitimacy of that single institution; in his final analysis, it was a quarrel about the very nature of human society, how it originated, how it ought to be organized, and how it would progress. And the dispute threatened to detonate a holy war between the godly and the infidels. "The parties in this conflict," Thornwell proclaimed,

> are not merely abolitionists and slaveholders—they are atheists, socialists, communists, red republicans, jacobins, on the one side, and the friends of order and regulated freedom on the other. In one word, the world is the battle ground—Christianity and Atheism the combatants; and the progress of humanity the stake. One party seems to regard Society, with all its complicated interests, its divisions and sub-divisions, as the machinery of man—which, as it has been invented and arranged by his ingenuity and skill, may be taken to pieces, re-constructed, altered or repaired, as experience shall indicate defects or confusion in the original plan. The other party beholds in it the ordinance of God; and contemplates "this little scene of human life," as placed in the middle of a scheme, whose beginnings must be traced to the unfathomable depths of the past, and whose development and completion must be sought in the still more unfathomable depths of the future . . . and with which it is as awful temerity to tamper as to sport with the name of God.

One side was religious, the other atheistic. One kept faith in Providence; the other misplaced its trust in the mad speculations of philosophers who wished to mold the world according to their fantastical whims. Thornwell thundered against the folly of the belief in human-directed progress: "Experiment after experiment may be made—disaster after disaster, in carrying out the principles of an atheistic philosophy—until all the nations, wearied and heart-sickened with changes without improvement, shall open their eyes to the real causes of their calamities, and learn the lessons which wisdom shall evolve from the events that have passed."[43]

Southern proslavery was thus a counter-vision of modernity, distinct from the liberalism of the North and the hopes of radical social change that had inspired the recent European revolutions and continued to menace the continent. Slavery was natural, universal, moral, and providential, and an economy constructed on the master-slave relation stood as the bulwark against the corrosive forces of market capitalism and its cash nexus and as a shield against revolutionary radicalism. Confidence was to be entrusted to the firm hand of divinity guiding human history and the imposition of order on a sinful humanity; those who dared dream reshape it were to be reckoned as infidels. Abolitionism was an anti-Christian ideology costuming itself in religious and moral garb, drawn not from the inerrant Word of God but from a rationalist philosophy that preached a false conception of humanity and human rights and promoted irresponsible and fantastic humanitarian schemes that, if they came to bear, would result not in justice but radical disorder. In a world corrupted by sin, the "traditional" institutions of their providentially ordered organic society, however imperfect, were the only certain hedge against the hubris of men and women and the anarchy that would be the consequence of the mad utopian schemes they dreamed up and strove to implement. "The very principles upon which we have been accustomed to justify Southern slavery," Thornwell told his Charleston audience, "are the principles of regulated liberty—that in defending this institution we have really been upholding the civil interests of mankind—resisting alike the social anarchy of communism and the political anarchy of licentiousness—that we have been supporting representative, republican government against the despotism of the masses on the one hand and the supremacy of a single will on the other."[44]

The implications of the quarrel, then, went further and deeper than the perpetuation of slavery in the South and its expansion into the territories. Abolitionism was just another manifestation of atheistic philosophy, which, combined with unbridled capitalism and the growing despotism of the masses, threatened to destroy the republic. Insofar as Christian ministers became abolitionists and demanded, as another proslavery theorist claimed, "an anti-slavery Constitution, an anti-slavery Bible, and an anti-slavery God," they have "ended in downright infidelity."[45] The battle over slavery was one front in a wider war. And the stakes were nothing less than the future of American—and Christian—civilization.

It was with this vision in his mind that Thornwell's student Benjamin M. Palmer pressed into the argument for secession shortly after Lincoln's election. Delivered on Thursday, November 29, 1860, in the First Presbyterian Church, New Orleans, Palmer's sermon was reprinted, summarized, and editorialized upon in newspapers throughout the South and published as a separate pamphlet and in an anthology of fast day sermons by both Southern and Northern preachers, launching his career as a preeminent clerical champion of the Confederate cause and morale.[46] The South, he declared, had been assigned a providential trust *"to conserve and to perpetuate the institution of domestic slavery as now existing."* "My own conviction is, we should at once lift ourselves, intelligently, to the highest moral ground, and proclaim to all the world that we hold this trust from God, and in its occupancy we are prepared to stand or fall as God may appoint," he said. "If the critical moment has arrived at which the great issue is joined, let us say that, in the sight of all perils, we will stand by our trust: and God will be with the right!"[47]

Palmer detailed the South's duty of self-preservation and protection of its own material interests (as slavery is "interwoven with our entire social fabric"), its duty to the slaves (who, on account of their "natural inequality," are fit for dependence and helpless unless under the protection of the patriarchal system), and its duty to the civilized world (that is to say, the looms of the North and of England are dependent on cheap Southern cotton). But most of all, Palmer proclaimed the Southern duty to *"defend the cause of God and religion"* against abolitionism, which was the leading edge of the atheistic spirit of the modern age:

> The demon which erected its throne upon the guillotine in the days of Robespierre and Marat, which abolished the Sabbath, and worshipped reason in the person of a harlot, yet survives to work other horrors, of which those of the French revolution are but the type. Among a people so generally religious as the American, a disguise must be worn; but it is the same old threadbare disguise of the advocacy of human rights. From a thousand Jacobin clubs here, as in France, the decree has gone forth which strikes at God by striking at all subordination and law. Availing itself of the morbid and misdirected sympathies of men, it has entrapped weak consciences in the meshes of its treachery; and now, at last, has seated its high-priest upon the throne, clad in the black garments of discord and schism, so symbolic of its ends. Under this

specious cry of reform it demands that every evil shall be corrected, or society become a wreck—the sun must be stricken from the heavens, if a spot is found on his disk. The Most High, knowing his own power, which is infinite, and his own wisdom, which is unfathomable, can afford to be patient. But these self-constituted reformers must quicken the activity of Jehovah, or compel his abdication. In their furious haste, they trample upon obligations sacred as any which can bind the conscience.

Such "fierce zealots," he continued, "working out the single and false idea which rides them like a nightmare, . . . dash athwart the spheres, utterly disregarding the delicate mechanism of Providence." They labored under the prideful delusion that they could remake the world according to their own imaginings and had chosen Southern slavery as their sacrificial victim. To counter this foe, Palmer demanded humility and submission to the providential order. "It is time to reproduce the obsolete idea," he said, "that Providence must govern man, and not that man should control Providence." The battle lines had been drawn between this "spirit of atheism," which, waving its tricolor of "liberty, equality, fraternity," prepares to "inaugurate its reign of terror," and the forces of Christian religion, truth, and order. And in this battle, "to the South the highest position is assigned, of defending, before all nations, the cause of religion and of all truth. In this trust, we are resisting the power which wars against constitutions, and laws and compacts, against Sabbaths and sanctuaries, against the family, the State and the church; which blasphemously invades the prerogatives of God, and rebukes the Most High for the errors of his administration, which, if it cannot snatch the reins of empire from his grasp, will lay the universe in ruins at his feet. Is it possible that we shall decline the onset?"[48]

The North, Palmer charged, had utterly succumbed to the infidel forces of antislavery. With the victory of the "sectionalist" candidate—"prejudiced against the established and constitutional rights and immunities and institutions of the South," and whose party had abolitionism as "its informing and actuating soul"[49]—the die had been cast. "If the South bows before this throne, she accepts the decree of restriction and ultimate extinction, which is made the condition of her bondage."[50] In his view, "this union of our forefathers" had already been abrogated. The two sections ought to separate from one another as Abraham did from Lot. Palmer called his fellow Southerners to "pledge each other, in sacred covenant, to uphold and perpetuate what they cannot resign without dishonor and palpable ruin," and to "take all the necessary steps looking to separate and independent existence, and initiate measures for framing a new and homogeneous confederacy."[51] "Under a full conviction that the salvation of the whole country is depending upon the action of the South," he concluded, "I am impelled to deepen the sentiment of resistance in the Southern mind, and to strengthen the current now flowing toward a union of the South in defence of her chartered rights." A newly constituted Southern Confederacy would replace the Union as God's New Israel—and prosecute a holy war to safeguard its destiny if need be.[52]

In his own fast day sermon, Thornwell mournfully reflected that it had been the mission of the Republic "to redeem this continent, to spread freedom, civilization and religion through the whole length of the land. Geographically placed between Europe and Asia, we were, in some sense, the representatives of the human race. The fortunes of the world were in our hand. We were a city set upon a hill, whose light was intended to shine upon every people and upon every land." Yet the North had broken faith with this sacred trust. "To forgo this destiny, to forfeit this inheritance, and through bad faith, is an enormity of treason equaled only by the treachery of a Judas, who betrayed his Master with a kiss."[53] Like his protégé, Thornwell proclaimed the South a redeemer nation that would now take its place on the world stage. "We shall have a Government," wrote the former Unionist in his final literary effort, "that acknowledges God, that reverences right, and that makes law supreme. We are, therefore, fighting not for ourselves alone, but, when the struggle is rightly understood, for the salvation of this whole continent." This was God's cause. Thornwell's parting words called on his countrymen to strive for a great victory: "The spirits of our fathers call to us from their graves. The heroes of other ages and other countries are beckoning us on to glory. Let us seize the opportunity, and make to ourselves an immortal name, while we redeem a land from bondage, and a continent from ruin." *Let us make us a name.* The learned Presbyterian divine must have known when he pronounced them that those were the words spoken by the builders of Babel.[54]

In that fiery sermon in November 1860, Reverend Palmer had incited his fellow Southerners to "throw off the yoke of this union as readily as did our ancestors the yoke of King George III, and for causes immeasurably stronger than those pleaded in their celebrated declaration."[55] Nearly a month later, the government of South Carolina announced its secession from the Union. Its "Declaration of

the Immediate Causes Which Induce and Justify the Secession of South Carolina from the Federal Union" appealed to the language of the Declaration of
Independence to justify its litany of complaints and its decision, as did many
of the secession documents of the states that followed South Carolina out of
the Union.[56] In his first inaugural address on February 18, 1861, President
Jefferson Davis invoked the Declaration of July 1776. "Our present condition,
achieved in a manner unprecedented in the history of nations," he proclaimed,
"illustrates the American idea that governments rest upon the consent of the
governed, and that it is the right of the people to alter or abolish governments
whenever they become destructive of the ends for which they were established."[57]
(He did not mention slavery, either directly or by euphemism, in that address.)
Near the end of his June 1861 fast day sermon, Palmer drew a parallel between
the current "glorious struggle" and the American Revolution. "The principles
involved in this conflict are broader and deeper than those which underlay that
of the Revolution, rendering it of far greater significance to us and to our
posterity and to mankind at large," he remarked. "Our fathers fought for no
abstract rights as men, but for chartered rights as Englishmen. They claimed
that the fundamental principle of English liberty was invaded, when the Colonies were taxed without representation. . . . But *our* Revolution rests upon the
broader principle laid as the corner stone of the American Constitution:"—and
here Palmer actually presumed to paraphrase Jefferson's words—" 'that governments derive their just powers from the consent of the governed; and that
whenever any form of government becomes destructive of the ends for which it
was formed, it is the right of the People to alter, or to abolish it, and to institute
a new government, organizing its powers in such form as to them shall seem
most likely to effect their safety and happiness.' " It was this argument of the
right of revolution and to begin anew that Palmer wielded against the North.
"This right is denied to us," he protested, "and its denial lays the foundation of
a despotism under which we cannot consent to live, for it was distinctly repudiated in the Declaration of 1776. We should be unworthy of our Fathers, if we
flinched from maintaining to the last extremity the one, great, cardinal principle of American constitutional freedom." And so Palmer approved the revolutionary conclusion of the Declaration while severing it from its revolutionary
premises, construing the founding statement of the United States to endorse
the "right" of some people to establish a self-government to hold others in
bondage. "The last hope of self-government upon this Continent lies in these
eleven Confederated States," the minister proclaimed. "Let us trust in God, and

with an humble self-reliance take care of ourselves; prepared to recognize gracious Providence which will work our deliverance."[58]

Such invocations of the Declaration of Independence and the American Revolution did not address the fundamental propositions on which the very right to break with old governments and form new ones was based. For while the actions of Congress in 1776 provided a precedent for the Southern states' decision to break from the Union and remake their political community, the "self-evident truths" that the Patriots had appealed to presented an obvious problem for the proslavery ideologues. Indeed, Palmer rejected the belief that the Declaration had spoken of "abstract rights of men," seeing it rather as an endorsement of the "chartered rights" of men such as himself. That was, of course, a denial of the plain meaning of that text.

While the Declaration of Independence had been composed as a public relations document for both foreign and domestic consumption to justify (and implore support for) the actions of the Continental Congress, in time Americans came to realize that its stirring words could be deployed for other causes. With its affirmation of the "self-evident" truths of human equality and unalienable rights detailed in the first sentences of the second paragraph and the political theory that emerged from them, the Declaration came to be a most formidable rhetorical weapon in the fight against slavery. As Carl L. Becker noted in his celebrated study, "The ideas of the Declaration survived as a living faith chiefly among those who felt that slavery was an evil requiring immediate and desperate remedies." If its claims were indeed "self-evident," then it self-evidently followed that no person could rightfully find himself or herself the property of another, that the institution of American slavery was both a sin against the Creator who endowed those rights and an affront to the American project. The statement of "the sacred and inalienable rights of all men" brightly illuminated the stakes of the matter. The words of the Declaration, rather than those of the Constitution, comprised the spirit of the "national covenant." They could well be appealed to as a "higher law," as Senator William Henry Seward famously put it in an 1850 speech, to which the "positive law," the Constitution itself, would have to be proved.[59]

"All honor to Jefferson," whose proclamation of human equality Abraham Lincoln took as his political creed. In what came to be known as his "Peoria Speech" (October 16, 1854), Lincoln appealed to those words to summon his audience to a political-spiritual revival, to "re-adopt the Declaration of Independence, and with it, the practices, and policy, which harmonize with it.

Let north and south—let all Americans—let all lovers of liberty everywhere—join in the great and good work." "The assertion that 'all men are created equal,'" he noted in response to the *Dred Scott* decision, was placed there to be "a stumbling block to those who in after times might seek to turn a free people back into the hateful paths of despotism."[60] Frederick Douglass asked in a speech to the Ladies' Anti-Slavery Society of Rochester, New York, in 1862, "Would you have me argue that man is entitled to liberty? That he is the rightful owner of his own body? You have already declared it." Indeed, he proclaimed that "the Declaration of Independence is the RINGBOLT to the chain for your nation's destiny. . . . The principles contained in that instrument are saving principles." Douglass went on, in that remarkable address, to protest that "the great principles of political freedom and of natural justice" were not extended to the nation's Black men and women, and to condemn the infidelity of the "most eloquent" proslavery divines ("They convert the very name of religion into an engine of tyranny, and barbarous cruelty, and serve to confirm more infidels, in this age, than all the infidel writings of Thomas Paine, Voltaire, and Bolingbroke, put together, have done"), the cowardice of the American church in general, and the hypocrisy of the country ("The existence of slavery in this country brands your republicanism as a sham, your humanity as a base pretence, and your Christianity as a lie"). But the nation's redemption could be found in the Constitution, "a GLORIOUS LIBERTY DOCUMENT," which contains "principles and purposes, entirely hostile to the existence of slavery."[61] Although the Framers of the Constitution had regrettably compromised on the issue to facilitate the formation of the Union, the antislavery vision embedded in the Founding was nevertheless clear, evidenced by their refusal to directly use the word "slavery" in the Constitution, by the sunset provision of the slave trade in Article I, Section 9, and by the prohibition of slavery in the territories by the Northwest Ordinance of 1787 (drafted in 1784, predating the Constitution itself).

While the radical abolitionist William Lloyd Garrison condemned the Constitution as a "covenant with death" and an "agreement with hell,"[62] his movement could still regard the Declaration of Independence as providing ammunition for their cause. The Declaration of Sentiments of the American Anti-Slavery Society, adopted in Philadelphia in 1833, opened with an appeal to its assertions as "the corner-stone upon which is founded the Temple of Freedom," and proclaimed, "With entire confidence in the overruling justice of God, we plant ourselves upon the Declaration of our Independence and the truths of divine revelation as upon the Everlasting Rock."[63] Religious abolitionists coupled the Declaration's self-evident truths to those disclosed by Christianity. Appeals to the spirit of Scripture *and* the letter of the Declaration came to be frequent refrains in antislavery discourse. Jonathan Blanchard stated that "abolitionists take their stand upon the New Testament doctrine of the natural equity of man. The one-bloodish of human kind:—and upon those great principles of human rights, drawn from the New Testament, and announced in the American Declaration of Independence, declaring that all men have natural and *inalienable* rights to person, property and the pursuit of happiness."[64] The "New School" Presbyterian Albert Barnes wrote that slavery "is a violation of the first sentiments expressed in our Declaration of Independence, and on which our fathers founded the vindication of their own conduct in an appeal to arms; it is at war with all that a man claims for himself and for his own children; and it is opposed to all the struggles of mankind, in all ages, for freedom." "Nothing can be more certain than that man was formed by his Maker for freedom, and that all men have a right to be free," he continued. "Nothing can be more true than the declaration in the immortal instrument which asserts our national independence, that 'all men are created equal; that they are endowed by their Creator with certain inalienable rights; and that among these are life and LIBERTY.' Nothing can be more certain than that God has implanted in the human soul a desire of liberty which is a fair expression of what he intends shall be the settled condition of things in the world." The argument that the Word of God endorsed slavery, he warned, would turn people to infidelity. " 'If such are the teachings of the Bible, it is impossible that that book should be a revelation given to mankind from the true God. . . . We want no book,' such men will go on to say, 'which proclaims other doctrines than these; we can embrace no book as a revelation from God which does not coincide with the great laws of our nature,—those laws which proclaim that; all men have a right to be free. No book which departs in its teachings from those great laws CAN POSSIBLY BE FROM GOD.' "[65]

Proslavery polemicists rebuffed such appeals to a "higher law"—whether understood as one's conscience or the claims of the Declaration—stating that there was no law higher that that revealed by God in Scripture. "These consistent men," proslavery minister Frederick A. Ross sneered, "have now turned away from the word, in despondency; and are seeking, somewhere, an abolition Bible, an abolition Constitution for the United States, and an abolition God."[66] Nevertheless, antislavery appeals to the Declaration left the defenders of slavery in a difficult position, having to dismiss the letter, so to speak, of that famous text.

Toward the end of his career, John C. Calhoun saw their quandary clearly. In his 1848 speech on the Oregon Bill, the South Carolinian warned his colleagues of the coming consequences of what he regarded as the Founders' original sin. "We now begin to experience the danger of admitting so great an error to have a place in the declaration of our independence," he said. "For a long time it lay dormant; but in the process of time it began to germinate, and produce its poisonous fruits. It had strong hold on the mind of Mr. Jefferson, the author of that document, which caused him to take an utterly false view of the subordinate relation of the black to the white race in the South; and to hold, in consequence, that the former, though utterly unqualified to possess liberty, were as fully entitled to both liberty and equality as the latter; and that to deprive them of it was unjust and immoral." If the South's peculiar institution was indeed in concord with God's revealed will and providential design, it was imperative to refute the errors of the nation's founding document.[67]

To do so, proslavery apologists employed a number of approaches. One was to accept the Declaration's formulations but to claim that the natural equality and endowment of rights referred solely to the white English colonists in their dispute against the British government, and not to the Negroes or the Indians, a point that was supposedly proven by the fact that the latter were not subsequently granted citizenship under the US Constitution. This argument was adopted by Judge Roger Taney in the *Dred Scott* decision.[68] Another was to argue that those now troublesome words were incidental to the argument for independency and now politically irrelevant. More simply, some dismissed those "self-evident truths" as neither self-evident nor true. "Notwithstanding our respect for the important document which declared our independence," Chancellor William Harper explained, "yet if any thing be found in it, and especially in what may be regarded rather as its ornament than its substance—false, sophistical or unmeaning, that respect should not screen it from the freest examination."[69] Jefferson's words set up a false understanding of the basis of government. Human beings are not born free but rather situated within complex webs of dependence. Thus, the natural inequality of human beings would persist even in the most free and popular of governments. What political privileges an individual may hold are not on account of natural right but are those granted by social convention. "The plain truth," the Episcopalian clergyman and lawyer Albert Taylor Bledsoe avowed, "is that although this notion of the 'inalienable right' of all to liberty may sound very well in a declaration of independence, and may be most admirably adapted to stir up the passions of men and produce fatal commotions in a commonwealth, yet no wise nation ever has been or ever will be guided by it in the construction of her laws. It may be a brand of discord in the hands of the abolitionist and the demagogue. It will never be an element of light, or power, or wisdom, in the bosom of the statesman."[70]

And then there was the argument that the Declaration's assertions of natural equality, endowed rights, and government instituted by the consent of the governed were simply contrary to what Christian revelation taught. The most sustained example of this argument was advanced by Frederick A. Ross, pastor of the First Presbyterian Church in Huntsville, Alabama, in his *Slavery Ordained of God* (1857). Slavery, Ross flatly stated in his preliminary remarks, "is part of the government ordained in certain conditions of fallen mankind. . . . *Slavery is of God*, and to continue for the good of the slave, the good of the master, the good of the whole American family, until another and better destiny may be unfolded." Attempts to argue otherwise, he held, lead straightway to infidelity.[71]

A good part of the work was composed of letters directed at Albert Barnes, the author of *The Church and Slavery.* In that book, Barnes had warned that the clergy's disavowal of the Declaration's principles would turn people away from Christian faith; Ross countered that it was the abolitionists' strained interpretations of Scripture that were the true cause of their infidelity. He accused them of "torturing the Bible for a while, to make it give the same testimony," "applying to the rack the Hebrew and the Greek," contorting the Hebrew word *ebed* and the Greek *doulosi* into "servant," all in order to have the prophets condemn slavery as "*a violation of the first sentiments of the Declaration of Independence.*" "You find it difficult to persuade men that Moses and Paul were moved by the Holy Ghost to sanction the philosophy of Thomas Jefferson!" Ross mordantly remarked. "You find it hard to make men believe that Moses saw in the mount, and Paul had vision in heaven, that this *future apostle of Liberty* was inspired by Jesus Christ."[72] The Declaration of Independence, rather, expressed an "infidel theory of human government."[73]

Ross conceded that if the five affirmations that comprised its second paragraph were true, then slavery would indeed be morally wrong. (None of this, he made clear, had any bearing on the document's purpose—to set forth the colonists' grievances against Great Britain and their right, so oppressed, to separate and form their own government.) But those affirmations were neither self-evident nor supported by the Bible:

God gives no sanction to the affirmation that he has *created all men equal*; that this is *self-evident*, and that he has given them *unalienable rights*; that he has made government to *derive its power solely from their consent*, and that he has given them *the right to change that government in their mere pleasure*. All this—every word of it, every jot and tittle—is the liberty and equality claimed by infidelity. God has cursed it seven times in France since 1793; and he will curse it there seventy times seven, if Frenchmen prefer to be pestled so often in Solomon's mortar. He has cursed it in Prussia, Austria, Germany, Italy, Spain. He will curse it as long as time, whether it is affirmed by Jefferson, Paine, Robespierre, Ledru Rollin, Kossuth, Greeley, Garrison, or Barnes.

Indeed, Ross suggested that that entire section of the Declaration was to be regarded as "an *excrescence* on the tree of our liberty"; accordingly, it ought to be cut away as one would surgically remove that parasite from a plant.[74]

A distinction needed to be made, Ross went on to argue, between two understandings of civil liberty: the liberty granted by God to human beings and a liberty that God does not endow. According to the Bible, God had ordained government over fallen humanity: first, the authority of Adam over his wife, extended to the institution of patriarchy, and then to that of monarchy. "God required the family, and then the state, so to rule as to give to every member the *good* which is his, in harmony with the welfare of the whole; and he commanded the individual to seek *that good* and NO MORE." Given the depravity of humankind, from time to time governments will violate their obligation to pursue the welfare of their subjects. And those so oppressed do retain the right to secure their good. However, in their struggle against such rulers, "they have ever been tempted to go beyond the limitation God had made, and to seek supposed good, not given, in rights, prompted by *self-will*, destructive of the state." Propelled by a sinfully deformed instinct for liberty, human beings desire to go beyond the measure granted by God.[75]

The Declaration of Independence, Ross claimed, invoked both conceptions of liberty. The first paragraph affirmed the godly right of the colonists to separate from Great Britain, nothing more than the right children who come to the age of maturity have to secure their good by separating from their parents to go and form their own families. The second paragraph, however, contained "*the affirmation of liberty claimed by infidelity*" (the very same infidelity, Ross noted, that motivated Korah, Dathan, and Abiram to rebel against the rightful authority of Moses and Aaron). That chain of affirmations—the four links of natural equality, endowed rights, government that received its just powers by the consent of the governed, and the right, if that government is destructive of those rights, to alter it or institute a new one—"teaches as a fact *that* which is not true; and it claims as right *that* which God has not given." "It is the old infidel averment," Ross contended. "It is not true in any one of its assertions."[76]

Those propositions were not self-evident truths but claims that could only be verified by means of reasoning, through experience, or vouchsafed by revelation. The entire chain was dependent on that first assertion of natural equality. And, according to Ross, Scripture taught no such doctrine but rather the ordained hierarchies of gender and of race. The creation of woman out of Adam's rib demonstrated the original relationship between the sexes: God had made "*the man the image and glory of God*, but the woman *the glory of the man. For man is not of the woman, but the woman of the man. Neither was the man created for the woman*, but the woman *for the man*" (1 Corinthians 11). The original inequality between the sexes became pervasive on account of the fall, as God placed the woman under the perpetual authority of her husband. Scripture also explained the differentiation of the races. After the flood, God dispersed human beings to different parts of the world, and the subsequent "natural history of man," in which all human beings have been born, proceeded "under causes of inequality, acting on each individual from climate, from scenery, from food, from health, from sickness, from love, from hatred, from government, inconceivable in variety and power."[77]

Ross was satisfied that if that first link in the chain could be refuted, the entire argument would collapse: "If all men are *not* created equal in attributes of body and mind, then the *inequality* may be *so great* that such men could not be endowed with right to life, liberty, and pursuit of happiness, unalienable save in their *consent*; then government over such men cannot rightfully rest upon their *consent*; nor can they have right to alter or abolish government in their mere determination."[78] He dispatched the three remaining assertions by arguing that Scripture taught that political authority was not derived from the consent of the governed but was bestowed by God (to Adam and Noah, directly to Israel, and indirectly to the other nations). "Government over men," he wrote, "whether in the family or in the state is, then, as directly from God as it would be if he, in visible person, ruled in the family or the state." The appeal to Romans 13 would appear to settle the case. So long as the government did not require one to violate God's word, one owed it one's obedience. One was also to submit, even if the government did not rule righteously, "*until* oppression has gone to *the point* at which *God makes* RESISTANCE *to be duty.*" (This, of course, raised the question as to whether one might regard the use of one's labor without one's consent as "oppressive," which in the case of people of African descent Ross apparently did not.) A person was obligated to submit to government not on account of some prior consent but because of the obligation to submit to God. "God gives no sanction to the notion of a SOCIAL COMPACT. He never gave to man individual, isolated, natural rights, unalienably in his keeping." "And, therefore," Ross concluded, "those five sentences in that second paragraph of the Declaration of Independence are not the truth; so, then, it is not *self-evident* truth that all men are created equal. So, then, it is not the truth, in fact, that they are created equal. So, then, it is not the truth that God has endowed all men with unalienable right to life, liberty, and pursuit of happiness. So, then, it is not the truth that governments derive their just powers from the consent of the governed. So, then, it is not the truth that the people have right to alter or abolish their government, and institute a new form, whenever to them it shall seem likely to effect their safety and happiness."[79]

On the same day Thornwell delivered his "Sermon on National Sins," the Reverend Thomas Smyth preached one in the Second Presbyterian Church in Charleston, in which he portrayed the crisis as a divine curse poured out on the nation. But what had provoked God's wrath, the nation's primal sin, was not the Constitution, which Smyth called "an embodiment of wisdom, patriotism, sagacity and prudential foresight and moderation; of sterling good sense; and of religion without restriction upon the full exercise of conscientious differences."[80] Rather, he pointed an accusing finger at the nation's founding statement:

> Now, to me, pondering long and profoundly upon the course of events, the evil and bitter root of all our evils is to be found in the infidel, atheistic, French Revolution, Red Republican principle, embodied as an axiomatic seminal principle—not in the Constitution, but in the Declaration of Independence. That seminal principle is this: "We hold these truths to be self-evident: that all men are created equal; that they are endowed by their Creator with certain inalienable rights; that among these are life, liberty, and the pursuit of happiness; and that to secure these rights, governments are instituted by God, deriving their just powers from the consent of the governed," and so on to inevitable consequences.

Smyth urged his audience not to be fooled by the appeals to the Deity that punctuated that document. "Now, though God is here introduced, the Declaration is Godless. God is introduced to give dignity and emphasis; to create man, and to ordain government; and then He is banished. The sceptre is torn from his hands, and fictions are substituted for facts." The claims the Declaration makes are false: the only equality among human beings is that they are all born in sin; government is ordained by God, and he alone determines the rights people have and the duties they owe. And "the progressive development of this atheistic, revolutionary and anarchic principle" has undercut the Constitution; it brought about expansion of suffrage, which "put the government of this country into the hands of a majority of many—and in some cases, of multitudes—who were ignorant, unlettered, unacquainted with its principles, altogether uninterested in its course of policy, and restrained by no love of truth, justice, or constitutional order and in consequence, the government of the majority." From this "it followed that majorities should absolutely govern, and should interpret and govern even the Constitution." Further, this principle had led to the Bible being interpreted according to the will of the majority, or popular opinion, and this interpretation was being enforced "as a higher law upon all who differ from it." And the principle of a "higher law"—"the views of this sectional majority"—was easily transferred to their interpretation of the Constitution.[81]

And not only that. The acceptance of the false principle of equality proclaimed by the Declaration of Independence had also led to "the rejection, by many, of the divine inspiration, and infallible, unalterable authority of the Bible, as the only standard of faith and practice, of right and wrong, of sin and duty. Hence, also, the doctrine of a self-developing morality." According to "this higher law principle, a majority of his creatures can decide for God, and against God, that slavery is, in its essential nature, absolutely sinful; further, that it is so essentially and hienously [*sic*] wicked, that in order to overthrow it, compacts may be broken, and robbery, murder, arson, treason, rebellion and massacre with all the hellish crew of bigotry, hatred, uncharitableness, excommunication, calumny, opprobrious vituperation, are let loose to devastate and destroy." Smyth warned of "anarchy, prodigality, profanity, Sabbath profanation, vice and ungodliness in every monstrous form, and in the end the corruption and overthrow of the Republic, and the erection, upon its ruins, of an absolute and bloody despotism, of which coercion, or in other words, force, is the vital principle. An anti-slavery Bible must have an anti-slavery God, and then a God anti-law, order, property and morality; that is no God but 'THE GOD OF THIS WORLD.' " On account of the nation's primal sin of the infidel Declaration of Independence, the members of his audience were "now partakers in the penal curse and consequences, and in all the disastrous results of violated faith, and in the aggressive encroachments of a cruel and crushing majority." He called on his fellow South Carolinians to turn back to their God in humiliation and prayer, and urged the South to build on the rock of her proslavery Bible. "God's word obeyed, and God's will followed, will secure for us that Divine succour, which is greater than all that can be against us."[82]

That the new Confederacy was founded on the renunciation of Jefferson's proposition of the natural equality of men was voiced by its vice president, Alexander H. Stephens. A former Whig, he had opposed secession as late as mid-November 1860 and privately confided that he preferred the Constitution of 1787 to the charter he helped usher out of Montgomery. But in extemporaneous remarks on March 21, 1861, in Savannah, Georgia, Stephens decided to pronounce explicitly what Jefferson Davis had evaded in his inaugural address. "The new constitution has put to rest, *forever*," Stephens declared, "all the agitating questions relating to our peculiar institution—African slavery as it exists amongst us—the proper *status* of the negro in our form of civilization." The Union had been founded on the false principle of human equality. "The prevailing ideas entertained by [Jefferson] and most of the leading statesmen at the time of the formation of the old constitution," he noted, "were that the enslavement of the African was in violation of the laws of nature; that it was wrong in *principle*, socially, morally, and politically."

> It was an evil they knew not well how to deal with, but the general opinion of the men of that day was that, somehow or other in the order of Providence, the institution would be evanescent and pass away. This idea, though not incorporated in the constitution, was the prevailing idea at that time. The constitution, it is true, secured every essential guarantee to the institution while it should last, and hence no argument can be justly urged against the constitutional guarantees thus secured, because of the common sentiment of the day. Those ideas, however, were fundamentally wrong. They rested upon the assumption of the equality of races. This was an error. It was a sandy foundation, and the government built upon it fell when the "storm came and the wind blew."[83]

By enshrining the legitimacy of slavery, Stephens said, the framers of the Confederate constitution had built better than their forebears. While the Union had been formed on the notion of human equality, "our new government is founded upon exactly the opposite idea; its foundations are laid, its corner-stone rests, upon the great truth that the negro is not equal to the white man; that slavery subordination to the superior race is his natural and normal condition. This, our new government, is the first, in the history of the world, based upon this great physical, philosophical, and moral truth," he boasted. This "truth" may have been slow to find recognition (Stephens did not claim that it was "self-evident"), but like the scientific theories of Galileo, Adam Smith, and William Harvey, which had been dismissed by their contemporaries, human inequality would in time become universally acknowledged. Those Northerners who clung to the erroneous notion of human equality were to be dismissed as "fanatics." "They were attempting to make things equal which the Creator had made unequal." It was on this principle of natural inequality—"in strict conformity to nature, and the ordination of Providence"—that Stephens proclaimed that "our social fabric is firmly planted." His description of the foundations of the new political order is worth pondering:

> The architect in the construction of buildings, lays the foundation with the proper material—the granite; then comes the brick or the marble. The substratum of our society is made of the material fitted by nature for it, and by experience we know, that it is best, not only for the superior, but for the inferior race, that it should be so. It is, indeed, in conformity with the ordinance of the Creator. It is not for us to inquire into the wisdom of his ordinances, or to question them. For his own purposes, he has made one race to differ from another, as he has made "one star to differ from another star in glory." The great objects of humanity are best attained when there is conformity to his laws and decrees, in the formation of governments as well as in all things else. Our confederacy is founded upon principles in strict conformity with these laws. This stone which was rejected by the first builders "is become the chief of the corner"—the real "corner-stone in our new edifice.[84]

These words loudly echoed the proslavery theology that the Southern Christians had forged. Stephens adorned his proclamation of the "great physical, philosophical, and moral truth" of human inequality with biblical allusions. His listeners and readers would have understood the references to the curse on Ham's son (Genesis 9:18–27) and the stars differing in glory (1 Corinthians 15:41). But most audacious was Stephens's reference to that once rejected "corner stone" (Psalms 118:22, quoted by Jesus),[85] which in other New Testament texts (Acts 4:11 and 1 Peter 2:6–7, using Isaiah 28:16 as a proof text) referred to Jesus Christ himself but in Stephens's oration signified the so-called truth of racial inequality upon which the new regime had been built in strict conformity. And the vice president predicted that neighboring states would soon break away from the decaying Union and join the rising Confederacy, "the nucleus of a growing power which, if we are true to ourselves, our destiny, and high mission, will become the controlling power on this continent"—the coming to be of a new redeemer nation as an Empire of Slavery.

It is against those proslavery heresies—the claim of a false beginning and desire for a new founding—that we can consider Abraham Lincoln's dedicatory remarks at Gettysburg on November 19, 1863. There, by the graves of those who fell in that battle, Lincoln succinctly reaffirmed his understanding of the American founding and its purpose. The new nation, he proclaimed, had been "conceived in Liberty, and dedicated to the proposition that all men are created equal." The Union soldiers who fought and died in the present war "gave their lives that that nation might live." And it was for the living to take up the unfinished work to ensure "that this nation, under God, shall have a new birth of freedom." The argument that had provided the case for separation from Great Britain was transformed into the announcement of a national endeavor.

The words "under God," which were not in the text prepared for delivery, would later, during a cold war, be called on to demonstrate the nation's recognition of and dependence on the Almighty.[86]

CHAPTER FOUR

The Crowning, Original Sin
of the Nation

The Religious Amendment Movements

In December 1863, a pair of ministers traveled to Washington, dispatched by their presbyteries to meet with the president of the United States and "lay before him the views of the Church in relation to what should be done to save the country in its emergencies and trials." The men, J. R. W. Sloane and A. M. Milligan, were introduced as "a delegation from the Church of the Covenanters" and, after an exchange of pleasantries, read their prepared statement: "Our church has unanimously declared, by the voice of her highest court, that the world has never seen a conflict in which right was more clearly wholly upon the one side and wrong upon the other, than the present struggle of this government with the slaveholders' rebellion. She has also unanimously declared her determination to assist the government by all lawful means in her power, in its conflict with this atrocious conspiracy, until it be utterly overthrown and annihilated." Members of "an antislavery church of the most radical school," they believed "that God, by his word and providence, is calling the nation to immediate, unconditional and universal emancipation." They therefore implored the president to enforce the Emancipation Proclamation to the "utmost extent" of his powers. "Let it be placed on the highest grounds of Christian justice and philanthropy. Let it be declared to be an act of national repentance for long complicity with the guilt of slavery."[1]

In the meeting, which lasted over an hour, Sloane and Milligan also took the opportunity to speak of the Reformed Presbyterian's long-standing complaint against the Constitution—its failure to acknowledge the authority of God, Christ, and his law. "This we deeply deplore as wholly inconsistent with all claim [*sic*] to be considered a Christian nation, or to enjoy the protection and favor of God." The president, they suggested, could "set the world an example of a Christian state governed, not by the principles of mere political expediency, but acting under a sense of accountability to God, and in obedience to those laws of immutable morality which are binding alike upon nations and individuals."[2]

Milligan noted Lincoln's "deep-set eyes steadfastly upon me, while his care-worn face assumed at once the expression of deepest attention," and how "more than once when allusion was made to the responsibility of his position, God's controversy with our nation, and the church's hope that he had been raised up to be our country's deliverer, he gave signs of evident emotion." Upon its conclusion, he recounted, the president "arose and received it, carried it to his desk and deposited it there, with the remark, that he would give it the attention due to the importance of the document and the high character of the body from which it came, and that, if his other duties would permit, he would prepare an answer; but added, that such was the pressure of business upon him that frequently the day passed without being able to *begin* some particular work to which it had been specially devoted." According to Milligan's report, the three men then engaged in a theologically charged exchange about the sin of slavery, providence, and the judgment coming down on the nation. The ministers asked, "Was it possible that any Christian man could doubt on which side of such a contest the righteous God was to be found; was there any attribute of his character which could take the side of such an iniquity as slavery." Lincoln answered that "he never could see slavery, in any other light than as an evil—an only evil, and that continually; that he viewed providence generally, and these providences particularly, as both an end and a means; that there was no doubt but God was visiting this nation, both North and South, with judgment for our sins, and that in the end He would bring about some result from these operations that would show he had a purpose, and that the result might be very different from what we expected or desired." The ministers were more certain of God's ways, responding that "this depended entirely upon ourselves; that if we repented under his judgments, and executed judgment in the morning, and delivered the spoiled out of the hand of the oppressor—if we would submit to

God, do homage to his Son, and give obedience to his law, we would be established as a nation; but if we refuse and rebel, we will be destroyed, for the mouth of the Lord hath spoken it."[3]

Even before the war, some of those hardline Old Light Covenanters had begun to reconsider their mode of engagement with the sinful nation. The Synod of the Reformed Presbyterian Church took a tentative step toward a more activist stance in 1859 when it met in Allegheny, Pennsylvania, and prepared a memorial to Congress. Writing that their church was "desirous to promote the best interest of the country," they warned the legislators that it was "convinced that our nation does not thus submit itself to God in its Constitution, and exposes itself to the denunciations of God's wrath," and appealed for them to amend the Constitution to include an acknowledgment of God, the nation's submission to Christ's authority, and "the paramount obligation of God's law, contained in the Scriptures of the Old and New Testaments." They called attention, as well, to the denomination's aversion to "the existence of any form of slavery within the national limits."[4] By this time, the Old Light Covenanters had added the failure to acknowledge the Bible as the source of law to their catalogue of the Constitution's defects. The notion that the state was a "moral person" and therefore accountable to God's judgment in history was also incorporated into their theological-political doctrine.[5]

The Synod's appeal fell on deaf ears in Congress. And it does not appear that the denomination's rank and file were very much roused by the effort; the memorial was promoted neither through the church's periodicals nor by its regional assemblies. But the action did signal a shift in the church's testimony of political dissent: from passive waiting to direct appeal for constitutional change.[6]

When the war came, the Covenanters learned they were not alone in thinking that the nation's trial was on account of a flawed Constitution. The Sunday following the debacle at Bull Run, the Hartford Congregationalist minister Horace Bushnell preached a sermon titled "Reverses Needed." Bushnell, one of the leading New England divines, endeavored to prepare his listeners for the "grand struggle" that lay before them, "to go over a calm revision of the matter of the war itself, showing what it means and the great moral and religious ideas that are struggling to the birth in it—possible to be duly born only in great throes of adversity and sacrifice."[7]

The conflict was foreordained. Slavery was, of course, its proximate cause, but its true origin lay deeper. "It is a remarkable, but very serious fact, not sufficiently noted, as far as my observation extends, that our grand revolutionary fathers left us the legacy of this war, in the ambiguities of thought and principle which they suffered, in respect to the foundations of government itself. The real fact is that, without proposing it, or being distinctly conscious of it, they organized a government, such as we, at least, have understood to be without moral or religious ideas; in one view a merely man-made compact, that without something farther, which in fact was omitted or philosophically excluded, could never have more than a semblance of authority." In the struggle between those two wings of the revolution—the New England Puritan and the Jeffersonian (shaped by "the writings of Rousseau and the generally infidel literature of the French nation"; it is curious that Bushnell did not mention the more profound influence of Locke)—it was the latter, the atheistic rather than the religious, that happened to succeed, founding a republic without God. "If we go back to the deepest root of the trouble, we shall find that it comes of trying to maintain a government without moral ideas, and concentrate a loyal feeling around institutions that, as many reason, are only human compacts, entitled of course, if that be all, to no feeling of authority, or even of respect." A "real nationality," he claimed, could never be forged on the basis of "the specious fictions we have contrived, to account for the government without reference to God, or to moral ideas. . . . We began with a godless theorizing, and we end, just as we should, in discovering that we have not so much as made any nation at all."[8]

Yet, in the coming adversity, in shared sacrifice and the bloodshed of "fighting the war out," Bushnell hoped a true nation would at last be forged. "And the victory, when it comes, will even be a kind of religious crowning of our nationality. All the atheistic jargon we have left behind us will be gone, and the throne of order, established, will be sanctified by moral convictions." It was not now the moment, he said, to agitate for "political reforms"; nevertheless, Bushnell dared to hope that the nation would "at some fit time, insert into the preamble of our constitution, a recognition of the fact that the authority of government is derivable only from God; cutting off, in this manner, the false theories under which we have been so fatally demoralized." But such a deed— "the everlasting expulsion of those basely, godless theories which our fathers let in to corrupt and filch away the principles of right and law-begirt liberty"— would only ratify what had already been born in blood.[9]

Bushnell's oration, widely published and excerpted in the Northern press, signaled a growing mood. In the months that followed, similar laments echoed throughout churches and lecture halls of the North.[10] As if to compensate for its former negligence, the government found ways to deploy religion in the war effort—Lincoln proclaimed three fast days and four days of thanksgiving; Congress made provision for the appointment of army chaplains; the US Mint struck the words "In God We Trust" on the two-cent coin.[11]

And so it was that the Covenanters undertook their mission to persuade the government to correct the Constitution—a practical expression of their testimony of political dissent. Unlike Bushnell, they believed that the crisis demanded immediate action on this front. The time had come for national repentance and to place the country on a proper theological foundation.

Lincoln did not take up Sloane and Milligan's proposal, but soon thereafter a national movement for a "Christian Amendment" to the Constitution began to take shape. It began somewhat haphazardly, at a "convention for prayer and Christian conference with special reference to the state of our country" held in February 1863 at Xenia, Ohio, one of the many ad hoc regional conferences organized by ministers and laymen to discuss the war and contemplate its religious meaning. Later accounts of that gathering, keen on demonstrating the movement's broad evangelical support, related it had been attended by participants from eleven denominations, but contemporary reports suggest it was in fact dominated by men from the Presbyterian fringe, though not convened as a Covenanter production.[12]

The proposal for a constitutional amendment was submitted during a session on "Religion in the Nation" by a successful layman named Mr. John Alexander, who at the time appeared to have attended a United Presbyterian church.[13] "In this, the day of our national calamity, it becomes us to inquire what the Lord would have us do," Alexander told the assembled. "In considering the way by which God has led our nation and the poor returns we have made to him for his distinguishing blessings, we are constrained to confess that we have been an ungrateful and backsliding people; and if the deserved judgments now upon us for our sins do not produce repentance and reformation, national division and prostration, if not destruction, are inevitable." While reliance on God and his authority was frequently acknowledged during the struggle for independence, "a fatal backward step was taken in adopting that otherwise noble instrument without any direct recognition of God or his authority and with a toleration of slavery, thus contradicting two of the noblest principles of the Declaration of Independence, viz.: Reliance upon Divine Providence, and acknowledgement of the equal rights of man." This failure to acknowledge God's sovereignty and his law was "the crowning, original sin of the nation, and slavery [was] one of its natural outgrowths"; the calamity of civil war was God's "just judgments." The nation needed "to repent and forsake our national sins, or be destroyed." It was long past time to correct this grievous error by amending the Constitution "so as to acknowledge God and the authority of his law." Alexander proposed doing so by revising its Preamble to read: "WE, THE PEOPLE OF THE UNITED STATES, recognizing the being and attributes of Almighty God, the Divine Authority of the Holy Scriptures, the law of God as the paramount rule, and Jesus, the Messiah, the Savior and Lord of all." The pulpit and the press and the "Christian patriotic sentiment of the nation" would then work in concert to pressure Congress and the state legislatures to adopt the measure.[14]

While Alexander's proposal occasioned a more heated discussion among those gathered than the later official histories of the movement suggest, it was greeted with enthusiasm sufficient to merit further discussion.[15] A follow-up meeting took place in Pittsburgh on July 4, but was attended only by Old and New Light Reformed Presbyterians. More successful and broad-based was the convening of a national convention, advertised to "all citizens favorable to the measure, without distinction of party or creed," the following January at Allegheny, Pennsylvania.[16] Those present resolved to work to amend the Constitution "as fully to express the Christian national character," hammered out a formula that would be acceptable to all parties, drew up a memorial and petition to Congress, and formed the National Association to Secure the Religious Amendment of the Constitution to obtain public support and lobby for the effort.[17]

On February 10, 1864, a delegation of ministers representing the association appeared at the White House for an audience with Lincoln. (That same week, Lincoln listened to the appeal of a three-person delegation of Reformed Presbyterians composed of the Reverends J. R. W. Sloane and S. O. Wylie and a layman.)[18] The men who comprised that "special committee"—three Old Light and two New Light Reformed Presbyterians, two United Presbyterians (including Alexander), two New School Presbyterians, and an Episcopalian— carried high hopes that the president would greet their proposal with favor. The delegation was chaired by Joshua Hall McIlvaine, a Presbyterian minister and professor at Princeton, who in 1859 had published a lecture arguing for a constitutional amendment to shore up the Protestant nature of the republic from Catholic encroachments.[19] Standing before the president, McIlvaine recited the Association's revision of the Preamble to the Constitution, which wove into the original wording a profession of Christian faith and language from the Declaration of Independence:

> We, the people of the United States, [humbly acknowledging Almighty God as the source of all authority and power in civil government, the Lord Jesus Christ as the Ruler among the nations, his revealed will as the supreme law of the land, in order to constitute a Christian government,] and in order to form a more perfect union, establish justice, insure domestic tranquility, provide for the common defense, promote the general welfare, and [secure the inalienable rights and the blessings of life, liberty, and the pursuit of happiness to ourselves, our posterity, and all people,] do ordain and establish this Constitution for the United States of America.

The first insertion incorporated the key aspects of Covenanter doctrine—the acknowledgment of God as the source of civil authority, of Christ as Ruler, of the Bible as the fountain of law. The inclusion of the phrase "inalienable rights" in the second insertion, perhaps a concession to those who wanted the amendment to include explicitly antislavery language, would have incorporated into the Constitution the goals of government as spelled out in the Declaration. The proposed text did not, however, include the Declaration's affirmation of the self-evident truth of human equality. In neither their appeal to the president nor their memorial to Congress did the clergymen deign to mention the "godly" Constitution of the Confederate States of America.[20]

The delegation informed the president that "our civil and religious liberties, our free institutions, and all our national prosperity, power and glory, are mercies and blessings derived from God to us through the channel of the christian religion," yet "we have omitted even the mention of His blessed name in the most significant and highest act of the nation." This was a failure of the nation to fulfill its obligation to the Creator. "His just displeasure, opened the floodgates of that political corruption which is the mediate, and given occasion to that prodigious development of the spirit of oppression and injury to the negro race, which is the immediate source of our present calamities and sorrows." The war was just chastisement. To repent of these "national sins," Americans must "return to our obligations as a christian people, by acknowledging the true God as our God in our fundamental and organic law." Ratification of the amendment would neither violate the principle of separation of church and state nor trample upon the religious liberties or rights of conscience of the people. "We ask for no union of Church and State—that is a thing which we utterly repudiate; we ask for nothing inconsistent with the largest religious liberty, or the rights of conscience in any man. We represent no sectarian or denominational object, but one in which all who bear the christian name, and all who have any regard for the christian religion, can cordially agree." And they emphasized that Lincoln had the political and moral standing to push the measure through Congress, having achieved "the confidence and affection of the christian people of this land, beyond all your predecessors, save only the Father of his Country." They told Lincoln that, in doing so, "you will have wielded that vast influence with which you have been clothed by Divine Providence and by the voice of the people." The clergymen did not mention in these remarks that the language of the proposed amendment had been informed by Covenanter political theology or the key role of Reformed Presbyterians in the movement. Nor was there any mention of that denomination's long and controversial testimony of political dissent.[21]

"The general aspect of your movement I cordially approve," Lincoln replied, according to the ministers' report. "In regard to particulars I must ask time to deliberate, as the work of amending the Constitution should not be done hastily. I will examine your paper in order more fully to comprehend its contents than is possible from merely hearing it read, and will take such action as my responsibility to our Maker and our country demands."[22] While the ministers were encouraged by this response, from what we know Lincoln ignored the proposal, as he had the Reformed Presbyterians' earlier appeal.

The memorial was introduced to Congress by Senator Charles Sumner, and the National Association launched an all-out petition effort to demonstrate public support for the measure. In June, the Association held its First Anniversary Meeting in Philadelphia, and later that year published its first statement to the public at large: a seventeen-page booklet setting forth the history of the Association, the rationale for the Religious Amendment, and their vision of a Christian America. The core of the booklet was an "Address of the Committee of Correspondence" to "the Christian People of the United States." "The terrible national calamities into which we have fallen, indicate that we do not, *as a nation*, possess those moral qualifications which secure the permanence and welfare of the Commonwealth," it asserted. Moral reform was necessary, on both a personal and national level. "Many Christians are convinced that we have failed to give our civil institutions that definite and practical religious character which is worthy of a Christian people and essential to national permanence and prosperity." The people had failed to recognize the "divine origin" of the government and to acknowledge their obedience to Jesus as Ruler and his law. "It is surely fitting that a Constitution framed by a Christian people should recognize a higher source of civil authority than the mere will or consent of the citizen." The text further asserted that "an irreligious government begets an irreligious people."[23]

But the American people had long considered themselves a Christian people under divine authority. Numerous historical precedents and national acts were enumerated—beginning with the Mayflower Compact and working through colonial charters and Revolutionary-era state constitutions. Why, then, did the "eminent men who framed the Federal Constitution" neglect to recognize God in their work? Hamilton was said to exclaim, "I declare we forgot it," but

> the only satisfactory explanation is found in their known anxiety to avoid the unsound and hurtful union of Church and State, and in their conception of civil government merely as a social compact and not as the ordinance of God. In guarding against unequal and unjust discriminations between citizens of various religious belief, they have absolved the citizens from all profession, even of the fundamental moral truths on which civil government rests. In guarding against the doctrine that constitutions, if established at all, are granted to the people by their rulers, and asserting the right of the people to frame their own Constitution, they forgot that the people were still dependent on the power of God, and that their national authority and rights are conferred by him.

The Constitution's defect was not a mere oversight but could be attributed both to the Framers' fears of religious establishments and to the influence of an erroneous political theory. The Christian character of American government had nevertheless been demonstrated in the appointment of congressional chaplains, fast and thanksgiving day resolutions, and "the divine ordinance of the oath." "If such implied recognition of God be proper and becoming, no objection can be urged against the express recognition which we propose," Alexander suggested. Further, instances such as the refusal of a president to "appoint a day of fasting and prayer in an hour of public calamity, because the nation in its constitution recognized no God" and the Treaty of Tripoli, which declared the United States was not a Christian nation, attested to the necessity of such an amendment. "Let us begin anew," this time building on the "true foundation," recognizing divine authority and the people's subordination, providing for "law, order, and stability in every department of the social fabric." The Association was "prompted by pure Christian patriotism, participated in by various Christian denominations, all of whom are opposed to any sectarian establishment of religion."[24] There was no explicit mention of the proposal's repressive consequences, though the proviso that "we also ask for any changes in the body of the Constitution, which may be necessary to give effect to these amendments in the preamble," provided a hint as to what might be in store if it were to be ratified.[25]

Also included in the pamphlet was John Alexander's address before the Philadelphia meeting, which briefly presented the complaint against the Founding and recounted the short history of the movement. Alexander suggested that "our fathers," fleeing persecution in the Old World for religious liberty in the New, thought that "the greatest safety lay in keeping religion and politics at the greatest distance from each other." But the nation was misled by the "philosophical sentiments" that "some of our talented statesmen imported from France," which led them to "the other dangerous extreme of attempting to set up a national government without that direct recognition of God, His law and His authority required from a Christian people." Alexander praised the "immortal Declaration of Independence," which recognized our "Reliance on the aid of Divine Providence," even as that document failed to acknowledge Christ and laid out the very secular social contract theory that he otherwise denounced. He then reiterated the "Original Sin" of a government established on those foreign secular principles:

> But alas for our ingratitude, being vainly confident in our own strength, we forgot the true source of our power, and set up a government in the name of "*The people.*" We respectfully submit that a false principle was thus assumed at the very foundation of our government,—viz: that "the people" are the source of all power and authority in civil government, and that civil government is the ordinance of man: whereas God has revealed himself as the source of all power and authority in civil government, and when properly constituted by the voice of the people, civil government is the ordinance of God. We as a nation have thus forgotten Him,—failed to acknowledge Him in our highest national act.

The current conflict was a sure indication of divine chastisement "by permitting a portion of his own people to rebel against the national authority, thus furnishing us with an example of the legitimate consequence of our original rebellion against Him."[26]

The aim of the Association was to encourage the nation to atone for its original sin and secure an amendment to the Constitution "so as to make it conform to the Christian character of the nation," expressing the Christian conception of the origin, nature, and purpose of government. Such a project was "of a broadly constitutional, patriotic and entirely unsectarian character," and Alexander was bullish about its prospects, suggesting that the unanimous adoption of the proposed amendment at the Allegheny meeting was "evidence of the Divine Spirit." But he took notice of the headwinds the movement faced as "the chief objection of this reform in the public mind lie in the very just and sacred regard of all true patriots of the Constitution itself." (Alexander himself spoke of "our noble Constitution.") The booklet closed with an appeal to "the Christian people of the land" to form local auxiliaries, circulate the memorial for signatures, and forward them to the National Association to present to Congress.[27]

By the end of 1864, the Association had settled on its fundamentals: the movement was nonsectarian and patriotic; it endorsed a vision of a divinely originated government against a state erected on mere human consent; this demanded that the Constitution conform with the Christian convictions of the people; to do so would require not a generic acknowledgment of God but the specific recognition of Jesus Christ as Ruler of nations and the authority of his revealed law; such an amendment would be no mere cosmetic alteration to the Constitution but would effect substantive changes in American governance and in the morality of citizens. Those potentially coercive implications were left unsaid.

The Reformed Presbyterians had long asserted that the United States had not been properly founded as a Christian state. As the Religious Amendment movement gained momentum, some members of the denomination found themselves increasingly uncomfortable with public statements displaying a reverent attitude toward the Constitution in tension with the traditional Covenanter position. Others suggested that such concessions were necessary if the movement was to broaden its constituency and have a real chance of success. Indeed, the founding of the National Association and the endorsements of its goals by some of the larger Protestant denominations suggested that their testimony against the Constitution was beginning to bear fruit.[28]

Public support was far from unanimous, however. Catholics, Jews, Unitarians, Seventh-day Adventists, atheists, and others feared the amendment would be a first step toward the official establishment of Protestant Christianity.

(Sumner withdrew his support from the proposal once Jewish friends expressed concern that it would lead to their disenfranchisement.)[29] In the end, opponents of the measure had little to fear. Neither the House nor Senate Committees on the Judiciary chose to take up the proposal. The chairman of the Senate Judiciary Committee, Lyman Trumbull, requested that the body be discharged from further consideration of petitions for the recognition of God in the Constitution of the United States: "The Committee deem it unnecessary to make the asked for amendment, as the Supreme Being is already recognized in the Constitution, in the requirement of oaths, and the prohibition of interference with the full exercise of religious opinions," the Senate report declared.[30]

The wartime endeavor for a Christian Amendment turned out to be untimely. Following the Union victory, confronting the spiritual waywardness of the nation seemed unwarranted. While the National Association's energy flagged in the years immediately following the war (it did not convene national conventions between 1864 and 1870), the Old Light Reformed Presbyterians kept the embers of the movement burning. The *Christian Statesman* was founded in 1867 as the unofficial organ of the movement with the Reformed Presbyterian ministers Thomas P. Stevenson and David McAllister as its editors and J. R. W. Sloane as its most frequent contributor. McAllister, who was aligned with men keen on maintaining the doctrinal purity of the amendment's text, was appointed general secretary of the Association in 1871 to coordinate its national and local efforts; he remained in that position until 1875.[31]

As it happened, the proponents of the Christian Amendment did not have to wait long to get another hearing. Postwar developments were disrupting long-standing Protestant dominance and calling into question the very place of religion in the nation's public life: mass immigration; urbanization and the growth of the power of labor; pervasive political corruption; the Mormon theocracy, practice of polygamy, and resistance to federal authority in the Utah Territory; the "idolatrous practices" of Chinese workers in the West; the brazen flouting of Sabbath laws (and the efforts of German American groups to overturn them); an expanding and increasingly assertive Catholic population calling for public funding for their parochial schools and wielding considerable influence in city political machines; the adoption of the doctrine of papal infallibility and the Vatican's demand that Catholics submit to the guidance of Rome even in civil matters; the rising visibility of Jews, Seventh-day Adventists, and adherents of new religious movements and "free thought"; the new intellectual currents of Darwinism and biblical criticism; the formation and popularity of secret societies. The United States was being transformed into a more heterogeneous and, indeed, more secular society. Whereas during the war the Covenanters and their allies had called for the amendment as an act of repentance for national sin, in the 1870s they promoted the measure as a matter of national defense, to shield a Protestant America increasingly under siege by foreign, non-Protestant elements.

The so-called Cincinnati "Bible War" of 1869–1870, and the "School Question" more broadly, provided fuel for the movement. A local dispute over the reading of the King James Version of the Bible and religious instruction in the public schools had national reverberations, causing old tensions between Protestants and Catholics to resurface and new ones from liberal Christians, non-Christians, and secularists to become evident. While Protestants and Catholics alike insisted on the importance of religion in education, Catholics were uneasy about the "nonsectarian" Protestantism being promoted in the public schools, and many Protestants opposed diverting public funds to Catholic parochial schools that they believed taught religious doctrines inimical to American democracy. Other voices argued that the public schools ought to eschew religious instruction altogether. As the public schools were the primary institutions through which civic morality was inculcated, control of the nature and means of that instruction was increasingly contested in the public square and litigated in the courts.[32]

The Cincinnati Board of Education's decision to prohibit the reading of the Bible and religious instruction and exercises (later upheld by the Ohio Supreme Court) provided an opening for the National Association to exploit. Its national convention in Pittsburgh on March 3–4, 1870, marked the return of the movement to the national stage and demonstrated renewed energy and mounting support. National and regional conventions attracted media attention, local auxiliaries formed, and hundreds of public meetings and lectures helped recruit and cultivate grassroots activists who assisted the petition drive and fundraising.[33]

The Religious Amendment would be no mere symbolic gesture, its supporters claimed, but a simple yet comprehensive solution to a complex and multifaceted problem. The constitution of a nation helped mold the character of its people. The modification of the Preamble of the Constitution would reframe the instrument, affirm the United States as a Protestant Christian nation, provide the legal foundation for its long-standing religious practices, and so protect the nation and public morality from the onslaught of those hostile forces—religious (non-Protestant) and secular, foreign and native. From such a remedy at the top, profound moral and social benefits would inevitably flow.

Even as the Association presented itself as a broad-based interdenominational movement, with well-known public figures elected as honorary officers,[34] the language of the proposed amendment continued to express the Covenanter political theology. Attempts by moderate members to remove the explicit references to Jesus as "Ruler of nations" and the Bible as the "supreme law of the land" in national conventions were vigorously opposed by Covenanters and their evangelical allies who demanded the measure remain doctrinally correct, and such revisions consistently failed in committee.[35] Nevertheless, the Association pledged that ratification of their amendment would not result in the establishment of any particular denomination but would rather safeguard an already Christianized nation. "Our movement has no tendency toward setting up a religious despotism, under which all who entertain dissenting opinions shall be deprived of their rights," McAllister wrote, "but, on the other hand its aim is to establish those very principles, and save from being swept away those very features of our civilization, which have made this nation conspicuous for its civil and religious liberty, and which have given to the men that seek to strike them down, the very rights and privileges which they now enjoy, and of which in their blindness they would rob both themselves and us."[36]

The amendment would thus serve "as a legal basis" to preserve and defend America's Christian culture and heritage (instantiated in such long-standing traditions as prayers at legislative assemblies, Sabbath and blasphemy laws, the use of oaths in court, Bible readings in public schools, and so forth) from contemporary and future challenges. The amendment would also restrain the national government and the states from passing legislation at odds with Christian morality and thwart the widespread political corruption that was plaguing the nation by ensuring the "right moral conduct" of those in public service. All of this was essential to protect the reputation of republican government and the maintenance of Protestant hegemony.[37] As Corresponding Secretary T. P. Stevenson remarked in his address at the Association's 1874 convention, "Our movement aims to preserve the Christian institutions which have descended to us from our fathers. It is the settled policy of the enemies of Christianity to deny the fact, and to disparage the importance, of any connection which exists between the American government and the Christian religion. . . . The success of our movement will be the introduction of a springing and germinant principle into the Constitution, which will yet redeem American politics from all unholy influences, and enable us to attain to a complete and consistent Christian character as a nation."[38]

The members of the Association saw themselves engaged in a fundamental struggle over the origin of civil authority and purpose of the state. The failure to acknowledge God in the Constitution was not merely a defect but illuminated a deeper problem. "There is a virtual denial—a principle taught which is at variance with the doctrine of the divine authority over the nation," A. M. Milligan told the national convention in 1873. The "Christian theory, the teaching of the Bible," instructs "that God is its author; that the power to set up and administer government is from Him; that the revealed will of God is the rule by which this divine ordinance should be constituted; that the magistrate is the minister of God; and that to resist government so constituted and administered is to resist God and incur His wrath." In contrast, the "infidel" theory "first proclaimed by Hobbes, the celebrated English infidel"—that other social contract theorist John Locke went unmentioned—"accepted by the infidel school of France, and taught in the French Encyclopedia ... proclaims that government is a mere human institution—a social compact—deriving all its authority from the consent of the governed, and having no higher law than the will of the people constitutionally expressed; that the magistrate is a mere servant of the people, having no higher obligation than to fulfill the will of his constituents, and responsible only to them." The challenge the nation faced, Milligan argued, was that the infidel theory was "obscurely, but really and effectively, taught in our national Constitution. True, that instrument does not declare '*There is no God*,' nor does it declare that human governments are not under divine authority. Such declarations would never have been accepted by the Christian people of this nation. Had such declarations appeared in that instrument, they would have raised such a storm as would have swept out of political existence the men who had offered the insult to our Christianity, and their names would have gone down with that of Thomas Paine to infamy. No; the infidel element which participated in the framing of that instrument had not the courage to hazard such an experiment." The Constitution had effectively made the secular theory of government operative. Milligan conceded that this idea "is not openly expressed but covertly disguised under the flattering idea that all power is in the hands of the people." The absence of an "allusion to any authority above 'the people'" in the Preamble and its prohibition of a religious test for office rendered the Constitution "a complete illustration of the theory of 'No God in Government.'" This needed to be corrected lest the people be educated to be political infidels and the country "lapse into atheism." "The nation will stand squarely on the one side or the other—either Christian in Constitution as well as character, or infidel in character as well as Constitution," he presaged. "Our relations to the Kingdom of Christ will be well defined and we will as a nation either crown or crucify him."[39]

McAllister struck a similar note in his account of the history and progress of the movement, describing the conflict between "two theories of the relation of civil government and religion." On the one side was the "purely secular theory of government," which imagined that government was based on popular sovereignty and established by a mere social compact. Believing that religion has nothing to do with the state, the secular theory attempts to separate, not only the church, but "all religion from the state." "Its 'demands' are revolutionary. Its watchwords are 'repeal,' 'abrogate,' 'discontinue,' 'abolish.' ... It demands the abrogation and abolition of everything in the nation's life which involves a governmental recognition of the religion of the fathers who settled the country, and of their sons whose Christian virtues have won for our nation whatever excellence and honor it may rightfully claim." All those laws supporting Christian practices are rendered unconstitutional. On the other was the theory that "civil government has a proper and necessary connection with religion." Such a connection did not entail "a union of Church and State." "All are agreed that the civil establishment and endowment of any ecclesiastical body would be an evil," McAllister acknowledged. "It is the relation of religion and the state, not of Church and State, which is the point in dispute." The purpose of the Religious Amendment was to formalize this "necessary connection," strip the Constitution of its French infidelity and make it impervious to challenges from unbelievers, and deepen the religious commitment of its citizenry.[40]

The Association's spokesmen audaciously presented their Christian theory of government as the traditional American view: "The movement for such an amendment rests on a fact and a principle: on the *fact* that the Government of the United States, as it is and always has been administered, stands in intimate relations with Christianity; and on the *principle* that the relations of a government to the religion of the people, as a unit, should be acknowledged in the fundamental law," McAllister remarked during the 1873 convention. Religion—"the most potent of all social forces"—had molded and pervaded their social, educational, and political associations and institutions, forging the common bond that held together a people who had immigrated to the country from across so many places throughout Europe. He appealed to a number of well-known European and American social theorists—"the highest authorities in political science and jurisprudence"—to support these contentions.[41]

His point was America had always been a "Christian nation" if not formally a "Christian state." The government had been founded on Christian principles; Christianity shaped its "real" if not its "formal" enacted Constitution. Such bonds of connection between Christianity and government had been manifest in Bible readings in public schools, government proclamations of fast and thanksgiving days, Sabbath laws, military and congressional chaplains. But "the written or formal Constitution fails to reflect the nation's spirit in not being conformed to the real or unwritten Christian Constitution of the nation, and for this reason it has in itself elements of weakness and of peril." The proposed amendment would correct this anomaly, align the "written fundamental law" with "the Christian *facts* of our national life," keep the state from becoming secular, and ensure the nation's progress in Christian civilization.[42]

The present danger, McAllister warned in his address opening the 1872 convention in Cincinnati, came from "the attack of enemies of our common Christianity upon the Christian features of our national life," a growing and increasingly emboldened alliance of the unrighteous and the ungodly:

> No thoughtful citizen can be ignorant of the assault made upon every act and observance in our national life. Avowed atheists and infidels, communists and papists, uniting like Herod and Pilate, have been plotting and working for years to expel religion from our schools, and turn our Sabbath into a holiday for revelry and parade. Shrewd, far-sighted men, who well know that state neutrality in religion is an utter impossibility, and who are determined to throw the influence of the nation squarely in favor of irreligion, have long and ever more loudly been demanding their "rights of conscience," as they are pleased to term them;—their "right" not to be insulted with religious ideas and usages in civil matters, their "right" not to have a Book which they hate read where their children go to be taught: their "right" not to have the government, with which they stand connected, in any way recognize a sacred day, a solemn oath, an exercise of prayer or anything of the kind, of which they do not approve.

Mormons, too, were appealing to the Constitution to protect their immorality. "They claim their so-called 'rights' under the ægis of the National Constitution," McAllister explained.[43] "The potent weapon with which they strive to smite down the religious observances and institutions of the country, is the United States Constitution." The "irreligious party" had located the nation's Achilles' heel. But those "enemies of Christianity" were not misinterpreting the Constitution; the secularization of America was a necessary consequence of the flawed founding. Though it was "the fruit of Christian civilization," the Constitution was being exploited as "the shield and sword of irreligion, communism, atheism, and infidelity," the very means to sever the organic connection between the government and Christian morality and wipe out all vestiges of true religion from public life. "Their weapon must be wrenched from their grasp," McAllister insisted. No longer could the nation simply rely on the Christian morality of its citizenry when such powers were so energetically working to stamp out the Christian composition of public life. The proponents of Protestant America needed to organize to do battle against an ever-advancing foe. What was coming was nothing short of a religious war: "It is too late to deprecate the agitation of the controversy. The demand has been made and most emphatically repeated. It is resisted. And the question is now raised. The issue is joined. The crisis is fast approaching. The advance guards of the opposing forces have met. There is no attempt to conceal or deny the fact that it is irreligion on the one side, and Christianity on the other. These are the respective rallying points. And the conflict thus begun must soon become general. There can be no indifference or neutrality here."[44] The following year, McAllister warned that "the written Constitution is to-day the spear and shield, the potent weapon of both offense and defense, of the foes of the Christian institutions of the nation." American Protestants could no longer stand on the sidelines of the conflict; it was time to choose. To decline to declare the nation emphatically for Christ would be to succumb to the mounting forces of "political atheism," forsaking the nation to immorality and anarchy. Only an explicitly Christian Constitution would protect America from this "aggressive irreligious party," articulate and preserve the nation's fundamental Christian character and traditional practices, and serve as the philosophical and legal basis for a broader program of Protestant social reform—promoting religious morals through law, education, and civic rituals, and ensuring that a Christian legislature elected by Christian citizens would make laws in accord with the Bible to be enforced by a Christian executive.[45]

There was, no doubt, no little irony in the fact that the men leading the charge to preserve the Christian character of the nation and its institutions had long dissented from what they regarded as an infidel American government.

But reforming the Constitution required assembling and maintaining a broad pan-Protestant front, and that in turn required obscuring the sectarian origins of the project. The calls for the Association's annual conventions demonstrated its national and interdenominational support, listing a broad range of prominent backers as honorary vice presidents and officers, including college presidents, mayors, governors, senators and judges, and Episcopal and Methodist bishops, and the endorsement of numerous clergymen and religious periodicals. The in-house reports of the organization's history (T. P. Stevenson's versions appeared in the 1872 and 1873 *Proceedings of the National Convention*; David McAllister's account was published in the 1874 *Proceedings*) elided the influence of the Reformed Presbyterians and their control over the amendment's language. In a similar fashion, in the "Testimonies to the Religious Defect of the Constitution" delivered at the 1874 national convention, McAllister compiled quotations from American political and religious leaders to demonstrate "an unbroken chain of testimony . . . from some of the ablest thinkers and most patriotic citizens of our country," stretching back as far as Luther Martin's 1788 complaint over the Constitutional Convention's exclusion of a mention of God or Christianity and Alexander Hamilton's well-known but apocryphal remark that it had "forgot" to acknowledge the Deity in the Constitution, as well as Horace Bushnell's "Reverses Needed" sermon. Only a tiny sample of Covenanter testimony (culled from the sermons of Samuel B. Wylie, Alexander McLeod, and James R. Willson) was among the more than two dozen citations McAllister chose to include, and of those, only McLeod's denominational affiliation as a Reformed Presbyterian pastor was acknowledged. The author of *Two Sons of Oil* was identified simply as a "distinguished scholar and divine, widely known from his honorable connection with the University of Pennsylvania," and Willson as a "rarely eloquent divine, at one time Chaplain to the Legislature of New York."[46]

While the National Association promised their Religious Amendment would preserve the nation's venerable Protestant character and traditions against the forces of religious pluralism and encroaching secularism, the Old School Reformed Presbyterians continued to hold fast to their vision of establishing a truly Christian polity. They would not be satisfied by a mere shoring up of the status quo ante. In their eyes, the amendment would deepen the Christian character of the nation. Perforce, the measure would have real repressive consequences, effectively annulling the prohibition on a religious test for federal office and curbing the First Amendment's protection of the free exercise of religious minorities. The disenfranchisement of non-Christians was the price of a nation's obligations to God (and would also encourage infidels to discover Christ). So the ratification of the Religious Amendment would essentially amount to a refounding. The reformed Constitution would announce a new national covenant, explicitly placing the nation and its citizens under the sovereignty of Christ and the authority of his law. And the declaration of a truly Christian government and its victory over the infidel theory would allow the Covenanters at long last to come out of their self-imposed political isolation.[47]

As it happened, by so vigorously advocating for the Religious Amendment, the National Association conjured up a countermovement—the very embodiment of the secular theory of government that they so deeply opposed. That theory came to be incarnated in the curious person of Francis Ellingwood Abbot and in the Liberal League he created. A graduate of Harvard and erstwhile Unitarian minister, Abbot had come to cast off any association with historic Christianity (which he regarded a "perversion" of true theism) and aligned himself with the cause of "free religion," promoting a "scientific theism" based on the authority of human reason rather than that of Scripture and superstition.[48]

In 1870, Abbot, along with Octavius B. Frothingham, a noted "theistic humanist" author, lecturer, and founder of the Free Religious Association, launched *The Index*, "A Weekly Paper Devoted to Free Religion." A "Prospectus" in the first issue plainly stated the periodical's agenda: "It will aim, above all things, to increase pure and genuine Religion in the world, to develop a nobler spirit and higher purpose both in society and the individual. It will aim, at the same time, to increase Freedom in the world,—to destroy every species of spiritual slavery, to expose every form of superstition, to encourage independence of thought and action in all matters that concern belief, character or conduct."[49] What unified heterodox thinkers of all sorts, Abbot realized, was an increasing anxiety about the malignant influence of Christianity in modern society and American government. The Religious Amendment movement perfectly exemplified that threat, and as its indefatigable editor and foremost contributor of original content, Abbot wielded *The Index* as a cudgel against it.[50]

In a March 1871 article noting the call of the National Association for its upcoming meeting in Pittsburgh, Abbot set a belligerent tone for the ensuing contest. "There is a BATTLE to be fought, every whit as fierce and perhaps as prolonged, as that between freedom and slavery," he wrote, "and we give these reactionists fair warning that the first organized action to introduce Christianity into the Constitution of the United States will be the signal for a struggle of which they little foresee the consequences."[51] Ten months later, he prophesized that "the country is on the eve of a great agitation of this question. The present attempts will probably fail. But new ones, and more powerful ones, will be made. There is no escaping this issue. Christianity is mustering its forces for open war against republican liberty, and the sooner the fact is recognized, the better."[52] And in response to the call for the 1872 national convention in Cincinnati, Abbot described the proponents of the amendment as "fanatics of the old Inquisitorial stamp, who, if they had the power, would relentlessly put you to the rack for rejecting their gospel, not because they are harder-hearted than other men, but because they would think themselves doing God service by destroying heretics." He wrote of the consequences of its ratification in apocalyptic terms:

> Nothing can be plainer than that the contemplated change, if made, will involve a POLITICAL REVOLUTION of the most sweeping and profound character. It will be the overthrow of the Free Republic and the erection of a Christian Theocracy in its stead. It will be the formal abolition of the great principle of the separation of Church and State, to which we owe the unparalleled civil liberty we enjoy. It will be the restoration to power and influence of the Christian clergy, as the recognized priesthood of a Christian State. It will be, sooner or later, the destruction of the rights of free speech and a free press, in the interest of Orthodoxy. It will be the return of the Dark Ages, of the persecution of science and free thought, of the frightful tyranny of ecclesiastical domination over the mind, the conscience, and the heart of the people. In short, it will be the utter and disastrous failure of the great American experiment of free popular government, and the earlier or later rehabilitation of ecclesiastical despotism.

The National Association did not aim simply to remedy a "defect" and to shore up those sundry Christian entitlements but to instigate an utter transformation of the American republic. Abbot focused on the particular theological-political claims that underlay their proposal, arguing that they were not only false but in fundamental contradiction to the American philosophy of governance (whereby governments are instituted by people and from the consent of the governed). "The proposed 'amendment,' " he wrote, "involves the overthrow of the Declaration of Independence root and branch, and the erection in its stead of the dismal catechism of the Westminster Assembly as the law of the land."

Christianity is conspiring against the existence of the State—as openly, as virulently, and, I believe in my very soul, as dangerously, as did the now extinct Slave Power of the South. This Call for a National Convention is a new Ordinance of Secession. It shows us that here, in the very heart of the Great Republic, we have a domestic foe in the Christian Church, conspiring openly and with deadly hatred against the whole framework of our political institutions; and it is even now trying to fire the Christian heart with the flames of treason. The parallel is complete. The Church proclaims the absolute dominion of Jesus over the nation, and teaches that every citizen belongs to him body and soul; what is this but to proclaim once the exploded infamy of "property in man?" It is slavery still that aims the deadly blow at the national existence. Once it was slavery of the body; now it is slavery of the mind. The difference is nothing—the principle is essentially the same. The conflict is between Christianity and Freedom—between the Christian Church and the Republic—between the Christian Creed and the Declaration of Independence. The object of the attack is an absolute Political Revolution—the subversion of all republican principles and the triumph of spiritual despotism. Let the true nature of the conflict be once understood, and the danger is past.

As he believed the National Association was seeking to overthrow the republic, Abbot was horrified by the array of distinguished political leaders, jurists, and university presidents who had offered their support to the movement, "undoubtedly ignorant of the real tendency of their attempt." He was even more amazed that ministers from the liberal Unitarian and Universalist denominations would align themselves with the cause. The response to such aggression, Abbot realized, was to rally his own troops to defend the republic.[53]

In January 1872, Abbot called for a counterpetition to "protest against such proposed amendments as an attempt to revolutionize the government of the United States, and to overthrow the great principles of complete religious liberty and the complete separation of Church and State on which it was established by its original founders."[54] By the end of February, that effort had amassed over ten thousand signatures.[55] (Two years later more than thirty-five thousand had signed; the petition, which had grown to 953 feet in length, was presented to Congress by Senator Charles Sumner on January 7, 1874.)[56] Abbot also dispatched a written protest to the National Association and then ventured to the association's annual convention in Philadelphia to deliver it in person. The association granted his request to speak.

"I respect this movement very sincerely," Abbot announced to the assembled clergy and laymen of the association. "It seems to me to have the logic of Christianity behind it, and if I were a Christian, if I believed in Christianity, I do not see how I could help taking my stand at your side." But he went on to speak of what he believed the movement's success would beget—"the establishment of a Christian oligarchy on the ruins of this free republic." He detailed the repressive consequences of the measure. "If the proposed changes are ever made in the Constitution," he said, "their necessary result will be to prevent all persons except Christian believers from holding any office, civil or military, under the American government. No honest disbeliever in the newly incorporated doctrines will be able to take the Oath of allegiance required from all United States officials and soldiers. Only Christian believers and dishonest unbelievers will be able to take it; consequently the entire power of the government, both political and military, will be constitutionally concentrated in the hands of those who believe, or profess to believe, the doctrines thus incorporated." Those who did not confess the Christian faith would be disqualified from office, disenfranchised, "robbed of rights which have been hitherto recognized as theirs from the very adoption of the Constitution. They would be degraded to a subject class, ruled by an aristocracy of Christian believers." The amendment would effectively annul the free exercise protections of the First Amendment, ushering in a regime of religious intolerance. "Whether intended now or not, oppressive persecution must be the consequence of the adoption of the proposed amendment. All your disclaimers of the intent or wish to persecute are utterly idle. The matter will not be in your hands. Persecution will grow like a cancer in the body politic just as soon as the coveted inequality of religious rights once poisons its blood." He warned the assembled that their "proposed usurpation of political power" would inevitably bring about another bloody civil conflict as "the great body of freedom lovers" would not idly submit to the destruction of "the equality of religious rights now guaranteed by the Constitution to all American citizens." And he prophesized that they would only serve to weaken the cause of Christianity—"for the reaction you will create will open the eyes of millions to the fact that Christianity and freedom are incompatible."[57]

A few months after this audacious appearance, Abbot drew up a platform for his secularist position—"The Demands of Liberalism." First published in

The Index as a reply to what he regarded as the "audacious demands of the 'National Reform Association,'" Abbot's manifesto was a clarion call for a radical separation of religion from government. Its nine demands insisted on the elimination of tax exemptions for churches and ecclesiastical property; employment of chaplains in Congress, legislatures, the military services, and public institutions; appropriation of public funds for "sectarian educational and charitable institutions"; religious services and Bible readings in public schools; proclamation of public religious festivals or fast days; judicial oaths; Sabbath laws; and "all laws looking to the enforcement of 'Christian' morality" (all laws instead "shall be conformed to the requirements of natural morality, equal rights, and impartial liberty")—all those displays of public religion that the National Association held up as proof that the United States was a de facto Christian nation and which it desired an amendment to preserve. It concluded with a demand "that not only in the Constitutions of the United States and of the several States, but also in the practical administration of the same, no privilege or advantage shall be conceded to Christianity or any other special religion; that our entire political system shall be founded and administered on a purely secular basis; and that whatever changes shall prove necessary to this end shall be consistently, unflinchingly, and promptly made."[58]

This was a call for the wholesale purging of Christianity from public life. The following January, Abbot asked his readers to set up local Liberal Leagues "to secure practical compliance with the 'Demands of Liberalism' throughout the country," and "to lay the foundations of a great national party of freedom, which shall demand the entire secularization of our municipal, state, and national government."[59] This was followed in 1876 by the establishment of the National Liberal League, whose "single fixed and easily comprehensible purpose" was "to accomplish the total separation of Church and State."[60] Supporters included such prominents as Wendell Phillips, William Lloyd Garrison, Robert G. Ingersoll, Robert Dale Owen, and Rabbi Isaac M. Wise.

In numerous lectures and articles, Abbot and his associates warned of the ongoing threat of Christianity (in Protestant and Catholic forms) to the nation and human liberty. The very project of American republicanism was grounded in the self-evident equality of human beings and popular sovereignty. Political authority emanated from the people, whose natural reason and conscience was altogether sufficient to provide the foundation for order and the freedom to work out the secular functions of government enumerated in the Preamble to the Constitution: "This is the foundation of the American government and the vital essence of the American idea ... the chief original product of the New World."[61] This doctrine was spelled out in a "Patriotic Address of the Liberal League to the people of the United States," delivered by the chairman, Damon Y. Kilgore, a Spiritualist, at the Centennial Congress of Liberals in Philadelphia on July 4, 1876, immediately following the National Reform Association's (NRA) national convention in the same city. Recalling the signers of "that sublime Declaration of Independence," the speaker set forth the Liberal League's understanding of the Founders' political project:

> The dominant purpose of their hearts and the proud achievement of their hands were the foundation of a free commonwealth on the *self-evident equality of all men with respect to their natural rights*. The Constitution which with consummate sagacity they framed for the execution of this purpose rests on no other basis; it was ordained and established in the name of "the people of the United States," and in no other name; it speaks by the collective authority of all the individuals who compose "the people"; it recognizes the will of "the people," carrying into effect the dictates of their natural reason and natural conscience, as the ultimate source and origin of all political power.[62]

The Constitution established a "purely secular" government that "deals only with the political interests of the people." The instrument was designed to protect and preserve the religious liberties of all. Americans must not be compelled to support the religious opinions and practices of others whether by taxation or any other means, nor should the state uphold policies that privilege any one religion over others. Without a total separation of church and state, "there could be no 'government of the people, by the people, for the people'; without it the liberties of the individual, the natural rights of man, would vanish altogether."[63]

As a free commonwealth presupposed the absolute separation of church and state (or, more precisely, the relegation of religion to a sphere altogether outside that of public life), all those government recognitions of Christianity, rather than expressing the people's authentic religious character, were "abuses," violations of the fundamental principle of secularism on which the state had been erected. They were not harmless concessions to the religious sensibilities of the people or vestiges of a bygone time, but provocations, their existence a continual threat to the very stability of the republic, for they served as "a standing invitation and summons to revolutionize the government, a perpetual temptation to disloyalty of a fanatical and therefore most dangerous kind."[64]

The status quo—the de facto nonsectarian Protestant establishment—was precarious, for there was, Abbot noted, a "profound and irreconcilable antagonism between the Church and the Republic." The "corner-stone of historical Christianity" was the claim that *"Jesus is the true Christ of God"*—that is, "the Divinely sent and Divinely appointed SOVEREIGN in the so-called 'kingdom of God' . . . with Divinely bestowed authority over all the individuals and nations of the earth." This faith, he averred, "has been, and still is, the very breath of life to all parts of the Christian Church." Indeed, the history of Christianity recounts attempt after attempt to incarnate the idea of divine lordship in the political realm—a project inaugurated by Constantine, maintained by the papal supremacy of the church over the state throughout the Middle Ages, and continued during the Reformation by Luther and Calvin. "To this day it is the essential doctrine of all divisions and subdivisions of the Church," Abbot proclaimed.

> It allied itself with the State, controlling legislation and dictating national policies, in every country of the Old World; and it governed the early colonies of the New World as absolutely as it governed the Old. Wherever it went, it upheld monarchy as the Divinely appointed system of government; it crowned all monarchs as "Kings by the grace of God"; it sanctioned the "powers that be" in every land as ordained by God; it everywhere frowned upon the impious pretentions of the people to govern themselves. It brought Christianity everywhere and always into alliance with monarchial claims, made it sympathize with royalty as by an unerring instinct, and compelled liberty lovers in Europe to see one single foe in the royal State and the royal Church.[65]

The United States had broken decisively from this dark history by prohibiting Christianity's unions with the state and denying the church "the reins of political power." "Thanks to the great free-thinkers of the Revolution," Abbot wrote, "this essential dogma of Christianity was thrust into the background, and America was baptized in the name of the people, not of the Christ. For the first time in human history, a great nation was born to be its own Christ, and to know no subjection to the King of all Christendom." American republicanism rested on the altogether different foundation of popular sovereignty. "Because here the idea of 'government of the people, by the people, for the people,' was made the organic law of the land, the Christ-claim of the Church became an anachronism and absurdity; royalty was an idea that could by no possibility be admitted under any form; and the Christian Church, which is royalty carried out to the farthest possible extent, abides here in America as an institution imported from the Old World, and fundamentally out of harmony with the government that protects it."[66]

Abbot's Liberal League was thus engaged in a war against theocracy conducted on two fronts—against Roman Catholicism and Protestantism. While Rome openly declared its opposition to the American project, the more insidious menace was a Protestantism "affirming republicanism in secular things and royalty in spiritual things." But this was an untenable position: "The whole faith and life of the Church is based on the monarchial theory of absolute submission to a Lord and King. The whole faith and life of the Republic is based on the democratic theory of freedom for the natural reason and conscience of man to govern himself unconstrained. These two theories are in utter contradiction." In time, American Protestants would be lured either by their faith toward monarchism or by their republicanism away from Christianity. Abbot did not see the possibility of any via media or modus vivendi. "The Church is awakening to her danger in America," Abbot avowed "and she will either commit suicide by trying to republicanize her own religion (an impossibility), or she will try desperately to adapt the Republic to herself by usurping control of it." And he observed that the church was coming to understand that "the chief cause of American 'infidelity' to-day is *not the influence of foreign thought, but the home influence of the unsectarian, non-Christian United States Constitution.* If she ever comes to see this fact in all its momentous significance, she will shrink back in horror from the governmental theory she has been upholding, and will make up her mind that, if republicanism tends to 'infidelity,' republicanism must be abandoned. That day will be one of great danger, either to her or to the Republic; for then must come in some shape a mighty struggle for existence."[67]

Accordingly, Abbot did not imagine the "fanatics" of National Reform would be satisfied with the mere ratification of their amendment; they would not rest until Christianity was rejoined with the state with Christ as King. And Abbot himself would not rest content with the secularization of the state and the complete cordoning off of Christianity to the private realm. As he believed the fundamental principles of Christianity and the American republic stood in contradiction, they could not exist side by side in perpetuity. He declared that "the Christian Church is a most dangerous enemy within the very citadel of American institutions, and that every enlightened patriot and every wise friend of humanity must desire for it a natural but speedy death; in other words, that the Christian Church and the American Republic cannot permanently coexist, but that one of the two must ultimately build its own safety on the total ruin of the other." The preservation and future prospects of the nation thus depended on the eradication of Christianity as a vital force in American public life. In a sense, religious freedom really meant freedom from Christianity. "Just so far as we are faithful to American principles, to democratic principles, to the principles on which the freedom and welfare of humanity depend," Abbot said, "we must stand in open and conscious opposition to the Christian Church and its ideas. For the sake of our own posterity, I hope we shall have courage and unselfishness enough to carry the republic forward in the path of its sublime destiny, and see to it that here, at least, one nation shall be governed only by humanity, freedom, and truth."[68] Abbot's Christian opponents appreciated his candor; his biographers recorded that "orthodox editors praised him for laying bare with such logical and unsentimental rigor the implications of abandoning the Christian confession."[69]

To uproot all those entanglements of church and state that were eroding the secular foundations of the republic, Abbot and his allies pursued the same instrument that their opponents at the National Association were using to defend and expand their Christian prerogatives—a constitutional amendment. In the same issue in which Abbot's lecture "Church and State" appeared, *The Index* published its proposal for an "enlargement of the First Amendment":

Section 1.—Congress shall make no law respecting an establishment of religion, or favoring any particular form of religion, or prohibit the free exercise thereof; or abridging the freedom of speech or of the press, or the right of the people peacefully to assemble and to petition the Government for a redress of grievances.

Section 2.—No State shall make any law respecting an establishment of religion or favoring any particular form of religion, or prohibit the free exercise thereof; or abridging the freedom of speech or of the press, or the right of the people peacefully to assemble and to petition the Government for a redress of grievances. No religious test shall ever be required as a condition of suffrage, or as a qualification to any office or public trust, in any State; and no person shall ever in any state be deprived of any of his or her rights, privileges, or capacities, or disqualified for the performance of any public or private duty, or rendered incompetent to give evidence in any court of law or equity, in any consequence of any opinions he or she may hold on the subject of religion.

Section 3.—Congress shall have power to enforce the provisions of the second section of this Article by appropriate legislation.

By prohibiting the individual states from interfering with the religious liberty of their citizens (by means of religious tests for public office or oaths for jurors and witnesses, for example), the amendment would "carry out the essential purpose, the fundamental idea, on which the whole Constitution rests." Its ratification "would be the death-warrant of all attempts to pervert the Constitution to the service of Roman Catholicism or any other form of Christianity," "ensure the final victory to the idea of the Republic," and "bequeathe to [our posterity] a supreme law freed from the last, lingering traces of a poisonous ecclesiasticism."[70]

For the next two years, the text of the Religious Freedom Amendment ran alongside "The Demands of Liberalism" on the front page of every issue of *The Index*. A revised version, responding to "inadequate propositions" of the Blaine Amendment then making its way through Congress, appeared in the January 6, 1876, edition, prohibited taxing the people for the support of any religious body, institution of learning, or charity. "This amendment is as comprehensive and as thorough as we can make it," *The Index* avowed. Curiously, neither its initial nor enhanced text explicitly prohibited the reading of the Bible in the public schools.[71]

An editorial introducing the revised amendment noted that the proposal was made necessary because of the actions of those "technical religionists of America" who falsely claimed "that this is a Christian country, that Christianity is the national religion of the United States." That position was belied by the Constitution itself. Judged by its own "authoritative utterances in its Constitution, treaties, and laws,"

> the United States cannot intelligently be declared to be a Christian country; or, if intelligently so declared, the declaration must be coupled with a demand to amend the Constitution in accordance with the alleged fact. For the Constitution, treaties, and laws of the United States, as a nation, render this country totally independent of Christianity and all its sacred authorities. . . . The Christian Church is not a national church, and the Christian religion is not the national religion; the attempt to make either of them a national institution is an attempt to deliver over this purely secular republic to a foreign power. And that is neither more nor less than *treason*.

Abbot admitted that "religion is the vital or formative principle of every great national organism." The United States, however, was animated not by Christianity but by "its own purely secular religion": "It is the religion of political and personal freedom, of widely diffused education, of equal and universal human rights, of justice between man and man and the brotherhood of universal benevolence which inevitably grows out of justice between man and man." To safeguard the republic from the subversive forces of Christianity (its "revelations," "supernaturalisms," and "ecclesiasticisms") and preserve the political system that the Constitution had intended to establish, "the imperfect guarantees of this political secularism, of this utter divorce of Church and State, need now to be perfected. The 'unfinished window' of the Constitution needs now to be completed." This would be accomplished with the instillation of an amendment that "shall make the separation of Church and State no longer a matter merely of national tradition or disputed inference, but a great principle fully and explicitly declared in the great charter of all our civil and religious liberties."[72]

Those members of the Liberal League who met in Philadelphia in July 1876 reaffirmed the necessity of such an amendment, as well as sundry other proposals, to complete their ideal of the absolute separation of church and state. They designated themselves as the defenders of the republic and the Framers' revolutionary vision. "We feel ourselves to be, in a peculiar sense, the heirs of the originators of American Independence," Abbot told the audience.

> The principle of the total separation of Church and State is the very corner-stone of the American Republic. So long as we are true to it, careful to preserve it, eager to extend it, just so long is our national welfare sure. But if we allow ourselves to be driven, seduced, coaxed, or in any way tempted from standing fairly and squarely by that principle, from that moment we may date the beginning of our national ruin. It is therefore because this republic was founded on the idea of total separation of Church and State, and because that idea is the innermost soul of the United States Constitution, that we have met here to demand of the American people, respectfully yet firmly, in the spirit of our forefathers, a new and necessary extension of that principle, its larger and wider application, and its better embodiment in our general political system.[73]

In another address, Abbot remarked that "the whole inspiration of our movement is its purpose to carry forward to perfection the structure of our National political system, to make it express more fully George Washington's bold ideal of a Secular State."[74] Another speaker stated that "the proposed amendment, being designed solely to preserve and perfect the existing secular character of the Constitution, is a thoroughly and wisely *conservative* measure, in the very best sense of the word." It was the supporters of the Christian Amendment who, moved by a "spirit of innovation upon its principles" against which "the venerated Washington has so solemnly warned us," departed from the ideals of American founding. If they succeeded, "it would be a revolution, the destruction of this democratic republic and the substitution of an ecclesiastical theocracy." Americans faced a fateful choice: secularism or Christianity; freedom or tyranny; they could bravely forge ahead in the New World or to fall back into the Old. "Two Constitutional amendments are offered to you for your choice, embodying two opposing principles between which human ingenuity will search in vain to find a mean. One fatally entangles the State with the Church, and plunges this young republic into all the bitterest embarrassments of the Old World. The other proclaims the absolute emancipation of the State from all these embarrassments, and sets her forever free, with her face to the future."[75]

There was, as we have noted, yet a third Constitutional amendment on the relation of church and state being discussed by the American people during that centennial year. The controversies over public funding of parochial education and nonsectarian religious exercises in the public schools got caught up in the tangle of presidential ambitions and partisan politics, as Republicans sought to make the question of public support for parochial schools a wedge issue in the 1876 elections, mobilizing nativist anti-Catholic sentiment to deflect from looming scandals.

On September 30, 1875, President Ulysses S. Grant sounded the alarm in a speech to a reunion of the Army of the Tennessee in Des Moines, Iowa. "If we are to have another contest in the near future of our national existence," he stated,

> I predict that the dividing line will not be Mason and Dixon's, but it will be between patriotism and intelligence on one side, and superstition, ambition and ignorance on the other. In this centennial year, the work of strengthening the foundation of the structure laid by our forefathers one hundred years ago, should be begun. Let us labor for the security of free thought, free speech, free press, and pure morals, unfettered religious sentiments, and equal rights and privileges for all men, irrespective of nationality, color or religion. . . . Leave the matter of religion to the family altar, the church, and the private school, supported entirely by private contribution. Keep the Church and the State forever separate.[76]

Grant repeated the call in a December 7 message to Congress, calling on legislators to adopt a constitutional amendment requiring states to provide public schools and preventing them from contributing public funds to sectarian schools. Congressman (former Speaker of the House and soon to be Senator) James G. Blaine of Maine, his sights set on his own run for the presidency, introduced a proposal a week later to do so.

The Blaine Amendment, as it came to be known, would have extended the protections of the religion clauses of the First Amendment to the states and specifically prohibited public funds from being "under the control of any religious sect." It was well understood that the measure was directed against Catholic parochial schools.[77] The Liberal League regarded the measure as "a compromise between the ecclesiastical and secular theories of government" that would fail to adequately remove religion from the public schools, not going far enough in enforcing the separation between church and state. If it had been ratified, they worried it would have formalized the de facto nonsectarian Protestant establishment.[78] The supporters of the Religious Amendment were initially apprehensive about the Blaine proposal. The *Christian Statesman* warned that "the adoption, without discussion, of the ambiguous declaration than no sectarian teaching shall be permitted in the schools, will be the signal for the opening of a baleful strife. The Christian religion and the English Bible will be denounced as sectarian. The provision for prayer and the readings of the Scriptures in the schools, will be declared to be the 'establishment of religion.' And the country will be plunged immediately and inevitably into a prolonged and pernicious controversy." But a massive last-minute NRA lobbying blitz resulted in a provision "requiring that the amendment could not be 'construed to prohibit the reading of the Bible in any (public) school or institution.' " With the explicit protection of Bible reading in place, the NRA supported the amendment as a means to advance their broader agenda. And with that provision, the Liberal League accused their opponents of attempting "with a Machiavellian ingenuity to introduce into the United States Constitution, *unsuspected*, the very essence, pith, and fundamental principle of the Christian Amendment." In the end, the revised Senate version tried to have it both ways: being both pro-Protestant (in favor of nonsectarian Bible reading) and anti-Catholic (opposed to public aid to sectarian schools).[79]

The Blaine Amendment easily made its way through the House, but after several versions were considered, it fell four yeas short in the Senate in a party-line vote. (Twenty-seven senators, including the newly appointed James

G. Blaine himself, failed to appear for the vote.)[80] Upon its defeat, *The Index* let out a sigh of relief, noting that "a direct mention and reverential recognition of the Bible, and, by implication, a reverential recognition of the Christian God and Christ of whom the Bible treats" would "destroy that absolutely secular character of the Constitution." The ratification of the amendment would have provided a great victory to "the Christianizers of the Constitution" and rendered moot hopes for the complete separation of church and state. "No words of ours could paint the magnitude of the disaster which the nation has so narrowly escaped, and which it could only have discovered when the remedy had become well-nigh impossible," *The Index* concluded.[81]

The Blaine Amendment was more about the partisan politics of the day than the deeper principles regarding the relationship of religion and the political order that so animated the members of the National Reform Association and the Liberal League. In the end, those groups' proposals for more radical changes to the Constitution fared no better. The House Judiciary Committee took up the Religious Amendment in February 1874. After consideration, it issued a report stating,

> That, upon examination even of the meager debates by the fathers of the Republic in the Convention which framed the Constitution, they find that the subject of this memorial was most fully and carefully considered, and then, in that Convention, decided, after grave deliberation, to which the subject was entitled that as this country, the foundation of whose government they were then laying, was to be the home of the oppressed of all nations of the earth, whether Christian or Pagan, and in full realization of the dangers which the union between church and state had imposed upon so many nations of the Old World, with great unanimity that it was inexpedient to put anything into the Constitution or frame of government which might be construed to be a reference to any religious creed or doctrine.

This was a straightforward reaffirmation of Framers' intention of a godless constitution. No notice was made of Abbot's "Counter-Petitions" in the committee report, which concluded by advising that "it is inexpedient to legislate upon the subject of the above memorial" and requesting the committee be discharged from any further consideration of the matter.[82] Though the National Association continued to advocate for the measure, the Religious Amendment was never to be seriously considered by either legislative body.[83]

Neither did the Liberal League make any headway with their proposal. The organization briefly toyed with the idea of forming a third national political party (the New Conscience Party) to advance the cause of secularism and counter the Protestant and Catholic influences on the Republican and Democratic parties. At their annual congress in Rochester on October 26, 1877, a platform for the 1880 election was adopted and a ticket comprising "the Great Agnostic" Robert G. Ingersoll for president and Francis E. Abbot for vice president was proposed, but Ingersoll declined the invitation and the initiative was suspended.[84] Soon, the Liberals fell victim to infighting over their response to Anthony Comstock's moral crusade against the dissemination of obscenity and materials promoting contraception, abortion, and "free-love." Having lost control of the movement he had brought into being, Abbot withdrew to private life, spending his days composing obtuse treatises on "scientific theism." The National Liberal League split into separate organizations for Freethinkers and Spiritualists. The American Secular Union, formed in 1884, continued the struggle for the Demands of Liberalism, but to no avail. The constitutional window remained unfinished; the religious civil war that Abbot had darkly prophesized failed to erupt.[85]

In the meantime, the National Association had rechristened itself the National Reform Association in 1875, the new name expressing the body's commitment to a broad suite of moral reforms "to maintain existing Christian features in the American government,"[86] joining forces with other Christian crusaders such as the Evangelical Alliance, the American Sabbath Union, and the Woman's Christian Temperance Union.[87] When Justice David J. Brewer (himself a staunch supporter of the Religious Amendment) declared America a "Christian nation" in *Church of the Holy Trinity v. United States* (1892), the NRA saw opportunity and launched another petition drive and testified before the House Judiciary Committee in March 1896. But if America was indeed a "Christian nation," the thinking went, no amendment attesting to that fact was necessary, and the proposal died in committee.[88] Despite the great organizational and financial exertions to acknowledge the Christian theory of government, the Constitution of the United States remained as stubbornly godless as it was when it was first drafted and ratified.

In an 1893 address to the faculty of Allegheny Theological Seminary, John Alexander lamented the difficulties his movement to amend the Constitution had faced. "The secular theory of government is so intrenched in many minds and Churches that it has always been a great obstacle to our movement."

No less powerful, he noted, was "the deep veneration almost akin to idolatry in which the Constitution is held by the American people."[89] But he made note of the movement's most steadfast advocates. "The Covenanter Church is the only denomination that has adopted our Association as one of its schemes or objects for which their Synod for many years has made liberal annual appropriations, and for the payment of which collections are made yearly in all their congregations," Alexander said.[90] Yet, as the Association joined those broader fights for moral reform, the Reformed Presbyterians struggled to retain their dogmatic boundaries and testimony of dissent. Those years of engagement in the movement and efforts to hammer out compromises with other Protestants had in the end brought to the surface long-standing tensions within the Old Light Reformed Presbyterians about the relation of the church to the state. In 1891, a new schism erupted as a number of its members found that their consciences allowed them at last to take up their duties as American citizens. A faithful remnant sustained the traditional posture of political dissent even as their country became more religiously pluralistic, and increasingly secular, stubbornly refusing to concede to their demands, turn in repentance, and become a truly Christian nation.

Let's consider another message from a pastor to a president and Congress. This one was delivered in a sermon on February 7, 1954, at the storied New York Avenue Presbyterian Church in Washington, DC, just a few blocks from the White House. Abraham Lincoln had attended services there during the Civil War, perhaps musing over the inscrutability of divine providence. On that winter morning in 1954, President Dwight D. Eisenhower sat in the very pew Lincoln had rented while Dr. George M. Docherty preached on Galatians 3:28. The occasion of the sermon was Lincoln's birthday, and Docherty's theme was "a new birth of freedom," the reverend suggesting that "the issues we face today are precisely the issues Lincoln spent his life seeking to resolve."[91]

But first, Docherty spoke of "the American way of life," waxing lyrical on those simple pleasures of mid-century America—attending ball games and eating popcorn and drinking Coca-Cola, shopping in department stores, driving cross-country, enduring television commercials, "setting off firecrackers on the Fourth of July," and "sitting for seven hours to see the pageantry of the Presidential inauguration." He spoke of fenceless gardens perfumed by honeysuckle and "the neighborliness of your neighbor," of "Negro Spirituals and Colonial Architecture" and "Thanksgiving Turkey and pumpkin pie," and described the country's vistas, its great rivers and plains, and Pittsburgh's factories and Chicago's Lakeshore Drive and New York City skyscrapers (and, incongruously, "the lonely proud statue of Lee on Gettysburg field"). And then his thoughts turned back home, to children wearing jeans and riding bicycles and to color comics and the Sunday *New York Times* and the creak of a wicker chair and "the solitary bugler playing taps, clear and long-noted, at Arlington." All in all, a vision of a bucolic America, a commercial America, an industrial America, and a domestic America, grand and good.

Such was Docherty's sentimental portrait of the American way of life and its wholesome, middle-brow culture, and he wanted those who sat in the pews that morning to understand from whence it came. "It has been with us so long, we have to recall it was brought here by people who laid stress on fundamentals," he told them. "They called themselves Puritans because they wished to live the pure and noble life purged of all idolatry and enslavement of the mind, even by the Church. They did not realize that in fleeing from tyranny and setting up a new life in a new world, they were to be the Fathers of a Mighty Nation." They had been shaped by the moral law revealed in graven tablets at Mount Sinai and the words of Jesus of Nazareth as they were recorded in the New Testament. "This is the 'American Way of Life.' Lincoln saw this clearly. History was for him the Divine Comedy, though he would not use that phrase. The providence of God was being fulfilled."

Docherty had opened his sermon with Galatians, but as he went on, it became clear that the actual text he was expounding was not from the New Testament but from American scripture—Lincoln's Gettysburg Address. "Wherefore, Lincoln claims that it is 'UNDER GOD' that the nation shall know a new birth of freedom. And by implication it is under God that 'government of the people, by the people and for the people, shall not perish from the earth.'" And from this binding of the American way of life to the watchful eye of divine providence, Docherty reached the purpose of his oration. For the Scottish-born minister's purpose was to suggest an alteration to one of his adopted nation's civic rituals. One day, when he asked his children what they had done in school, they described to him "in great detail, and with strange solemnity, the Ritual of the Salute to the Flag," and as he, an immigrant to the country, pondered those words for the first time, he came to realize that something fundamental was missing.

What was missing, Docherty informed his audience, was "the characteristic and definitive factor in the 'American Way of Life,'" the religion which he believed undergirded the American way of life, that belief in God that distinguished the United States of America from other republics, especially from the Soviet Union. ("I could hear little Muscovites repeat a similar pledge to their hammer and sickle flag in Moscow with equal solemnity," he confessed.) And this was why he had fastened on Lincoln's words at Gettysburg. For Lincoln had "seen clearly" that American freedom, in its first and in its new birth, was a freedom "under God"; Lincoln was "simply reminding the people of the basis upon which the Nation won its freedom in its Declaration of Independence."

Lincoln's address was a war sermon, as was Docherty's. The Civil War, Lincoln said, was a test of whether a nation so conceived could endure. Then the question was slavery. Now the great threat to the American way of life was "a militantly atheistic Communism." But Communism posed such a danger not because it was "godless" but precisely because it was a dynamic, messianic faith. The Cold War was no mere jockeying for geopolitical dominance; it was fundamentally a spiritual conflict. "We face, today, a theological war," Docherty proclaimed.

> It is not basically a conflict between two political philosophies—Thomas Jefferson's political democracy over against Lenin's communistic state.
>
> Nor is it a conflict fundamentally between two economic systems between, shall we say, Adam Smith "Wealth of Nations," and Karl Marx "Das Capital."
>
> It is a fight for the freedom of the human personality. It is not simply, "Man's inhumanity to man." It is Armageddon, a battle of the gods. It is the view of man as it comes down to us from the Judao-Christian [*sic*] Civilization in mortal combat against modern, secularized, godless humanity.

"To omit the words 'Under God' in the Pledge of Allegiance," he said, "is to omit the definitive character of the 'American Way of Life.'"

And so Docherty called on his audience to realize the nature of the conflict and reaffirm the theological foundation of the nation, and of democracy, by incorporating the words "under God" (words themselves added at the last minute) into the Pledge of Allegiance. The patriotic ritual needed to become an explicitly religious one. (Docherty suggested that the revised text ought to read "one nation, indivisible, under God," a more grammatically felicitous phrase than the one ultimately settled on by Congress.) So amending the

Pledge would not infringe on the First Amendment's prohibition on the establishment of religion, which demands a separation of church and state but not "a separation of religion and life." ("What the Declaration says in effect," he averred, confusing the documents in question, "is that no state church shall exist.") And he stressed he was not advocating that the inserted phrase be "Under the Church" (for which church would that be?), or "Under Jesus Christ," or "Under the King of Kings." "It must be 'UNDER GOD,'" he said, so "to include the great Jewish Community, and the people of the Moslem faith, and the myriad of denominations of Christians in the land." A formulation capacious (and ambiguous) enough to encompass most Americans (monotheists, polytheists, and pantheists, too).[92]

But even that formulation had its limits. Docherty raised the case of "the honest atheist," referring to that "new type man" who has emerged in the modern age—"we call him a 'secular.'" Could he, too, be a proponent of American liberty and justice? Docherty's answer was simple: "An atheistic American is a contradiction in terms." While he could personally vouch for excellent and honorable men who did not profess belief in God, they were, all considered, "spiritual parasites" who "[live] upon the accumulated Spiritual Capital of a Judaio-Christian [sic] civilization." Good and decent people they may be, but in the end, living in accordance with "the American ideal of life" requires faith in "the God who revealed the divine principles upon which the ethics of this Country grow." "If we deny the existence of the 'God who gave us life,'" Docherty asked, "how can we live by 'the liberty he gave us at the same time'?" The oath that every naturalized citizen takes to his or her adopted nation concludes with the words "so help me God," the pastor, himself still a foreign national, reminded his audience.

There remained some ambiguity in Docherty's discussion. For even as he declared that American freedom is the product of Judeo-Christian civilization, at the same time American citizenship was not limited to Christians or Jews; "one of the glories of this land is that it has opened its gates to all men of every religious faith." Docherty appealed to Emma Lazarus's "word of welcome to these shores" at the base of the Statue of Liberty; those "huddled masses yearning to breathe free" do not have to pass a religious examination upon disembarking, nor do they face religious persecution in this land. Believing in God (or gods?) is sufficient—so long as it is belief in a power who endowed human beings with the rights to life, liberty, and the pursuit of happiness. Docherty was affirming a sentiment similar to what then President-elect

Eisenhower had shared with the Freedoms Foundation in December 1952: "Our form of government has no sense unless it is founded in a deeply felt religious faith, and I don't care what it is. With us of course it is the Judeo-Christian concept, but it must be a religion that all men are created equal." A vision in which all who came to these shores were invited to graft themselves onto the tree of the American way of life.[93]

Docherty concluded his oration fusing Paul's words to the Galatians, Lincoln's reflections at Gettysburg, and Francis Bellamy's pledge in a proclamation of American unity and the nation's providential mission: "In this land, there is 'neither Jew nor Greek, neither bond nor free, neither male nor female,' for we are one nation indivisible under God, and humbly as God has given us the light we seek liberty and justice for all. This quest is not only within these United States but to the four corners of the globe wherever man will lift up his head towards the vision of his true and divine manhood." The same faith that had in the previous century animated the fight against slavery would now sustain them in their struggle against Communism. America's Protestants, Catholics, and Jews would stand together "under God," brought together under the sacred canopy of this common civil religion. So unified, these children of light would prove victorious in the spiritual Cold War they were waging against the children of darkness.[94]

Reverend Docherty was not the first to advance that proposal to transform what had been a secular patriotic exercise into one with an explicitly religious dimension. The Catholic fraternal organization the Knights of Columbus had already amended the Pledge to include the words "under God" for its own purposes back in 1951; a year later its members appealed to Congress to make the change official, and in April 1953 Louis Rabaut, a Catholic congressman from Michigan, had introduced legislation to do so. But Docherty's sermon, coming "from the center of the core of the mainstream establishment," as Martin E. Marty put it, had its desired effect, and Congress jumped into action. With President Eisenhower's blessing and buoyed by an outpouring of public support, some seventeen bills in the House and one in the Senate jockeyed for consideration. And so the legislators amended the secular text originally composed by a former Baptist minister and Christian socialist nativist, and the president signed the successful bill into law on June 14 (Flag Day), proclaiming, "From this day forward, the millions of our school children will daily proclaim in every city and town, the dedication of our nation and our people to the

Almighty. To anyone who truly loves America, nothing could be more inspiring than to contemplate the dedication of our youth, on each school morning, to our country's true meaning." The newly outfitted Pledge, "reaffirming the transcendence of religious faith in America's heritage and future," whose theological-political abstraction could appeal to conservatives and liberals and could well be uttered by Protestants, Catholics, and Jews, was now added to the nation's arsenal of "spiritual weapons" to be deployed in its crusade against that "materialistic philosophy of life" abroad and at home.[95]

The Eisenhower era was high time for such spiritual mobilization. Eisenhower opened his cabinet meetings with prayer. The US Capitol added a nondenominational prayer room in 1955. A year after inserting "under God" into the Pledge of Allegiance, Congress unanimously passed legislation to engrave the phrase "In God We Trust" on all US currency (demonstrating that capitalism was fully in accord with the created order) and then ordained the phrase the official national motto (displacing "E Pluribus Unum," which long had that honor unofficially). The first annual National Prayer Breakfast was held in 1953 with more than five hundred dignitaries in attendance. Throughout the country, pastors and politicians and business leaders declared the importance of civic piety, spoke of American democracy as the providential product of Judeo-Christianity, and emphasized the importance of the people remaining steadfast to their faith. Such spiritual foundations needed to be shored up as the nation faced the millennial threat of a militant atheistic Communism. "Recognition of the Supreme Being is the first, the most basic, expression of Americanism," President Eisenhower, now the high priest of this American civil religion, told the American Legion's "Back to God" program in 1955. "Without God, there could be no American form of government, nor an American way of life."[96]

But even as such a nonsectarian Judeo-Christian "civil religion" was being promoted by the president and Congress, Francis Ellingwood Abbot and the Liberal League's dream of the secularization of the public square was being partly realized, as the protections of the First Amendment were extended to the states not by means of a constitutional amendment but by the Supreme Court, through its "incorporation" by the due process clause of the Fourteenth, and by the constitutional doctrine of strict separationism.

Again, the primary theater of conflict was the nation's schools. The controversies involved public aid to parochial schools, time release for religious instruction, and mandated prayer exercises and Bible reading. The process of secularization commenced with *Everson v. Board of Education of Ewing Township* (1947), a dispute over the reimbursement of transportation fare to Catholic parochial school students. While the court in a 5–4 decision technically found in favor of the school program, it nonetheless announced in sweeping language what legal scholar Noah Feldman has called "the credo of legal secularism":

> The "establishment of religion" clause of the First Amendment means at least this: neither a state nor the Federal Government can set up a church. Neither can pass laws which aid one religion, aid all religions, or prefer one religion over another. Neither can force nor influence a person to go to or to remain away from church against his will or force him to profess a belief or disbelief in any religion. No person can be punished for entertaining or professing religious beliefs or disbeliefs, for church attendance or non-attendance. No tax in any amount, large or small, can be levied to support any religious activities or institutions, whatever they may be called, or whatever form they may adopt to teach or practice religion. Neither a state nor the Federal Government can, openly or secretly, participate in the affairs of any religious organizations or groups, and vice versa. In the words of Jefferson, the clause against establishment of religion by law was intended to erect "a wall of separation between Church and State."

The rationale for such a "wall," the court maintained, was to protect religious minorities from governmental discrimination and abuse. In his opinion, Justice Hugo Black reflected on the long, dark history of religious persecution in Europe. "With the power of government supporting them, at various times and places, Catholics had persecuted Protestants, Protestants had persecuted Catholics, Protestant sects had persecuted other Protestant sects, Catholics of one shade of belief had persecuted Catholics of another shade of belief, and all of these had from time to time persecuted Jews." Such practices, Black contended, "were transplanted to, and began to thrive in, the soil of the new America"; religious establishments were authorized by the British government and with them came "a repetition of many of the old-world practices and persecutions." "These practices became so commonplace as to shock the freedom-loving colonials into a feeling of abhorrence," he wrote, and "it was these feelings which found expression in the First Amendment." The dissenters in *Everson* agreed with the majority on the interpretation of the Establishment Clause as requiring church-state separation but disagreed on its application in the case. For the minority, even the mere support for transportation to Catholic schools (where the basic purpose of education is religious) amounted to a violation of the hallowed principle, a "breach" in the wall the court insisted "must be kept high and impregnable."[97]

The court reaffirmed the principle of strict separationism the following year in *McCollum v. Board of Education*, extending it to prohibitions of release-time programs for religious education that utilized public facilities. In 1952, a divided 6–3 court backed off a bit, permitting a release-time program at off-school locations in *Zorach v. Clauson*, while still holding that the First Amendment "reflects the philosophy that Church and State should be separated."[98] In the early sixties, the court turned its scrutiny to the questions of Bible readings and school prayer. In 1962, a 6–1 majority held in *Engle v. Vitale* that a nonsectarian New York State Board of Regents prayer was unconstitutional, as it "officially establishes the religious beliefs embodied in the Regents' prayer." Further, the opinion cited "the indirect coercive pressure upon religious minorities to conform to the prevailing officially approved religion."[99] A year later, in an 8–1 decision in *School District of Abington Township, Pennsylvania v. Schempp*, the court determined that Bible readings in public schools did not have "a secular legislative purpose and a primary effect that neither advances nor inhibits religion." "The place of religion in our society is an exalted one, achieved through a long tradition of reliance on the home, the church and the inviolable citadel of the individual heart and mind," the majority concluded. "We have come to recognize through bitter experience that it is not within the power of government to invade that citadel, whether its purpose or effect be to aid or oppose, to advance or retard. In the relationship between man and religion, the State is firmly committed to a position of neutrality." By means of such decisions, the old nonsectarian Protestant quasi-establishment was dismantled; a secular state would govern a more and more religiously diverse nation.[100]

The public school cases had brought together an alliance of militant secularists such as Vashti McCollum with liberal Protestant and Jewish organizations. Those Protestants were driven by long-standing suspicions of Catholic power and its putative threat to American democracy. Jewish Americans, reflecting back on a history of persecution in Christian Europe and the recent atrocities committed by the Nazis and their collaborators, regarded their continued flourishing in the United States—indeed their very safety and security—as dependent on the existence and maintenance of a fundamentally secular public sphere.

Yet, other religious minds, such as the neo-orthodox Reinhold Niebuhr and his allies, lamented the decisions in *Everson* and *McCollum*, fearing the court's novel doctrine of absolute separation of church and state would undermine the critical role of religion in public life. As intended, the First Amendment, they claimed, prohibited the state's favoring of this or that religious body but did not rule out cooperation between churches and the government, particularly in the moral formation of children by means of education, public and private. The court's "hardening of the idea of 'separation,'" a group of prominent Protestant leaders warned, would "greatly accelerate the trend toward the secularization of our culture." And that process, they feared, would inevitably lead to the weakening of American democracy.[101]

For how could a "secular nation" maintain its system of self-government and face and defeat the Communist menace? It was not enough that its citizens proclaim a civic piety to underwrite their "American way of life." For Will Herberg, a convert from ardent youthful Communism to a Reinhold Niebuhr–inspired style of Jewish neo-orthodoxy, only an authentic, "God centered" "prophetic faith"—based on the awareness of God's transcendence, which illuminates the human being's ambivalent dual nature (created in the image of God yet corrupted by sin that manifests in "idolatrous self-love") and the relativism of all earthly pursuits and institutions, including democracy, all finally subject to a higher law and God's judgment—would safeguard the experiment of American democracy from the relentless temptations of atomistic individualism on the one hand and totalitarianism ("the self-deification of society incarnated in the state") on the other. "Every attempt to establish an equalitarian ethic in exclusively nonreligious, humanistic terms must fail, since aside from their God-relationship there is literally nothing in which all men are 'created equal,'" he warned.[102] As democracy derived from and depended on such religious conviction, secularism—"the perennial effort of sinful man to establish himself in his self-sufficiency against God"—posed a real and ongoing threat to the nation's well-being. Secularism had become "the official voice of our culture" and "the cultural climate of our time," having even "penetrated deeply into church and synagogue." Removing religion from public life, relegating it to "a carefully sheltered private 'spiritual' domain," separating the American political life from its biblical foundations, would, in the end, create a vacuum that some ersatz religion would necessarily fill.[103] The spiritual challenge of Communism ("the great substitute-faith of our time," "the apotheosis of secularism"[104]) could not be met under the banner of some secular "religion of democracy." "Democracy, we are told, is not merely a social and political order, a *means* whereby men can fashion their lives in freedom and responsibility; it is itself an end, the Way of Life, the highest truth, the ultimate commitment of all free men. It is a religious absolute." But democracy so understood is stripped of its religious presuppositions; it has become both idolatrous and totalitarian—if not immediately, then potentially—as the object of human beings' absolute devotion.[105] The American people (Protestant, Catholic, and Jewish) must always regard the republic as being under God's sovereignty and judgment. "Democracy acknowledges a 'higher law' and a higher sovereignty; were it to make absolute pretentions as an ultimate principle of life, it would turn itself into a demonic self-idolatrizing ideology, repugnant alike to the true democrat and to the man of biblical faith."[106]

And then there were still those who believed that the well-being of the republic, the struggle against Communism, and Christianity itself required that the nation explicitly commit itself to Christ. Despite past failures, the National Reform Association had not given up its dream of remaking the Constitution to acknowledge God and the rulership of Christ.[107] In 1945, the Reformed Presbyterian Church of North America launched a monthly periodical, the *Christian Patriot*, dedicated to the amendment effort and soon thereafter formed the Christian Amendment Movement (CAM) to lobby for the measure. The fledgling National Association of Evangelicals came out in support of the campaign in 1947 and in 1954.[108]

In May 1954, as the bill to incorporate the words "under God" into the Pledge of Allegiance was making its way through the halls of Congress, the Senate Judiciary Subcommittee on Constitutional Amendments convened to discuss a proposal for a "Christian Amendment" brought by Senator Ralph Flanders of Vermont. The text under consideration was not, as in past efforts, a rewriting of the Preamble but a discrete amendment that set out the theological-political formula and its practical confines:

> SECTION 1. This Nation devoutly recognizes the authority and law of Jesus Christ, Savior and Ruler of nations through whom are bestowed the blessings of Almighty God.
>
> SEC. 2. This amendment shall not be interpreted so as to result in the establishment of any particular ecclesiastical organization, or in the abridgment of the rights of religious freedom, or freedom of speech and press, or a peaceful assemblage.

SEC. 3. Congress shall have power, in such cases as it may deem proper, to provide a suitable oath or affirmation for citizens whose religious scruples prevent them from giving unqualified allegiance to the Constitution as herein amended.[109]

The hearings, held on May 13 and 17, were not particularly well-planned events, which gives us a sense of how seriously the measure was taken on Capitol Hill—especially when compared with the hustle and bustle over the legislation to add "under God" to the Pledge of Allegiance. The only senator who bothered to attend was William Langer of North Dakota, chairman of the subcommittee. He was joined by the subcommittee's counsel. Senator Flanders himself did not show up.[110]

In their testimony before the committee, the professional supporters of the measure, including leadership from the NRA and CAM and the president and president emeritus of Reformed Theological Seminary in Pittsburgh, reiterated many of the movement's old talking points, scriptural warrants for the measure, and the historical documentation of the nation's traditions, supplemented with some recent materials (sermons by Peter Marshall Sr., Senate chaplain and former pastor of New York Presbyterian Church, and Billy Graham, the popular evangelist),[111] described how the measure would serve as a foundation for all those Christian features and as the basis of moral action on the part of the government. This was all the more urgent in light of the nation's global leadership in the struggle against Communism. "The Marxian program presents a unified and self-confident philosophy of life, a complete world view," declared John Coleman, a professor of political science at Geneva College. "How much stronger would be our appeal if we presented the splendid realities of a God-made, God-governed, and God-redeemed world in contrast to the view which sees the world grinding on forever like a mill with no purpose, heart, mind, or will?" S. Bruce Willson, president of Reformed Theological Seminary in Pittsburgh, emphasized that the amendment would not result in "an establishment of, nor the preferential recognition of, any denomination or sect," but would simply reaffirm the attitude implicit in American traditions and "provide for an explicit declaration of the religious, moral, and spiritual foundations upon which democratic government must rest." The constitutional guarantee of the separation of church and state, he noted, did not require that the state be a "secular institution, utterly removed from the sanctions of moral law and order." Remo I. Robb of CAM testified that the amendment would neither infringe on religious freedom nor discriminate against religious minorities. He added, however, that "the Nation, this organic living America, which outlives all its citizens, has national obligations which transcend the rights of some or even all of its citizens." R. H. Martin, president of the National Reform Association, maintained that "it would make the Bible the lawbook of the Nation, not on theology and baptism and all things in the sacraments, but as the fundamental law on morals. . . . It is the greatest book on political science or on government that the world has."[112]

Even as the supporters of the amendment "Recognizing the Authority and Law of Jesus Christ" claimed that there was widespread approval of the measure, they did not expect it to go unchallenged. "We have lived too long away from God as a Nation to unanimously approve of the placing of Christ at the head of our government," one of the CAM officers conceded.[113] And the Senate committee did indeed receive statements from numerous organizations opposing the resolution: Protestants and Other Americans United for Separation of Church and State (POAU) stated that the measure would "virtually repeal the first amendment to the Constitution," reduce "non-Christians to second-class citizens," and "work a revolution in the American way of life" and "set the clock back by centuries and lose for America her coveted role of civilized leadership"; the American Ethical Union wrote that "wisdom dictates, that legislators center their concern about legislation in the interest of all the people and leave theology to the theologians"; the American Civil Liberties Union protested that the amendment "would violate our traditional doctrine of separation of church and state, which has done much to protect the freedom to worship as one pleases."[114]

The witnesses that showed up before the Senate committee to testify against the amendment, Rabbi Isidore Breslau of the Synagogue Council of America and Leo Pfeffer, a prominent litigator on church-state issues, were representing American Jewish establishment organizations.[115] Pfeffer was a leading proponent of "strict separationism."[116] "Under this system of the separation of church and state and religious freedom, religion has achieved in the United States a high estate unequalled anywhere else in the world," Pfeffer concluded in his monumental book *Church, State and Freedom* published a year earlier. "History has justified the great experiment, and has proved the proposition on which it was based—that complete separation of church and state is best for church and best for state, and secures freedom for both."[117] In their testimony, Breslau and Pfeffer argued that, notwithstanding the claims of its proponents, the amendment would have detrimental effects on religious minorities, reducing Jews and other non-Christian Americans to the status of second-class citizens, and would open the door to the teaching of Christian dogma in the public schools and religious tests for civil activities. That it provided an "escape clause" allowing Congress to make suitable provisions for non-Christian citizens was not reassuring. (Did this mean that an immigrant would have to become a Christian in order to take the oath of naturalization? asked Pfeffer, himself a naturalized citizen.) They reflected on the difficulties Jews historically experienced living in "so-called Christian nations" and were skeptical of expressions of "Christian love" toward them. They noted, too, that similar proposals had been rejected in the past as "basically alien to the American tradition," citing the 1874 recommendation of the House Judiciary Committee. And they appealed to the Founding Fathers and American traditions to endorse their position of church-state relations, citing Thomas Jefferson's Statute of Religious Freedom and President Washington's letter to the members of the Newport Synagogue, which "expressed the spirit of the new nation which proposed that men should be completely equal before the law without any distinction as to religious affiliation or doctrinal conviction." "I think nothing that the United States has done compares as a contribution to western civilization with the launching of the unique experiment of absolute and complete separation of church and state and complete religious freedom. That was unique. That never existed before 1789," Pfeffer declared. The regime of separation of church and state was put into place to protect the new republic from "the sectarian conflicts, persecution bitterness, and religious warfare which plagued the Old World for centuries." The proposed amendment thus not only was a menace to American Jewry and other religious minorities but also "threatens to undermine the foundation of our democracy and to bring upon the American people the very evils which the constitutional fathers sought to prevent." Freedom to choose and practice one's own religion was a right granted by God and secured by the Constitution's provision of religious liberty, "a mantle of protection" for the Christian and non-Christian alike.[118]

Pfeffer's statement that religious liberty was granted by God demonstrated that strict separationism did not entail political atheism. "We are not against the suggestion of the inclusion of the idea of God in our Government and our American life," Rabbi Breslau responded when Dr. Martin asked him if he believed that all the "religious features in our national life" needed to be abandoned. "We do believe, however, that the propagation of a religious idea, of religious teaching, is not the function of the Government but the function of the individual, the family, in his own communal organization and such other organizations as he establishes for the advancement of culture need of his own family." When questioned by Willson if "there is distinction between a recognition of the basis of technical and moral civil government and a union of church and state," Pfeffer maintained that the amendment violated the separation of church and state as it had been understood by Jefferson and Madison. When Willson suggested that the times demanded that Americans "now declare the basis of our moral and religious freedoms," Pfeffer replied that the threat then emanating from Communism was not so different from what the Framers themselves had faced.

> History has a peculiar way of repeating itself because our principle, our concept, our Constitution was adopted at a very similar period just when the forces of atheism, revolution, were coming out of France. . . . It was just during that period when people were making the same argument, is it not now the time to declare ourselves free and independent from those atheists, those secularists of the French Revolution who are going out to change the towns and abolish God, and so on? Then as now our forefathers knew that the best way, the surest way, to preserve the moral foundation on which religion is based is to make sure that religion and state do not intervene in each other's affairs, that religion will not be sullied by being descended into the mire of political life.

This was, no doubt, a retort deliberately calibrated to those who argued that the godlessness of the Constitution was the unfortunate result of French influence.[119]

Indeed, Pfeffer had an inkling whom he was up against. He had briefly sketched out the history of the NRA and CAM (though not realizing they continued as separate organizations) in his *Church, State and Freedom*, clearly noting the intolerant agenda of the supporters of the Religious Amendment.[120] In his remarks before the committee he recalled "a group of Presbyterians" who refused to vote until such a time as the Constitution was amended but did not draw the connection between those radical Presbyterians during the early republic and those men who were testifying before the Senate committee. The NRA and CAM witnesses did not explicitly mention the Covenanters and their testimony of political dissent. The issue emerged only obliquely in an exchange among the witnesses when Professor Coleman mentioned that his forefathers, who had helped slaves escape on the Underground Railroad, "could not take an unqualified oath to the Constitution unless it allowed them to say 'subject to my supreme allegiance to the Lord Jesus Christ.' "[121]

The Jewish organizations Breslau and Pfeffer represented opposed the measure not on account of anti-Christian or anti-religious animus but because they believed it to be "contrary to the spirit and to the philosophy of the American way of life." Despite the assurances of the NRA and CAM officers that they were not "anti-Semeitics [*sic*]" (they had many friends who were Jewish—McKnight made sure to declare his friendship with Harry Houdini), that their proposal was not motivated by any enmity toward them but would, in fact, be good for the Jews (as their religious freedom was dependent on Christianity), the representatives of American Jewish organizations had sufficient reason for concern. Earlier in the hearings, the committee listened as a pair of concerned women from California representing the Christian Patriotic Rally of Reseda, California, argued that the amendment was now necessary "to protect Christianity from the attacks of anti-Christians." The Constitution, they argued, had failed to declare the United States a Christian nation as a number of the Framers had adopted the "Jacobian atheistic theories of the French Revolution of 1789." Even so, America had been and is "a Christian not an atheistic nation." And that nation needed to be protected from its enemies.[122]

And who were those anti-Christians and what were their assaults on Christian "teachings and practice"? Communists, of course. That much was obvious. But there was yet another, more insidious threat, and representatives of that foe were sitting right there among them. The women submitted an article from a 1951 publication by the American Jewish Committee (AJC) describing the organization's efforts, conducted with the Anti-Defamation League of B'nai B'rith (ADL), to recommend the removal of inaccuracies, misconceptions, and distortions in public and religious school textbooks and provide materials to promote a positive image of Judaism and Jewish life and "the remarkably close relationship of the Jewish religious ideals to American democracy." One of the women submitted a commentary by the Christian Patriotic Rally which contended that such undertakings were part of a Jewish endeavor to control Christian religious education and, in doing so, undermine Christianity itself. "For all Christians who share the belief in the incompatibility of the Christian Gospels with the Jewish Talmud and its antisocial laws, it may come as a sad shock to have to admit the fact that even the religious teaching of Christians is controlled by Jews whose spiritual life is based upon the books of the Talmud wherein, not only the divinity of Christ, the virgin birth, but the whole life of Our Lord and His crucifixion and [*sic*] blasphe-mously derided." The document also noted the opposition of those Jewish organizations, as well as the Central Conference of American Rabbis, to release-time arrangements for religious instruction and Bible reading and religious observances in public schools.[123]

For those "Christian Patriots," members of far-right antisemitic outfits who believed in "the incompatibility of the Christian Gospels with the Jewish Talmud and its antisocial laws" and warned of Jewish organizations' "planned determined infiltration and control of Christian education through the exploitation of misguided tolerance," the promotion of "Interfaith" and "Judeo-Christianity" was part of a larger Jewish plot against America and its Christian people. In acqui-escing to Jewish interests, Christian leaders had "delivered their fold to the enemy bent on the annihilation of Christianity, through corruption of its very core." This amounted to "religious treason." The Christian Amendment was therefore vitally necessary to protect Christian Americans from "the intrusion and injec-tion of the Talmudist spirit" and the denial of Christ's divinity into religious education.[124]

The spokesmen for the NRA and CAM appeared embarrassed by the "patriotic" women whose testimony kicked off the hearings and the antisemitic conspiracy theory they propagated. But that testimony revealed that, for a not insignificant number of its supporters, a nation explicitly committed to Christ would be one that would not be so congenial to religious minorities—especially Jewish Americans.

The hearing adjourned at 4:45 p.m. Nothing further came of the proposal during that Congressional session. Like all those past efforts to put God, Christ, and the Bible into the Constitution, this one, too, proved unsuccessful.

CHAPTER FIVE

A Derailment of the Christian Political Tradition

The Confessional Tribe

The sociologist Robert N. Bellah opened his influential article "Civil Religion in America" by suggesting why so obvious a phenomenon had thus far received so little attention. This civil religion was to be distinguished from Christianity and the "generalized religion of 'the American Way of Life.' " Bellah saw a "religious dimension" of American life that "actually exists alongside of and [is] rather clearly differentiated from the churches," even as that dimension incorporated biblical symbols and tropes into its own myth and ritual. He mused that scholars may have been disinclined to confront the matter on account of "the controversial nature of the subject," noting how conservative groups had for decades "argued that Christianity is, in fact, the national religion" and "proposed constitutional amendments that would explicitly recognize the sovereignty of Christ." Those efforts were opposed by groups "defending the doctrine of separation of church and state" who therefore "denied that the national polity has, intrinsically, anything to do with religion at all." (Both parties could well be described as "heretics" of the civil religion.) Even as they accepted and cherished the long-standing tradition of the state supporting religion, the "moderates on this issue," Bellah noted, nevertheless failed to appreciate "the positive institutionalization" of civil religion that his article set out to explore. He noted, too, that "part of the reason this issue has been left in obscurity is certainly due to the peculiarly Western concept of religion as denoting a single type of collectivity of which an individual can be a member of one and only one at a time." A sociologist who was influenced by "the Durkheimian notion that every group has a religious dimension" and who had spent time researching in Japan was perhaps better situated to recognize and analyze a genuine "set of religious beliefs, symbols, and rituals" shared by Protestants, Catholics, and Jews in the United States.[1]

When Bellah set out to present his evidence for the existence (albeit waning) of this American civil religion, he submitted Kennedy's inaugural address as Exhibit A. Presidential inaugurations, "the religious legitimation of the highest political authority," are significant ceremonial events in American public life, and Kennedy's address, he observed, was framed by three references to "God." Such appeals to the divinity, not at all uncommon in the proclamations of American politicians, were not of mere "ceremonial significance" but revealed a set of ideas about the nature of American democracy and the purpose and destiny of the nation. Kennedy opened his remarks affirming the oath of office he had just taken—"For I have sworn before you and Almighty God the same solemn oath our forebears prescribed nearly a century and three-quarters ago"—and bridged present to past as he acknowledged taking upon himself the obligation to uphold the Constitution, a vow made before the people and God. That the oath is made before God demonstrates that while the will of the people is "the operative source of political authority, it is deprived of an ultimate significance." God is the true sovereign. "This is the meaning of the motto 'In God we trust,' as well as the inclusion of the phrase 'under God' in the pledge to the flag," those Cold War innovations making explicit this older understanding of the relationship of the American people to the divine. The point is emphasized further in the subsequent paragraph, where Kennedy spoke of "the same revolutionary beliefs for which our forebears fought are still at issue around the globe—the belief that the rights of man come not from the generosity of the state but from the hand of God," an allusion, of course, to the Declaration of Independence (the foundational text of the American civil religion). The conflict between the free and Communist worlds had at its root the question of the ultimate ground of political legitimacy and the origin of "the rights of man": Were such rights bestowed by the state or divinely endowed and thus prior to and inalienable by any government or human agency? And the speech worked up to an appeal to the "transcendent"—albeit this-worldly—"goal for the political process," as Kennedy called on the new generation of Americans, "the heirs of that first revolution," to commit to the protection and promotion of those human rights "at home and around the world" and continue this revolutionary task on the global stage, to take up their "role of defending freedom in its hour of maximum danger." Such was the divinely ordained national endeavor. Kennedy concluded with these words: "With a good conscience our only sure reward, with history the final judge of our deeds, let us go forth to lead the land we love, asking His blessing and His help, but knowing that here on earth God's work must truly be our own." All told, as expressed in Kennedy's address, the civil religion was "a general vehicle of national religious self-understanding," of its origin and purpose, despite the formal separation of church and state.[2]

Bellah found it notable that the country's first Roman Catholic president's address powerfully expressed "the very activist and noncontemplative conception of the fundamental religious obligation which has been historically associated with the Protestant position." At his inauguration, Kennedy performed as a high priest of this civil religion, so he did not speak as a Catholic (or even as a Christian, for that matter), as his private religious beliefs were not "relevant in any direct way to the conduct of his public office." The American civil religion, one might say, transcended the formal separation of church and state (which "guarantees the freedom of religious belief and association but at the same time clearly segregates the religious sphere, which is considered to be essentially private, from the political one").[3] It was this commitment to that dimension of the American system that Kennedy the candidate was forced to address during the heat of the campaign against Richard M. Nixon.

Throughout his quest for the presidency, Kennedy had been dogged by the same question that had hounded New York governor Al Smith during his bid in 1928: Was the candidate's commitment to Catholicism compatible with faithfulness to the Constitution? The senator directly addressed the question in a speech in the fall of 1960 when he crossed into the lion's den of the Greater Houston Ministerial Association and preached the gospel of separationism. Before the assembled pastors, Kennedy affirmed his twin convictions—his Catholic faith and his belief "in an America where the separation of church and state is absolute" and "in a president whose religious views are his own private affair, neither imposed by him upon the nation, nor imposed by the nation upon him as a condition to holding that office." As president, he would be the servant of the American people and loyal only to the Constitution of the United States. "I would not look with favor upon a President working to subvert the first amendment's guarantees of religious liberty," he said. "Nor would our system of checks and balances permit him to do so—and neither do I look with favor upon those who would work to subvert Article VI of the Constitution by requiring a religious test—even by indirection—for it." Kennedy reaffirmed his opposition to an ambassador to the Vatican and state aid to parochial schools.[4] He said he would make policy decisions "in accordance with what my conscience tells me to be in the national interest, and without regard to outside religious pressure or dictates." And he vowed that if any conflict should appear between his "conscience" and "the national interest," "then I would resign the office; and I hope that any other conscientious public servant would do the same." He closed his remarks pledging that should he be elected, he "shall devote every effort of mind and spirit to fulfilling the oath of the Presidency" (similar to the one he had taken in Congress) and will "to the best of my ability preserve, protect, and defend the Constitution . . . so help me God."[5]

In preparation for the Houston ordeal, Kennedy's aide and speechwriter Ted Sorenson thought to consult the noted Catholic theologian John Courtney Murray, SJ. The Republican-leaning Jesuit had no doubt taken notice of the anti-Catholicism the campaign had predictably roused and the exploitation of such sentiments by the Nixon camp. Sorenson read a draft of the address over the phone, and Murray proffered some advice on distinguishing between the church's legitimate instruction on faith and morals and the realm of public policy. While not incorporated into his prepared remarks, Kennedy echoed Murray's language during the Q and A.[6]

Father Murray was not an advocate of the separationism Kennedy had confessed to the Houston ministers. A believer in "cooperation" between state and religious institutions, he was disturbed by the increasing secularity of American society and its validation by the Supreme Court. In his view, in *Everson v. Board of Education* (1947) and *McCollum v. Board of Education* (1948) the court had instituted a novel doctrine of absolute separation of church and state (that is, of "no aid to religion"—despite the actual holding of *Everson*) that challenged the historic meaning of the First Amendment and the long-standing practices of the American people. These decisions would have the effect of pushing the nation "in the direction of secularism," he told an audience in Wilmington, Delaware, soon after the *McCollum* decision.

Murray was troubled, too, by "the development of the 'religion of democracy' as the national religion of the U.S., by law established." That religion, the Jesuit claimed, "whose church would be the public school," was "a secularist system of values, constructed without reference to God or to any human destiny beyond this world, that presents itself as a higher, more unifying religion than all 'sectarianism.'" This "contemporary nationalist myth" was the real present danger, the common enemy of Protestants, Catholics, and Jews alike.[7]

And yet so many liberal Protestants, Jews, and secularists were joining together not against secularism but against the specter of "Catholic power." Much of this anti-Catholicism, Murray averred, was based on entrenched misunderstandings and reflected lingering nativist bigotry. But he recognized that the traditional Catholic teaching on the church-state issue did not conform as neatly to the American system in theory as the American Catholic leadership supposed it did in practice; "the theory of church and state expressed in Catholic writings on politics could disturb the Protestant mind," he conceded.[8] Pope Pius IX's notorious *Syllabus of Errors* (1864) denounced, among other falsehoods, the proposition "The Church ought to be separated from the State, and the State from the Church," and the anathemas concluded with a denial of the proposition "The Roman Pontiff can, and ought to, reconcile himself, and come to terms with progress, liberalism and modern civilization."[9] The "Syllabus" provided much fuel for anti-Catholicism for decades to come. Kennedy was questioned directly by his Houston inquisitors whether its denunciations of the separation of church and state, freedom of religion, and the freedom of conscience were still binding.[10]

There was also the matter of the Catholic counter-vision. Rome professed the ideal of a "confessional state" that would cultivate the true faith and repress heresy. Church and state were separate and independent institutions, each enjoined with authority over its own circumscribed jurisdiction, existing in an "orderly connection" and "mutual co-ordination." The state is assigned the duty to recognize and care for the "one true religion" and accordingly is responsible for the suppression of error (for "error has no rights")—that is, of the propagation of all "false religions." Prudential considerations may require a state to extend a degree of tolerance to non-Catholics. But false religions would not enjoy state sanction or support. Catholicism would be the sole licit public religion. The "confessional" state is perforce a regime of religious coercion and intolerance.

Such was the ideal arrangement, "the thesis," in theological parlance, laid out in Pope Leo XII's 1885 encyclical *Immortale Dei*. This could not be realized in all situations—say, under a non-Catholic monarch or in democracies where the majority were not (or not yet) Catholic. Under such unfortunate circumstances the "hypothesis" would pertain: the Roman Catholic Church demands the freedom of worship and to evangelize. This would be a tolerable arrangement (and surely a lesser evil than if the church were not granted its freedom or attempted to impose the thesis over a recalcitrant populace), but only to be endured until such a time as circumstances change so as to permit the implementation of the thesis.[11] If—or rather when—the church were to be successful in its apostolic mission and a Catholic majority came to be (and many a Catholic clergyman anticipated the eventual decay of Protestantism in America), it would be incumbent on the state to do so. And with the formal establishment of the one true religion, the liberties that had been extended to false religions would consequently be restricted. For error, the church teaches, has no rights.

Roman Catholicism consequently appeared to many worried Americans as not only an alien transplant but an antithesis to their political ideals. By the mid-nineteenth century, Catholicism had grown to be the nation's largest denomination, and Catholics were busy building up an American subculture made up of parochial schools, orphanages, hospitals, and charitable and welfare institutions. A Catholic political party such as those that arose in Europe never did take shape, but Catholics (the Irish in particular) were able to assert considerable political power to defend and advance their interests by means of bloc voting and assembling urban political machines, practices that long offended the sensibilities of the defenders of republican Protestant America. For them, that compounding Catholic population was still a foreign element and a chronic threat to the stability and endurance of their free and democratic institutions.

In the late nineteenth century, the so-called Americanists in the Catholic hierarchy—such as John Ireland, archbishop of St. Paul; John J. Keane, bishop of Richmond and later the first rector of Catholic University of America; and Cardinal James Gibbons of Baltimore—proclaimed the harmony between Catholicism and American republicanism and endorsed the robust participation of Catholics in public life. Yet the Americanists could not really offer a theological defense of the nation's church-state arrangement. While they may not have advocated for the thesis loudly, they did not publicly disavow the teaching.[12] The Vatican didn't provide much assistance to their efforts at rapprochement. In his 1895 encyclical to the archbishops and bishops of the United States, *Longinqua Oceani*, Leo XIII praised "the prosperous condition of Catholicity" within "the well-ordered Republic" but cautioned that "it would be very erroneous to draw the conclusion that in America is to be sought the type of the most desirable status of the Church, or that it would be universally lawful or expedient for State and Church to be, as in America, dissevered and divorced." While the pope applauded the "good condition" and growth of the church, he remained adamant that "she would bring forth much more abundant fruits if, in addition to liberty, she enjoyed the favor of the laws and the patronage of public authority."[13] The Americanists continued to press their cause, but Rome remained convinced that the advance of such modern democratic ideas within the church needed to be halted. In 1899, Leo XIII condemned a set of opinions he dubbed "Americanism," even as they were probably not even held by the Americanists themselves. His warning against "the principle of these new opinions"—that "in order to more easily attract those who differ from her, the Church should shape her teachings more in accord with the spirit of the age and relax some of her ancient severity and make some concessions to new opinions"—followed by Pope Pius X's condemnation of "modernism" (as "the synthesis of all heresies") in his 1907 encyclical and the subsequent purging of biblical scholars and theologians engaged with modern scientific methods of inquiry, may well have stifled intellectual life within the church and retarded the development of a liberal Catholicism in America and elsewhere. Neo-scholasticism remained the framework for Catholic thought for decades to come; censorship, surveillance, and discipline would ensure orthodoxy and suppress deviance. The conservatives had received the imprimatur for their counter-society.[14]

Following World War II, however, that counter-society was beginning to weaken, as American Catholics enrolled in the nation's secular colleges and universities, entered the middle class, and set out from their urban enclaves for the suburbs. By the mid-fifties, Will Herberg could confidently announce in his *Protestant-Catholic-Jew* "the transformation of a group socially and culturally alien into a thoroughly American religious community." It helped, too, that the Vatican was seen as a valued ally in the Cold War crusade against Communism. Yet official Catholic commitment to the foundational principles of the American republic still appeared equivocal.[15] Even the liberal "Right Reverend New Dealer" John A. Ryan included *Immortale Dei* (with his commentary) in his seminary textbook on Catholic political thought. (As if to demonstrate the ongoing incoherence, the volume also included a 1913 paean to American democracy, "Catholicism and Americanism.") In his commentary on the encyclical, Father Ryan acknowledged the "traditional teaching" of religious intolerance but tempered it by avowing that "the event of its practical realization in any State or country is so remote in time and probability that no practical man will let it disturb his equanimity or affect his attitude toward the Church because they fear that some five thousand years hence the United States may become overwhelmingly Catholic and may then restrict the freedom of non-Catholic denominations." Still, Ryan maintained the validity of the "thesis": "We cannot yield up the principles of eternal and unchangeable truth in order to avoid the enmity of such unreasonable persons. Moreover, it would be a futile policy; for they would not think us sincere."[16]

Such statements were not reassuring to those predisposed to fear Catholic power and distrust the intentions of the hierarchy. The hierarchy's stances—its stubborn contention that Roman Catholicism was the "one true Church," consequent refusal to participate in interfaith associations and good-will partnerships, and insistence in seeking assistance for parochial schools from public coffers—were not approaches well designed to win friends and influence Protestant pastors. Those who insisted that there was a fundamental contradiction between Catholic doctrine on church and state and American political ideals still had plenty of evidence to exhibit. Paul Blanshard may have overstated the case in his bestselling *American Freedom and Catholic Power* (1949), but the tensions were real and could not simply be swept under the rug.[17]

And here Father Murray stepped in to attempt to revise the terms of the conversation. In October 1950, he penned a memorandum to the Vatican secretariat of state in which he pointed out the obstacle "in the present state of development of the Church's doctrine on Church-State relationships." "This doctrine has not yet been vitally adapted to modern political realities and to the legitimate democratic aspirations, especially as they have developed in the United States," Murray wrote. He warned of the devastating consequences if such a doctrinal adaption was not quickly pursued; "the result will be a progressive alienation of the American mind from the Catholic Church, with consequent damage to the apostolic activity of the Church."[18]

The Jesuit was candid about the problem the church faced in the United States: "There is a widespread belief that the Catholic Church does not fully and sincerely affirm the human and political values of a democratically organized political society; that American Catholic support of the principles of the U.S. Constitution is basically incompatible with certain tenets of Catholic faith; in a word, that Americanism and Catholicism are fundamentally in conflict." This attitude, he noted, was not completely unwarranted, as the present state of the church's teaching on church-state relations gave the impression that it has accepted the American settlement "only provisionally, and on the grounds of expediency." "A very widespread impression has been created that only the Spanish religio-political system can in principle command the support of the

Church; that any other solution is sheer 'hypothesis,' a reluctant and opportunistic acceptance of a situation of fact." The church thus appeared more comfortable with dictatorships than with democratic regimes, and non-Catholic Americans were troubled by the political implications of the "thesis," the determination of the church to use the coercive power of the state to suppress the religious beliefs and practices it finds erroneous when it finds it is possible to do so. That position on religious freedom had alienated Protestants and provided fodder to the secularist claim that "the Church is the enemy of democracy," and the atmosphere of fear and distrust it encouraged was an obstacle to the church's apostolic efforts and to working out an equitable solution to the vexed school question, even as the fight against Communism provided robust opportunities for respect and collaboration among religious communities.[19]

The current crisis provided an opportunity for a rethinking—a vital adaptation—of Catholic teaching on the church-state relationship. Murray hoped to advance the teaching beyond the stage of development that reflected the previous century's conflict between the church and Continental liberalism, in particular the anticlerical and anti-Catholic Jacobian democracy that emerged from the French Revolution. The threat to the church now came from totalitarian Communism, and democratic regimes ought to be considered in a new light. The church needed to free itself from the "dichotomies, 'thesis vs. hypothesis,' or 'union of Church and State vs. separation of Church and State' " that shaped the nineteenth-century dispute and develop a doctrine that drew from the long tradition of Catholic teaching, engaged with mid-twentieth-century realities, and attended to the unique history and virtues of the American political tradition and the situation of the church within it. Such an endeavor would not bring forth a new "ideal" but could affirm the principles of the American constitutional system as valid within the contours of traditional Catholic principles. And it would demonstrate "what is principle and what is contingent application of principle, what is permanent demand and what is legitimate temporary expedience, what is required by the universal Church and what is required by the Church in certain nations."[20]

Murray took up the task himself, excavating a deeper account of the Catholic political tradition and its relationship to the American project that would demonstrate to Americans that Catholicism was not inimical to the political values of the republic (and assure the church that the American project was not inimical to Catholicism). In a series of scholarly articles published in the 1950s in *Theological Studies*, the Jesuit journal that he edited, Murray argued that the core of Catholic political teaching was not the ideal of a confessional state—a Catholic establishment—called for since the nineteenth century. It was, rather, the "Gelasian thesis," which distinguished the sphere of civil government and that of the church. Further, rather than ushering in a radically new order, the American constitutional framework was actually a manifestation of this veritable political tradition.

Murray's revisionist account was greeted with stiff resistance in some conservative circles. Fearing his work was undermining a key teaching of the church, Joseph Clifford Fenton and Francis T. Connell, both on the faculty of Catholic University of America, enlisted the support of Cardinal Alfredo Ottaviani, the secretary of the Holy Office in the Roman Curia, in an effort to silence the Jesuit. In 1955 Murray was directed by his superiors in Rome to cease writing on the subject (he was advised to take up poetry in its stead).[21] But the winds in Rome were shifting. Soon after the election of Pope John XXIII in 1958, the censorship of Murray was lifted, and he resumed his labors on the church-state question. In late October 1960, a month after Kennedy's Houston speech and just days before the election, Father Murray presented his case to a candid nation. *We Hold These Truths: Catholic Reflections on the American Proposition*—the title alluding to the Declaration of Independence and Lincoln's Gettysburg Address—brought together in a single volume the arguments he had been laboring over for more than a decade.

The proposition Lincoln proclaimed at Gettysburg, Murray wrote, "rests on the more traditional conviction that there are truths; that they can be known; that they must be held; for, if they are not held, assented to, consented to, worked into the texture of institutions, there can be no hope of founding a true City, in which men may dwell in dignity, peace, unity, justice, well-being, freedom."[22] Murray conceded that religious pluralism was "the native condition of American society," and unlike thinkers such as Reinhold Niebuhr and Will Herberg he did not appeal to some shared "Judeo-Christian" tradition that might serve as a common denominator of civil faith. Indeed, the Jesuit went so far as to state frankly that Jews, Protestants, Catholics, and secularists "have no common universe of discourse." Despite such fundamental divisions, the nation had been established on a "public consensus" regarding certain truths, "whereby we are made 'e pluribus unum,' one society subsisting amid multiple pluralisms."[23]

The Declaration of Independence ("that landmark of Western political theory") announced the first truth of the "American Proposition": "the sovereignty of God over the nations as well as over individual men." Murray held that the document "radically distinguishes the conservative Christian tradition of America from the Jacobin laicist tradition of Continental Europe," which began by asserting the autonomy of human reason as "the sole principle of political organization." By contrast, "the first article of the American political faith is that the political community, as a form of free and ordered human life, looks to the sovereignty of God as to the first principle of its organization." This idea echoed throughout American political history; it could be heard in the pronouncements of presidents and has been affirmed by the Supreme Court. (The contemporary secularist dissent from this principle was just that—"a dissent" from the "authentic voice of America.") The American consensus was "in fundamental continuity with the central political tradition of the West"—that is, "the tradition of natural law and natural rights." What's more, this "constellation of principles" concerning "the origin and nature of society, the function of the state as the legal order of society, and the scope and limitations of government" emerged from the medieval Catholic tradition. The celebrated phrase "a free people under limited government," Murray quipped, could well have been uttered by "the first Whig, St. Thomas Aquinas."[24]

American constitutionalism could thus be regarded as a transposition of the "Great Tradition" into a modern register, its great innovation being its written constitution. The principle of the consent of the governed had its roots in "the medieval idea of kingship" and "the ancient principle of popular participation in rule." The protection of free speech and a free press emerged from this "political faith" of self-governance and not from "the thin theory proper to eighteenth-century individualistic rationalism." American political institutions also affirmed the classical distinction between the state and society, a distinction that had collapsed under European absolutism and was obliterated in "the modern omnicompetent society-state."[25]

Having disclosed those things "agreed upon," Murray turned to the other aspect of American pluralism—the things not agreed upon, "the problem put by the plurality of conflicting religions within the one body politic." Murray considered the religious differences between Protestants, Catholics, and Jews (and secularists, for that matter) to be fundamental and irreconcilable. "Religious pluralism is against the will of God," the Jesuit lamented. "But it is the human condition; it is written into the script of history. It will not somehow marvelously cease to trouble the City." So the problem had to be faced squarely. The question, as he put it, was how to manage the situation so as "to dissolve the structure of war that underlies the pluralistic society, and erect the more civilized structure of the dialogue." As no "official" religion could possibly be agreed upon at the federal level, it was incumbent on the Framers to come up with a new mechanism to manage the relationship between the churches and the new state.[26]

Their solution to the problem of pluralism took form in the First Amendment. It was a solution that flowed naturally from the people's commitment to limited government. But what did the religion clauses of the First Amendment demand? Murray distinguished between those who regarded the religion clauses as "true articles of faith"—that is, statements of religious truth deposited as dogmas of an American orthodoxy, "to which one must conform on pain of some matter of excommunication"—and those who regarded them "only as law," statements devoid of any "religious content," which required "rational civil obedience." Those who read into the religious clauses "certain Protestant tenets," or "ultimate suppositions of secular liberalism," or "an identification of their Protestantism with American secular culture,"[27] distorted the original intention and meaning of the provisions.[28] If it were the case that to endorse the First Amendment it was necessary to assent to certain "sectarian" principles, "the very article that bars any establishment of religion would somehow establish one." Correctly understood, the First Amendment simply demarcated the federal government's power. Rather than "articles of faith," the religion clauses were to be accepted as "articles of peace" intended to ensure the stability of a political community marked by fundamental religious disagreement. This did not mean that the arrangement was devoid of religious value, for seeking peace is itself a "Christian imperative." So Murray could conclude that "to speak of expediency here is altogether to misunderstand the moral nature of the community and its collective moral obligation towards its own common good. The origins of our fundamental law are in moral principle; the obligations it imposes are moral obligations, binding in conscience."[29]

The "Gelasian thesis" carefully distinguished the spheres of government and that of the church, limiting the government to its secular purposes and denying it competence in the realm of religion. The church maintains its *libertas Ecclesias*. This principle allowed for different legitimate models of church-state relations to take shape in varying historical contexts. As it maintains this classical distinction, the dualist American arrangement—in which the churches remain free in their spiritual jurisdiction and "fully independent and immune from interference by political authority"—ought to be more amenable to Catholics than constitutional arrangements that extended the powers of the state over or against the church. (The "thesis of the juridical omnipotence and omni-competence of the state" was, Murray reminded his readers, "the central object of the Church's condemnation of the Jacobin development.") Americans were rightly anxious about "illegitimate" unions of church and state that had emerged in Europe following the Reformation—whether they be "Calvinist theocracy, Anglican Erastianism, Gallican absolutism"; that anxiety revealed the contin-uing sway of the classical Christian political tradition.[30]

Further, Murray contended that the First Amendment had proven itself at the bar of American history as "good law." The American experience had demon-strated that "political unity and stability are possible without uniformity of reli-gious belief and practice, without the necessity of any governmental restrictions on any religion."[31] That could not be sustained absent an enduring consensus regarding "the rational truths and moral precepts that govern the structure of the constitutional state, specifically the substance of the common weal," of course. But that required a narrower ground of agreement and excluded such questions as regard "the total life and destiny of man" from the political conversation and policy discussions.[32] Poring over the political treatises of the Founding era, particularly *The Federalist*, Murray observed that the authors "were not engaged in broaching a political theory universal in scope and application, a plan for an Ideal Republic of Truth and Virtue."[33] Rather, they intended to construct a place where human beings could enjoy their freedom, and so the jurisdiction of the state over the pursuit of the common good was limited to agreed-upon mundane ends. This has been an advantage to religion. While the churches do not benefit from government privileges, neither do they suffer persecution when the direc-tion of political winds shift. All told, the price the church has paid for religious freedom in America was better than what it had shelled out for its privileges else-where. Deeply informed by the Christian tradition (and not dependent on Lockean liberalism), the American system had established lasting social peace among potentially warring groups and ensured the freedom of the (true) church to pursue her mission. This did not mean that the American arrangement was the best of all possible regimes. But, given the nation's native and enduring condition of pluralism, it was a very good solution and a worthy modus vivendi, one greatly superior to the "sectarian Liberalism" of nineteenth-century Europe, the "totalitarian democracies" of the twentieth, and the situation that obtained in ostensibly Catholic confessional states such as Spain and Portugal.[34]

Here at long last was that full-fledged Catholic theological case for the legitimacy of American constitutional order. The nation's Fathers and Framers were "building better than they knew," Murray suggested, alluding to the statement of the 1884 Third Plenary Council of Baltimore, on the solid foundation of natural law.[35] Catholics could be at home in the nation because it was a home that had been built according to the blueprints provided by their tradition. "Catholic participation in the American consensus," Murray wrote, "has been full and free, unreserved and unembarrassed, because the contents of this consensus—the ethical and political principles drawn from the tradition of natural law—approved themselves to the Catholic intelligence and conscience. Where this kind of language is talked, the Catholic joins the conversation with complete ease. It is his language. The ideas expressed are native to his own universe of discourse. Even the accent, being American, suits his tongue."[36]

We Hold These Truths was arguably the most important and influential book of American Catholic thought of its time.[37] The author appeared on the December 12, 1960, cover of *Time* magazine; a glowing profile announced him as "the intellectual bellwether of this new Catholic and American frontier."[38] In 1963 he was invited to serve as a theological advisor to the Second Vatican Council, where he was instrumental in drafting its 1965 Declaration on Religious Freedom, *Dignitatis Humanae*, one of the documents that articulated the church's coming to terms with modernity.

Murray was not altogether sanguine about the prospects of the American experiment, however, and he worried whether the ideas on which the consensus was based still maintained "the same hold upon the American mind," as Protestant theology and modern rationalism had turned away from the tradition of natural law. So if there came to be "widespread dissent" from the American consensus that had held for nearly two centuries, its perseverance would hang on the nation's Catholics, who "would still be speaking in the ethical and political idiom familiar to them as it was familiar to their fathers, both the Fathers of the Church and the Fathers of the American Republic. The guardianship of the original American consensus, based on the Western heritage, would have passed to the Catholic community, within which the heritage was elaborated long before America was."[39] All human beings had access to natural law, but it was Catholics who continued to teach and learn the tradition in their schools and affirm it in their religious lives. If other Americans no longer recognized the foundations of their republic, it would be the responsibility of their Catholic compatriots to remind them.

In his 1950 memorandum to the Vatican, Murray had observed that "the wide propagation" of the "secularist thesis that the Church is the enemy of democracy" has not only been accepted by many Protestants but has led to Catholic counterreactions, "especially among the laity," in the forms of "excessive and sentimental protestations of 'Americanism,'" on the one hand, and "a certain Catholic 'integrism,' a certain aggressive willingness to be 'the enemy,' with its consequent exclusion from a full participation in the national life," on the other.[40] Even as Murray's new vision of Americanism was gaining ascendency, an aggressive group of Catholic traditionalists came together in resistance. They did not regard American culture as hospitable to Catholic ideals and aspirations or see their role as Catholics to uphold a putative consensus. By contrast, they pitted themselves as enemies of the infidel regime. "If she is to protect herself and if she is to abide by her divine mandate to teach all peoples," they proclaimed, "the Catholic Church in America must break the articles of peace, she must forthrightly acknowledge that a state of war exists between herself and the American political order."[41] To encourage their fellow Catholics to do so, they launched a magazine.

This endeavor—which they dubbed *Triumph*—carried on a nearly decade-long literary crusade against the country's secular liberal order and an American Catholic Church all too willing to acquiesce. Following the call of Vatican II's *Decree on the Apostolate of the Laity* (1965), the editors regarded themselves as the vanguard of a new "counter-reformation" preparing to fill the spiritual vacuum opened by the secular liberal order and set out into the world to rally the faithful and reeducate wayward Catholics. The voices published proudly proclaimed their "radically Christian" vision, which they set against secular liberalism as well as against the heresies put forward by the modernizers at such magazines as the lay-run *Commonweal* and the Jesuit *America*.[42]

The energetic mind behind this crusade was that of L. (Leo) Brent Bozell Jr. Bozell had been one of the wunderkinder of the new conservative movement that had coalesced in the mid-1950s. At Yale, Bozell met William F. Buckley Jr., who became his debating partner, facilitated the young Nebraskan's conversion to the Roman Catholic Church, and introduced him to his sister Patricia, whom Bozell later married. Soon after graduating, Buckley made a name for himself with his assault on the liberal academy, *God and Man at Yale*. In 1954, he and Bozell published *McCarthy and His Enemies: The Record and Its Meaning*, a defense of the senator's controversial anti-Communist antics. The following year, Buckley launched the *National Review*. The magazine soon became the organ of the New Right, bringing together the various ideological factions—libertarians, cultural and religious traditionalists, anti-Communist Cold War hawks—all united in their antipathy to New Deal liberalism at home and Communism abroad.[43] Bozell worked as a speechwriter and advisor for McCarthy until the senator's death in 1957. He then joined his brother-in-law's venture, first as a contributor, then as a senior editor, writing prolifically on national politics (his frustration with the overreach of the Supreme Court, the liberalism of the Eisenhower administration and the moderate Republicans, and the ongoing menace of Communism), forecasting to a too-complacent country its coming doom and helping found the Young Americans for Freedom to stave it off. On account of these bona fides, Bozell was tapped to ghostwrite Barry Goldwater's political manifesto, quickly penning *The Conscience of a Conservative.* That paean to heroic individualism and its struggle against state paternalism, together with the fantasy vision of a stunted federal government and muscular confrontation with the Soviet menace, was an instant classic, launching the Arizona senator as the star of the burgeoning movement. The work was not an exercise in moderation. A supporter of the senator later styled the book as "an accurate distillation of Goldwater's past statements and speeches liberally spiked with 200-proof Bozell."[44]

In early 1961, the Bozell family decamped to Spain so as to live cheaply while Brent focused on a critical book on the Warren Court. During that two-year sojourn in the waning years of Franco's regime Bozell came to experience what he dubbed "the Catholic thing." Enchanted by the incense and pageantry of that "magic kingdom," the author of the most celebrated libertarian manifesto began to rethink his prior certainties. Though he and his family returned to the United States, his heart never left Spain. He had become thoroughly infatuated with the ideal of "Christendom"—the dream of a holistic Catholic social order.[45]

Given his Catholic commitments, Bozell found himself increasingly at odds with the big-tent conservatism that his brother-in-law was trying to stage-manage over at *National Review*. Despite their mutual abhorrence of Communism, Catholic traditionalists who respected the social teachings of the church and free-market libertarians who worshiped the invisible hand made strange bedfellows and unreliable allies. A *National Review* witticism illuminated the strain. Finding Pope John XXIII's 1961 social encyclical *Mater et Magistera* insufficiently critical of Communism and too supportive of the welfare state, the magazine quipped, "Going the rounds in Catholic conservative circles: 'Mater sí, Magistra no.'" Liberal Catholics, the types that wrote for and read *Commonweal* and *America*, were not amused by the allusion to the well-known slogan of Cuban exiles, "Cuba, sí, Castro, no." Though he was a critic of the liberalizing trend in the tradition (that same issue featured his article "The Strange Drift of Liberal Catholicism"), Bozell was put off by the magazine's impudence, an opinion he privately shared with Buckley. He also grew frustrated with the magazine's relaxed positions on contraception and birth control.[46] Bozell articulated his new theological-political outlook against what he called the "fusionism" of his conservative comrades who were futilely trying to square the circle of reconciling libertarianism and traditionalism. Over at the *National Review*, Frank S. Meyer had been making the case for a recovery of "that earlier synthesis of belief in transcendent value and in human freedom which the Founders of the Republic embodied in their lives and actions, discursively expressed in their writings and their debates, and bequeathed to us in the body politic they constituted." The limited state ("restricted to its natural functions: the preservation of domestic peace and order, the administration of justice, and defense against foreign enemies") preserved the possibility of individual freedom, for the individual to make "the free choice of good over evil." It was wrong, therefore, "to look upon the state as unlimitedly instituted to enforce virtue, thus abnegating the freedom of the individual."[47]

In a lengthy response, also published in *National Review*, Bozell argued that the attempt of a "fusion" of libertarian and traditionalist stances in the end sacrificed virtue to individual liberty. "The goal of man is virtue—the fulfillment of the potentialities of his God-oriented nature," Bozell wrote. "The chief purpose of politics is to aid the quest for virtue." He went on to explain the necessity of religion in this endeavor:

> Man's nature is such, however, that he, uniquely among created beings, has the capacity to deviate from the patterns of order—to, as it were, repudiate his nature: i.e., he is free. So viewed, freedom is hardly a blessing: add the ravages of original sin and it is the path to disaster. It follows that if individual man is to have any hope of conforming with his nature, he needs all of the help he can get. That is why the role of grace is so vital to the Christian view of things, not only supernatural grace, but the natural grace that springs forth from man's constructs: his institutions, his customs, his laws—the ones that have been inspired by his better angel and that remain in time to give nourishment to all of the human race. And that, in turn, is why the Christian view, which begins in despair, ends in optimism.

The institutions that make up the commonwealth—especially (but not exclusively) the state—ought to provide external inducements to assist human beings in their quest to become virtuous. The commonwealth, then, should be arranged so as to follow the instruction of the Gospel: " 'Go . . . and teach all nations.' These are the marching orders of Christianity, and, from a theological viewpoint, its central operational command. God's purpose, if we may put it so, is twofold: to give the widest possible access to supernatural grace—that is, to magnify the Christian Church; and to establish temporal conditions conducive to human virtue—that is, to build a Christian *civilization*." In contrast, Meyer's position that the role of government is to preserve freedom led to abandonment of the quest for virtue. "The urge to freedom for its own sake is, in the last analysis, a rebellion against nature; it is the urge to be free from God." Bozell concluded, "The story of how the Free society has come to take priority over the good society is the story of the decline of the West."[48]

The idea that became *Triumph* was conceived in the summer of 1964.[49] Just off of a failed bid for a congressional seat in suburban Maryland (he apparently perplexed potential supporters by stating that the "Gnostic heresy" was the country's most serious domestic crisis), Bozell initially proposed launching a new political party, an idea soundly vetoed by the editors of *National Review*.[50] In 1965, along with Frederick ("Fritz") D. Wilhelmsen, a professor of philosophy specializing in medieval scholasticism at the University of Dallas, Bozell formed a "Committee for a Conservative Catholic Magazine."

Bozell and Wilhelmsen were joined by the Hungarian émigré Thomas Molnar, then a professor at Brooklyn College, John Wisner (like Bozell, a convert to Catholicism), and Gary Potter, who all signed on as founding editors. Michael Lawrence (who met Bozell while a law student at Catholic University of America) came on as business manager, later serving as editor of the magazine from 1970 until it folded six years later. A procession of traditionalist contributors helped fill *Triumph*'s pages. Many who became associated with the project were, like Bozell, not "cradle Catholics" with deep familiarity with the tradition from their youth, but those who "swam the Tiber" as adults, their commitment to the church ideologically charged.[51]

A fundraising letter was not modest about the purpose of their project: "Our goal is the resurrection of Christian civilization, the triumph of God's Church, the Future: Christ Himself."[52] The editors had planned to call the magazine *Future*, but it turned out that name was already taken by a publication of a trade organization. Confronted with a lawsuit, they quickly settled on *Triumph*.[53]

The first issue appeared in September 1966. It had been scheduled to come out a month earlier, but as it was going to press, the printing plant was struck by lightning, resulting in a delay of several days.[54]

Triumph had announced itself as a traditionalist alternative to the modernist-directed Catholic press. For the first year or so, its articles defended the conservative position in various "intra-Church battles"—contending over the Latin Mass (the loss of which they regarded as an abandonment of the idea of a universal Christian civilization) and the church's teachings on divorce, birth control, and abortion—from the liberalizing currents gaining strength in the wake of Vatican II. The editors were greatly relieved by Pope Paul VI's proclamation of the Credo of the People of God and the encyclical *Humanae Vitae* reaffirming the church's traditional position on contraception in 1968.

Within a few months of its existence, *Triumph* also began to challenge the notion that there could be a comfortable correspondence between the American conservativism and Catholicism. As one of its editors later reflected, "There is not only not a 'seamless fit' between the American tradition—even as refracted through the conservative lens—and the Catholic tradition; the American experiment itself, not merely in its contemporary flowering but from its conception, was and fundamentally is irreconcilable with the Catholic Thing."[55] Early supporters and subscribers had expected a conservative Catholic publication, a sort of religious supplement to the *National Review*; *Triumph* announced itself as a "radically Christian" one, refusing all innovations and attempts to strike accommodations with the times. In editorial after editorial, column after column, article after article, *Triumph* inveighed against the modern secular-liberal (neo-pagan) order, its bogus anthropology, crass materialism, and pluralist ethos. The magazine broke with American conservatism over an array of issues and policy positions, endorsing the social teachings of the church over a commitment to unfettered capitalism, criticizing American military policy and the war in Vietnam, and opposing nuclear weapons. Bozell and his writers nostalgically recalled a lost golden age and recounted narratives of decline, just-so tales of wrong intellectual turns that led by an inevitable logic to the current cultural and moral abyss, epitomized by sexual revolution, student rebellion, urban riots, political assassinations, and, most hideously, the growing social acceptance—and legalization—of abortion. While the conservative movement he had helped his brother-in-law organize and cultivate sought to rescue the nation from the New Deal consensus liberalism and restore its "original" constitutional order, Bozell had come to realize that the fatal turn had come much earlier than the scribblers at the *National Review* could dare admit. The problem wasn't the liberal departure from the American idea; it was the American idea itself. By the late 1960s, it was evident to the editors that the bill of liberalism was coming due. It was well time for a reckoning. The editors understood the counter-cultural dimension of their mission. As Michael Lawrence later confessed, "The project that became central to TRIUMPH was the on-going effort to expose the besetting characteristic idolatry of Americans, which consisted (and consists) in worship of: America; and to invite the Catholics in America to see themselves as 'the people set apart,' 'the city on a hill,' whose providential mission is to help their fellow Americans throw off their bondage to their strange god and return to allegiance to the Lord our God."[56]

As it happened, it was the obstinacy of America's "race problem" that motivated the editors to focus on the condition of the American regime and to conclude that liberalism had failed beyond repair. Reflecting in the wake of the urban riots of "the long, hot summer of 1967," a *Triumph* editorial opined that the violence evidenced the collapse of the civil rights movement as well as "the secular establishments' confidence in its own ability to govern the country." The disorder on the streets illuminated the much deeper disorder of the American project. Rather than arguing that the disturbances called for the restoration of "law and order," *Triumph* diagnosed a liberal establishment that was simply unable to govern.[57] Conservatives fared no better in *Triumph*'s judgment. While "artificially imposed integration" would not alleviate the problems of "the Negros," the editors scoffed at the existing system of "artificially imposed segregation." "Integration-segregation is a false competition, an unnatural, puritanical dispute that could only arise in a stunted culture that never knew or had forgotten the fullness and freedom of the human person." Further, the conservative "superstition" that free-market economics would provide a "social cure" was delusional, as was the liberal confidence that a cure could be achieved by means of government welfare programs. Liberals and conservatives all failed to understand that the fundamental problem African Americans struggled with was not material but moral and spiritual. So the solution would not be found in the implementation of this or that social or economic policy. The riots demonstrated that "the Negro" was no longer satisfied with the false promises made by the liberal order. "The rebellion is *not* a revolution of rising expectations. It is a rebellion against liars, against the false, cynical and unspeakable (because they are unkeepable) promises that have heretofore managed to buy the black man's submission to the social order. The Negro now knows, instinctively and empirically, what he could have learned from grace: the Promised Land is not anywhere in the Rand-McNally Atlas, certainly not in the technocratic empire that now sprawls over the American landscape; it is a place of the soul. The rebellion is a search for civilization."[58]

The violence heralded another great awakening. Since they believed that all civilizing came from Christ, *Triumph*'s editors took a somewhat sanguine view of that "peculiar institution," which, for all its attendant evils, at least had the virtue of introducing the enslaved to Christ and providing them "moral and cultural discipline." The sins that accompanied slavery, they hastened to add, "also reflected . . . the distorted version of Christian doctrine called Calvinism which, for all of the individual Protestant's concern for the Negro's soul, poorly understood such matters as charity, mercy and the equal dignity of all men before God." Nowhere in this essay did the writers pause to consider how African Americans cultivated their own "Christianities," which in many ways departed from the religion set on them by their masters. Nor did they care to expound on "the mixed nature of the American Christian approach to the Negro"—the post-Reconstruction installation of white supremacy, buttressed and sustained by the laws of Jim Crow and state and vigilante violence. They had cast a different agent for the role of villain. It was liberalism that "destroyed civilization." "As liberalism spread over the country and broke down Christian social institutions, it freed the Negros, like white men, not only from moral necessity, but also physical necessity; and gathered them together in large numbers in the large urban centers where liberalism is most powerful." In the liberal city, the African American was systematically demolished. "All culture, breeding, and moral character is stripped from him. He is flung into a dirty slum to fend for himself. Gone are the models of civilized men on whom he leaned for guidance, encouragement, and protection." In their view, "he is reduced to that isolated and abstract individual, whose innate virtue, according to the liberals, is supposed to be able to face all eventualities of life by itself. He has no responsibilities and no duties: he is perfectly free. . . . The result, in the main, is that the liberal conception of liberty has gone a long way toward barbarizing those whom the Christians had civilized." This was, to be sure, a breathtakingly tendentious account of the history of the race problem in America, utterly bypassing the sins of white supremacy and racial terrorism. The editors held out some hope for the "stabilizing influence" of the old Southern Protestantism but took a dim view of the "political" use of religion by the leaders of the civil rights movement such as Martin Luther King Jr. ("Because the secularization of all Protestantism has served to marry the faith with a political program, a failure of the politics inevitably weakens the faith"). The fundamental error of the civil rights movement was that its leadership sought integration with secular liberal America rather than submission to the sovereignty of Christ.[59]

The editors of *Triumph* were, however, sympathetic to the spiritual, one might even say prophetic, quests of the "revolutionary Negro" who "filled the ghetto air with contempt for the pretentions of the secular-liberal political creed."[60] Black Power revealed a vivacious, if misguided, rebellion against the secular liberal order. While Black Muslims may have been seduced by "a heresy of a foreign heresy," they were rightly attuned to the virtues of discipline, order, and authority, and they well understood that the "race problem" would not be solved by secular liberalism and "the sterile legal and material satisfactions offered them in the name of equality." They sought instead "some dimension of the Real that transcends the banalities of Secular City and that will allow a man to feel and display the real dignity of their being."[61] *Triumph* anticipated that "the Negro is destined to play a prominent role in leading America and the rest of the Christian West from the rule of men to the rule of God."[62] A few months earlier, the editors suggested that "the Negroes, with a prudent utilization of the notion of Black Power, can implement the Christian thesis, perhaps even can play a leading role in breaking up the secular behemoth and so restore liberty and human dignity to America."[63]

Further, the attraction of African Americans to such radical movements illuminated the past and present failures of the apostolic effort of the Catholic Church. While understandable on account of the church's long-standing struggles within the dominant Protestant culture, the disinclination and ineptitude of the church in reaching out to African Americans was nonetheless inexcusable, "an abandonment in our own land of Christ's apostolate." The article concluded with a call for Catholic assertion, as a harbinger of a postliberal order: "It is for Christians to point out that the cure for a diseased social order is not to burn it down, or carve it into pieces, but to put it under the care of a political order that has time for the soul, because it is founded on the laws of God. It is the moment to start fashioning a new politics for America."[64]

Soon *Triumph* was prophesizing the imminent collapse of the secular liberal order. "Anyone who is not aware that the liberal Republic is coming down, and that it could be a matter of months, at most a few years, before the wreckage is visibly upon it, is too insensate to hope to draw into profitable conversation." Surveying the turmoil in June 1968—the race riots, student revolts over Vietnam—the editors concluded that liberalism had run its course. "Liberalism, which began by believing in everything, has ended by believing in nothing. It must, then, disappear."[65] They could not help but take a swipe at Frank S. Meyer, who still maintained a tempered optimism that some "national renewal of leadership and moral authority" might yet emerge. Meyer's determined hope "thus voices the key premise of American conservatives that repriming the well-springs of the country's origins is the way to achieve national virtue and health. It is this premise that prompts the dogged conservative reluctance to identify liberalism with America, and thus perpetuates a distorted picture of history." Conservatives may operate under that delusion, but *Triumph* understood that America was indeed liberal at its core; "its present doctrines" were simply "an elaboration and fulfillment of the original deposit." And that really amounted to a wholesale rejection of the Christian revelation:

> Now the central tenet of liberalism, yesterday and today, is that man is on his own. His personal life is neither dependent on nor answerable to any external Authority; nor, in his own sphere, is the public order he constructs. It follows, as the necessary antidote to disillusionment and despair, that human life and human society are perfectable [*sic*] by the agency of man. But since man, by himself, cannot function in the realm of the spirit, he is directed by liberalism to seek his goals in the realm of matter. That search, in turn, requires experimentation under the standard of utility; thus the famous American pragmatism which may, in some circumstances, counsel rugged individualism and self-reliance, but in others, recourse to the collectivity, or to the support of technology. Still, liberalism recognizes that matter may not be everything and thus urges man to *reach* for the spirit—for truth: on the understanding, however, that one man's reach is as good as another's (Meyer's relativism): and on the consequent understanding that any affirmation of Truth must be denied (Meyer's nihilism).

"This may be the shortest synopsis of liberalism on record, but it is complete," the editors submitted. "It is also a synopsis of the American creed. It comes down to a revolt against God." So-called conservatives such as Meyer could hope for a return to "moral authority," but such talk was vain so long as they refused to ignore the "*source* of morality." "Moral authority implies, in the absence of the Author, the authority of man; and that is the beginning and the end of all of our troubles." Proclaiming belief in God is not enough. Belief demands obedience to his authority. Bend the knee. Punish the rebellion. Renew the world in Christ.[66] Failing to do so, the country was doomed to collapse into the anarchy of mob rule or the tyranny of a police state.[67]

It wasn't just American conservatives who could not read the signs of the times. In the same issue, *Triumph* also called attention to "the signs of demor-alization in the Roman Catholic Church in America." Commenting on a summary of the American bishops' semiannual meeting held in St. Louis in April, the editors lamented that "*in the epochal moment for Church and country . . . the bishops of the United States could think of nothing distinctively Christian to do and nothing distinctly Christian to say to their fellow Catholics or to their fellow countrymen*." While the bishops had issued a statement on the crisis of Amer-ican racism that endorsed the findings and policy suggestions of the Kerner Commission, they were silent on abortion, which the editors regarded as the preeminent moral issue of the day. This demonstrated that "the bishops of the United States have lost faith in the *mission* of the Church: the task of sacramen-talizing the world, of raising it to the dignity that the Incarnation promised to Creation." The secularization of the West had brought about "a loss of confi-dence in the feasibility of this mission. . . . As defeat whittled away the Church's confidence and its nerve, it also increasingly drove important segments of the Church to draw up articles of peace with the momentary victors—with the secularist order that succeeded Christendom. When Christians lost faith in their capacity to make history, they naturally became interested in the success formulas of those who *were* making history, or seemed to be. They became inter-ested in liberalism." This was unquestionably a swipe at the work and legacy of the late John Courtney Murray, SJ. In *Triumph's* view, "the American bishops now feel able to take a stand on a public issue only when they concur with the consensus of the national secular establishment. Which means: the American Church has married the American state, is committed to its secular values and goals, is an arm of a political order which . . . is down on one knee before history—but not genuflecting; falling." The bishops who ought to be shepherds have revealed themselves to be sheep; the good news was that as liberalism declined, so would their power and influence.[68]

In February 1968, Bozell published what could be regarded as his declaration of independence from the American conservative movement that he himself had helped create. Back when he still regarded himself as a "conservative," Bozell had believed that the Framers were "perhaps the only group of men in modern history to have set their minds to the task of constructing a common-wealth on the basis of prudence, and therefore free from ideology," that "they deserve considerable reverence, and are a fit object for imitation,"[69] and that the country could be saved—it was a matter of getting back to the American foun-dations. His book *The Warren Revolution* attempted to demonstrate how, since 1954, the Supreme Court had stepped beyond its assigned role and introduced a new type of constitution-making—"to transfer the solution of some of the most momentous problems of contemporary public policy from the fluid consti-tution to the fixed constitution—by judicial decree" (rather than defer to the constitutionally mandated amendment process that depends on a nationwide consensus). At that time, Bozell contended that the answer to the overindul-gences of the liberal Warren revolution would be a conservative counterrevolu-tion, a return to the traditional practices of constitution-making. He pledged to discuss "what concrete demands the Restoration will make upon us" in the book's sequel.[70] That sequel was never to be. Instead, in an essay titled "The Death of the Constitution," Bozell argued that "the Constitution was no longer an operative charter of government" and there was no point in attempting "a revival of constitutional government," that careful orchestration of "checks and balances" thrown out of whack by the Warren Court. For even if the Constitu-tion were to be rescued from the usurpation of the court, the ills that troubled the nation would not be cured. For that to happen, "the *causes* of the country's spiritual and moral decline must be searched out; and where better to begin than at the country's beginnings, with the Constitution itself?" He assessed the "first principles" on which the American *res publica* rested and concluded that they were not good. If Murray thought the Framers had "built better than they knew," Bozell found that they built much worse than he had once thought.[71]

While the Framers were "an exceptionally learned and politically sophis-ticated group of men who were entirely at home with the grand concepts of the *res publica*: the ideas of Authority and Sovereignty; of Power and the ways of limiting it; of Freedom and Order; of the Rights of citizens and their obligations—and especially with the recent development of such ideas in the literature and experience of the West," they did not feel obliged to state explicitly the first principles of the new political system in the document that set out the "machinery of government." To find "an explicit statement and systematic elaboration of such principles"—that is, of "the ideas of Authority and Sovereignty"—one had to look elsewhere, to "the writings of the principal spokesperson of the period," but "above all to the two great documents that framed the Constitution in a single historical and ideational setting, the Declaration of Independence at one end and *The Federalist* at the other." A consideration of how the Framers imagined their machinery of government would illuminate the fundamental defect of their project, a project that was now coming to its inevitable bad fruition.[72]

The Declaration of Independence, Bozell wrote, "has the virtues for these purposes of having stated flatly and unequivocally the principle of authority under which the adopters of the federal Constitution performed the act of sovereignty that set up the American republic. '*Governments*,' the Declaration asserts, derive '*their just powers from the governed*.'" This he contrasted with "the Christian principle of authority," as explicated by Pope Leo XIII in *Immortale Dei*, in which political power proceeds from God and by way of nature delegated to human rulers. Divine sovereignty thus restricts the power wielded by sinful human beings. The will of the ruler—whether it be a monarch, an oligarchy, or the people themselves—needed to be fixed in accordance with the divine will; "the divine authority must be kept in view as a *limitation* on the sovereignty of 'the governed,' on *their* claim to authority." To assert otherwise, as the Declaration's claim that legitimate political authority emerges solely from the people appeared to do, means that "the civil order is in rebellion against the divine order, and must be prepared to accept whatever consequences such rebellion may entail."[73]

The signatories of the Declaration of Independence had thus rejected the Christian principle of authority. This was not to say that they had "understood themselves to be repudiating God." But all those acknowledgments of divinity in the Declaration amounted to nothing more than sundry rhetorical attempts "to summon God as a witness to their virtue and as an ally." "God was made the patron of America in much the same sense that Catholic countries adopted this or that saint as their patron. . . . God's authority in political affairs (as distinct from his existence) was denied; and the American republic came into being as

an autonomous entity answerable only to itself." The Declaration was a statement of rebellion not only against George III but also against the true King.
The birth of the United States thus marked a decisive break from the political
principles of medieval Christendom; the new state was an incarnation of the
unholy doctrine taught by Machiavelli, Hobbes, and Locke: "the idea that Man
is Lord of the world." "It is not a mysterious oversight by the Framers, as many
have imagined, that God is not mentioned in [the Constitution], let alone
treated as an authority," Bozell alleged. " 'We the People' (the Declaration's
'governed') are, in the premises, entirely sufficient authority for creating a
government and defining its powers. We the people do not mean to slight God,
to be irreverent; he simply does not figure, according to the conventions now in
force, in our civil order. . . . We do not by any means ordain an agnostic state;
we do not intend to abandon Christian 'values,' as they are presently understood; we simply propose to be fully free, as men are supposed to be, to make
our own history: we adopt this charter of government precisely to assure such
freedom."[74]

The other set of documents that framed the Constitution and elaborated
its principles of government, *The Federalist*, fared no better in Bozell's account.
The champions of the proposed Constitution promoted another false political
premise—a "constitutional morality." The very self-interest of the people, they
believed, could be exploited to keep the powers of government in check. Madison's theory was really just a "Calvinist rationalization" expecting that "the self-
aggrandizing tendencies of men occupying rival power centers would provide
reciprocal obstacles to misgovernment and tyranny; we would not have to
depend on, or even ask for, a *conscious* dedication to the common good." But
Madison did not consider the possibility that "the interests of the rival power
centers" might at some time come to coincide. What if, Bozell asked, "the President, the courts, Congress and the states came to the common conclusion that
it was inconvenient to resist secular-liberal demands to turn the American
republic into an officially agnostic state?" This was, of course, not a mere theoretical question. "The ultimate defect of our constitutional morality," Bozell
concluded, was that the people "had cut themselves off from the divinely
ordained restraint on civil power, and the only source of civil virtue—from the
Authority that is the final cause of the civil order." And so that order was now
collapsing. "The Constitution has not only failed; it was bound to fail. The
architects of our constitutional order built a house in which secular liberalism
could live, and given the dominant urges of the age, would live." America did not

enjoy a Christian-influenced founding as Murray had proposed, nor even a founding that Catholics could honestly accommodate themselves to as the "hypothesis." Restoring the nation's original foundations would not rescue it from its decline. The people needed "to leave that house and head for home." And that home was the one built on Peter's rock. America did not need a counterrevolution; it needed a counterreformation.[75]

A year later, the man who had voiced for Goldwater that "conservatism holds the key to national salvation" published a requiem for the movement. "Your supposed enemy, secular liberalism, has fallen," Bozell wrote to his erstwhile comrades, but they had not emerged from the struggle triumphant. The conservative program (summed up as anti-statism, nationalism, anti-Communism, and constitutionalism) had been abandoned; the movement had run out of energy. The reason for this failure, Bozell averred, was that both conservatism and secular liberalism were really branches of the same rotten tree, both nourished by the same flawed understanding of human beings and political life taught by nineteenth-century liberalism. (He acknowledged the "traditionalist" strain of American conservatism but regarded it as a nostalgic minority report.) Both shared "the parent ideal of self-fulfillment" that had "emerged as a modern, essentially un-Christian notion, from the Renaissance." The ideal of self-fulfillment, to be sure, had a spiritual dimension, but that could not be sustained without the moral discipline provided by the church—"man's fallen nature, unsupported by grace, tends to animalhood." The human's assertion of self-sufficiency (and denial of his status as a fallen creature) was a revolt against God, truth, and the divinely instituted order. The decadence and barbarism of secular liberal modernity is the inevitable consequence. This false anthropology of self-sufficiency shared by both left and right branches of liberalism lies at the basis of the American project and its overconfident faith in human liberty. American conservatives may regard themselves friendly to religion, but by relegating that dimension of our existence to the sphere of private life, they ignore that "the public life, as it now exists, is an enormous obstacle to virtue, if not to salvation" and "have not acknowledged the Christian teaching that the proper goal of the orderers of public life is to help open men to Christ."[76]

Given the evident failure of liberalism, Bozell imagined three possible avenues available for American conservatives: "You will find a place in the establishment as Nixon has, offering common-sense criticisms and suggestions which may be proximately useful. You will retire, perhaps to care for one of those moribund ideological projects like keeping America a republic because it is not a democracy. Or you will be driven (whether wittingly or no, I do not predict) to swell the ranks of a protofascist reaction to the collapse of secular liberalism. This last may have a political future of sorts." Bozell, however, did not believe that any of these possibilities would have any real impact. "The future," he told his former collaborators, "belongs only to those who keep touch with reality—that is, those who manage to keep open to Christ, who is Reality." He acknowledged that "old Christian forms for sanctifying the public life have become obsolete and thus do not provide a sufficient guide for the future." Other forms would need to be discovered.[77]

Other *Triumph* contributors echoed and elaborated on Bozell's views. William H. Marshner, for example, wrote that "America shares with all post-Catholic states the mistake of trying to put the state above religion and to substitute the distinction between public and private for that between political and supernatural." And yet, observing the revolutionary forces of the time (and those radicals within the church itself), he noted that the privatized morality would not remain so, but would fuel a "moral crusade" and a "new politics" striving to overthrow and replace the old "immoral" order and to abolish "the distinction between private and public." "Then, as in ancient totalitarianism, the political order absorbs the divine and divinizes its masters." This would no doubt come to pass—unless Catholics, whose tradition rejects "the attempt to put the state above religious differences," put their "politics [that is, the political order] first!"[78] Michael Lawrence contended that the American project ought to be regarded as a radical break with the Christian political tradition that had regarded as the primary purpose of politics helping human beings be virtuous "in a world flawed by evil," by means of "the infusion of Christianity into the world's political and social institutions so that those institutions become intrinsically and organically Christian, become, in fact, vehicles by which God's grace is communicated to man." While he conceded that the Puritans had attempted to bring about a new beginning for Christendom in their New England commonwealths, Lawrence held that the political vision of the United States was shaped by the quite different experience of Virginia, whose Declaration of Rights (1776) established a "wedge" separating the political from the religious orders. This was "a *derailment* of the Christian political tradition," in which path the Philadelphia Convention later followed. The American project rested on a misplaced confidence in the ability of the people themselves to maintain a virtuous government. Its conception of the relationship of the governed to the government reversed the "natural hierarchy of the Christian political order; it located the value of religion in the service it could offer to the government." Americans wrongly believed that "government ... is *not* to be infused with Christianity, not to be made a vehicle of divine grace." "We are a people who have banished God to a transcendence utterly divorced from the world," Lawrence lamented. "We have annulled Christendom's marriage of the transcendent to the immanent." What America needed, he announced, was nothing less than a new founding: "In symbolic terms, we are back on the boat, about to set foot for the first time in the New World. Our course must be to make a new compact; among ourselves and between ourselves and God, we are obliged to pledge that this land will be suffused far and wide, in every root and stone and in every artifact of our own devising, with the grace of God, who is the Most High and Awful Lord: and our most intimate companion in this New World."[79]

Triumph looked forward to that new founding, endeavoring to articulate a vision of a Christian politics and the order it could build to replace the decaying liberal regime. *Prayer as a Political Problem*, a little book by the French Cardinal Jean Daniélou, SJ, provided some inspiration. A Christian life and a Christian people, Daniélou argued, were only possible within a truly Christian civilization. Christendom is the medium through which the Christian message is communicated.[80] "The public life is supposed to help a man be a Christian," Bozell reflected in the second part of his "Letter" to his erstwhile comrades on the Right. "It is supposed to help him enter the City of God, and meanwhile it is supposed to help him live tolerably, even happily, in the City of Man." Unlike liberalism, which was premised on the false distinction between public and private life, a Christian politics would regard public life "as an extension of the interior life." (Bozell dryly noted that "John F. Kennedy became the liberal *par excellence* by announcing that his religion would not affect his presidency because it was 'a private affair.'") Sinful humanity requires not only order but also direction. As Daniélou had put it, "*It is practically impossible for any but the militant Christian to persevere in a milieu which offers him no support.*" And so the state would not be limited to the securing of public order and administration of justice. The state is to help conform its citizens to Christ, cultivate virtue, and orient them toward salvation. And such a politics would reach beyond the state, to the sacralization of all of life. "Christian politics is free to regard family and school, play and work, art and communication, the order of social relationships and the civil order, as integral parts of a whole: as integral and therefore mutually dependent aspects of civilization." Finally, a Christian politics would be attentive to the "quality" of this broadened public life and would look to provide *"sensible expressions of truth and beauty and love"* and *"sensible signs of the divine."* Art would be of especial importance to this endeavor.[81] "The success of that politics," Marshner avowed, "would make everything else fall into place: abortion, drugs, pornography, ecology, nuclear arms, economic justice—even Catholic dissidence"—that is, the radicals within the church, such as the Berrigan brothers and the then leftist Michael Novak, who mistakenly confuse and collapse supernatural salvation into political "liberation."[82]

Such a politics would not only use the mechanism of the state to inculcate virtue but would bring about the re-enchantment of the world, an entirely different way of being in the world. In his musings, Fritz Wilhelmsen struggled to express what an "incarnational politics" might look like. The Roman Catholic Church, he observed, "proclaims, through its faith in the Incarnation, a vocation to fashion creation anew and hallow all things so that they might participate in the Redemption of Our Lord Jesus Christ." Such activity, whether it be the anointing of kings or the blessing of fishing boats, was "the *civilizing* aspect of the Incarnation." Christians had once answered the call "to incarnate the Truth and the Grace of Christ in a civilization whose lineaments bore the mark of the Faith." Their public acts disclosed Catholicism as an "exoteric" religion. "Sacramentalizing the real includes the political and social orders," Wilhelmsen argued, "and our general vocation to redeem the world is specified in a human fashion by a call to rear up a truly Christian Order of Things."[83]

The striving for this *res publica Christiana* was based on a more optimistic, activist vision than the Christian politics of St. Augustine. The *City of God* only comprehended the inheriting of pagan institutions by Christian functionaries—"a Roman Empire led by Christian princes and staffed by Christian magistrates and soldiers." But the bishop of Hippo did not imagine "the possibility of a new cluster of institutions, themselves temporal, which would be integrally Christian." While Augustine distinguished the "city of man" from the "city of God," regarding the citizens of the latter as pilgrims wandering through the former, Wilhelmsen conceived of the city of man being drawn toward the city of God by means of Christians' sacramentalizing activity, shaped by "the public recognition that the only Sovereign in Christendom is Christ the King to whom all kings owed whatever portion of power and authority might be theirs." The result of their labors was "Christendom"—the civilization of medieval Europe. Wilhelmsen surveyed with wonder the manifold achievements of that civilization: "the preeminence of the family and the hallowed place of women; the gradual conversion of the slave into a serf and the serf into the free peasant; the free university whose authority stood so high that kings consulted it on the moral authority of political adventures; the sacredness of customary law; the institution of chivalry and the Christianizing of the profession of arms; a society of families governed by fathers, expressed politically in the popular Christian dynasty, and unencumbered by the quasi-totalitarian character of the pagan polis," and so on.[84]

But then came the deluge. The Protestant revolt against Rome resulted in the abandonment of the church's civilizing and sacralizing vocation. Luther commenced this process with his announcement of an utterly transcendent God and his rejection of Thomas Aquinas's "analogy of being." This severing of the linkages between human and divine, between nature and grace, had baleful consequences; human sinfulness required a secular power to maintain order, but that power was no longer charged with helping guide souls toward salvation. The exoteric dimension of Christian faith—its outworking in cultural productions and social institutions—was lost to the cribbed minds of the Reformers. Across the Channel, the Church of England effected "the subordination of ecclesiastical to the political," a move perfectly in tune with the emerging principle of nationalism. By misconceiving creation as corrupted, Calvinism "blocked any sacramental view of the world or of society." Calvin shattered the medieval unity by regarding God as "Totally Other," devaluing creation and casting out natural theology, and forging the this-worldly restlessness of the Puritan. These formations of Protestantism—heresies all—were unable "to call man to the specifically Christian task of civilizing the world," which could flow only from the true church's "highly sacramental view of creation." The Counter-Reformation came close to restoring the unity of European Christendom that had been disrupted by the Reformation, but by then it was really too late, those modern currents having become too powerful to resist. "The Protestant principle of the primacy of the individual conscience over the authority of the Church has become a public orthodoxy of the Secularized West," Wilhelmsen lamented. "This new orthodoxy has outlawed any corporate incarnation of Christian principles in the social and political order. The sacral universe has itself been outlawed." The now wholly secular state appropriated from religion the vital "horizontal task" of fashioning the world, consigning to the churches only the human being's "vertical" relationship with God.[85]

And so the unhappy story went . . . from Marsilius of Padua's *Defensor Pacis* to Thomas Hobbes's *Leviathan* to the authors of the *Federalist Papers*, all of these men aiming to diminish the end of politics from the "high virtue" once proclaimed by the pagans of antiquity and preached by the spiritual authorities of medieval Christendom. In the American case, the *Federalist* "urged upon our forebears the accumulation of wealth and the cultivation of private interests because these activities drain off enthusiasms that otherwise might harden into religious fanaticism which could lead the various factions to make the nation a battleground for their respective creeds." So far as religion was concerned, the attitude was the more the merrier: "Let creeds multiply merrily, the American 'solution' proclaimed: latitudinarianism will eventually dilute conviction; religion will retreat to the 'private sphere'—to the attic of the individual conscience, and to the sacristies whose doors are closed to the public forum." "The American founders wrote wisely from their point of view. They brought forth the only great power in history that has not been guilty of anything so indecent as a religious war," Wilhelmsen quipped.[86]

Meanwhile, the secularist conquest of Europe—its "de-Christianizing of the social order"—carried on unabated. True, its advance faced the determined resistance of the "splendid Catholic rally" and the valiant refusals of Popes Pius IX, Leo XIII, and St. Pius X to accommodate the church's teaching to the modern age. But they lacked the "secular arm" to back their vision with temporal power. In the end, the liberalism of the past two centuries had accomplished the "purposeful dismantling of the civilization that the Catholic Church had erected over fifteen hundred years." Those vestiges of Christian order (Wilhelmsen had authoritarian Spain and Portugal in mind) were looked on by the liberal governments with suspicion and hostility.[87]

What, then, was to be done by a people whose Faith demanded their civilizing activity in history and through public institutions? How does one re-enchant a disenchanted world? Wilhelmsen understood well that his mediations were untimely. "No democratic politician could conceivably get himself elected if he ran on a platform of sacramentalizing the political order. In most nations, including the United States, such an ambition would be tantamount to treason." All opportunities and avenues to the church's "civilizing" mission—in the universities, development programs, and so on—had been taken over by or surrendered to secular authorities. In such an environment "in which Catholics find themselves cut away from a role in history," Catholics face the temptation to relinquish the exoteric dimension of their religion—the idea of Christendom—and withdraw into esoteric mysticisms or, if they are still able to hold on to its activist character and to externalize it in contemporary social and political movements, to attempt "to graft the Church onto a tree whose roots are utterly foreign to the Faith." "Robbed of their own culture," Wilhelmsen lamented, "they have accepted an ape of the real thing, and have launched an elaborate campaign to accommodate the Church to secular society. Just as the French royalty in the last century attempted, with far more justification, to identify Throne and Altar, our liberal Catholics today identify Democracy and the Meal Table." But all such attempts in the end must fail at realizing the church's calling "to raise up a society integrally Christian in character."[88]

Nevertheless, Wilhelmsen remained optimistic. The impending collapse of the secular liberal order would present the opening for the next Christian era. "For nothing is clearer to men capable of evaluating history than that secularism—the process of desacralizing the real—is nearing the end of the road. The modern world is in its last agony; the age that began with the Renaissance is thrashing on a bed of death prepared by history itself," he wrote. Change was going to come; the sacral and secular would soon be rejoined into some new Christian unity.[89]

The professor may have been a monarchist at heart (he particularly revered the Spanish Carlists, who, in recognition of his efforts for their cause, made him a Knight of the Grand Cross of the Order of the Banished Legitimacy), but he was clear-sighted enough to realize that the trappings of a grand monarchial past could not be restored but might, as "symbolic figures," "serve as an inspiration for a future Christendom." That society would need to develop a novel, postmodern political form.[90] He thus cautioned his readers away from the restorationist approach of "Integrism," which he regarded not as a living possibility for an incarnational politics but as an "ideology of despair."[91] "Integrism tends to freeze Catholic political order, to identify it as necessarily bound up in the *forms* of some privileged moment in human history, usually the Middle Ages, occasionally the Age of the Fathers or even the baroque seventeenth century. For this reason, Integrism is marked by a despair of victory in the political order. . . . Integrism is elitist by nature. It tends to be excessively moralistic and to read damnation everywhere on the broad screen of the contemporary world: We—the chosen ones—have the key to the truth; we alone know what it means to be Catholic in a truly dense and incarnated fashion." And when the advocate of Integrism looks about the world and realizes that the restoration he hopes for will not come, as it is impossible to return to the old forms that have long become obsolete, such a person inescapably despairs. Such an ideology entrances an elite to turn inward, abandoning the Catholic mission to evangelize the world.[92] Neither did Wilhelmsen advocate the classical Augustinian tactic, now taken up by the members of Opus Dei, to "infiltrate the going order and Christianize it from inside itself." Rather than look wistfully to pasts that could not be recovered, he counseled traditionalist Catholics to embrace a postmodern future. A friend and enthusiast of the Canadian media theorist Marshall McLuhan, Wilhelmsen envisioned that new "electronic" technologies such as television might present opportunities for the Catholic spirit to exploit, providing "the technical ground" for a figure (the head of a new dynastic family?) who could represent the "personalist order" of incarnational politics. For the moment, however, the professor could only make vague gestures: "Let us accept the new barbarism and Christianize it. . . . We must seize this moment for the sake of Eternity."[93]

"America today is not a Christian country," Bozell declared in a programmatic essay in 1970. Indeed, he said that it had never been a Christian country publicly, much less a Catholic one. But "is it not time to make America a Christian country?" To his own question, Bozell answered in the negative—"that time has passed; it is time to do something else."[94] And so the visionaries of *Triumph* hoped to gather and fashion a cadre of committed American Roman Catholics, to forge a countercultural theological-political vanguard prepared to usher in a new sacral politics as the secular liberal order collapsed around them. While they labored on the margins of the American political scene, they did not advise the faithful to wait out the deluge or to take their cues from a dispirited hierarchy but rather to join a "confessional tribe."

Their strategy was not narrowly political. ("What Incarnational politics needs far more fundamentally than a political program is a political philosophy," Wilhelmsen suggested.)[95] They did not look to the formation of a "Christian" political party (or the takeover of an already existing third party) that would work to implement policies through the democratic process.[96] The ground was simply not prepared for such a program. "America is separated from Christendom, which is the political expression of Christian belief, by more centuries than the nation has existed," Bozell admitted. "There is no shared standard or goal. What is more, the American experience has cultivated highly sophisticated and deeply engrained civilizational habits antithetical to Christianity, which have become a second nature to the vast majority of its population." American citizens were not yet open to a truly Christian program and would not "shake off such habits" overnight. They had first to learn and cultivate Christian habits. And then they needed to transform the "American way of life" to a Christian one.[97]

Rather than trying to compete within a collapsing political order, American Catholics needed instead to have the "spiritual *lebensraum*" from which to build up a "city hospitable to Christian living," first in their imaginations and then in the world, in which the church—as first citizen—would be "the anchor for the whole public thing," its laws serving as the city's basic constitution (to which all human laws would comport), its liturgical calendar of ceremonies and feasts and fasts setting the "rhythm of public life," its arts decorating and perfuming its avenues and streets. In such a city, the family would be hallowed, contraception would be prohibited, divorce discouraged, and the abortionist would face "the coldest fury of the public justice." As this city "would view life as a training ground for sanctity," its schools would be Christian, which would "convey to the young the unity of truth, the role of every part of creation in the orchestration of salvation." The city's other social arrangements would be configured so as to provide "sensible supports for the virtues taught in family and school." ("The city would not have a First Amendment," Bozell duly noted.) Its foreign policy would be "imperialist," its mandate to go and teach the nations as instructed by Christ's Great Commission. Wars would from time to time erupt—for on this side of paradise there will tragically always be rivalries among nations—but would be faithfully prosecuted according to just war doctrine. But such a city "would never really know defeat. For in success or in failure it would have been obedient to the victory on the Cross."[98]

But that city was a long way off. And the secular city in which they currently resided was in rebellion against the King. The "formal public agnosticism" of the American system demanded the exile of Christ "from the public life which He came to occupy at the Incarnation." In this sense, America was no different from officially atheistic Soviet Union. Perhaps, Bozell mused, the situation was even worse here, as American Christians were "not blessed with an active persecution" that would fortify their souls.[99]

The exile of Christ was most evident in the "expropriation of his most intimate possession"—that is, of human life itself (by means of birth control and abortion). "By asserting the power to control and manipulate the production of human life—by usurping authority over what ontologically belongs to the King, because its destiny is the King—this city has escalated the war against Christ to the highest level. American law requires Christians to support this usurpation."[100] Under present circumstances, "the question is not whether America is able to become Christian, but whether Christians are able to be Americans."[101]

But perhaps that, too, was the wrong question. Social orders were still transforming; what had been "the dominant form of organization—the national state" was "giving way to something else." While some "less perceptive" observers (but really "ideologues") believed that the trend was toward global unity, Bozell saw the world moving toward greater "separateness." What was on the horizon as "the successor arrangement to the national city is not the world city, but the tribe." He delineated the differences between the city (based on "force") and the tribe (based on "affinity"), the latter "essentially *exclusive*," producing "a common style of life that flows organically out of the bond," and the former ostensibly accommodating but eventually assimilating the "diverse styles of life" that come to reside within its borders. He called on Christians to think of themselves as members of a worldwide tribe apart from the nations. They were people who "salute the Cross, before any flag." Theirs would be a new kind of movement whose postmodern purpose "is not to reform the American system. It is not to destroy the American system. The movement's purpose is to be the Christian system"—that is, "to establish the temporal conditions hospitable to the Gospel life."[102] "Christians must renounce modernity's lust for wealth and power—for secular redemption—and turn to their preeminent vocation, to the most militant form of Catholic Christianity: the imitation of Christ and the reconversion of the world to the Cross," he announced a few months later. By rallying together as a "confessional tribe," Bozell and his allies could raise the spiritual consciousness of their coreligionists and prepare the inauguration of a new Christendom.[103]

While sympathetic to Bozell's deep critique of contemporary America, some of *Triumph*'s most distinguished readers were nonetheless perplexed by his dream of forging a counterrevolutionary Catholic vanguard to bring about some future theocratic order. The intellectual historian Stephen J. Tonsor, for example, called "The Confessional Tribe" "a gloriously wrongheaded piece. . . . Well-intentioned, serious, windy, mistaken and tacitly insane." Bozell's program, he wrote, was based on "a false notion of the Church and the role of the Church in relation to secular society." He chastised *Triumph*'s editor for yielding to "the temptation to translate religion into politics and politics into religion" and "dressing up in the rags of Spanish romantic politics." And he cautioned him about the danger of sacralizing the secular order: "I believe you should have no illusions about the purposes of civil government. It is not to make men good, it is not to save their souls, but simply to enable men to live together with a minimum of strife and disorder. Beyond this it cannot go and wise men ought to refuse the temptation to enact their faith and their moral sensitivities into law."[104] Will Herberg, the Jewish theologian and religion editor at the *National Review*, wrote that "your goal—'to be the Christian system,' even to reconstitute the 'Christian tribe'—seems to me genuinely Christian. But it seems to me also to raise very difficult, perhaps insurmountable, problems on the civil and cultural planes." He advised Bozell to pause and reflect on the paradox of "Christian politics" as set forth by Augustine in *City of God*.[105]

Bozell was not deterred. To further the apostolate, he and his associates with the Society for the Christian Commonwealth launched a number of initiatives, most prominently the Christian Commonwealth Institute (CCI), a summer institute for college students held at El Escorial in Spain, a guild program, a lecture bureau, and a number of smaller newsletters.[106] The CCI became the basis of a later endeavor, the four-year liberal arts Christendom College, established in 1977 in Front Royal, Virginia. Bozell also helped organize the ecumenical pro-life lobbying group Americans United for Life, which led the June 6, 1970, antiabortion demonstration at George Washington University Hospital in Washington, DC. Following a Mass of the Holy Innocents at nearby St. Stephen Martyr Church, some three hundred protestors carrying processional crucifixes and papal flags made their way toward the hospital. Their number included a score of young activists from the University of Dallas calling themselves Los Hijos de Tormenta ("The Sons of Thunder," an allusion to Mark 3:17), bedecked in khakis and red berets and rosaries and Sacred Heart patches in the manner of the Carlist Requetés. Wilhelmsen addressed the crowd in such a prophetic pitch that one of his students feared he might suffer a stroke. Seven of the protestors, including Bozell and one of his sons, made their way past the police and into the clinic, chanting, "Viva Cristo Rey!" After a scuffle with the authorities, they were charged with unlawful entry and damaging property. They were found guilty but got away with only suspended sentences and five years' probation. Such were some of the Acts of the Confessional Tribe.[107]

Such radicalism in thought and deed had intriguing parallels with the anti-war Catholic Left but was worlds away from the concord between Roman Catholicism and American republicanism that had been advocated by Father John Courtney Murray.[108] The Americanist controversy of the late nineteenth century, Michael Lawrence reminded his readers, was a struggle over "whether one could be both truly Catholic and truly American." The proximate question was whether Catholics ought to pursue education in parish schools or seek accommodations within the public school system. But the deeper one was over the Catholic embrace of American political forms. Yet both sides in the quarrel—the Americanists as well as their conservative opponents—maintained their mission was to convert the people to the true religion, to make the nation Catholic. Lawrence maintained that "the essential error of

Americanism" was "the belief that the Church can not only survive under the American political arrangement, but can thrive, prosper and flourish more fully under that arrangement than any other." But Catholics could not maintain both "a commitment to the politics of Americanism" and a commitment to "the evangelizing requirements of Roman Catholicism." America did not meet the condition of the "hypothetical case"—the "tolerable political arrangement"— of the church's teaching on the relation of church and state. For in such a case "the non-confessional state is a tolerable political arrangement, provided that the state does not interfere with her freedom to teach—does not interfere, that is, with her efforts to convert the political order." However, rather than providing the conditions of the Catholic "hypothesis," American pluralism stood in "an aggressive contradiction" to it. "Pluralism," Lawrence contended, "may be defined as a theory of politics that envisions an on-going competition among its constituent units for recognition as Possessors of the Truth, which denies, however, the possibility of ever recognizing a winner of the competition." The First Amendment demands that "the competition must go on." Put another way, a society organized around maintaining freedom over submission to the Truth as the highest good is one in which the Truth has no rights.[109]

But "Catholics don't believe that truth is relative. If they are sure about anything, it is that Christ did not come into the world to announce to men that they could believe whatever they like," Lawrence declared.[110] They understand the hypothesis to be "a transitional arrangement" that would pertain only so long as to convince enough people of the Truth so that the thesis could be implemented. And such a political order "will endorse and sanction those truths, will hold them as she holds them—will 'confess' them as an outward sign of a God-centered morality." This would necessarily entail the termination of the American way of religious pluralism. The honest Catholic "would admit that if he could, he *would*, in due season, make certain adjustments in the American system."[111] To believe in the Truth—and to act on such beliefs—was to be, in the eyes of American pluralists, un-American. Which brings us back to Father John Courtney Murray and his attempt to relieve this tension and shield American Catholics of the charge of hypocrisy:

> Fr. Murray's adjustment of Catholic theory was marvellously uncompli-
> cated. It simply turned the thesis-hypothesis doctrine upside-down.
> Henceforth the thesis—the ideal arrangement—would be pluralism;
> and the hypothesis—the tolerable, but ultimately unsatisfactory

arrangement—would be the confessional state. The ultimate goal of all enlightened Catholic peoples, in short, would be to emulate the American pluralist society. From now on a suspicion of hypocrisy might be directed at, say, the Spanish Catholic who pledged allegiance to a confessional state while conceding its ultimate undesirability. But Americanist Catholics would be blissfully free from the appearances of inconsistency. Having been married to the American theory of Freedom, they could now not only practice what they preached, they could convincingly preach what other Americans preached.

"Father Murray's field was not political theory, but etiquette," Lawrence quipped, "his purpose in abandoning the confessional state having been to make it possible for Catholics to be sociable."[112] *Mater, sí; Murray, no.*

This was not, to be sure, an entirely accurate account of Murray's argument and its influence. Lawrence elided the Jesuit's appeal to natural law and his nonideological interpretation of the First Amendment. And he incorrectly suggested that it was somehow on account of "the Murray dispensation" that John F. Kennedy "could make it to the American presidency by believably disowning any intention to use the office to defend Catholic moral positions on education, birth control or abortion." Lawrence was incensed with what he saw as the effect of Murray's revision of Catholic political teaching whereby "the Americanist Church in general, several years later, could believably disown any ambition to convert the country to Catholicism."[113] Indeed, John Courtney Murray served as a convenient symbol for the kind of American Catholicism *Triumph* disdained. In any event, by that hour Murray's vision of Americanism was already in decline; even if there had ever been an "American consensus," which the *Triumph* tribe would deny, it was now self-evident that a good number of the people no longer held those truths. Moreover, demographically America was moving beyond the "Protestant, Catholic, Jew, secularist" configuration that defined the 1940s and '50s. Murray himself had worried that it was breaking down. Did it even make sense to speak of consensus anymore?[114]

The Catholics of *Triumph* subscribed to a much different vision. Their dream was of course the nightmare of those Lyman Beechers, Josiah Strongs, and Paul Blanshards, and all who regarded Romanism as an existential threat to the republic. Catholicism and American institutions—insofar as the former taught universal and timeless truths and the latter were manifestations of the modern secular liberal worldview, of error—were indeed ultimately at loggerheads. The fervent Catholic ought to aspire to win over his fellow citizens to the Truth and, when that has been sufficiently accomplished, to work to implement the "thesis." William F. Buckley Jr. decried *Triumph* as "an organ of militant Catholicism" that had become "an organ of militant anti-Americanism"—in the words of a correspondent, "as hostile to the American ethos as any revolutionary organ on the hard Left."[115] The *Triumph* tribe may have replied: extremism in the defense of virtue was no vice. Reflecting back on the pronouncements of the summer of 1968 from the vantage point of the autumn of 1973, Bozell conceded that in the heat of the moment the editors might have gone too far; their judgment against the republic "probably entailed too great a tilt towards nihilism," a desire to give it "a small, last shove." Yet, while their prediction of the republic's imminent demise was premature, the "basic diagnosis of the disease" and the prognosis were nevertheless correct.[116] To accept that the church needed to make peace with secular liberal modernity— "to adapt herself somewhat to our advanced civilization, and, relaxing her ancient rigor, show some indulgence to modern popular theories and methods"[117]—would be a betrayal of its very mission. Catholicism did not need to figure out a way to become more relevant to or come to terms with the world; the world rather needed to reconcile itself to the universal and eternal verities that had been vouchsafed to Rome. Bozell and his associates dreamed that their counterculture would ultimately transform the culture, recasting America as a Catholic-dominated—and Catholic-saturated—society. "We Catholics are not in the business of making peace with the American political order. We are in the business of converting the people of this land, and of sacramentalizing its institutions."[118] But it was telling that the Catholics of *Triumph* had a difficult time describing what their hoped-for confessional sacramental state would actually look like and how it might come to be.

In the meantime, America (Protestant, Catholic, Jew, and otherwise) remained recalcitrant, oblivious to the allures of that vision of Christendom. Even Spain, the imagined bastion of the old order, was succumbing to the temptations of liberalism. The scribes of the confessional tribe continued to fulminate, but the secular apocalypse that Bozell had prophesized had not come to pass. Ten years after it was launched and after much sound and fury, the magazine quietly folded, having failed to realize the triumph of radical Christianity over American secularism.

CHAPTER SIX

The Constitution Cannot Save
This Country

The Theonomists

"Let us never forget," the Reverend Jerry Falwell exclaimed near the outset of his 1980 book, *Listen, America!*, "that as our Constitution declares, we are endowed by our Creator with certain inalienable rights. It is only as we abide by those laws established by our Creator that He will continue to bless us with these rights. We are endowed our rights to freedom and liberty and the pursuit of happiness by the God who created man to be free and equal."[1]

This was a remarkable statement, both for its (con)fusion of America's foundational texts and for its implication that those very rights of life, liberty, and the pursuit of happiness were not truly unalienable but granted condition-ally, contingent on the people's piety and obedience. The words may have been Jefferson's, but the spirit was Moses's. In Falwell's view, America was indeed a chosen nation, a "New Israel." (For those who had ears to listen, it was easy to catch in the title of the book the allusion to Deuteronomy 6:4—"Hear, O Israel!") A page later Falwell declared that "I am positive in my belief regarding the Constitution that God led in the development of that document, and as a result, we here in America have enjoyed 204 years of unparalleled freedom." That merging of the Declaration of Independence into the Constitution allowed Falwell to elide the scandal of the "godless Constitution" that had vexed so many earlier conservative Christians. No amendment was necessary.[2] The problem was not a flawed founding but the people's apostasy. "Our religious heritage and our liberty can never be separated," Falwell wrote. "America is in trouble today because her people are forgetting the origin of their liberty, and questioning the authority and inerrancy of the Bible."[3]

Falwell was a relative newcomer to the political scene. For years, the founder of the Thomas Road Baptist Church had styled himself a "separatist, premillennialist, pre-tribulationist sort of fellow," staying aloof from politics, whether that be in fighting Communism or supporting civil rights. "The Christian has his citizenship in the Royal Nation of Heaven," he proclaimed in a 1965 sermon titled "Ministers and Marchers." "Preachers are not called to be politicians but to be soul-winners." Falwell himself went about preaching the Word at Thomas Road, cultivating a national television audience with his *Old-Time Gospel Hour*, and founding a Christian academy and college. In the bicentennial year 1976, however, Falwell had a change of heart and journeyed along with his Liberty Baptist College choir from state to state to headline a series of "I Love America" rallies on the steps of capitols and state houses. Three years later, the politicized pastor was recruited by conservative activists to organize the Moral Majority. The organization pitched a big tent for its revival, hoping to gather together fundamentalists, evangelicals, and other conservative Protestants and join hands with similarly concerned Roman Catholics, and even Jews and Mormons, to rescue the nation from moral and political decline. Falwell renounced his previous apolitical separation from the world as "false prophecy." The times required that internecine theological disputes and quarrels between faith traditions be set aside for cultural and political cobelligerency.[4]

Several factors goaded fundamentalists like Falwell who had long eschewed political engagement (and kept their distance from non-fundamentalist Christians) to enter the fray and join the cluster of organizations with names like the Moral Majority, Religious Roundtable, and the National Christian Action Coalition that came to comprise the "New Religious Right." There was, of course, still the decades-old crusade against godless Communism to be won. But there were also the Lord's enemies at home who needed to be exposed, confronted, and vanquished. The Supreme Court, by deciding long-standing religious exercises such as nonsectarian prayer and Bible reading in the public schools were unconstitutional, had cast God out of the schools.[5] The anti-Christian counterculture of the sixties had become the dominant culture of the seventies. Feminists brazenly inveighed against the patriarchal order; the growing acceptance of homosexuality and other forms of sexual deviance exposed America's disobedience to God and his created order. Rising divorce rates and the increasing number of children being born out of wedlock were bringing about the collapse of the "traditional family." And in 1973, the Supreme Court licensed the murder of innocent unborn children with its decision in *Roe v. Wade*. Pornography and drug use were rampant. America's continuing struggle with racial inequality also figured in the mix. While the major battles of the civil rights movement had concluded, the Civil Rights Act of 1964 and the Voting Rights Act of 1965 having put an end to the Jim Crow regime, the federal government's attempts to enforce those provisions, leading to the Supreme Court rulings in *Green v. Connally* (1972) that revoked the tax-exempt status of institutions practicing segregation (and the subsequent IRS enforcement against the fundamentalist Bob Jones University), were regarded by the New Religious Right as an assault on their religious liberty.[6] They saw before them a landscape of disorder, decadence, and degeneration. As one observer summed up the anxiety, "America is the last launching pad for world evangelism, and if it falls to Communism— as a result of its own moral decay—that will mean the end of Christianity."[7]

From their pulpits and over the airwaves, the prophets of the Right pronounced jeremiads on the people. A once-righteous nation had lost its way, seduced by the false creed of "secular humanism" (which had become the established religion of the land).[8] Its moral and political foundations were being undermined by the impious elites who had captured the courts, the universities, and the media. Americans had broken the covenant and had gone whoring after strange gods, worshiping with promiscuous abandon the idols of the self, sexual liberation, and material satisfactions. They needed to turn back to God in repentance or face retribution.

Behind all this was a grand national mythology, a story of providential planting and covenantal founding, of a good and godly nation chosen as an instrument for the salvation of the world. The Puritan settlers' covenant with God and one another set the pattern for civil government and laid the foundations "not merely of American democracy, but of the Kingdom of God in America."[9] The American Revolution was a just and holy war fought by pious Christian men against British tyranny. The Constitution was designed on biblical principles to establish a godly republic. "Any diligent student of American history finds that our great nation was founded by godly men upon godly principles to be a Christian nation," Falwell wrote. "Our Founding Fathers were not all Christians, but they were guided by biblical principles. They developed a nation predicated on Holy Writ."[10] He recounted the Christian background of the early English settlements and the influence of the revivals of the Great Awakening on the colonists' attitude toward the British rule. He called attention to the Reverend Jacob Duché's prayer at the opening of the First Continental Congress and one of his 1775 sermons (neglecting, of course, the clergyman's later political apostasy) and enumerated statements of religious piety by Benjamin Franklin, John Adams, Patrick Henry, and George Washington—all of this to bestow the impression of a nation that had from its very beginning acknowledged its dependence on God. The Founding Fathers "based our system of government on the First Commandment," so that citizens would "serve God, not the state," that the people would "govern themselves under God's laws." The Constitution founded a "republic" and not a "democracy" (which he defined simply as a regime based on the rule of the majority).[11] Congress adopted the First Amendment so as to prevent the establishment of a state church, not to separate religion from government and establish instead a secular state. The so-called wall of separation between church and state did not entail the wholesale divorce of religion from government or the silencing or removal of religious voices from the public square. Those mid-twentieth-century Supreme Court decisions that prohibited some of these practices were based on an inventive and erroneous reading of the First Amendment and marked a tragic departure from the country's veritable traditions. A restoration of the original settlement would heal the nation of its ills, vanquish its domestic enemies, and make America great again.[12] This story—that the United States was founded as a Christian nation, governed by a Constitution penned by a team of devout Christian men and premised on and shaped by Christian principles—was promoted by other propagandists of the New Christian Right such as Tim LaHaye, John W. Whitehead, Homer Duncan, and John Eidsmore.[13] Some went so far as to say that the Framers were inspired men, the document that they produced the result of the "Miracle in Philadelphia."[14]

"While it is true that we are not a theocracy, as was ancient Israel, we nevertheless are a nation that was founded upon Christian principles, and we have enjoyed a unique relationship to God because of that foundation," Falwell claimed.[15] And, as it was in ancient Israel, the answer to America's present disorder was repentance and restoration of that "traditional America." The people needed to recommit themselves to Christ, and their chosen yet prodigal nation needed to repent and reaffirm its covenant. As Falwell put it, "America must not turn away from the God who established her and who blessed her. It is time for Americans to come back to the faith of our fathers, to the Bible of our fathers, and to the biblical principles that our fathers used as a premise for this nation's establishment." His proof text was 2 Chronicles 7:14, a perennial of American Christian nationalism. "The answer to every one of our nation's dilemmas is a spiritual one," Falwell wrote. "When we as a country again acknowledge God as our Creator and Jesus Christ as the Savior of mankind, we will be able to turn this nation around economically as well as in every other way." He concluded his manifesto weaving together his conception of biblical morality, the faith of the Founders, and the American way of life: "Right living must be re-established as an American way of life. We as American citizens must recommit ourselves to the faith of our fathers and to the premises and moral foundations upon which this country was established."[16]

The revival would not be solely religious. Committed Christian patriots were not only to return to the Lord in prayer and repentance; the aim of the New Christian Right was to get them registered and to the voting booth. A coming great awakening would manifest itself in political mobilization. The moral concerns of the New Christian Right dovetailed perfectly with the Republican Party's policy priorities on such issues as taxes, government regulation, defense spending, and foreign policy.[17] The leaders of the New Christian Right also proudly proclaimed their staunch support for the State of Israel, their Christian Zionism shaped by multiple considerations—premillennial dispensationalist prophecy, religious belief that God would bless those who blessed the great nation that had come from Abraham (Genesis 12:1–3), and the regard for the Jewish state as a civilizational ally and a bastion against the Soviet Union. (Ostentatious displays of pro-Israel sentiment did not, however, inhibit preachers such as Falwell from regarding Jews as "spiritually blind" and in need of salvation through faith in Jesus Christ.)[18]

This was, as historian Mark Silk noted, "a gospel . . . of the Reagan dispensation."[19] In 1980, these defenders of America's moral order hitched their hopes for restoration to the Republican Party and its standard-bearer. While the self-proclaimed born-again Southern Baptist Jimmy Carter had enjoyed much support from evangelicals four years earlier, his administration's progressive views on the family and civil rights alienated many. His Republican challenger, though divorced, formerly pro-choice, and religiously heterodox, was loudly speaking their language, preaching against Communism and America's moral decline and promising a restoration of a "shining city on a hill," and running on a platform that endorsed constitutional amendments to ban abortion and congressional initiatives to restore voluntary prayer in public schools.[20] The mobilization of conservative Protestants, by means of voter registration drives and direct mail advertisements, helped Reagan take the White House, and they emerged a prominent GOP constituency. With their newly gained access to the corridors of power, would they be able to roll back the advances of secular humanism and restore the nation to its moral foundations? Or was the situation such that more drastic, possibly revolutionary action would be required to make America holy again?

That was the question raised by the man who had come to be regarded as "the intellectual guru of the Christian Right," Francis A. Schaeffer IV.[21] A youthful convert to Christianity, Schaeffer had enrolled for a few years at the conservative Westminster Theological Seminary, where he studied with Cornelius Van Til, an influential professor of apologetic theology. After a stint under the tutelage of fundamentalist radio preacher Carl McIntire, Schaeffer took leave of the United States to work as a missionary in Switzerland, where he established in the mountains a Christian educational retreat called L'Abri (The Shelter). L'Abri opened its doors to welcome spiritual seekers of all stripes. The countercultural guru preached the gospel in terms that spoke to readers of existentialist philosophy and listeners of pop music, and he expounded a throughgoing critique of modern Western civilization. In numerous books and the film series *How Shall We Then Live?* (directed by his firebrand son, Franky), Schaeffer popularized the notion that the spiritual decline and moral chaos of the West was the inevitable consequence of the emergence and steady advance of "secular humanism." The foundations of Christianity that Western civilization had been built on had been eroding ever since Thomas Aquinas smuggled Aristotle back into European thought and, by liberating human reason from the dictates of revelation, opened the floodgates of a philosophy that placed humankind at the center of all things.

Though he had become something of a pop celebrity among evangelicals on account of his books and films, Schaeffer may well have remained ensconced in his Alpine retreat, spending his days in his lederhosen lecturing backpackers on the decline of the West, had he not been coaxed by his son to take a leading role in the battle against abortion. Schaeffer committed his energies to shepherding heretofore reluctant evangelicals into what was at the time still a largely Catholic movement. With Franky and the renowned pediatric surgeon C. Everett Koop, Schaeffer made a four-hour documentary, *Whatever Happened to the Human Race?*, which depicted the procedure in graphic detail and prophesied a nation increasingly desensitized to the murder of innocents, the old, the infirm, and the unwanted. Such were the poisonous fruits of the false religion of secular humanism.

Schaeffer's political efforts culminated in a slender volume titled *A Christian Manifesto*. Published in 1981, just as Ronald Reagan was settling into the White House, the book set out to explicate "the Christian's relationship to government, law, and civil disobedience."[22] It sold hundreds of thousands of copies, becoming, according to one commentator, "the single most significant statement of Christian conservative political thinking." (Falwell saw fit to include a copy in his "God Bless America Survival Kit" sent out to sixty-two thousand contributors.)[23]

In *A Christian Manifesto* (its title a righteous retort to the *Communist Manifesto* and the *Humanist Manifesto I* and *II*), Schaeffer marshaled the arguments he had developed in his earlier work into political service. He depicted a contest between two totalizing worldviews: the Christian and the "humanist" ("based on the idea that the final reality is impersonal matter or energy shaped into its present form by impersonal chance," which results in the delusion that "man is the measure of all things"). "We live in a democracy, or republic, in this country which was born out of the Judeo-Christian base," Schaeffer claimed, but without a "Christian consensus to contain it," America's "form-freedom balance in government" would devolve into chaos or usher in tyranny.[24]

The key figure in Schaeffer's historical reconstruction was the president of the College of New Jersey, Presbyterian minister, and leading Patriot John Witherspoon. Witherspoon was a signatory to the Declaration of Independence, an advocate of the Constitution of the United States, and a teacher of many leading lights of the revolution and of the republic that it brought into being, and his work demonstrated that the "linkage of Christian thinking and the concepts of government were not incidental but fundamental." And Witherspoon, Schaeffer alleged, had been influenced by the seventeenth-century Scottish Covenanter Samuel Rutherford, the author of the treatise *Lex, Rex, or The Law and the Prince* (1644), which argued that the king and government are subject to God's revealed law. Schaeffer further suggested that Rutherford's theological-political thought had profound influence on Thomas Jefferson by way of John Locke's secularization of the political theology of *Lex, Rex*. Thus, even the seemingly "Enlightenment" basis of American political thinking was dependent on the Scottish Reformation. Schaeffer concluded that the drafters and signers of the Declaration of Independence and the framers and ratifiers of the Constitution were consequently its political heirs. "These men really knew what they were doing," he wrote. "We cannot say too strongly that they really understood the basis of the government which they were founding. Think of this great flaming phrase: 'certain inalienable rights.' Who gives the rights? The state? Then they are not inalienable because the state can change them and take them away. Where do rights come from? They understood that they were founding the country upon the concept that goes back into the Judeo-Christian thinking that there is Someone there who gave the inalienable rights."[25]

Yet, even as the country was deeply rooted in Christian ideas, those ideas needed constant tending and support. For too long the American churches had failed to maintain their role as the "salt and light in our culture and our society." And so the inevitable decline—the movement away from this Judeo-Christian (but really Reformed) basis of government and "the takeover of our government and law by . . . the materialistic, humanistic, chance world view." Despite his appeal to the "Judeo-Christian" tradition, Schaeffer hinted that religious pluralism had been part of the problem, the mid-nineteenth-century influx of immigrants (specifically Catholics and Jews) having brought about "a sharp increase in viewpoints not shaped by Reformation Christianity." The reality of religious diversity was then exploited by humanists to endorse their own moral relativism. Their doctrine ("There is no right or wrong; it is just a matter of your personal preference") came to be taught in the schools and promulgated by the media and had taken over the law and the courts, as evidenced by the Supreme Court's arbitrary *Roe v. Wade* ruling (which is to be lamented not only because it licenses murder but also as it reveals that "the law and the courts became the vehicle for forcing a totally secular concept on the population"). The First Amendment had been ratified so that there would be "no established, national church" and no federal interference with the free exercise of religion, but Schaeffer claimed that the separation of church and state "is used to silence the church" and "is used today as a false political dictum in order to restrict the influence of Christian ideas." Indeed, "*it is the humanist religion* which the government and courts in the United States favor over all others!"[26]

The election of Reagan presented what Schaeffer called "an open window"—the opportunity for conservative Christians to push back against the humanist worldview and the advances it had made in culture, law, and government. But that window would not remain open for long, he warned, and those early victories might not bring about sustained cultural and political conquests. He worried, too, that many who supported the Reagan Revolution did so not out of Christian principles but out of their own material self-interest ("the two bankrupt values": to secure their "personal peace" and "to increase their own affluence"), and that if those gains did not materialize, "some form of an elite authoritarianism" (most likely through the courts) would come to be, putting into place policies that would more deeply encroach on the rights not only of conservative Protestants but of conservative Catholics and Jews as well. Whatever one thought of the Moral Majority (and having spent some time with the likes of Jerry Falwell and Pat Robertson, Schaeffer was ambivalent about the movement, its leadership, and its commitment to a number of Republican policy preferences), its foot soldiers had taken a stand in the tradition of Rutherford; they "carried the fact that law is king, law is above the lawmakers, and God is above the law into this area of life where it always should have been."[27]

And here the radical and potentially violent facet of Schaeffer's *Manifesto* came to light. If that open window was to be forced shut, if the state was to turn its powers against Christianity, then Christians must be ready to defend themselves and their convictions, by means of resistance if necessary. Schaeffer sought to prepare righteous minds for the possibility of some revolutionary action, drawing the parallel between the tyranny the Founding Fathers opposed and the situation confronting contemporary Christian conservatives. He noted that the Christian teaching of submitting to instituted authority (citing that cluster of classic New Testament proof texts: Matthew 22:21; Romans 13:1–4; 1 Peter 2:13–17) did not require obedience to injustice. "God has ordained the state as a *delegated* authority; it is not autonomous. The state is to be an agent of justice, to restrain evil by punishing the wrongdoer, and to protect the good in society. When it does the reverse, *it has no proper authority*. It is then a usurped authority and as such it becomes lawless and is tyranny." Schaeffer evoked the martyrdom of early Christians cast to the lions for their refusal to worship Caesar as a god, but disobedience could play out in different ways. "In almost every place where the Reformation had success there was some form of civil disobedience or armed rebellion." "*The bottom line*," he decreed, "is that at a certain point there is not only the right, but the duty, to disobey the state."[28]

Again, Schaeffer appealed to *Lex, Rex* as he "set forth the proper Christian response to nonbiblical acts by the state." When the state acted contrary to the principles of God's law, in an immoral and tyrannical manner, relinquishing its legitimate function as a ministry of justice, Christians have both the right and duty of resistance. Now, a magistrate was not to be removed from office on account of a single transgression against this rule. "Only when the magistrate acts in such a way that the governing structure of the country is being destroyed—that is, when he is attacking the fundamental structure of society—is he to be relieved of his power and authority." "That is exactly what we are facing today," Schaeffer declared. "The whole structure of our society is being attacked and destroyed. It is being given an entirely opposite base which gives exactly opposite results. The reversal is much more total and destructive than that which Rutherford or any of the Reformers faced in their day."[29] Just as Rutherford had called on Scottish Presbyterians to depose tyrants, and the American Patriots acted in self-defense in their "conservative counter-revolution" against the British,[30] so too contemporary Christian patriots needed to gird their loins for battle. "Simply put, the Declaration of Independence states that the people, if they find that their basic rights are being systematically attacked by the state, have a *duty* to try to change that government, and if they cannot do so, to abolish it."[31] The Christian tradition of resistance manifested in the Declaration of 1776 provided the warrant for civil disobedience or regime change today. "*If there is no final place for civil disobedience, then the government has been made autonomous, and as such, it has been put in the place of the Living God,*" Schaeffer thundered. "If there is no final place for civil disobedience, then the government has been put in the place of the living God, because then you are to obey it even when it tells you in its own way at that time to worship Caesar. And that point is exactly where the early Christians performed their acts of civil disobedience even when it cost them their lives."[32] Schaeffer did not specify the differences between the early Christian martyrs willingly going to their deaths for their refusal to worship the Roman cult, the American Patriots who chose to toss off the yoke of British imperial rule over a tax dispute, and contemporary pro-life activists.

But what should replace the secular humanist regime? Even as he called on Americans to return the nation to its Christian foundations,[33] Schaeffer took pains to explain that "we must make it definite that we are in no way talking about any kind of theocracy. Let me say that with great emphasis. Witherspoon, Jefferson, the American Founders had no idea of a theocracy. That is made plain by the First Amendment, and we must continually emphasize the fact that we are not talking about some kind of theocracy." While ancient Israel had been structured as "a theocracy commanded by God," Schaeffer emphasized that "there is no New Testament basis for a linking of the church and state until Christ, the King returns. The whole 'Constantine mentality' from the fourth century up to our day was a mistake," for it confused allegiance to Christ with loyalty to the state. And so he cautioned against the blending of Christianity with American nationalism: "We must not confuse the Kingdom of God with our country. To put it another way: 'We should not wrap Christianity in our national flag.'" Schaeffer believed that the First Amendment was not meant to separate religion from the state but had established a regime of religious freedom for all (or at least for Christians and Jews). "It is then up to Christians to show that Christianity is the Truth of total reality in the open marketplace of freedom," he announced, confident that his religion would ultimately prevail in the competition.[34]

But there were those who believed that a theocracy was precisely what America needed. In a critique of *A Christian Manifesto*, Gary North and David Chilton took Schaeffer to task for not following through on the logic of the argument.[35] "*Dr. Schaeffer's manifesto offers no prescriptions for a Christian society,*" they complained. Schaeffer rightly understood the Christian foundations on which the American project had been established and rightly opposed the ostensibly neutral but truly immoral humanistic state that had come to be, but he was unwilling to endorse the alternative of a comprehensively Christian regime. Schaeffer had hoped that breaking the secular humanistic stranglehold on the state would bring about the restoration of "the original purpose of the First Amendment," the freedom of all religion, but failed to realize that the godly society could not be achieved under the conditions of pluralism.[36] Truth, North and Chilton remarked, does not compete in the "Free Marketplace of Ideas." By advocating "religious liberty," Schaeffer had, in the end, come to sanction the position of "neutrality," thereby fatally undercutting his case for Christianity against secular humanism. In doing so, he had thus revealed himself to be an "intellectual schizophrenic." Schaeffer's so-called "Christian" manifesto "hesitates between two incompatible views: a society built in terms of the myth of neutrality and a society built upon the specifics of God's revealed law." He had appealed to Rutherford but failed to acknowledge that the author of *Lex, Rex* was "an uncompromising theocrat," who had called on the magistrate to enforce both tables of the Mosaic law. His refusal to call for theocracy in America lay in his premillennialist eschatology, the erroneous doctrine that only with the second coming of Christ would the godly kingdom emerge. The problem wasn't only secular humanism; it was bad religion.[37] Unlike the *Communist Manifesto*, Schaeffer's lacked a clear plan of action. He was unable to answer the question "What is to be done?"

North and Chilton had the answer. They were to prepare not merely for "resistance" against a "theocratic humanism" but for victory, by planning "a successful full-scale Christian counter-offensive to be launched *and completed* against the humanist civilization of our day."[38] Members of the small yet influential Christian Reconstructionist movement, they believed they were called to take dominion. The New Christian Right, however, was intellectually schizophrenic, deficient in epistemological self-consciousness, unable to go off to battle against the foe well-armed and with true aim. North, Chilton, and their comrades were already collecting stones as they marched off with their slingshots to take on the modern Goliath. And they were ready to cast them. They would not be satisfied with merely converting souls and hoping to restore the moral norms of a bygone era. They had a grander vision. Christian Reconstructionists maintained that the restoration of law and order would require a return to the ultimate source of law and order—submission to the sovereignty of the triune God. "Christ or chaos, God's law or tyranny" was their slogan. The vocation of the Christian was to help build up the kingdom through the work of dominion, to reorder—reconstruct—all aspects of human society according to the law of God as revealed in the Old Testament. As Gary North and Gary DeMar put it in their manifesto for the movement, "Christians are being challenged by God to reclaim the political realm for Jesus Christ. We must publicly declare the crown rights of King Jesus."[39]

At the head of the Christian Reconstructionist movement stood the formidable figure of Rousas John Rushdoony. "Rushdoony is the Marx of this movement," North once told an interviewer. "I'm trying very hard to be the Engels."[40] *Christianity Today* declared him to be one of the "most impressive" political theologians of his generation.[41] He was also one of the most controversial. A number of scholars of American religion concurred. Michael J. McVicar described Rushdoony "not only as a major influence on the Christian Right but also as the movement's most dangerous patriarch."[42] In Molly Worthen's assessment, he was "a strange brand of theological genius whose ideas proved robust enough to sustain an intellectual movement."[43] "Rushdoony was one of [the religious right's] intellectual godfathers," Julie J. Ingersoll noted, "but he is often treated like a crazy uncle."[44] North and Chilton complained that Schaeffer obscured the source of his historical claims. Not only he but "virtually every prominent leader of the so-called 'Christian right'" had been influenced by Rushdoony's work. "Without admitting it," they declared, "they are getting much of their

material, their insights, even their slogans, from the Christian Reconstruction-
ists." Why did they refuse to admit his influence on their thinking? Because
Rushdoony was a fearless advocate of theocracy. And in their inadequately
Christian America, that was considered heretical.[45]

Rousas John Rushdoony—Rush, as he was known to his friends and
colleagues—was, according to family lore, descended from one of the first Armenian families to convert to Christianity back in the fourth century. His father,
Yeghiazar Khachadour Rushdouni, grew up in the ancient city of Van. After his
family was killed by Ottoman forces in 1896, Rushdouni found shelter in an
orphanage established by an American missionary. There he converted from his
native Armenian Orthodox Christianity to Presbyterianism. After studying
theology at the University of Edinburgh, he returned to his native land in 1914
to engage in missionary work. But the young pastor was not to remain there
long. The following year, as the violence unleashed during World War I between
ethnic Turks and Armenians intensified, the family fled to Russian territory and
then to the West. They landed in New York City, where Rousas John was born in
1916. Soon thereafter, the family (now Rushdoony) resettled in California near
Fresno.

Rousas attended the University of California at Berkeley. He later
remarked that he was not impressed by most of his courses. "It took me a while
. . . to say, 'I don't care what everybody says. These may be classics, but they are
classics of depravity, classics of degenerate cultures. What they offer at their
best is evil.' To me this came to be epitomized in a book I had to spend an
entire semester studying, Plato's *Republic*," he told an interviewer. But he did
happen to come under the tutelage of the German-Jewish émigré scholar Ernst
H. Kantorowicz, whose work on "political theology" had a profound influence
on his own thinking. He went on to complete a master's in education and then
enrolled at the Pacific School of Religion, a Congregationalist and Methodist
Seminary awash with modernist trends in Christian theology. Following ordination as a Presbyterian minister in 1944, he set out to Nevada, where for eight
years he served as a missionary to the Paiute and Shoshone Indians.[46]

Along with Kantorowicz, the work of Cornelius Van Til had a decisive
influence on Rushdoony's intellectual formation. One of the conservative theologians who took flight from Princeton Theological Seminary to join the faculty
of Westminster Theological Seminary in Philadelphia, Van Til was the founder
of a school of apologetic theology that became known as presuppositionalism.[47]
As Van Til put it, "The best, the only, the absolutely certain proof of the truth of

Christianity is that unless its truth is presupposed there is no proof of anything. Christianity is proved as being the very foundation of the idea of proof itself."[48] For the Christian, that "presupposition" is the absolute sovereignty of God and the gap between the Creator and all created beings. God is the source of knowledge, and therefore adequate human knowledge is derived from revelation as recorded in Scripture. Presuppositionalist epistemology was not so much conservative as radical; it eschewed any and all appeals to human reason, custom, tradition, or experience. Jerusalem had absolutely nothing at all to do with Athens. Natural law was a myth. The Thomist synthesis of reason and revelation was a fraud. The Scottish "common sense" philosophy, long relied on by American Presbyterian theologians, was to be cast aside. And there was no "neutral" standpoint from which human beings could reason with one another.[49]

Rushdoony's first book, *By What Standard* (1958), was a study of Van Til's apologetics. In two subsequent volumes, *Intellectual Schizophrenia: Culture, Crisis and Education* (1961) and *The Messianic Character of American Education* (1963), he developed a foundational critique of public education in America. Since there is no neutrality—all "knowledge" is necessarily partisan—who controls the educational system and to what ends it is directed are of utmost importance. Insofar as the state had usurped the authority of the family over education, all those quarrels about prayer and Bible reading in public school classrooms were in the end irrelevant. The public school itself was the problem—the "church" where the established religion of humanity was catechized.

During his tenure as a missionary, Rushdoony came to be a fierce critic of government intervention and the welfare state, and in the early 1950s he began associating with pro-business, anti–New Deal networks such as Spiritual Mobilization and the Foundation for Economic Education that were powering mid-century conservativism and its blending of the gospel with the spirit of capitalism. (A grant from the William Volker Charities Fund, a major sponsor of thinkers on the American Right, helped support his research for *Intellectual Schizophrenia*.) While he shared the free-market principles being promulgated by the Austrian School, Rushdoony rejected the "amoral utilitarianism" of its proponents. Ludwig von Mises, Fredrich A. Hayek, Murray Rothbard, and the like might base their libertarianism on the efficiency of the market or the rights of property owners; Rushdoony's was grounded in an account of political theology and divine law.[50]

Rushdoony discovered the metaphysical basis for his anti-statism in the historic creeds and confessions of the church. Having studied with

Kantorowicz, Rushdoony understood that theological ideas have political consequences—abstract ideas about the divinity and cosmic order shape particular social and political institutions. The christological formula worked out at the Council of Chalcedon in AD 451 defined Christ as "two natures without confusion, change, division, or separation." In Rushdoony's reading, this was the essence of Christian political theology and its teaching about the state. Rushdoony published a version of his study, "Foundation of Western Liberty," in L. Brent Bozell's *Triumph* in March 1967. His book *The Foundations of Social Order* appeared in 1968.[51]

The bishops who hammered out this formula were working to settle a controversy regarding differing conceptions of the divine-human nature of Christ then circulating within the schools of Antioch, Alexandria, and Western Christianity.[52] But the question of Christology, Rushdoony argued, also involved the power, purpose, and legitimacy of the social order and the state. "Behind the problem stood the resurgence of Hellenistic philosophy in Christian guise and the claims of the state to be the divine order on earth, to be the incarnation of divinity in history." While Hellenistic philosophy conceived the cosmos as an undivided chain of being, "the Christian distinction between the uncreated being of God and the created being of man and the universe placed an infinite gulf between the two, a gulf unbridgeable by nature and bridged only by grace, by grace unto salvation and by grace permitting a union of community of life, not of substance." For the Greek mind, salvation was "not an act of grace but of self-deification" and could be imagined in terms of a mystical union with the divine or an absorption into the corporate body of the state "as the highest point of power in history manifests the nascent or incarnate divinity of being either in the body politic, the rulers, or their offices." In Rushdoony's reckoning, then, Christology had crucial political implications. How the divine and human natures of Christ were comprehended would determine whether Christians regarded their salvation as coming through Christ or under Caesar (as a divinity incarnate in the state). "The problem was God or man, Christ or the state, who is man's savior, and how is divinity incarnated?"[53] By defining Christ "in two natures, without confusion, without change, without division, without separa-tion," the Chalcedonian formula distinguished Christian faith from pagan reflections on nature and being, closed off the route of personal mystical union with the divine, and guarded against a collective absorption into the human institution of the state. (If the human and divine natures of Christ were confused, human beings would aspire to divinization, to unite the two orders.)[54]

After Chalcedon, "statist theology" was heretical. From this point on, the state "could not claim to be the ultimate or comprehending order. Man, as God's creature, transcended the state by virtue of his citizenship in God's eternal Kingdom."[55] Rushdoony declared that the creed therefore established a great divide in world history: "*The state was thus placed under God, not in the being of God as in paganism.* The state, in terms of the Council of Chalcedon, could not be regarded as the order of man's fulfilment or the means of his redemption. Rome fell in 410, and the Council of Chalcedon met in 451. The two events are not unrelated. What the barbarians did to the City of Rome, the Council did to the idea of Rome, and of all states and empires."[56]

The Chalcedonian formula, then, was both a statement of belief in the nature of Christ and a political theology that set out the correct understanding of the state and the human being's relation to it. The state was acknowledged in the cosmic order as a limited institution, a ministry of justice—complemented by the church as a ministry of grace—under the transcendent God. The council thus set "the Christian foundation of Western culture and made possible the development of liberty. Chalcedon handed statism its major defeat in man's history."[57] Yet, while the creed ought to have restrained Christians from pursuing salvation by means of the state, Rushdoony conceded that the struggle between the Christian and pagan understandings of salvation and the state "is endemic to Western history, with empires and states warring against the liberty of Chalcedon, and the state seeking again to become the saving order."[58] "The history of the Christian era has been largely the struggle in some sense to establish the divine and unitary state," he remarked in another essay.[59] Political forms as diverse as absolute monarchy (the "divine right" of the king) and mass democracy ("vox populi, vox Dei") were in truth only alternative forms of "statism," revivals of the ancient pagan error.[60]

In the modern era, this error—now known as "humanism"—is proclaimed by those who believe that the state holds the solution to the problems of humanity. "The goal of politics today is messianic: its purpose is paradise regained, a perfect world order by means of law and technology," Rushdoony wrote. "Man's problem is not seen as sin but as a backward environment which science can correct. Statist theology sees all problems answered by statist action; the goal of all men of good will must therefore be social legislation. More power must be given to the state in order to realize the city of man." Human planning replaces predestination. This modern posture was a sweeping rejection of Christian teaching. "On the foundation of Chalcedon, the formulation of Biblical Christology, Western liberty has been built. Ignorance and neglect of Chalcedon has been basic to the decline of the Church. Strange voices in Christendom assert the necessity for Christian relevance, but the relevance they have in mind is not to Christ and His Kingdom but to the reviving pagan statist theology and the attempts by the pagan humanistic state to lead man into a paradise without God. But the reduction of man to the dimensions of the state, to the dimensions of time and history, is the enslavement of man, not his liberation."[61]

"When the foundations are provided, the general form of the building is determined," Rushdoony concluded. "When the creed is accepted, the social order is determined. There can therefore be no reconstruction of the Christian civilization of the west except on Christian creedal foundations." The great ideological battle was not the political-economic struggle between (American) democracy and Communism but the deeper theological one between Christianity and (pagan) statism. American Christians needed to reject the false creed of humanism, and the pseudo-messianic Leviathan it supported, and return to Chalcedon. Only by accepting this creed could they work to advance the kingdom of God on earth.[62]

Rushdoony launched the Chalcedon Foundation, hoping to build it into a Christian college, an alternative to all those faith-based colleges and universities that had become compromised by liberalism and modernism over the years. The school never materialized; the Chalcedon Foundation became instead a kind of personal think tank and the intellectual headquarters for what would become Rushdoony's project of "Christian Reconstruction."

In the early 1960s, Rushdoony composed a series of essays to elucidate the American past and evaluate its present. *This Independent Republic*, based on lectures he had delivered at the Intercollegiate Society of Individualists' Conference at St. Mary's College in California in August 1962, was published in 1964; another collection, *The Nature of the American System*, followed a year later. Rushdoony regarded these essays as "studies in Christian revisionism," written from the standpoint of "the central point of human history," the incarnation of Christian revelation—based on his understanding of Chalcedon—rather than by the methods of modern secular historiography. "Their purpose," he noted, "is to call attention to those aspects of American history currently neglected, namely, the Christian foundations which still militate against the present Gnostic and messianic movements."[63] This was an idiosyncratic approach, with sometimes tendentious results. The essays collected in these volumes were larded with tirades against equality, democracy, the social gospel, neo-orthodoxy, Darwin, Marx, Freud; Rushdoony expressed particular contempt for those avatars of democratic man, the pornographers the Marquis de Sade and Henry Miller; the dark sexual perversities they celebrated exposed, he claimed, the true demonic nature of the religion of humanity. In time, these books became staples of Christian academies and homeschool curricula.

It was Rushdoony's contention that the United States had enjoyed a most Christian founding—in continuity with the Puritan planting. In his telling, the nation's "origins are Christian and Augustinian, deeply rooted in Reformation, medieval, and patristic history,"[64] "markedly different from the doctrines of John Locke, Whig politics, and the political faith of the Enlightenment."[65] Unlike the Enlightenment-inspired French and Russian Revolutions, both of which aimed to overturn the established regime, forge a new humanity, and inaugurate a totally new order in history, the American "Revolution" was really a "conservative counter-revolution," aiming at the restoration of the Christian feudal system, "more deeply rooted in the Christian West than Europe itself."[66] The American Patriots were battling against Parliamentary encroachments on colonial self-rule and the further imposition of the Church of England. Theirs was a struggle against centralization and absolutism. With the Constitution of 1787, they endeavored to establish not a centralized national state but merely a federal union of the thirteen already existing—and Christian—states. The Constitution's doctrine of limited powers, its checks and balances and mechanisms to diffuse power, Madison's musings on factions in *Federalist* No. 10, demonstrated a distrust of human beings, a Calvinist conception of human nature.[67] Further, neither the Declaration of Independence nor the Constitution proclaimed the *legal* sovereignty of the people or the government; for the Framers, Rushdoony argued, sovereignty was recognized to be God's alone.[68] They understood the state to be a moral order that rested on theological order and assumed the American people shared a Christian, specifically a Calvinist, ethos. The Constitution thus only appeared to be a "secular" instrument; it was, rather, "designed to *perpetuate* a Christian order."[69]

Rushdoony was well aware that these claims would be considered dubious by many mid-century Americans. To those who might suggest that the absence of any reference to God or Christianity in the Constitution or the religion clauses of the First Amendment were evidence against the idea of such a "Christian" founding, he countered that these simply revealed the Framers' recognition of the states' standing jurisdiction over matters of religion. "All the constituent states had in some form or other either a Christian establishment or settlement, or specifically Christian legislation," he noted. "Religious tests for citizenship, blasphemy laws, singular or plural establishments, and other religious settlements were the rule, jealously guarded and prized, first against British interference, then against Federal usurpation. To preserve the integrity of freedom of the specific forms of Christian statehood of the constituent states, the Constitution forbade any jurisdiction to the Federal Union in the area."[70] (We should note that this explanation sidesteps the question of why the Framers' declined to acknowledge God in the Constitution.) Given this understanding of the original meaning of the First Amendment—which "forbade the Federal Government to enter the area of religion to impose *or* forbid any establishment or settlement alien to the states"—the proper response to "the present federal interference" in religion (those Supreme Court decisions on public school prayer and Bible reading) would not be the ratification of a Christian Amendment "but the restoration of the prior jurisdiction of the states."[71]

Rushdoony's declension narrative involved many villains, but what they all had in common was heresy. America's problem was not a bad founding but the spread of bad religion. Every departure from "orthodox Calvinism"—the enthusiasms of the Great Awakenings, Arminianism, deism, the social gospel, revivalism, and so forth—seduced the people away from a political order grounded in true religion (the holy commonwealth of the Puritans, founded on "the sovereignty of God and His kingship"[72]), reasserting the sovereignty of man and the state, setting them on the road toward statism and tyranny. Unitarianism especially bore responsibility by promoting the idea that government is a divine (rather than divinely ordained) institution—a humanistic distortion of the holy commonwealth idea. The public school that emerged under its aegis was a "radical and dangerous innovation" to subvert the old order and expand the power and the reach of the state, in time becoming its true established church.[73] The Unitarian spirit later fueled the rise of abolitionism, socialism, temperance, and feminism. But as orthodox Calvinism receded in New England, it took on new vitality in the South. Rushdoony approvingly quoted at length from Benjamin M. Palmer's November 29, 1860, incendiary and influential call for disunion as a defense of a Christian people against an infidelity disguised as "Christian idealism." Palmer, he noted, saw the coming conflict as "the forces of false theology, of atheism and of the French Revolution, of the religion of humanity . . . arrayed against a Christian people dedicated to faith in Jesus

Christ as Lord and Savior, and to Constitutional government."[74] And he defended the Confederacy's action: "The anti-Christian, Jacobin attack on slavery had to be fought, and slavery defended, because the revolutionary reordering of society would be far worse than anything it sought to supplant."[75] The conflict between the North and the South, Rushdoony claimed, was not fundamentally about slavery but between orthodox Christianity and "the religion of humanity."[76]

The war between the states was a decisive turning point in American history; a powerful national state ("the Union") arose only during this period,[77] and "from the Civil War to World War II, the goals of the state were secularized and nationalized. The purposes of law became increasingly not the reflection of God's justice, without respect of persons, but social justice, the triumph of humanism."[78] With the North's triumph, the long modern pagan assault, now conducted under the varied banners of "free thought," Darwinism (which provided the warrant for economic predations of the neo-mercantilist Gilded Age industrialists), socialism, women's suffrage, and so forth, continued unabated. The offensive was culminating with the legal secularization of the state. American churches, whether they preached the social gospel, neo-orthodoxy, or "our Judeo-Christian" heritage, that nondenominational revivalism which strives to "Save America," had succumbed to the dark spell of "the religion of humanity."[79] This had brought about "another and more radical Babylonian captivity of the church."[80] Rather than finding their salvation in Christ, American Christians sought their redemption in the "caretaker state [that] seeks to transcend or abolish history; it seeks to create the final and perfect order and usher man into paradise regained, and regained without God."[81] By the time of his writing, this false creed "had become not only the religion of most churches, preached from pulpits, and resounding from papal encyclical and from world church groups, but it was also in effect the established religion of the courts and of most states the world over. It was also the implicitly established faith of the United Nations. . . . By its omnipotence in most news and communications media, and its presence in church and state, it is working to weaken the moral fiber of the people."[82]

And democracy? Just another attempt of human beings to free themselves from obedience to God and his revealed law. "Democracy is 'vox populi, vox dei.' There is no standard other than the will of the people, which can include all things. It is 'the people, yes.' " And the will of the people inevitably meant the will of the state. Rushdoony concurred with his nemesis John Dewey:

democracy was indeed a counter-faith, a denial of Christianity's division of humanity into "the saved and the lost."[83] The false teaching of equality was likewise to be rejected. The Declaration of Independence (inspired by the Virginia Bill of Rights) was not making a universal claim; "the equal men were free-born colonial men."[84] (Rushdoony downplayed the Declaration's importance in the Founding as well and sidestepped the values it enunciated: its "legal meat," as he put it, "is not in its opening generalities but in its specific demonstration that a legal, contractual, and feudal relationship with George III had been violated and set aside by him.")[85] "Equalitarianism is a modern politico-religious concept: it did not exist in the Biblical world, and it cannot with any honesty be forced onto Biblical law," Rushdoony wrote in a later work. "Equalitarianism is a product of humanism, of the worship of a new idol, man, and a new image carved out of man's imagination." Christianity taught contrariwise that "all men are *not* equal before God; the facts of heaven and hell, election and reprobation, make it clear that they are not equal."[86] Democratic equality accordingly brings about the end of morality and values: "Total war must be raged against God, against all meaning, value, morality, law, and order, in short, against anything that divides men in terms of an absolute standard." The ensuing chaos was ushering in the tyranny of the "total state." A new Tower of Babel was being erected; a "new Islam" was being enforced. "Against all this," Rushdoony insisted, "the only refuge and strength of man is in the sovereignty of God and His infallible word, in the absolute law of God. We are either believers in this God, or we take a road which leads to radical and total democracy. The weakness of the United States today is its halfway position, a stand lacking the strength of either faith."[87]

Acknowledging American's deeply Christian—that is to say, Calvinist—past had crucial implications for thinking about the country's future: "The revival and growth of the historical American settlement depends therefore on the Christian renewal of the citizenry and the renewal of the centrality of the local units of government."[88] Rushdoony argued that "the restoration of that first revolution, *and* its *extension*" required "the Christian renewal of the citizenry," a return to orthodox Christian faith, the recognition of Christ as King, the establishment of Christian schools, and the devolvement of government to localities.[89] Such a "Christian renewal" was to be more radical—and more political—than the calls to conversation made by contemporary neo-evangelical leaders like Billy Graham. (Rushdoony often disparaged the religious posture of Graham and the neo-evangelicals as "pious irrelevance, anti-nomianism, phariseeism, and a general immoralism.")[90] It would not do for Christian Americans to await patiently (or impatiently) Christ's return to establish his kingdom. They needed to abandon their premillennialism ("pessimillennialism") and realize that, justified by faith, they themselves have been called to transform a world already conquered by Christ. "Their faith must be more than churchianity: it must rather be the declaration of the crown rights of King Jesus in every area of life," he later declared.[91]

But what would it mean for Americans to recognize and live under the sovereignty of God rather than the secular state? Van Til had been a "demolitions expert" who blew up shaky foundations; Rushdoony was searching for the blueprints for (re)constructing the new (old) order.[92] "The heresy of democracy has ... worked havoc in church and state, and it has worked towards reducing society to anarchy."[93] While the moral majoritarians dreamed of a restoration of an imagined America of the 1950s, Rushdoony had come to envision something more radical—an absolute transformation of the country into a new holy commonwealth. This would be accomplished under *theonomy*—the rule of divine law. The moral and civil laws God delivered to Moses (excepting those explicitly abrogated in the New Testament) remained binding. They comprised, one might say, the ur-constitution that lay behind all legitimate governments. That law, and not the pseudo-messianic state with the manifold laws that humans arrogantly legislated for themselves, was the only true foundation of social order and mechanism of justice. (Law is always "religious in origin," Rushdoony liked to remind his audiences, whether the true religion of Christ or the false religion of humanity. The source of a society's law is its god.) Against what he regarded as the heresy of antinomianism (that "faith frees the Christian from the law"), Rushdoony argued that "the purpose of grace is not to set aside the law but to fulfil the law and to enable man to keep the law." Against the heresy of premillennialism, it was that very law which provided the blueprints for the godly society. Christ's atonement for Adam's sin has restored the justified "to their position of righteousness under God" (of law-keeping and covenant-keeping) and thereby to their vocation to subdue the earth and exercise dominion over creation (Genesis 1:26–28) in preparation for Christ's return. "Man has been re-established into God's original purpose and calling. Man's *justification* is by the *grace* of God in Jesus Christ; man's *sanctification* is by means of the *law* of God."[94] The postmillennial kingdom was to be built up on the basis of that law. To hold dominion over and subdue creation—this was the original charge to Adam and the meaning of the Great Commission, the purpose of the covenant God had established with humanity.

In 1973, Rushdoony announced his vision for Christian Reconstruction with the publication of the massive first volume of *The Institutes of Biblical Law.* The book was based on sermons he had been working on since 1968. (Subsequent volumes followed in 1982 and 1999.) Knowledgeable readers were likely to catch in the title the allusion to John Calvin's *Institutes of the Christian Religion*, one of the foundational works of the Reformation. That was certainly audacious, but Rushdoony thought that Calvin did not go far enough in his Geneva in establishing a true Christian republic under God's law.[95] In any event, Rushdoony was not looking to restore some former state of affairs. His was a program to build, from the ground up, the coming theocracy.

For many, Rushdoony's teaching appeared as a new and strange doctrine. Certainly, the very term was open to misunderstandings.[96] In calling for theocracy, Rushdoony was not advocating the rule of the church or of a clerical elite. Nor did he regard theocracy as limited to, or even primarily concerned with, the state and civil government but rather viewed it as "a government over every institution by God and His Law, and though the activities of the free man in Christ to bring every area of life and thought under Christ's Kingship." All of human life is subject to God and to be organized in accordance with his revealed law, within the differentiated "spheres" of governance—the individual, the family, the church, and the civil sphere—and directed to man's original purpose to exercise dominion over creation. There is no "secular" sphere of human existence. Christians needed to recognize and accept that they were already living under God's rule (even as they believed they were autonomous). They then needed to work to coax a people that had rebelled against this law back into its yoke. As it was founded on divine law, reconstructed society would have no place for religious pluralism and religious liberty. All society would be fundamentally and fully Christian.[97]

Governance here meant first and foremost the self-governance of the Christian man, and his governance over his family and its economic life, in line with biblical law. The state's role is merely ministerial, not legislative, limited to the execution of justice and defense; it would "further the Kingdom of God by recognizing the sovereignty of God and His word and conforming to the law-word of God." The state would not have the authority to tax its citizens; the biblically mandated tithe would provide sufficient funding for schools, hospitals, and other social institutions. Nor would it have any part in the moral and religious formation of its citizens; the task of education, of cultivating Christian men and women, is assigned to the spheres of the family and the church. In a reconstructed society, public ("government") schools would be abolished. So too would government welfare programs, as the church would oversee the dispensing of charity (for those deserving of assistance). Such a conception of "theocracy in Biblical law," Rushdoony asserted, "is the closest thing to a radical libertarianism that can be had."[98]

Perhaps the most notorious aspect of the Reconstructionist program was its teachings concerning biblical crimes and punishment. In the *Institutes*, Rushdoony enumerated eighteen capital offences, many of which he believed would be reinstated in the theonomic society, including for male homosexual behavior, incorrigible delinquency, propagation of false doctrines, and sacrificing to false gods.[99] (Contemporary liberals' "hostility to the death penalty is humanism's hostility to God's law," Rushdoony contended.) For other crimes, biblical law mandated economic restitution, not incarceration. If the offender proved unable to make amends, "bond service" (slavery) would "work out the required restitution." The emergence of the prison system in Christendom, Rushdoony wrote, was "an ugly, bastard compromise" with the pagan system of punishment.[100]

With the appearance of the *Institutes*, all the fundamentals of Christian Reconstruction—the Calvinist notion of the sovereignty of God and regeneration by grace, Van Til's presuppositionalist epistemology, the metaphysical anti-statism of Chalcedon, postmillennial eschatology, the dominion mandate, and theonomy—were in place, and Rushdoony set out to put his neo-Puritan vision into practice. A cadre of disciples helped expound and disseminate the reconstructed gospel throughout the conservative Protestant world, in the United States and beyond. Gary North, a PhD in history from the University of California, Riverside, who regarded himself as Rushdoony's first full-time disciple (he also happened to be Rushdoony's son-in-law), focused his efforts on explicating the biblical laws of economics (he launched his own outfit, the Institute for Christian Economics, in 1975); Greg Bahnsen wrote on apologetic ethics; David Chilton toiled on postmillennial exegesis; and Gary DeMar was instrumental in the popularization of Reconstructionist ideas through his books, many written for homeschoolers, and his work with American Vision, a nonprofit organization devoted to promoting the "Biblically-based" Reconstructionist worldview. In countless talks, sermons, newsletters, journals, books, and materials for Christian academies and homeschools published in the monthly *Chalcedon Report* and the more scholarly *Journal of Christian*

Reconstruction, Rushdoony and his associates set out to describe their vision of a theocratic society and how to apply the principles of biblical law to contemporary circumstances. The ten-volume Biblical Blueprints series, edited by North, detailed the Christian Reconstructionist positions on government and political action, economics, social and welfare programs, international relations, education, family life, and divorce and remarriage.[101]

These "dominion men" were confident of their ultimate victory as it had already been assured. Guided by the Holy Spirit, the work of Reconstruction would move inexorably forward, even if it did so at a seemingly glacial pace. As North noted, "We have time on our side; our opponents don't. We have a sovereign God on our side; our opponents don't. We cannot afford to be complacent; we can, however, afford to be confident, and for the same reasons that David was. Plus, we have word processors and mailing lists. That makes all the difference. A dozen men armed with word processors can inflict enormous damage on those whose paradigms are in a state of collapse."[102] (The amount of writing composed by the small number of Christian Reconstructionists is indeed enormous. It is as if they believed they could defeat their heretical opponents simply by the amount of ink they spilled.) North estimated it would take "about a thousand years, not much more" for the reconstructed society to come to be.[103] They emphasized that their movement did not advocate seizing power by means of a coup d'état or revolution but simply by working within the democratic process, supporting candidates who would legislate in a biblical fashion. So far as Christian resistance to the tyrannical state was concerned, North demurred from violence, suggesting to his followers that they study Saul Alinsky's *Rules for Radicals*.[104]

So the prophesized theocracy would emerge from the bottom up rather than being imposed from the top down (in the manner of statism), requiring first the regeneration of individual human beings, who would then realize the political demands of their religion. Reconstructionists called on Christians to rouse themselves from their pietism, which stressed their immediate spiritual relationship with God. To remain committed to their "escape religion" (the soul saving of much of American evangelicalism) was to be an ally to and a collaborator with the secular humanists and their "power religion." They heaped scorn on premillennial dispensationalists, who they claimed cast off the unchanging Word of God for the "polytheistic" notion of a God who would choose to deal with humanity in different ways in different historical eras, eschewing the responsibility of dominion for the hope of personal rescue from a doomed creation. They pointed out the eschatological schizophrenia of working to Christianize the social order while believing that its decadence and depravity was a sign of its imminent demise. Only postmillennialists could truly build up a Christian America. So they called on American Christians to choose: Would they be the sons of the Puritans or the sons of the Great Awakenings?

But even as Christian Reconstructionists were assured of their own theological correctness, optimistic of their ultimate victory, and tireless in their efforts to spread their gospel, they turned out to be a disputatious bunch. North relocated his Institute for Christian Economics to Tyler, Texas, where he and his associates at Westminster Presbyterian Church and Geneva Divinity School developed a church-centered conception of Christian Reconstruction that diverged from Rushdoony's emphasis on the extended patriarchal family and promulgated their views in books, newsletters, and audiotapes. Rushdoony's Chalcedon Foundation continued to pump out material from Vallecito. Figuring out how to interpret and apply laws from ancient Israel to modern America was no mean feat and led to many quarrels among the faithful; differences regarding political engagement and confrontation also caused dissension within the ranks. Large egos and strong personalities amplified these disputes. By the summer of 1981, tensions between Rushdoony and North had come to a fever pitch—a rejected journal article led to a hostile exchange of letters and accusations of blasphemy, culminating with Rushdoony sacking North from his editorship at the *Journal of Christian Reconstruction.* Not to be outdone, North launched his own journal, *Christianity and Civilization.* Ties between Chalcedon and Tyler were severed. Despite persistent entreaties from friends and colleagues, Rushdoony and his son-in-law were never to speak again.[105]

Even so, by the 1980s the various labors of the Christian Reconstructionists were beginning to bear fruit as their theological, economic, and political ideas penetrated the wider ecosystem of American evangelicalism and helped shape Christian political engagement. Rushdoony made guest appearances on Pat Robertson's and D. James Kennedy's tele-ministries, and his *Institutes of Biblical Law* was assigned reading in Christian law schools. Rushdoony also served as an expert witness in numerous legal suits over Christian schools and homeschooling. Such schools were a tool to pry youth from the state, preparing their students not only to resist the dominant secular humanist culture but also to take back the country for Christ. Reconstructionist ideas were springing up throughout the conservative Christian American landscape: in the Christian patriarchy movement, in Howard Phillips's Constitution Party, and in the work of the Christian nationalist "historian" David Barton. And the rhetoric of "dominion theology" began to infiltrate Pentecostal and charismatic churches and ministries and was popularized in the "Seven Mountain Mandate" movement.[106] Many who began to speak in the Reconstructionist tongue may not have known its source; others did not want to admit that they had been influenced by Rushdoony and his school. Rushdoony was known to grumble that his own role in conservative Christian political activism was being obscured by those who were unwilling to acknowledge his intellectual influence. In one of his essays, Gary North mentioned a conversation with a member of the Moral Majority at the National Affairs Briefing Conference sponsored by the Religious Roundtable. (It was there that candidate Ronald Reagan famously said, "I know you cannot endorse me, but I endorse you and everything you do.") "We were speaking of the conference, and what a remarkable event it was," North recalled. "We agreed that it was unfortunate that Rushdoony was not speaking. He said: 'If it weren't for his books, none of us would be here.' I replied: 'Nobody in the audience understands that.' His response: 'True, but *we* do.' "[107]

True, Rousas John Rushdoony, Gary North, and Greg Bahnsen were not household names, even within conservative Christian circles; nevertheless, things got to such a point that the editors of *Christianity Today*, the flagship magazine of American neo-evangelicalism, felt the need to stage an intervention. February 20, 1987, *Christianity Today* published a cover story provocatively titled "Democracy as Heresy." After a brief sketch of Christian Reconstructionism's distinctive theological doctrines, the author argued that the movement posed a distinct threat to American Christianity—and to American democracy. "In the Reconstructed society," he informed his readers, "there will be no federal government. Nor will there be a democracy, which Reconstructionists regard as a 'heresy.' . . . In a Reconstructed society, government will be republican, with the Bible as the charter and constitutional document." This would involve the reinstitution of tithing, "biblical" slavery, and capital punishment for an assortment of crimes, including "sodomy, Sabbath breaking, apostasy, witchcraft, blasphemy, and incorrigibility in children." After assessing the ties of leading Reconstructionist thinkers to major televangelists, the appeal of their political theory in conservative Protestant circles, and their boasts that their "fusion of theology and social and political concerns" had provided the intellectual foundation for the New Christian Right, the report concluded that "there is clearly much cause for concern and disagreement."[108] As Michael J. McVicar noted, the article "portrayed [the Reconstructionists] as political heretics out of touch with contemporary evangelicalism and, worse still, contemporary American political sensibilities."[109]

Despite the "window" cracked open by the Reagan administration, through the mid-1980s the New Religious Right could boast few substantive achievements. Proposed constitutional amendments to restore prayer in public schools and to ban abortion went nowhere. *Roe v. Wade* was still the law of the land. The steady march of secular humanism continued apace.

Yet perhaps there were restorative victories to be had on the horizon. A cluster of interpretive approaches to the Constitution under the broad rubric of "originalism" that had been gaining traction in conservative legal circles charted a path through the courts.[110] In 1982 conservative law students at Yale and the University of Chicago founded the Federalist Society to promote originalist thinking in a legal academy largely committed to the progressive, living constitution tradition, bringing the ideas, and the lawyers and scholars who held them, to prominence. In a pair of speeches delivered in 1985, Attorney General Edwin Meese III announced the administration's policy to endorse "a Jurisprudence of Original Intention." Arguing against those court decisions that appeared to be "more policy choices than articulations of constitutional principle," Meese proclaimed that "the text of the document and the original intention of those who framed it would be the judicial standard in giving effect to the Constitution."[111] "Constitutional fidelity" required judges to interpret the document according to its original meaning as established by its "letter" (the voice of the Framers ratified by the people) and not by appeal to some "spirit" (a "vision" or "concepts of human dignity" or "penumbras") or a "living constitution" imagined by progressive law professors and judges.[112] In such a way, judges could preserve the Framers' goal of establishing a "limited but energetic government." Meese was particularly perturbed by the Supreme Court's Establishment Clause jurisprudence and its doctrine of incorporation, which he said rested on an "intellectually shaky foundation" and was a "politically violent and constitutionally suspect" blow to the principle of federalism. He reminded his audience that it wasn't until *Everson* that the Establishment Clause was mistakenly made to apply to the states. "This is striking," he said, "because the Bill of Rights, as debated, created and ratified was designed to apply *only* to the national government."[113]

Meese's formulations obscured the many and complex debates being waged among the various camps of constitutional scholars and legal theorists—interpretivists and noninterpretivists, textualists and intentionalists, loose and strict constructionists, those who looked to the intents of the Framers, or the ratifiers' understanding, or the text's original public meaning. But in his call for a jurisprudence of original intent, he set forth the general terms by which the decisions of the Warren and Burger courts on church-state issues and abortion could be rolled back and the brakes put on the discovery of additional "rights" (especially those of gays and lesbians and other historically marginalized minorities)—a secular constitutional theory that could serve Christian restorationist ends and was well suited to their hermeneutical sensibilities. And the Reagan administration was determined to place judges who adhered to some version of this orientation on the federal bench—a commitment demonstrated by the appointment of Antonin Scalia (who was, technically speaking, a textualist rather than an intentionalist in his approach) to the Supreme Court and the elevation of William H. Rehnquist to chief justice the following year.[114]

While the originalist call for a "return to the Constitution" (and for judges who would merely "apply the law" and not "legislate from the bench") had many evangelical (and Catholic) culture warriors rejoicing, Rushdoony registered reservations. America's profound moral and spiritual crisis would not be solved simply by a return to the Constitution. As religious order was anterior to the constitutional order, the Constitution needed to be complemented by a "higher law," that of the law of God as revealed in the Bible. In an essay published in his *Journal of Christian Reconstruction* (the entire issue devoted to the Constitution and political theology), Rushdoony spelled out his position: "The U.S. Constitution gives us no substantive morality, only a procedural one. It does not claim to be a moral code; rather, it presupposes faith and morality on the part of the people. What this means is that the defense of the republic is not primarily legal and constitutional but rather religious. If the people lack Christian faith and morality, the Constitution becomes meaningless."[115] While he continued to hold the Constitution in high regard, he reminded his readers that "it is not the Bible; it is not inerrant; and it has faults." It is "an excellent though imperfect document." The Constitution is not divinely inspired, and it does not have an "unchanging meaning"; its "intent" changes when altered by an amendment— "the later laws govern the earlier ones."[116] Despite the hagiographies promoted by some Christian Americans, the Framers were, as all people, fallible, and realizing that the instrument they were drawing up, as the product of their human minds, could not be perfect, they wisely included the amendment provision for its correction. However, in doing so they allowed for even more fallible people to transform the meaning of the Constitution, sometimes in deleterious ways. Rushdoony singled out the Sixteenth Amendment (for legalizing involuntary servitude to the state by permitting Congress to collect taxes on income) as a particularly noxious example. Yet, even had it remained in its original form, the Constitution could not make sinful men good and "has not preserved the United States from the depravity of man." "The Constitution is not a mechanism which guarantees us justice or freedom. Too many people have believed that constitutions can save a country, whereas only the godly faith and action of a people can do so." America's fundamental problem was infidelity, the people's allegiance to bad religions and to false gods. "A 'return' to the Constitution means nothing, unless there is first and last a return to Jesus Christ as King, Priest, and Prophet, and to God's law as the only word of truth and justice."[117]

The Constitution had presupposed the "faith and morality" of the citizenry and contained implicit Christian notions. Rushdoony noted the presidential oath of office stipulated in Article II, Section 1, calling it "an important religious act." (He passed over the prohibition of religious tests in Article VI, Section 3.) The problem was that the religious character of Americans had rapidly declined. Rushdoony noted that the church had been weakened during the Revolutionary War, and the generation of the Founders was not immune to all manner of corruptions. The Constitution could only maintain a godly social order if "we the people" were indeed a righteous people committed to orthodox Christianity. But the people had apostatized. American Christianity had become increasingly antinomian. As their pastors turned away from holding dominion over this world to "soul saving" for the next, the people degraded religiously and morally, over time surrendering their power and responsibilities (to tithe, educate, and provide the gamut of social services) to the humanist state, their false god of "big government," and demanding expanded rights to defend their perversities. So how could contemporary Christians take the Constitution literally and in accordance with its "original intent" when they failed to do so with Scripture? Accordingly, "the basic battle of our times is to overcome the antinomianism of the churches. . . . The Constitution can restore nothing, nor can it make the courts of the people just." The way to rescue the republic was not to turn back by means of the application of a jurisprudence of original intent but to move forward through the project of forging a Christian people. "What we need . . . is an appeal to the church to be Christian, to be faithful to the whole word of God, and to begin again its task of dominion by training men to work to bring every area of life and thought into submission, not to the church nor the state, but to Christ."[118]

Gary North was quick to pick up on the inconsistency in his erstwhile master's position. In his massive 1989 volume *Political Polytheism: The Myth of Pluralism*, he accused Rushdoony of relinquishing the very epistemic principles he acquired from Van Til and refusing to recognize the Founders for who they were—men of the Enlightenment, "Deist (proto-Unitarian) in outlook," who utilized natural law philosophy to undermine Christian orthodoxy—and their Constitution for what it was, a heretical covenant. "In a showdown between his theonomic theology and the U.S. Constitution," North sneered, Rushdoony "chose the Constitution." In the end, the godfather of Christian Reconstruction lacked the courage of his convictions. "If a defense of the U.S. Constitution as being somehow inherently Christian, or in some way fundamentally conformable to Christianity, is the position of the Christian Reconstruction movement," North asserted, "this means the suicide of Christian Reconstructionism."[119]

North's complaint against Rushdoony took up a twenty-nine-page appendix to the nearly eight-hundred-page work—an extended argument against so-called Christian alternatives to biblical theocracy that included lengthy broadsides against Francis Schaeffer, Surgeon General C. Everett Koop, and the evangelical historians Mark A. Noll, Nathan O. Hatch, and George M. Marsden for their capitulations to secular humanism, intellectual schizophrenics all. The centerpiece of the massive tome was North's argument that the US Constitution was not originally intended to establish a Christian republic or even maintain the states' establishments. Rather than the result of a "miracle at Philadelphia," the Constitution was the product of a grand Masonic conspiracy, an illegal coup that overthrew the standing Christian order of states and over time ushered in the regime of humanism. (Why did Joseph Smith, the Mormon prophet, proclaim that the Constitution was divinely inspired? Because he was a Freemason, North revealed.)[120]

The radical secularism of contemporary America was the logical and intended consequence of the design drawn up in 1787. The authentic "Founding Fathers" of the nation were not the men like Washington, Madison, and Hamilton but early Puritan leaders such as John Winthrop of the Massachusetts Bay Colony. Dissenters such as Roger Williams (whose "alternative to the theocracy of the Massachusetts Bay Colony . . . was the birthplace of modern political pluralism") were its first heretics. But the heretics had indeed won the day; the spirit of apostate Rhode Island had conquered the other twelve

Christian commonwealths. North drew a direct line from Williams to the Framers of a Constitution that was "a covenantal declaration of independence from the God of the Bible." The work of those conspirators in Philadelphia marked the beginning of a long war against Christianity that had culminated in the secular humanist state decided by the Supreme Court in the 1960s. "The Framers at the Constitutional Convention issued a death warrant against Christianity, but for tactical reasons, they and their spiritual heirs refused for several generations to deliver it to the intended victims," North alleged. But it was clear that their warrant had been executed and their dream had been realized.[121]

That the Constitution was intended as an anti-Christian covenantal document was evident in the opening words of its Preamble announcing the nation's commitment to a new sovereign—that "We the People"—to be incarnated in the federal government, the state. Rushdoony believed that the Constitution admitted no doctrine of "sovereignty," thus implicitly maintaining sovereignty as an attribute of God. North rejected this view as entirely fanciful. "The Framers were operating under the legal fiction that the sovereign People, not the God of the Bible, had authorized the new national covenant. 'We the People' were not the vassals of the Great King in this treaty; 'We the People' *were* the great king, and there shall be no other gods beside 'We the People.'" In North's telling, the conspirators at Philadelphia traded the deist god the Patriots appealed to in the Declaration of Independence for this new idol of popular sovereignty.[122]

And this, North argued, was the real reason why Article VI, Section 3, of the Constitution (a "seemingly innocuous provision") stipulated that officers "shall be bound by Oath or Affirmation, to support this Constitution" but prohibited religious tests as a qualification for office. That provision set in place the anti-Christian religious character of the regime; it was, North said, the judicial basis of Jefferson's "wall of separation." Civil officers would not be bound by an oath to the God of the Bible but to another god, a "national god." "That god is the American People, considered as an autonomous sovereign who possesses original and final earthly jurisdiction." The Fourteenth Amendment's granting of birthright citizenship opened political participation to all men, regardless of religious conviction—"citizenship without God." And North observed that now the "will" of "We the People" is simply what a majority of Supreme Court justices decides.[123]

North waved away all the arguments typically submitted for the Christian nature of the Constitution. There was no evidence that the Framers had studied

Samuel Rutherford; the Reverend John Witherspoon's influence was as a proponent of the Scottish Enlightenment, not as an orthodox Calvinist; his student James Madison was "a covenant-breaking genius," a "Unitarian theocrat," an American Rousseau who dreamed of creating a "secular republic."[124] The Constitution was an outgrowth not of colonial Puritanism but of the modern Enlightenment. North belittled the argument that the appearance of the phrase "in the Year of our Lord" indicated the document's Christian character.[125] Conservative Christians had long been duped by the myth of a Christian founding. Rather than imagine traces of Christian influence where there were not, North advised they bravely acknowledge that the Constitution is indeed apostate. "Let us cut our losses now. It is time to scrap this particular revisionist effort. It has produced nothing but confusion in the minds of Christians and ridicule from the humanists who have the footnotes on their side in this confrontation." North compared "the interdenominational American civil religion" to the idolatrous altars King Jeroboam of Israel erected at Dan and Beth El—a religion to serve the needs of the state. "The worship of the U.S. Constitution has been a popular form of this ancient practice, especially in conservative Christian circles. It is not seen as a flawed tool in need of revision but as a holy witness to the truth of the moral validity of permanent political pluralism." It was long past time to renounce this false god, tear down the idol, and affirm a Christian national covenant. There could be no Christian compromise with the pluralism that rested at the very foundation of the American experiment. "To admit the historical truth of 1787–89 would mean that a restoration of so-called 'original American Constitutionalism' would change nothing covenantally. The nation would still rest judicially on an apostate covenant."[126]

What was needed was a new founding.

Christians who wish to restore covenantal continuity with the nation's original Puritan founders ought to excommunicate Freemasons from their churches, pull their children from the public schools, and work toward correcting the apostate Constitution, participating in the democratic process to put forward and ratify an amendment acknowledging God as sovereign and the Bible as the ultimate source of the law. "A constitution's Preamble is the appropriate place to declare this publicly," North suggested. "The Preamble should be a nation's Declaration of Absolute Dependence on the Trinitarian God of the Bible. The Preamble should therefore declare the Bible as the unchanging law of the land. It should declare this law as being immune to any subsequent alteration. Thus, any public rejection of this judicial standard would be identifiable as a breaking of the national covenant." "What is needed," North proclaimed, "is a very simple modification of the U.S. Constitution." To wit,

> First, the Preamble should begin: "We the people of the United States, **as the lawful delegated agents of the Trinitarian God of the Bible,** do ordain and establish. . . ." Second, Article VI, Clause 3, should state "The Senators and Representatives before mentioned, and the Members of the several State Legislatures, and all the executive and judicial Officers, both of the United States and of the several States, shall be bound by Oath or Affirmation, to support this Constitution; and **a Trinitarian religious Test shall be required** as a Qualification to any Office or public Trust under the United States."

"These minimal steps," he added, "would mark the overthrow of the Masonic revolution of 1787–88."[127]

North expected that this suggestion "will be attacked as immoral, unamerican, and tyrannical. It will be attacked as being undemocratic—the greatest political sin of this dying era." Yet he maintained it was completely in accord with "the fundamental principle of political pluralism: the legal right to change the system to non-pluralism."[128] He conceded that he did not regard democracy as a legitimate form of political order but insisted that the allegation that Reconstructionists sought the abolition of democracy was misleading. Their theocratic society would indeed come about through "democratic" means: "Democratically, meaning a bottom-up movement initiated by the Holy Spirit, voters will progressively enact the whole law-order of God. This will probably take several centuries." He explained:

> What the critics of theocracy always assume is that the imposition of God's law in civil government has to be anti-democratic, i.e., opposed to the principle of political representation. It assumes that civil rulers impose God's law on recalcitrant citizens, who are somehow deprived of their right or actual ability to bring negative political sanctions against their rulers. But if the Spirit of God moves a vast majority of men to confess Jesus Christ as Lord and Savior, and if they return to the Old Testament in search of biblical blueprints, then the resulting theocratic republic will be legitimate in terms of democratic theory. That this idea is antithetical to the eschatological visions and schemes of humanists, amillennialists, and premillennialists does not refute the theory. Nevertheless, humanists, amillennialists, and premillennialists continue

publicly to misinterpret the position of Christian Reconstruction because these critics are intellectually incapable of equating *theocracy* with *democracy*. They do not believe that it is possible for large numbers of people voluntarily to become theonomists; after all, *they* haven't!

According to North, a democracy of Christians guided by the Spirit would come to vote itself out of existence. This would, of course, spell the end of liberalism and pluralism in America. At such a time, only orthodox Christians in good standing in their churches would be citizens of the theocratic republic.[129]

The volatile atmosphere of the late twentieth century was ripe for such a transformation, North believed. Manifold social, economic, political, technological, and environmental crises were weakening the resistance of the establishment's political pluralism/polytheism and preparing minds for postliberal ideas. "*God has been plowing up our ethically erosion-prone world since World War I, and this process is accelerating,*" he wrote. "This has created a unique opportunity for Christian revival, but this time the revival could lead to a broad-based cultural transformation. Revival could produce an international revolution: family by family, church by church, nation by nation. For a true social revolution to take place, there must be a transformation of the legal order. This transformation takes several generations, but without it, there has been no revolution, only a *coup d'etat.*" In the end, his vision was global: "Politically, the only legitimate long-term biblical goal is the creation of a worldwide theocratic republic."[130] In the meantime, North became more and more convinced that the world was on the verge of economic collapse (in the late 1990s, he was a vocal proponent of the coming Y2K computer glitch disaster), and in his publications he advised his readership to prepare by stockpiling food, gold, and firearms. In ways he sounded like a premillennial catastrophist, but instead of social collapse presaging the immediate return of Christ he forecast an opportunity for reconstruction by means of survivalism. He also made a good deal of money peddling his advice to the worried.

North dedicated *Political Polytheism* "to the members, living and dead, of the Reformed Presbyterian Church of North America ('Covenanters') who for 190 years have smelled a rat in Philadelphia." That was the locution Patrick Henry is said to have used to explain his refusal to attend the Constitutional Convention in 1787.

Gary North's emphatically negative evaluation of the Framers and their Constitution was very much a minority report in Reconstructionist circles.[131] Whether for substantive or tactical reasons, most associated with the movement embraced some conception of a Christian founding, arguing that the ideas behind and the structure of the Constitution had been derived from Scripture and the Reformed tradition.[132] The Reconstructionists did not look to restore some past America but instructed Americans to commit themselves to Christ and transform the nation in the future. An explicitly Christian Constitution would not have made the people Christian or sustained their religious devotion. Gary DeMar suggested that even if the Constitution had a Christian preamble, it would not have prevented "the nation's draft into secularism," for even the various acknowledgments of God in the state constitutions failed to "reinforce Christian character of the people." Christianity could not be legislated from the top down. Constitutional reform would only come after religious revival.[133] That America's spiritual climate was such that a constitutional change was impossible in the present moment was a point that the Reformed Presbyterian advocates of a Christian amendment conceded, even as they maintained the value of making their case "to educate individualist American Christians, who practice a privatized religion, that Christ rules public as well as private matters."[134]

The Reconstructionist movement nevertheless attracted some latter-day remnants of the National Reform Association. The NRA developed working relationships with Rushdoony and his followers, publishing in each other's periodicals and speaking at each other's meetings and conventions.[135] The Reverend P. Andrew Sandlin, once president of the NRA, became editor of the *Chalcedon Report*; in the late 1990s, he called the association's leadership "a strong working coalition of Reformed Presbyterians and theonomists."[136] The NRA had moved beyond the big tent it had pitched in the 1860s and '70s to shore up longstanding Protestant privileges. Influenced by the Reconstructionists, some of its members realized that the national confession acknowledging the sovereignty of God and the lordship of Christ would not be sufficient to establish a truly Christian commonwealth. The Constitution also needed to acknowledge the specific authority of biblical law and the policies that would be consequently implemented in accordance with its dictates. If the nation was under the sovereignty of Christ (rather than the sovereignty of "the people"), was not it also subject to the King's law? Otherwise, a national confession could be understood to endorse the heretical policies of the social gospel or liberation theology or the positions of the World Council of Churches. And they criticized those evangelicals who compromised with American culture by advocating for pluralism and religious liberty—that is, the liberty of false religions—and for using such equivocal language as "family values" and the "faith of the founding Fathers" and "natural law." These "politically correct" churches refused to preach Christian civil government and had surrendered biblical truth so as not to offend the infidels. "The antidote to the evangelical political compromise is repentance and a return to the biblical truth of the lordship of Jesus Christ over all nations—his mediatorial reign, and the authority of biblical law—theonomy."[137]

In the end, perhaps the nature of the Founding was irrelevant. Whether they believed that the Constitution of 1787 was the product of a Calvinist ethos or an anti-Christian conspiracy, the Reconstructionists all agreed that there was no accommodation with the current American regime to be had. The postmillennial theonomic vision required a wholesale rejection of the American constitutional order of the separation of church and state and religious liberty. Between Christianity and humanism there was to be no détente. The choice was Christ or chaos. "Democracy" was approved only as a means to the ultimate rule of God's law. Rushdoony and his disciples were not restorationists. They didn't hope to restore America to what they believed was its true founding. Nor did they long for the golden age of Christian America being preached by the leaders of New Christian Right. They were, rather, preparing the ground for a glorious theocratic future, though it may take a thousand years to come to be.

In May 1990, in the third issue of his journal *First Things*, Richard John Neuhaus pondered the persisting allure of Christian Reconstructionism. In the wake of evangelical disappointment that the Reagan administration had failed to bring about their hoped-for Christian America, the theonomists appeared to provide "the promise of a rationale for continued political engagement after yet another god had failed." There was also something "deeply American" about their project—its optimism, its can-do attitude. Theonomy could be considered the manifestation of "muscular Christianity," which was also part of its appeal. Yet Neuhaus also suggested the movement touched a deeply rooted desire: the honest and irrepressibly Christian yearning for the coming of the kingdom. Theonomy "manifests an abiding temptation in our Judeo-Christian history" to immanentize the eschaton and implement a Christian politics that would bring heaven down to earth. Like Thomas Müntzer and his followers in the sixteenth century, the modern social gospel movement, and contemporary "radical evangelicals" and "liberation theologians," they were pursuers of the millennium.

Father Neuhaus had been a radical Lutheran pastor in his youth, a supporter of civil rights and a fierce opponent of the war in Vietnam, but during the seventies he migrated to the right politically and in faith to Catholicism (he was received into the church in 1990). Catholics, Protestants, and Jews could join forces in articulating a public philosophy and re-sacralizing what had become "the naked public square," thereby renewing America's democratic order. Like John Courtney Murray, Neuhaus believed that natural law (rather than evangelical appeals to the Bible or religious feeling) could provide the basis for the American consensus. With this agenda in mind, he judged Reconstructionism "a dull heresy peddled to disappointed people who are angry because they have not received what they had no good reason to expect," but worried about its enduring influence, in particular over evangelicals who lacked a "theologically informed political philosophy that could sustain long-term engagement in public contest over the ordering of society." "There is little doubt that theonomy is an aberration of historic Christianity," Neuhaus mused, "but whether it is at all that temporary is another matter. As it has moved from eccentric marginality to a position of some influence, so it could, just conceivably, go on to become the dominant system of thought on the religious right. Such a development would have inestimable consequences for the relationship between religion and American public life."[138]

Perhaps Neuhaus was right to be concerned. The ideas and visions of political Christianity generated by the Reconstructionists were still flowing into the larger stream of American Christianity, inspiring political initiatives to retake America from the secularists. By rejecting the legitimacy of liberalism, democracy, and religious pluralism and envisioning the advent of a republic under God and God's law, Reconstructionism, we might say, could be considered a grave American heresy as well.

CHAPTER SEVEN

A Mistake with Lasting Consequences

Postliberals and National Conservatives

"The Constitution promises liberty to all within its reach, a liberty that includes certain specific rights that allow persons, within a lawful realm, to define and express their identity," announced Justice Anthony Kennedy at the opening of his majority opinion in *Obergefell v. Hodges* (2015), recognizing the constitutional right for same-sex couples to marry with "equal dignity in the eyes of the law" and receive the legal and material benefits that flow from government recognition of the relationship.[1]

The dissenting judges took issue with the majority's interpretation of the Fourteenth Amendment's Due Process and Equal Protection Clauses and worried about the decision's chilling consequences for religious liberty. But they also argued that the ruling was a departure from the American tradition itself. In his dissenting opinion, Justice Antonin Scalia lamented that Kennedy's decision was a "judicial Putsch" and "a threat to American democracy," which "robs the People of the most important liberty they asserted in the Declaration of Independence and won in the Revolution of 1776: the freedom to govern themselves." It was, in his view, "a naked judicial claim to legislative—indeed, superlegislative—power; a claim fundamentally at odds with our system of government." Justice Clarence Thomas, in his own dissent, added that the court's decision was "at odds not only with the Constitution, but with the principles upon which our Nation was built." The majority had misunderstood the liberty the Framers of the Constitution had sought to protect ("freedom from government action, not entitlement to government benefits") and, further, wrongly believed that their action could "advance the 'dignity' of same-sex couples." Kennedy's reflection on dignity, in Thomas's account, "rejects the idea—captured in our Declaration of Independence—that human dignity is innate and suggests instead that it comes from the Government"— paradoxically appealing to Jefferson's assertions of natural equality and inalienable rights (even as he elided mention of "the pursuit of happiness") to argue against the right of gays and lesbians to marry the partners of their choice.[2]

Obergefell was predictably celebrated by progressives and denounced by religious conservatives. In a symposium published in *First Things* the day after the ruling came down, contributors soundly bemoaned what the court had wrought. Princeton legal scholar and political theorist Robert P. George called *Obergefell* "a lawless ruling," "an egregious act of judicial usurpation" on the order of *Roe v. Wade* and *Dred Scott*, and recommended that its opponents look to Lincoln for inspiration and encouragement as they prepared for another long struggle not only for traditional marriage but for the very principle of democratic self-government. He was not alone in that assessment. Several of the respondents admitted to not being surprised by the court's decision, however disappointed they were by it. And some realized that the decision was not simply "an act of raw judicial power" but a reflection of where the culture had been heading. The argument that by recognizing a constitutional right to same-sex marriage the Supreme Court had short-circuited the democratic process assumed that the will of the people had indeed been overruled. But it appeared in fact that those five justices in the majority had interpreted the Constitution to find a right that an increasing majority of Americans approved of. And that majority included many *religious* Americans. Even before June 2015, same-sex marriage was legal in thirty-six states and the District of Columbia, made so by legislation, state court rulings, and voter referenda. Support for such measures was no longer countercultural; indeed, the winds of American culture were in their sails. *Obergefell* was not so much an act of judicial usurpation as a dénouement. As Reformed theologian Peter J. Leithart conceded, "Orthodox Christianity has lost all cultural potency in the United States." "We lost the culture long before we lost the Supreme Court," the conservative writer Rod Dreher sighed.[3]

The nation's pivot to support for same-sex marriage was swift and, for religious conservatives, jarring. With *Obergefell*, some feared that their decades-long culture war might be a lost cause. In their eyes, the decision did not merely announce an expansion of rights to gays and lesbians (providing legal sanction to a lifestyle they deemed sinful) but amounted to the remaking—or destruction—of the very institution of marriage, premised on a novel understanding of human nature and the purpose of the family. The legal protection of homosexual marriage, aside from its increased social acceptance and widespread cultural celebration, effectively announced the United States as a post-Christian, even anti-Christian, order and portended the persecution of the faithful. The expected election of Hillary Clinton in 2016 would solidify that liberal triumph and ensure civilizational collapse.

A way of coping with such defeats was what pollster Robert P. Jones called a "conditional surrender"—appealing to the First Amendment's Free Exercise Clause and the Religious Freedom Restoration Act of 1993 for protection from an increasingly hostile secular culture and the overweening demands of the liberal state. While the First Amendment had been long understood to protect the rights of religious minorities, the religious conservatives' strategy was to use it to demand exemptions from government mandates and antidiscrimination laws. The groundwork for this position was laid back in the 1970s, when the religious conservatives lobbied legislators to carve out conscience exemptions for health-care providers and institutions and deployed claims of religious freedom against challenges to the tax-exempt status of segregated religious schools. But, as Jones observed, "the new doctrine of religious liberty asserts that individuals should be able to carry religious objections from their private life into their public roles as service providers, business owners, and even elected officials."[4] And in case after case, the Roberts Court proved disposed to granting their wishes, extending religious liberty exceptions not only to religious orders and schools but also to bakers of wedding cakes and enormous for-profit corporations.

Extending constitutional protections of free exercise in many of these cases amounted to a significant, and activist, turn in First Amendment jurisprudence (and required overruling decades of well-established precedent). Yet for some religious conservatives, that was not sufficient to protect their interests. The trend lines were clearly running in the wrong direction. America's religious conservatives had long been frustrated that their victories at the ballot box did not translate into policy achievements. The so-called windows opened by two terms of Ronald Reagan and two of George W. Bush had failed to roll back a half century of liberal advances. *Roe v. Wade* was still officially the law of the land (even if abortion rights were being significantly curtailed in many red states). You could not achieve goals by democratic means if liberalism was always expanding the rights of ever more unencumbered individuals at the expense of traditional values.

Jerry Falwell and Francis Schaeffer had longed to restore an erstwhile Christian America. But what if the seeds of post-Christian American had been planted at its founding?

In his contribution to the *First Things* symposium on *Obergefell*, the conservative editor and commentator Rod Dreher suggested that "the common culture—insofar as we have one—is so far gone into decadence and individualism that the only sensible thing for us to do is to strategically retreat from the mainstream to strengthen our Christian commitments, and our church communities." A convert (from Methodism to Roman Catholicism to Orthodoxy), Dreher fancied himself a countercultural conservative in the mold of Russell Kirk and Wendell Berry, and for several years had been calling for a "communal withdrawal . . . for the sake of sheltering one's faith and family from corrosive modernity and cultivating a more traditional way of life."⁵ For Dreher, same-sex marriage was the decisive battle in the culture war, and the Supreme Court's landmark *Obergefell* decision became "the Waterloo of religious conservatism." He thus pronounced the American culture war concluded, with "hostile secular nihilism" the victorious and "traditional, historical Christianity" the defeated. "The cultural left—which is to say, increasingly the American mainstream—has no intention of living in a postwar peace," he forewarned. "It is pressing forward with a harsh, relentless occupation."⁶ Finding shelter was now even more urgent.

Dreher made his case at length in his bestselling 2017 book, *The Benedict Option*. While Dreher regarded the contemporary cultural battles over gay (and now transgender) rights as a consequence of the Sexual Revolution of the 1960s, he had come to believe that they were end-stage symptoms of a disease that had infected the West centuries ago. Once upon a time, in those happier Middle Ages, European Christians resided in a world of shared meaning and purpose; "men construed reality in a way that empowered them to harmonize everything conceptually and find meaning among the chaos."⁷ This he christened a "sacramental" worldview, and it had its highest expression in the metaphysical realism of the Scholastics. But this worldview and the religious, moral, and cultural unity it underwrote did not hold. Taking up the narrative advanced by historian Brad S. Gregory, Dreher told how this vision of the immanent and "integral connection" between God and his creation, the transcendent and the material, was severed by the nominalist philosophers of the fourteenth century, and the medieval dreamtime evaporated. The shattering of this vision of reality inexorably brought about the decoupling of science from theology, the this-worldly humanistic striving of the Renaissance, the Reformation challenges to religious authority and the shattering of Christian unity in Europe, the Enlightenment ("the decisive break with the Christian legacy of the West"), and the subsequent privatization of religion, the rise of democracy and capitalism, and the Sexual Revolution. What had begun with the abstruse metaphysical speculations of some overthinking theologians had, in this legend of the fall, ended with our present cultural disintegration.[8]

"It is far more important to me to preserve the faith than to preserve liberal democracy and the American order," Dreher once confessed, and it's not hard to see why he believed his conceptions of orthodox Christianity and the American project were fundamentally at odds.[9] The problem wasn't simply the overreach of the courts but something much deeper and more ingrained. The United States was indeed a secular, liberal, Enlightenment polity, and it was founded on the false and dangerous Enlightenment program—the attempt to rely on reason alone to "create a secular morality," "impose man's natural will upon nature," and unleash "the freely choosing individual." Dreher noted the nefarious influence of Enlightenment deism, which rejected supernatural revelation and the God of the Bible for a "God that is a cosmic architect who created the universe but does not interact with it." "Most of the American Founding Fathers were either confessed Deists like Benjamin Franklin (also a Freemason) or strongly influenced by Deism (e.g., Thomas Jefferson)," he claimed. "Deism was a powerful intellectual force in eighteenth-century American life." John Adams, for what it's worth, was "a practicing Unitarian." The intellectual godfather of the Founding, John Locke, though "technically not a Deist," nevertheless developed a political philosophy "strongly consonant with Deist principles." "The U.S. Constitution, a Lockean document, privatizes religion, separating it from the state." In doing so, it "profoundly shaped the American religious consciousness" and "laid the groundwork for excluding religion from the public square"; the government it established "has no ultimate conception of the good, and it regards its own role as limited to protecting the rights of individuals." America was already potentially post-Christian at its founding, as the very ideas behind it "contained the seeds of Christianity's undoing." Whatever Christian commitments and values Americans may have shared at that time could not withstand the forces unleashed against them by democracy, capitalism, and unconstrained sexual desire. What this story disclosed was that "the disorder in American public life derives from disorder within the American soul." Given the nation's constitutional foundations, how could things have turned out otherwise? America was destined to become a new Babylon.[10]

The "end point of modernity," in Dreher's recounting, was already announced by Justice Anthony Kennedy in his 1992 decision in *Planned Parenthood v. Casey*: "At the heart of liberty is the right to define one's own concept of existence, of meaning, of the universe, and of the mystery of human life." Dreher acidly observed that the pronouncement was a celebration of "the autonomous, freely choosing individual, finding meaning in no one but himself." Such was the fundamental maxim of our decadent post-Christian era. It heralded the arrival of a new dark age. Decisions like *Obergefell* were not betrayals of the founding ideas but really the logical outworking of them. There could be no way to reconcile a truly authentic Christian life with liberal modernity.[11] America's churches were no longer capable of holding off the onslaught of the decadent secularist hordes. Indeed, by now, all too many of America's nominally Christian churches had utterly abandoned orthodox teaching and had become corrupted by "a sneaky kind of secularism." This secularism in religious garb Dreher identified as "Moralistic Therapeutic Deism," a term coined by sociologists Christian Smith and Melinda Lundquist Denton. The theology professed by this "pseudo-Christianity"—something to the order of God exists and wants us to be happy and nice to one another—is far from the spiritual and moral teachings of the true faith.[12] By taking up and preaching this "new civil religion," which blesses and sanctifies the secular liberal order, the churches had effectively capitulated to the dominant and anti-Christian culture. "We have allowed our children to be catechized by the culture and have produced an anesthetizing religion suited for little more than being a chaplaincy to the liberal individualistic order," Dreher lamented.[13]

And so Dreher proposed a postliberal project: an "antipolitical politics" whereby the truly faithful might turn away from the fleshpots of America, to engage in "a strategic withdrawal . . . to gain the church militant a space in which to regroup, retrain, and reengage in the long struggle."[14]

Dreher dubbed this "the Benedict Option," elaborating on something the moral philosopher Alasdair MacIntyre wrote at the end of his influential book *After Virtue*.[15] Lamenting the loss of a moral consensus, MacIntyre suggested that those who endeavored to live serious and ordered lives might choose to establish "local forms of community within which civility and the intellectual and moral life can be sustained through the new dark ages which are already upon us." MacIntyre famously closed his meditation with the pronouncement "We are waiting not for a Godot, but for another—doubtless very different—St.

Benedict."[16] That historical Benedict had instituted a monastic "rule," the practical instructions to keep Christian learning and virtues alive as Rome declined.
Some three and a half decades following the initial publication of *After Virtue*,
Dreher had come forth as that new Benedict with his own rule—bestowing
instructions on how to build such arks in which to wait out the floodwaters that
"liquid modernity" unleashed. American Christians were not to retreat to
monasteries, of course, but to establish intentional communities, rooted in
theological orthodoxy and shared moral values, ideally situated in remote rural
parts of the country, far from the turbulence and temptations of the secular city
and the public school system. There they would reside in internal exile in a
post-Christian world, prepared for the possibility of marginalization, poverty,
and even martyrdom, as they awaited the dawn of a new Christendom.[17]

The political theorist Patrick J. Deneen arrived at a similar conclusion in his
2018 book, *Why Liberalism Failed.* Deneen charted the course of "liberalism"—an
abstraction granted almost sinister agency—from its emergence in the seventeenth century ("a wager that political society could be grounded on a different
footing"[18]) to its fruition in contemporary Western society, a story of success that
culminated in moral, social, environmental, and spiritual disaster. A bracing yet
somewhat sour read, *Why Liberalism Failed* turned out to be widely read and highly
praised by conservative commentators and beyond. Former president Barack
Obama recommended it as a summer reading selection. "I don't agree with most
of the author's conclusions," Obama wrote, "but the book offers cogent insights
into the loss of meaning and community that many in the West feel, issues that
liberal democracies ignore at their own peril."[19]

Liberalism was, in Deneen's account, an intentional project—and it had
become the operating system of the modern West. "The foundations of liberalism," he claimed, "were laid by a series of thinkers whose central aim was to
disassemble what they concluded were irrational religious and social norms in
the pursuit of civil peace that might in turn foster stability and prosperity, and
eventually individual liberty of conscience and action." The project commenced
with a shift in the way we think about and understand ourselves. Liberals (and
pre-liberals such as Francis Bacon and Thomas Hobbes) set out to remake the
world according to a new—and false—anthropology. They conceived of human
beings as "rights-bearing individuals who could fashion and pursue for themselves their own version of the good life." But they really aspired to free the individual from authority, culture, and tradition—even human nature itself.
Liberalism undermined all the bonds of human solidarity that had been forged

over time by the family, the church, and the whole range of social associations and institutions embedded in localities. In the place of all that, liberalism has produced an increasingly centralized and tyrannical state to "protect" the radically unencumbered individual's enjoyment of rights, property, and pursuit of consumption. "As liberalism has 'become more fully itself,' as its inner logic has become more evident and its self-contradictions manifest, it has generated pathologies that are at once deformations of its claims yet realizations of liberal ideology," Deneen claimed. "A political philosophy that was launched to foster greater equality, defend a pluralist tapestry of different cultures and beliefs, protect human dignity, and, of course, expand liberty, in practice generates titanic inequality, enforces uniformity and homogeneity, fosters material and spiritual degradation, and undermines freedom." Intrinsically incapable of establishing and maintaining a virtuous commonwealth, liberalism has succeeded in dismantling all settled forms of human community and establishing in their stead our present *res idiotica*. We now find ourselves forced to be free (or, rather, disordered) within the iron cage of this madhouse prison.[20]

In Deneen's account, liberalism's "political architecture that proposed transforming all aspects of human life to conform to a preconceived political plan" was first put into effect by the American founding. The Constitution is the " 'applied technology' of liberal theory," intentionally designed not only to establish a liberal government but also to "shape a distinctly different modern human." Understanding that "the first object of government is the protection of 'the diversity in the faculties of men,' " the Framers hoped to optimize "the sphere of individual liberty." Madison and his associates intended to undercut traditional affinities and local attachments, relocate power from the locality to the center, and remake the people into "individuals who, above all, would strive to achieve our own individual ambitions and desires." (Those more sympathetic to the Madisonian project might say that the Constitution "rearranges" or "displaces" those prior attachments or overlays them with others of individual choice.) "The ancient commendation of virtue and aspiration to the common good was to be replaced by the basic motivation of modern republicanism—the pursuit of self-interest that leads to the overall increase of power and thus fulfillment of desires," Deneen noted. (In his analysis, he appealed nearly exclusively to Madison's argument in *Federalist* No. 10 as the animating spirit of the Constitution.) The political tribes of progressives and conservatives that have emerged and now compete represent "different sides of the same counterfeit coin." American "conservatives" who believed a "return to the governing philosophy of the Constitution" would solve the nation's contemporary problems simply did not understand the very nature of that system. For the Framers were motivated not by timeless and universal wisdom but by the modern and specious ideas they took from the writings of Bacon, Hobbes, and Locke. The United States was born as a fundamentally liberal project and as such was doomed from the start; the baleful consequences suffered today were preordained. The nation's political ideology was and continues to be at odds with the Christian tradition and culture in which it was planted and which it has denatured.[21]

Deneen did not foresee a happy future for the nation, as least in the short term. Liberalism's all-too-apparent failures—growing economic inequality, social conformism, environmental degradation, political tyranny—are paradoxically symptoms of its very success that no further application of liberal measures will ameliorate. Indeed, as its reign continues to expand, liberal society will become more and more illiberal, taking "the form of the administrative state run by a small minority who increasingly disdain democracy," a "liberalocratic despotism." Alternatively, mounting frustrations and discontent may at some point bring about the collapse of the liberal order and its replacement by another type of regime. "Some form of populist nationalist authoritarianism or military autocracy seems altogether plausible as an answer to the anger and fear of a postliberal citizenry," Deneen presaged.[22]

Deneen hoped some "humane alternative" might yet emerge from our confusion but cautioned against seeking political redemption from the degradations of liberalism in some new or repurposed ideology. We must resist the temptation of concocting a political theory that might replace liberalism; instead, we must gird ourselves to pass through liberalism as a damaging but necessary stage of human history and try to build on its accomplishments even as we learn from its failures. In the meantime, we might find solace in "the remnants of orthodox religious traditions" and in the founding, not of a new political regime, but of "alternative communities and new cultures that will live outside the gathering wreckage of liberalism's twilight years." Presumably, such localist communities (and the "better" social, cultural, and economic practices that they nurture) would not be molded by false anthropologies and would not reproduce liberal individualists. Although nowhere explicitly mentioned in the book (Deneen appealed vaguely to the "classical" and "Christian" traditions), it is not difficult to discern the traditionalist Catholic commitments that lay behind Deneen's critique of liberalism and all its works.[23] Deneen understood that America was founded as a liberal regime—by and for a broadly Protestant people; it was, he remarked elsewhere, "essentially the first Protestant nation."[24]

Yet he appeared reluctant to acknowledge that liberalism—the secular regime it imagines, its commitments to human dignity and freedom, and its unceasing project of progress—is in some way an outgrowth of Christian ideals. Nor did he appear to grant that liberals, too, have families and friendships, join religious organizations and civil associations, forge deep bonds of solidarity, and participate in all sorts of projects aimed at some conception of a common good.[25]

Coming after such a furious indictment, Deneen's rather modest proposal may strike the reader as anticlimactic. For what did such a retreat to localism amount to but a kind of failure of nerve, a concession to some new modus vivendi with liberalism, even in its twilight. (One thinks of the Catholic enclaves of yore.) Critics noted that such experiments in traditional living would always be subject to the forbearance and munificence of the liberal regime (even the attempt to cultivate local economies would depend on the larger depersonalizing modern economy). Then again, the very existence of such communities is underwritten by the field of liberty that the liberal regime established and maintains. Dreher himself conceded that the protections of religious liberty granted by the liberal order that he so despises at least provide the possibility to build those communities of virtue and meaning and to insulate those communities from that very same liberal order.[26] Even so, doing so might be easier said than done (all those Amish and ultra-Orthodox Jewish communities did not spring up overnight); the members of such communities would not be able to seal themselves off hermetically from the wider world and would still have some exposure to its many temptations and corruptions, freedoms and opportunities. Would those raised within such Benedict communities choose to remain within their sacred precincts? Some may long to go home, but others yearn desperately to escape the confines of their upbringing.

In an influential review of *Why Liberalism Failed*, Harvard law professor Adrian Vermeule praised Deneen's diagnosis of the problem but suggested his proposed remedy was inadequate—indeed, a "relapse" into the very liberalism he had so masterfully exposed. The reason for this shortcoming, Vermeule suggested, was that Deneen intuited but did not fully recognize liberalism for what it really is, and was therefore incapable of proposing a way out of the "interim stage we currently occupy." For liberalism is not only an ideology but "a world religion" (and, as Vermeule wrote elsewhere, "an imperfectly secularized offshoot of Christianity, ... an odd and distinctive mix of Pelagianism and Gnosticism"), "a fighting, evangelistic faith," replete with its own liturgy (its liberal-democratic creed proclaiming commitments to individual autonomy, egalitarianism, secularism), sacraments (its original ritual being the French Revolutionary Festival of Reason in 1793, but nowadays performed in protest marches, confessions of privilege, declarations of allyship, and denunciations and cancelations of the recalcitrant and unrepentant), a soteriology (the Enlightenment myth of progress) that "immanentizes the eschaton," and its own backsliders, apostates, and heretics. Liberalism, Vermeule contended in a later essay, is also "a lived and very concrete type of political-theological order," yet one that is fundamentally disruptive, as its public "liturgy" must always challenge "the traditions, the mores and life-ways, of the broad mass of the population" in the name of freedom overcoming darkness. "The relentless dynamic of liberalism [that is, the interminable demand for 'progress'] tends to undermine the 'peace, security and order' that liberalism itself promises," thus generating destabilizing populist backlash, and its "uneasy alliance" with democracy itself comes under increasing strain. Liberalism, as presented by Vermeule, is an order fundamentally at odds with "the natural principles of rule" (as articulated by the early modern Catholic tradition of *ragion di stato*); from this perspective, liberalism fails to recognize itself as the theological-political order of disorder (which is why liberalism will fail).[27]

Vermeule was thus dissatisfied with Deneen's advocacy of a tactical retreat to a "vague communitarian localism," noting that the illiberal communities exist only by the pleasure of the liberal regime and in the end are materially and ideologically defenseless against it. An expert in administrative law whose own spiritual journey had brought him to Rome, Vermeule pitched, in what he called a bit of "fan fiction," a more audacious proposal that he believed to be "more consistent with Deneen's own argument": a quiet coup against the liberal "imperium." He suggested that motivated and well-trained postliberal elites, rather than retreat from the world or try to build democratic majorities to reshape policy, ought to "strategically locate themselves within liberal institutions and work to undo the liberalism of the state from within," and then use the machinery of the administrative state to impose upon the country their "substantive comprehensive theory of the good." A great restaffing, as it were, replacing the liberal technocrats and functionaries with traditionally minded ones who would work to steadily transform the state and society. (To take dominion, as others might say.) Vermeule weirdly presented the Old Testament characters of Joseph, Mordecai and Esther, and Daniel as exemplars of infiltrators of the state, and Paul of the New Testament, who "preached the advent of a new order from within the very urban heart of the imperium." (To be sure, those characters from the Hebrew Bible were not out to remake those empires into Jewish theocracies, and the notion of Paul setting his followers off to burrow themselves into the Roman bureaucracy in order to convert the empire and bring about the kingdom of God is a bit whimsical.) Vermeule's point, however, was that there was no need to withdraw to enclaves or dream of building a new order from scratch when they could deploy the administrative state and bureaucracy that liberalism had constructed as "the great instrument with which to restore a substantive politics of the good." "It may thus appear providential that liberalism, despite itself, has prepared a state capable of great tasks, as a legacy to bequeath to a new and doubtless very different future," Vermeule mused. The law professor was not coy about the possibility of state coercion in such a scheme: "It is a matter of finding a strategic position from which to sear the liberal faith with hot irons, to defeat and capture the hearts and minds of liberal agents, to take over the institutions of the old order that liberalism has itself prepared and to turn them to the promotion of human dignity and the common good." Citizens may have to be forced to be virtuous. The law is a pedagogue, and sometime pedagogues require firm rulers.[28]

A few years later, in a provocative essay appearing in *The Atlantic* (soon expanded into a short book), postliberalism's leading legal mind articulated a constitutional doctrine to legitimate such a future takeover of the American state.[29] For too long American jurisprudence had been held captive by two competing and erroneous theories of constitutional interpretation—left-liberal progressivism and originalism. While originalism (or, more precisely, the many varieties of "originalism") had allowed constitutional conservatives to push back against the excesses of the Warren and Burger courts and the advance of progressivism and "to survive and even flourish in a hostile environment" (and, in doing so, becoming something of a "creed . . . to which potential nominees could pledge fidelity"), Vermeule argued that it outlived its usefulness and now stood as "an obstacle to the development of a robust, substantively conservative approach to constitutional law and interpretation."[30] An essentially defensive tactic, originalism could not be called on to produce truly conservative ends, bound as it is to a narrow focus on positive law. (It does not appear that jurists with purportedly originalist views have been as constrained by their theory as Vermeule appears to suggest.) With the recent ascendency of conservatives in the courts, Vermeule suggested it was time for them to show some initiative and adopt a new doctrine.

What Vermeule was proposing was closer to the progressive notion of a "living" constitution, its meaning ever evolving as judges adapt its fundamental principles in light of new problems and changing attitudes. But progressives, he observed, were aiming at the wrong end—namely, "the relentless expansion of individual autonomy." A "substantive moral conservativism," or "illiberal legalism"—not "enslaved to the original meaning of the Constitution" and "liberated from the left-liberals' overarching sacramental narrative"—by contrast, would "be based on the principles that government helps direct persons, associations, and society generally toward the common good, and that strong rule in the interest of attaining the common good is entirely legitimate."[31] Those were the principles that "officials (including, but by no means limited to, judges) should read into the majestic generalities and ambiguities of the written Constitution,"[32] Vermeule wrote (mocking Justice William J. Brennan Jr.'s well-known encomium: "[The Constitution's] majestic generalities and ennobling pronouncements are both luminous and obscure. This ambiguity of course calls forth interpretation, the interaction of reader and text"[33]). "These principles," the law professor explained, "include respect for the authority of rule and of rulers; respect for the hierarchies needed for society to function; solidarity within and among families, social groups, and workers' unions, trade associations, and professions; appropriate subsidiarity, or respect for the legitimate roles of public bodies and associations at all levels of government and society; and a candid willingness to 'legislate morality'—indeed, a recognition that all legislation is necessarily founded on some substantive conception of morality, and that the promotion of morality is a core and legitimate function of authority. Such principles promote the common good and make for a just and well-ordered society." This approach to the Constitution would only make clear that "promoting a substantive vision of the good is, always and everywhere, the proper function of rulers"—rather than "the liberal goal of maximizing individual autonomy or minimizing the abuse of power."[34]

"Common good constitutionalism," Vermeule contended, would really be a return to the nation's original understanding of the nature of law and justice, a retrieval of the "classical legal tradition," a vision of the law "as a rational ordering to the common good."[35] This was "the fundamental matrix for the thinking of the whole founding generation," which had been forgotten and overtaken by modern legal theories of progressivism and originalism.[36] The Founding, in his view, did not involve a radical break with this tradition but was a conscious articulation of it. "Both progressives and (reacting to them) originalists, imagining themselves mortal enemies, cut themselves off from the classical heritage of our law, constructed imagined pasts, and invented traditions that projected their own premises backward in time, erasing the classical law for present purposes."[37] An overcoming of our constitutional amnesia would break the progressive and originalist duopoly. To achieve these ends, the Constitution didn't need to be supplemented by something like a Christian amendment, because a deep account of the common good was already embedded within it. This account simply needed to be recovered and acted on. Where the text says the purpose of the Constitution is to "promote the general Welfare," Vermeule read "the common good"—writ large.

Despite his claim that "common good constitutionalism" was only the recovery of an older, "classical" tradition of American jurisprudence, Vermeule's proposal might well be understood as an audacious reimagining of history, less a restoration than an attempt at a refounding.[38] Rather than advise anti-liberal traditionalists to take flight from the battle and withdraw into an impotent localism, Vermeule proposed they use the force of the law, enthused and well-placed bureaucrats of the administrative state, and a powerful executive to orient the polis toward his conception of the common good—and the highest good. And he dismissed any commitment to democracy as a "regime-form." A particular regime is legitimate only insofar as it is "oriented to the common good." And the legal order is prior to the regime itself. The "foundation of the American polity," its "living sovereignty," is not "the positive will of We the People embodied in the constitutional text enacted in 1788" but the *ius gentium*.[39] This claim involved lifting the Constitution out of its historical context and placing it into an entirely different framework, reading into it a political morality that opens up the possibility of religious authoritarianism utterly inconsistent with the document's values. Consider this chilling passage:

> Unlike legal liberalism, common-good constitutionalism does not suffer from a horror of political domination and hierarchy, because it sees that the law is paternal, a wise teacher, and an inculcator of good habits. Just authority in rulers can be exercised for the good of subjects, if necessary even against the subjects' own perception of what is best for them—perceptions that may change over time anyway, as the law teaches, habituates, and re-forms them. Subjects will come to thank the ruler whose legal structures, possibly experienced at first as coercive, encourage subjects to form more authentic desires for the individual and common goods, better habits, and beliefs that better track and promote communal well-being.[40]

Note well Vermeule's choice of "rulers" and "subjects" here and throughout, an implicit rejection of the very idea of democratic sovereignty.

Vermeule did not bother with the many problematic aspects of those other classical regimes—the institution of slavery and the sanctioned violence directed toward religious dissenters and minorities, for example. Further, his not infrequent references to such reactionary luminaries as Joseph de Maistre and the German jurist turned Nazi apologist Carl Schmitt raise uncomfortable questions about his true sentiments and intentions.[41] In his imagination, the Founders and Framers were more like Thomas Aquinas than Robert Bork or Antonin Scalia, let alone John Locke or Montesquieu. He wrote as though Article VI, Section 3, and the First Amendment did not exist. In his constitutional world, "the claim, from the notorious joint opinion in *Planned Parenthood v. Casey*, that each individual may 'define one's own concept of existence, of meaning, of the universe, and of the mystery of human life' should be not only rejected but stamped as abominable, beyond the realm of the acceptable forever after."[42] Vermeule's conception of the "common good" was already known and could be known to all. He did not explicitly state its origin, but it was clear that it would not come about by means of democratic deliberation. His inventory of "rights" that would be curtailed (free speech, sexual liberties, reproductive autonomy, for example) appeals to the concepts of solidarity and subsidiarity, and references to texts by Augustine, Thomas Aquinas, and Popes Leo XIII and Francis suggested otherwise.

In other fora, Vermeule stated his convictions more forthrightly. "The political Catholic wants to order the nation and its state to the natural and divine law, the tranquility of order, precisely because doing so is the best way to protect and shelter the localities in which genuinely human community, imbued with grace, can flourish. . . . The political Catholic thinks that not even the smallest particle of creation is off-limits to grace, which can perfect and elevate any part of nature, even the state and even the market."[43]

This counter-liberal proposal was, in short, a call for an American *ralliement*, to infiltrate and transform the liberal regime over time into a fully Catholic one, taking over the state bureaucracy (and sidestepping democratically elected representatives) so that it might rightly reorient its citizens.[44] The goal was not to restore the consensus that John Courtney Murray had discovered in the American founding but to usher in a better regime—a new Christendom. A Leonine option, if you will. And in this dream he was not alone. Vermeule is one of the more prominent of a new cadre of American Catholic "integralists" (notably the political theorist Gladdin Pappin and theologian C. C. Pecknold) who are repurposing the reactionary theological political argument of the late nineteenth century for the early twenty-first.[45] These men have no desire to forge an accommodation with the liberal order; they believe that liberalism forbids the church from being "catholic" (and God from being sovereign), allowing it to exist only as one religious "denomination" alongside the others (of which one may choose voluntarily to be a member, or not).[46] They reject the liberal regime's claim of substantive neutrality and the pluralism it preserves and adjudicates. And they aspire to remake the political order and have public policy promote the common good—as articulated in the moral, social, and economic teachings of the Roman Catholic Church.[47]

Not long after *Why Liberalism Failed* came out, Deneen realized that the collapse of the liberal order he believed to be inevitable was happening more quickly than he had previously envisaged. While he had earlier called for the recovery of traditional practices and the development of new communitarian ones, ahead of the development of wholesale new ideologies, in a preface composed for the new edition he stated that "epic theory becomes necessary when [the existing] paradigm loses its explanatory power, and events call forth a new departure in political thinking." It was time, he announced, for some new St. Augustine to get to work on a *City of God* for our soon-to-be postliberal age (an odd analogue, when you think about it, as the fifth-century bishop was writing in the wake of the collapse of a Christian empire; given that Deneen was dreaming of a new Christian dispensation, perhaps Eusebius would be a more appropriate model).[48]

An "epoch-defining book" like *City of God* requires some time to compose. But Deneen gave it a go and published his follow-up in the spring of 2023. He had since come around to Vermeule's view that the age of liberalism's failure required more than "the patient encouragement of new forms of community" on the small scale but called for out-and-out "regime change." Deneen imagined the (peaceful) overthrow of the liberal elites and the dislodging of their "ideological pursuit of progress," replacing the corrupt liberal regime with one that would provide "stability, order, continuity."[49]

Picking up on Vermeule's strategy of integration from within, Deneen suggested that "existing political forms can remain in place, as long as a fundamentally different ethos informs those institutions and the personnel who populate key offices and positions." The ethos informing the constitution would no longer aim at protecting individual rights by means of a system of checks and balances, the playing of faction off of faction, the messy working of democratic pluralism, but would be directed at their common good, by means of a blending of the interests and ethos of the two competing classes (the many and the few, or the common and the great) into "an internal harmony." He called this old-new theory of a mixed constitution (whose "deep origins lie in the classical and Christian traditions of the West") "aristopopulism"—"a better aristocracy brought about by a muscular populism and then, in turn, an elevation of the people by a better aristocracy."[50]

"What is to be done?" Deneen asked à la Lenin. This process of mixing the few and the many and replacing the current regime, its corrupt elites, and the totalizing power of "Woke Capitalism" (the "unholy alliance" of progressive individualism and corporate power) by common-good conservatism and its *aristoi* would require, in Deneen's judgment, "Machiavellian means to achieve Aristotelian ends"—that is, "the raw assertion of political power by a new generation of political actors inspired by an ethos of common-good conservatism" (a new confessional tribe?). He laid out a catalogue of policy proposals that he believed might help do so: a massive enlargement of the House of Representatives and the relocation of federal agencies out of Washington to places in the flyover country; a shift from primaries to caucuses in choosing candidates for public office; mandatory national service; government support of manufacturing industries; the "inculcation of civil virtue" by means of media shaming or outright censorship; weakening the power and influence of the universities (the factory and proving grounds of the liberal elite) and increasing resources to vocational education and the trades; expansion of pro-family (that is, "traditional family") policies (such as have been put into effect in Orbán's Hungary); and a "forthright acknowledgement and renewal of the Christian roots of our civilization," as "public acknowledgement and celebration of those Christian roots are essential to the creation of an ethos of genuine service by elites on behalf of those who do not share their advantages."[51] Unlike Vermeule, Deneen didn't argue that the Constitution had emerged from the classical Christian legal tradition, which, though it had been obscured, could simply be recovered. But proposing a new constitutional convention was perhaps too radical a proposal, one that, given the current condition of the *demos*, might not result in what was most needful.

And here Deneen's ultimate vision snapped into focus: while he might harken back to Aristotle for inspiration for his theory, in the end his championing of ordinary people demanded "a politics infused with the West's Christian inheritance." What was required was "a pervasive form of *postliberal integration*" to draw back together what liberalism had rent asunder (in Deneen's view, literally "all embodied and situated forms of human membership"). Americans needed to turn from the Lockean emphasis on the individual's "self-fashioning" announced in the Declaration of Independence, in which the commonwealth is established to secure our individual rights, to the Christian vision, described by Paul in 1 Corinthians 12–13 and John Winthrop in "A Model of Christian Charity," in which "inequality based on differences in talent, interest, and achievement is . . . a sign of our deeper solidarity, a window into our mutual need and insufficiency." And they needed to cast off liberalism's separation of religion and politics that had pushed out "considerations of an objective 'good' from political life." The emergence and spread of "wokeism" and its totalitarian ambitions, Deneen wrote, is "the consequence of the most fateful and fundamental 'separation': the so-called separation of church and state" ("so-called," for every political order, even liberalism, "rests on certain theological assumptions"). To overcome the disintegration brought about by liberalism, Deneen called for a restoration of Christendom.[52]

In the book's closing pages, Deneen turned to reflect on Jean Daniélou's *Prayer as a Political Problem*, a work that, incidentally, also had significant impact on L. Brent Bozell and the editors of *Triumph*. Daniélou spoke of the necessity of a comprehensively Christian society, a milieu that could forge and sustain a Christian people. And so Deneen closed what had become a theological-political treatise wistfully imagining "politics as a place for prayer, since politics is how we together seek to realize the good that is common." The hope, in short, for a politics that does not simply provide the means for human beings to exist together in the here and now but trains us toward eternity, a politics that would be redemptive, the possibility that liberalism's false promise of progress and freedom of religion obstructs.[53]

As they prophesize the advent of some postmodern, postliberal Christendom, a restoration of "the ordered community of tradition"[54] that will rescue us from an unbounded yet ultimately unfree liberal order, and as they labor from their professorates to inspire and forge a virtuous new elite to go out and capture the institutions of cultural and political power, America's integralists not only reject liberalism but dream to overcome the situation of religious pluralism that liberalism tries to manage, repudiating the approach of John Courtney Murray and his neoconservative epigones (such as Michael Novak, George Weigel, and Richard John Neuhaus) who labored to reforge an American consensus based on natural law.[55] Liberalism may weaken or it may fail, but it does seem safe to predict that the underlying condition of pluralism is here to stay. While it may—or may not (as Murray lamented)—be God's will, religious pluralism is unquestionably the American situation and, perhaps, a perennial aspect of our human situation.

The integralists' European forerunners yearned for an alliance between throne and altar. But America has no throne to restore. Vermeule proposed that the Constitution could be strongly read and the administrative-confessional state put in the service of the formation of virtuous citizens (and the restraint of their sins). But it's hard to imagine a cabal of traditionalists successfully infiltrating the ranks of the federal bureaucracy and transforming the United States into a Catholic confessional state—a stage, as Vermeule fantasized, in the formation of a hemispheric Empire of Our Lady of Guadalupe and eventually (a man can dream) a Catholic world government.[56] In their public pronouncements, Vermeule and his allies do not appear to seriously consider that they are dreaming within a historically Protestant country (and one with a long and deep-seated suspicion of Catholic ambitions), or that many of the illiberal Americans they hope to rally to their standard may be motivated by their own particular religious convictions, cultural preferences, and nationalist feelings rather than by a vision of Catholic universalism. (When it comes to immigration policy, the tensions between the prerogatives of nationalism and the universal pretentions of the church become readily apparent.) Or do they perhaps expect the populace to be tutored and trained by wise and enlightened rulers and their functionaries to recognize and comprehend their common good?

Suggesting that such proposals to convert the nation are improbable should not dull us to the authoritarianism that proponents of "political Catholicism" (a moniker that obscures the true nature of their ideology) celebrate and commend and the democratic values that they repudiate and revile. This has been observed even by those who generally share their deep critique of liberal modernity. Rod Dreher, for example, worried that the integralists did not appear interested in obtaining the consent of the governed; the hope that they could simply "re-Christianize the lost lands of Christendom by executive action" was delusional. "The more I read about integralism, and listen to integralists, and see the way integralists treat those who question them, the more I run smack into a big reason why liberalism arose in the first place: to provide a way for people who disagree on the nature of the Good to live together in relative peace," he confessed.[57] In the past century, reactionary Catholics in Europe and Latin America often made common cause with fascist movements and authoritarian leaders; let's recall, too, that L. Brent Bozell Jr. and his *Triumph* tribe found much to admire in Generalissimo Franco's seeming achievement of a confessional society in Spain. Given their appeal to and confidence in strong and dynamic executive power and the administrative state it commands to realize their aspirations, the neo-integralists appear all too enthused by the spiritual possibilities of authoritarianism.[58]

"Today's widespread yearning for a strong leader, one with the will to take back popular control over liberalism's forms of bureaucratized government and globalized economy," Professor Deneen mused near the beginning of *Why Liberalism Failed*, "comes after decades of liberal dismantling of cultural norms and political habits essential to self-governance." Toward the end of the book, he warned that "liberalism itself seems likely to generate demotic demands for an illiberal autocrat who promises to protect the people against the vagaries of liberalism itself." Those who struggle to resist its onslaught will clamor for a strongman who would wrest control of the regime, drain the swamp, vindicate their values, and safeguard their way of life. Or, at the least, would "own the libs," as they say. Liberalism, he darkly prophesized, will in the end be demolished by authoritarian backlash to its success.[59]

As it turned out, it would be Donald J. Trump—whose very "brand" had for years been gold-plated decadence—who emerged as the avatar of populist resentments and conservative Christian hopes. While this turn was surprising to some, a number of commentators have shown that the ground of nationalist evangelical Christianity had been well prepared for his arrival.[60] Already a celebrity businessman, Trump achieved political notice and notoriety as a purveyor of the racially charged "birther" conspiracy theory, and on the campaign trail he demonstrated an uncanny ability to tap into deep veins of populist anger and distrust (of "elites," "experts, "the deep state," and so forth) and secure the devotion and loyalty of millions of heretofore "values voters." His political rallies were likened to old-time revival meetings; he spoke to his supporters like a televangelist to his network flock. The slogan he chose for his movement, his political *raison d'être*, "Make America Great Again," is a restorationist sentiment; it was complemented by his vow to put "America First!" These exhortations were in turn rounded out by Trump's often-repeated assertion that "I alone can fix it." The long-aggrieved would have their hopes fulfilled and fearful Christians their rights protected by the edicts of a charismatic strongman. "Christianity will have power," the candidate told an audience in 2016. "If I'm there, you're going to have plenty of power, you don't need anybody else."[61] The "chaos candidate," as one prominent dominionist dubbed him, manifested to his most fervent devotees as a national savior; "prophets" proclaimed the thrice-married, playboy real estate developer a modern-day King Cyrus, raised up and anointed by God, sent to protect a righteous people under siege.[62] His early disciples came from the loosely organized and often multiracial charismatic churches; they would become the vanguard of Christian Trumpism. (The leaders of the Christian Right establishment were relatively late converts to the cause.)[63] Instructed to regard the tussle of politics as spiritual warfare, a contest between the supernatural forces of good and evil, Christian Trumpists saw the election as a "miracle," the unlikely president a providentially given instrument to shatter their enemies and restore an imagined Christian America. Under Trump's leadership, they would dominate the heights of government, one theater in a broader war to liberate all the spheres of human endeavor and social influence from Satan and his minions, and from such vantages to work to bring about the kingdom of God in the United States and throughout the world. The discipling of nations was their Great Commission.[64]

During his theatrical tenure, Trump granted many of the wishes of his supporters on the new and newer Christian Right: installing believers such as Dr. Ben Carson, Betsy DeVos, Rick Perry, and Mike Pompeo in his cabinet; appointing Federalist Society–cultivated federal judges and Supreme Court justices; moving the US Embassy to the State of Israel from Tel Aviv to Jerusalem; and releasing an executive order "promoting religious liberty."[65] He tapped prosperity televangelist Paula White to oversee a reinvented White House Faith and Opportunity Initiative and assembled an "Evangelical Advisory Board" to inform policy.[66] (Trump was less disposed to fulfilling his populist policy promises of massive infrastructure projects, repealing and replacing Obamacare, and bringing back American manufacturing jobs.) What may have begun as a transactional relationship with his evangelical supporters had during his term blossomed into something like love. "Nobody's done more for Christians or for evangelicals or frankly religion itself than I have," Trump boasted in an interview with the Christian Broadcasting Network in 2018. (The former president repeated the statement nearly verbatim in 2021.) Many evangelicals were inclined to agree. This may help explain Christian Trumpists' unwavering support for their president, despite his evident immoralities and ethical lapses; their tolerance of the scandals, corruptions, incompetencies, and mishaps of his administration; and their willingness to accept his vices as virtues and fabrications as truth ("believe me!"). Some of the country's most conspicuous evangelical figures such as Franklin Graham and author and radio host Eric Metaxas continued to voice their support and claim God's blessing for the chosen leader. Much more than Ronald Reagan, for whom the Religious Right first rallied, or George W. Bush, who spoke their language fluently, it was "the Donald" who had proved to be their champion. The "baby Christian" was more importantly a holy warrior. Christ was their King, but Trump was their president. And they were well accounted for among the masses that came to Washington, DC, on January 6, 2021, shock troops intent on halting—by prayer and by deed—the peaceful transition of power that is a hallmark of a constitutional republic, to preserve, by violence if need be, the power of their political savior. The insurrection at the Capitol was fueled in good part by such religious passions, a manifestation of spiritual warfare to fulfill a prophecy in danger of failing.[67]

In any event, those books advocating a strategical withdrawal were composed during what appeared to be the high tide of liberalism and now seemed untimely. The advent of Trump (and the enduring spirit of MAGA) suggested that reconquest was possible. Why build arks when you can command battleships? Why endure the liberal American order when you can found a better one? Perhaps we await not a new St. Benedict but another—doubtless very different—Emperor Constantine?

Perhaps it should not be surprising that those who had soured on liberal democracy found themselves favorably disposed to political leaders willing to champion traditional Christian values and impose policies reflecting them through illiberal means if needs be. Hungarian prime minister Viktor Orbán in particular had become a darling of the postliberal set. Could America's paladin of postliberalism be Donald J. Trump?

Some of liberalism's cultured despisers saw in Trump's unexpected 2016 electoral triumph a disruption that might halt the onslaught of the Left, an occasion to reengage the culture war and, on a deeper level, an opportunity to reframe the argument about the means and ends of American politics. As the new administration settled in, the intellectuals got to work theorizing the new dispensation and suggesting ways to channel the energies Trump unleashed and the movement he mobilized to remake and redeem America. Did he enjoy the popular support and have the executive will to break the liberal order and usher in something new? If so, new alliances would have to be forged to direct the revolution, replacing the old and failed fusionism, so proclaimed the manifestos. It was time, as Sohrab Ahmari notoriously put it in *First Things*, "to fight the culture war with the aim of defeating the enemy and enjoying the spoils in the form of a public square re-ordered to the common good and ultimately the Highest Good."[68]

One such attempt to forge a new conservative consensus began to take shape under the banner of "national conservatism," a movement that brought together commitments to moral and cultural traditionalism rooted in religion, a nationalist-populist economic policy, protectiveness of national sovereignty, and hostility to supranational institutions. If anti-Communism was the force that bound together the old consensus, the new one was animated by anti-liberalism. A good measure of religious and cultural uniformity was necessary for social cohesion and flourishing and political legitimacy, order, and security.

The leading theorist and impresario of national conservatism was the Israeli American political theorist Yoram Hazony. Along with David Brog, former executive director of the Christian Zionist organization Christians United for Israel, Hazony founded the Edmund Burke Foundation in January 2019. The organization was soon hosting "NatCon" conferences in London and Washington (2019), Rome (2020), Orlando (2021), Brussels and Miami (2022), and again in London (2023), featuring talks by such prominent postliberal intellectuals as Deneen, Dreher, and Ahmari; Fox News host Tucker Carlson; *National Review* editor Rick Lowry and *First Things* editor R. R. Reno (both of whom penned books on nationalism around this time); Dr. Albert Mohler, president of the Southern Baptist Theological Seminary; Senators Ted Cruz, Josh Hawley, and Marco Rubio and Governor Ron DeSantis; European politicians Viktor Orbán and Marion Marechal of France's National Front; and Ryszard Legutko, the Polish philosopher and head of the Law and Justice party's delegation to the European Parliament. Even as Hazony and his American NatCon comrades have been called "the intellectual vanguard of the MAGA right," they also aimed to organize and cultivate a "Nationalist International."[69]

Hazony set out his new-old vision in a pair of volumes—*The Virtue of Nationalism* (2018) and *Conservatism: A Rediscovery* (2022)—in which he made his case for the "national state" as the optimal form of political organization and international order possible and for conservatism as the national state's foundation and spirit. Both nationalism and the conservative standpoint, he contended, were rooted in the wisdom of ancient Israel as recorded in the Hebrew Bible, a book, Hazony suggested, that ought to be read not only as a religious text but also as a philosophical one (the authority of which would be based on human reason rather than divine revelation) with much to say about "the nature of the world and the just life of man." The historical recounting of the rise and fall of the Israelite kingdoms put together by the exilic editors for consolation, commitment, and hope and vision of future restoration presented not only a theological argument about the covenantal relationship of Israel and their God but also an "instructional narrative" about the nature, purposes, and ideal form of government and the best way of organizing the international order. The past experience of Israel offered crucial lessons for the nation's future—indeed, for the other nations as well.[70]

Hazony developed his teaching in *The Virtue of Nationalism.* Like Deneen's *Why Liberalism Failed,* the book found a large readership, receiving acclaim and criticism in good measure. Nationalism, Hazony argued, is not a modern phenomenon but an ancient ideal, one first proposed by the Hebrew Bible. That "new political conception" was "a state of a single nation that is united, self-governing, and uninterested in bringing its neighbors under its rule." In this view, "the distinctive Israelite institution of the national state" formed by the confederation of the tribes, sharing a common language, religion, and history, and living within set borders peacefully alongside other free nations, was paradigmatic, even if ancient Israel's own history was unique. This "national state" charted a middle way between the "anarchial" form of political order of tribes and clans—the form of order that existed prior to, and whose instabilities brought about, the centralized state, with its bureaucracy and standing military—and the "imperial state," a political order "which seeks to bring peace and prosperity to the world by uniting mankind, as much as possible, under a single political regime." The Bible presents these political forms—in the experience of the Israelite tribes prior to their unification, transformation into a national state under a king, and the prophets' warnings against the ambitions of the despotic and expansionist empires of Egypt, Assyria, and Babylonia."[71]

Hazony remarked (in a footnote) that the Israelite national state was not initially presented by the Hebrew Bible as God's preferred political order; that would have been a primitive theocracy under the episodic leadership of charismatic chieftains—that is, an "anarchial" form. The difficulties of sustaining that model are copiously recorded throughout the book of Judges, and under the corrupt administration of Samuel's sons, the elders of Israel clamored for a king, "like all the nations," and God acquiesced to their plea (1 Samuel 8). While the Hebrew Bible taught the advantageousness of a permanent state, the legitimate regime was one in which the power of the monarch was bound by "an independent standard of justice and goodness" (set out in

Deuteronomy 17:14–20) and the nation set within proscribed borders and without further territorial ambitions. That the borders of the promised Land of Israel are described variously in the Hebrew Bible and don't correspond to the actual borders of the Israelite kingdoms is worth noting. So, too, are the problems of who determines national borders and what happens when there is more than one nation contesting the same territory. Indeed, the biblical narrative itself recounts the conquest of the Land of Canaan (and the commanded yet incomplete annihilation of its inhabitants) by the Israelite tribes in the book of Joshua.[72] Be that as it may, this simplified distinction between national states and universalistic empires provided the framework for Hazony's understanding of political organization and advocacy of nationalist projects around the world.

Christianity had burst into the world as a Jewish sect but alongside the Hebrew Bible developed its own collection of sacred writings and a theological vision that focused on the salvation of humanity. Once it became the official religion of the Roman Empire, Christianity—in the form of the Roman Catholic Church—took up "the aspiration of establishing a universal empire of peace and prosperity," universalist (imperialist) political concepts of classical thought taking the place of the Hebraic political preference for the national state. In short order, Islam followed suit. In the modern era, secular universalist salvation theories such as liberalism, Marxism, and Nazism (which Hazony claimed had been mistakenly understood as a form of nationalism) likewise served "as engines for the construction of empire." One might say that they all preach a particularist doctrine of universalism, while the Hebrew Bible advances the universalist truth of national particularism.[73]

Hazony did not have much to say about the theological-political teachings of the New Testament, but it is clear that he believed a good political order required restraining the tendencies toward universalism inherent in "the Gospel's message of salvation and peace."[74] Such a corrective was achieved by Protestant Reformers of the sixteenth century, particularly in England, Scotland, and Holland. Whatever else the Reformers believed, whatever theological, ecclesiastical, and ritual innovations they introduced, their main contribution from his point of view was retrieving the importance of the Old Testament, providing the foundation for the assertion of sovereignty of the national states of England, Scotland, and the Netherlands, who modeled their struggles after the paradigmatic case of ancient Israel, and the emergence of what Hazony called "the Protestant Construction of the West." That "Protestant construction" derived two principles from the Hebrew Bible: a "moral minimum" of legitimate government—that is, the obligations rulers have to their people, which Hazony located in the Ten Commandments—and the right of independent nations to govern themselves according to their particular national traditions and constitutional arrangements without foreign interference or impositions, an alternative to the claim of a universal Christian empire promoted by the Roman Catholic Church. By the mid-seventeenth century, those principles had "refounded the entire political order," having come to be enshrined in the post-Westphalian European order of independent national states; in time, they helped bring the United States into being.[75]

This was, in Hazony's view, an altogether salutary development, for "the world is governed best when nations are able to chart their own independent course, cultivating their own traditions and pursuing their own interests without interference." Such a world order ought to bring about stability and peace among nations. That it hadn't in actuality was a problem Hazony conceded but quickly glossed over, confidentially declaring that "an order based on the principle of national freedom . . . provided a basis for the eventual remediation of many of its deficiencies." The problems generated by nationalism could be ameliorated by ever more nationalism.[76]

Rather than dwell on the continued conflict of those early modern national states (and their transformation into empires), Hazony turned to narrate a different tale of decline. The Protestant construction was soon contested by yet another vision of political order, "the liberal construction of the West." Shaped by Enlightenment rationalism, liberal thinkers imagined a regime focused on the preservation of individual freedom. Liberalism's most influential authority was John Locke, whose *Second Treatise of Government* set forth a fanciful account of the state emerging from the agreement of free and unencumbered individuals seeking to preserve their lives, liberty, and property. Locke's was "a rationalist view of human political life that has abstracted away every bond that ties human beings to one another other than consent" and led to a utopian vision of the individual liberated from the constraints of traditional obligations and institutions, even the national state—all those "bonds of loyalty and common purpose" that had emerged from family and religion and which formed the basis of political obligation. "Without intending to, the dream-world offered by Locke's *Second Treatise* rendered most of the Protestant order senseless and superfluous," Hazony concluded. The German philosopher Immanuel Kant pushed the project further, dreaming of the moral maturity of humanity by means of the integration of nations into a world federation. In this manner, the

liberal construction of politics eventually transformed into a new form of imperialism powered by a universal salvation theory striving "to establish conformity
and break down the effects of countervailing considerations, not only among the
nations that are subjected to them, but also in the soul of the individual." But
rather than opening up a regime of tolerance for different forms of living and
conceptions of the good, liberalism generates a fanatical hatred of all particularities that refuse to submit to its particular utopian vision of salvation. In
short order, Hazony warned, the liberal imperium will come after "the teaching
and practice of traditional forms of Judaism and Christianity." Ancient Israel
had to face the empires of Egypt, Assyria, Babylonia, Persia, and Rome; the
modern national state has to confront the liberal global order of American
power and multinational institutions such as the European Union and the
United Nations which is set on stamping out national particularities—as well
as the corrosive liberalism within.[77] To resist the liberal imperial project of
globalism, Hazony called for the restoration of the nationalist vision and of
nationalist states, a messianic dream of a slowly yet steadily emerging postliberal international order. (Not all nations would enjoy the right independence
and self-determination in a national state, Hazony acknowledged. Prudence
requires that some "weaker" ones settle for the status of a "protectorate" under
the beneficent domination of a more "powerful neighbor." Who decides which
nations deserve to be states and which do not—there's the rub.)[78] And in Brexit,
the ascendency of Trump in the United States, and a State of Israel unapologeti-
cally protective of its sovereignty, Hazony perceived the signs of the times.

This was, as many critics have pointed out, a partisan and unbalanced
caricature of liberal theory and practice. (The book could have easily been
subtitled *The Vices of Liberalism*.) Hazony did not bother to examine why liberal
political concepts emerged in the first place, and why many found them attrac-
tive or advantageous in managing the internecine tensions and conflicts religious and other differences generated within those "national states." He ignored,
too, how those ideas helped shaped the formation of modern nations and
became part of the Western inheritance. He simply dismissed as "a myth" the
"neutral" or "civic" state that purports to separate the nation from the state and
claims that political community can be maintained on the basis of commitment to shared ideals or principles rather than a deep-seated loyalty to one's
own tribe. A "liberal nationalism" would be a contradiction in terms.[79]

As the national state provides political form, "conservativism" contributes
its content—the values, mores, and norms that shape and govern people's

private and collective lives. In the American situation, a restoration of nationalism and the extirpation of the liberal heresy would require a revival of the nation's authentic Anglo-American (as opposed to its "right-liberal") conservative tradition as its animating force. A "Protestant reconstruction of the United States," we might say.[80]

Hazony spelled out the particulars in his subsequent book, *Conservatism: A Rediscovery*, an ambitious work of history, political theory, advocacy, and memoir.[81] Hazony reconstructed an account of a distinct, biblically infected Anglo(-American) national conservative tradition, *avant la lettre*, stretching back to the fifteenth-century jurist John Fortescue and up through the centuries to Richard Hooker, John Selden, and Edmund Burke, the celebrated eighteenth-century British statesman. The principles of this tradition included a commitment to historical empiricism over philosophical rationalism, the centrality of the nation, the importance of religion to public order, a limited executive, and the guarantee of individual liberties by law that laid the foundation of English constitutionalism. Transplanted to America, it was this conservativism—not Lockean liberalism or the classical Christian natural law tradition—that was incarnated in the Constitution of the United States, put into practice by the leaders of the Federalist Party such as George Washington, John Adams, Alexander Hamilton, John Jay, and Gouverneur Morris in the early days of the republic. It was "the force that made America." But this storied tradition had been displaced by "liberal democracy," the modern apotheosis of Enlightenment liberalism, which, in turn, was now on the verge of being ousted by a revised Marxism (in the form of "progressive" or "woke" ideology). Hazony hoped to arrest this development, pointing the nation back to this intellectual foundation and suggesting an alternative regime of "conservative democracy" that could be put in place.

By placing this conservative tradition at the center of his account of American political history, Hazony downplayed the importance of and indeed vilified liberalism as a false and dangerous countertradition. During the early days of the republic, American "nationalists" who admired the English constitutional order and looked to it as a model for the new state faced off against liberal radicals who pledged to build on the "dictates of universal reason" and tried to resist the unification of the states under a strong centralized national government. The two conflicting approaches could be clearly seen in its founding documents. The Declaration of Independence, Hazony acknowledged, was a liberal statement proclaiming "the Lockean doctrine of universal rights as 'self-evident' before the light of reason."[82] The Constitution of 1787 and the Bill of Rights, on the other hand, were fashioned by men deeply influenced by the English conservative tradition who looked to history and experience rather than speculative reason for political guidance; they regarded human beings as bound together by ties of mutual loyalty and respect, and society as hierarchically structured and maintained by long-inherited religious beliefs and practices, customs, and institutions.[83] The American Revolution may have been animated in part by rationalist liberal ideas (and one wonders whether Hazony would regard the Patriots' actions as justifiable or prudent, as many of his assertions sound as though they could have been taken from a Church of England Loyalist's sermon), but the framing of the Constitution and its ratification amounted to a restoration of traditional order and the assertion of national unity and purpose.[84]

National conservativism, then, with its focus on "maintaining a nation and strengthening it through time," was America's dominant political tradition, animating the Federalists and later the Whig and Republican Parties, establishing "an American consensus that lasted well into the twentieth century." Hazony even audaciously deputized Lincoln to his cause, despite the sixteenth president's well-known appeals to the ideals of the Declaration of Independence as the very foundation of his understanding of the American political order. By contrast, Hazony claimed that the idea that America is a "creedal nation" defined by the sentiments of the Declaration is "a myth promoted in the service of liberal dogma." Those who emigrated from elsewhere were adopted by and into the nation, taking on its language, assimilating into its culture, identifying with its history, rather than becoming citizens of a "neutral" state.[85]

In the United States, liberal Enlightenment ideas had been largely "held in check" by the Anglo-American conservative tradition. And that was a good thing, Hazony maintained, as liberalism is a counter-faith, a "substantive belief system," and an "alternative foundation" based on a system of dogmas such as the self-sufficiency of human reason, the free and equal individual, and government by consent. Failing to promote belief in God, the authority of Scripture, the sanctity of the traditional family, and "the national state as the best form of political order"—ideas that could not "be derived from liberal premises"—liberalism inevitably brings about a dissolution of "traditional institutions," national cohesion, and even the very commitment to national independence. And Hazony observed that "while the Bible teaches that all are created in the image of God, thus imparting a dignity and sanctity to each human being, it says nothing about our being by nature perfectly free and equal." Even as he decried American slavery as an evil and ignoble stain on the nation's history, it is worth noting that his critique of the ideals of the Declaration of Independence has clear parallels to the arguments of the proslavery theologians who maintained that its assertions of natural equality and natural rights contravened Scripture and were destabilizing to traditional society. One wonders how Hazony would manage the problem that the same Bible that teaches all people are created in the image of God and celebrates the liberation of the Israelites from Egyptian servitude also countenances and regulates the institution of human bondage, and the further problem that it was under the banner of the Declaration of Independence that Americans fought to end the injustice and struggled for continued integration of Blacks into the political community. It's unclear how this could happen under the auspices of Hazony's conservatism (or if he believed African Americans would remain a "tribe" within but not an integral part of the white American nation).[86]

In Hazony's view, America had been "a traditional society—and it remained so, in many respects, until the upheaval of the two World Wars."[87] Submitting this claim, which at face value seems considerably at odds with American history and culture, required overlooking the sweeping social and economic transformations that made such a national conservativism difficult to sustain. And so it's not surprising that Hazony did not have much to say about developments that clearly challenged his thesis, and that his text simply side-stepped the problem of a conservative slaveholding South. Rather, his story jumped from the Federalists of the early years of the republic to the Cold War era, when the not-entirely-suppressed liberal countertradition began to gain ascendency. It's another tale of *la trahison des clercs*. While President Franklin D. Roosevelt could be regarded as upholding America's Christian inheritance, framing World War II as a struggle between " 'God-fearing democracy' and its enemies"—that is, "a war about religion"—"such expressions of traditional Anglo-American nationalism would soon come to an end." By the mid-1960s, Congress and the Supreme Court, with support from the nation's elites, came "to embrace Enlightenment liberalism as the sole legitimate foundation for American government." The 1947 *Everson* decision, which determined that the intention of the Establishment Clause was to protect religious minorities from the threat of persecution ("a new story of the American founding—one broadly hostile to government encouragement of religion"), proclaimed the false teaching on the separation of church and state and inaugurated the great unraveling. The court's subsequent decisions on religion "signaled the end of Christianity as a decisive and legitimate influence on public life in America," solidifying the nation's "transition" from what had been "a God-fearing democracy to a liberal democracy," an entirely novel regime with Enlightenment liberalism supplanting Christianity as the nation's "public religion." That Establishment Clause jurisprudence, along with the court's 1954 decision in *Brown v. Board of Education* and congressional legislation such as the Civil Rights Act (1964) and the Immigration and Naturalization Act (1965), which, Hazony informs us, were bent on "erasing distinctions based on race and religion," amounted to nothing less than "a bloodless revolution in which the old assumption of a Christian nation rooted in the English legal tradition was replaced by a liberal state modeled on the social contract theories of Enlightenment rationalist philosophers." This attempt to radically remake the nation and rescue it from its national conservative inheritance was primarily motivated by that generation's "revulsion over Hitler's racial policies." From Hazony's telling, you would not know how deeply and bitterly contested these developments actually were.[88]

In any case, the wrong instrument (Enlightenment liberalism) was brought in to correct a historical injustice (the mistreatment of Black Americans). And so the "dream-world" of Locke and Jefferson had returned with a vengeance, aided and abetted by "prominent liberal scholars" who busied themselves rewriting American history to declare it "a liberal nation from its birth" and to obscure or blot out its conservative heritage and support the new regime. It was assisted, too, by the Cold War anti-Communist alliance between traditional conservatives and so-called "right-wing" liberals (influenced by such thinkers as the economist Fredrich von Hayek and the scholar of political philosophy Leo Strauss) that William F. Buckley Jr. tried to assemble at the *National Review*. Echoing L. Brent Bozell's earlier critique, Hazony noted that the so-called fusionism advanced by Frank Meyer shunted considerations of tradition and the cultivation of virtue to the private sphere. The right-wing liberals who celebrated individual freedom were the dominant party in the relationship; the believers in "maintaining the religious and natural traditions of the people" were relegated to second fiddle. Rather than providing a vital alternative to liberal democracy, "Cold War conservativism itself became an important part of this liberal hegemony." And so the proponents of this much-vaunted American conservative alliance were, in the end, collaborators with the liberal project. Granted, President Ronald Reagan governed more or less in the national conservative mold, and the alliance succeeded in defeating the Soviet Union, but in the post–Cold War era, the movement quickly fell victim to its own contradictions. American neoconservatives lost all touch with reality, becoming all-out Enlightenment liberal utopians announcing the end of history under the aegis of American empire, engaging in such quixotic misadventures as the wars in Iraq and Afghanistan, and bringing about much bloodshed, misery, and national shame. Given their deviations from the tradition of the Federalists and Burke, that was bound to happen. In the meantime, those faithful to authentic Anglo-American conservativism "were sent into political exile."[89]

The nation's apostasy was bringing about its decline. And thus the contemporary hegemony of "liberal democracy." Even as it was "unleashing the principles of individual liberty and equality to do their work of uprooting and destroying the inherited evils of the past," liberal democracy did not vanquish its ideological foes and inaugurate the end of history. Rather, having abandoned its traditional Christian foundations and on account of its own inherent contradictions, liberal democracy was now making way for, or was itself being overcome by, a "woke" neo-Marxism whose conquest of America—the steady march of "Progressive" "Anti-Racist" "Social Justice Warriors" across academia, culture, business, media, and government—appears preordained. Unless. To save themselves from the barbarians within their gates, Americans and other Westerners must forsake the failed experiment in liberal democracy and restore a regime based on true foundations and firm borders (without that old, unfortunate ugliness of slavery and racism, of course).[90] Hazony, too, was against the dead consensus. And, with his vision of a restoration of a restoration, he had a dreamworld of his own to promote.

So Hazony set forth his proposal for "repentance" (note the word's religious connotations)—the return to an "alternative political framework" he called "conservative democracy" (but we might fairly dub "illiberal democracy"), which would supplant liberal democracy root and branch. Such a regime would be characterized by its commitment to a distinct national identity (as opposed to being rooted in some abstract "creedal" formula); preservation of the nation's particular legal tradition (and not theories of universal rights); policies that support the "traditional family" (built on "the lifelong bond of a man and a woman ... [and] between a father and mother and their children ... [and] consist[ing] of multiple generations in daily contact") and preferred religious communities; parental responsibility over education; a free market tempered by concern for national cohesion and public morals; a limited immigration program favoring assimilation into the national tradition; and a generally noninterventionist foreign policy and disengagement from international bodies.

Among these sundry proposals was the endorsement of "public religion" as an "indispensable purpose of government"—a religion that would serve as a conservative and legitimating, rather than "prophetic," force.[91]

Hazony's "conservative paradigm" rested on a scriptural account of the origin of moral and political obligations and the limitations of human knowledge. Biblical monotheism—the idea that there is one God who created the heavens and the earth—discloses that there is "only one normative order." "What is true or right in God's eyes is a standard independent of all local standards, and consequently of the claims made in the name of the gods of a given place," Hazony noted. By contrast, polytheism and atheism lead necessarily to moral relativism. Scripture further teaches that human beings are born into and embedded in collectives—"families, tribes, and nations"—and that God had established a covenant with the nation of Israel. The biblical notion of covenantal community was extended to the other nations of the world through Christianity. Hazony acknowledged that Christian nations "have their own unique understanding of both God and the Bible"; nevertheless, Orthodox, Catholic, and Protestant ones "all are in possession of the same broad framework." The "God of Scripture" provided the "metaphysical foundation" of (Anglo-American) conservatism, which also looked to inherited tradition for guidance on what is good and what is true. By contrast, Enlightenment rationalism proclaimed its confidence in human reason's ability to determine universal moral and political principles. Denying the "chasm between the reasoning individual and knowledge of the true character of reality" that Scripture discloses, rationalists hold to be universal what is only the product of their own limited perspectives. Conservatives, by contrast, are secure with the moral objectivism and epistemic humility that they learn from the Hebrew Bible, which teaches that human knowledge and understanding is limited and fallible. So the Bible, and the Christian religion that issued from it, was a key part of the cultural inheritance that ought to be revered and passed down to future generations. Yet Hazony had nothing to say about the religion that emerged from Jesus's life, ministry, and crucifixion (there is no mention of Jesus in either book), the Christian tradition's distinctive beliefs and practices, or the numerous and conflicting political theologies that it spawned. His conception of religion and political theology is fundamentally Hebraic, stressing the centrality of Moses as lawgiver, Israel as the paradigmatic national state, and the Hebrew Bible as the fount of the conservative disposition. The universalist tendency of the New Testament always needs to be tempered by the national particularism and epistemic humility sanctioned by the Old. In other words, Christian nations need to remain tethered to Hebraic thought (and to read the Hebrew Bible not only through the theological lens of the New Testament but on its own terms—or, more precisely, Hazony's—in a sense against the grain of the Christian tradition itself) lest they succumb to the universalist and imperialist potentialities of Christianity's distinctive revelation and the influence of classical thought upon it. (In having this fundamental relationship to the Hebrew Bible, Christianity is distinct from other universal religions and political ideologies, which possess no analogous check on their ambitions.)[92]

Consequently, Hazony maintained that the national state ought to promote "the national religion" to serve as "an overarching frame of reference" that teaches and inculcates those conservative values and virtues. He approvingly quoted a long passage from Edmund Burke's *Reflections on the Revolution in France* declaring the necessity of "the consecration of the state by a state religious establishment" for good political order, noting its salutary effects on both those of "exalted situations" who exercise power and the citizenry who should come to look upon it with awe.[93]

The constitutional settlement of 1787, which Hazony had celebrated as a restoration of national conservativism, had failed in this decisive respect, despite the Framers' own commitments to public religion and their favoring of "an alliance between Christianity and the state." "Perhaps the most striking innovation in the American nationalists' Constitution of 1787 is the absence of any explicit mention of religion," he sighed. Even though it had not been their intent to remove Christianity from public life, "with hindsight I think we can say that the failure to acknowledge God and religion was a mistake with lasting consequences." After all, there is no such thing as a "neutral state"; the political order is based on and shaped by some overarching framework. And by neglecting and not rightly honoring religion, the federal government had in fact weakened it domestically and had set a bad example for other nations. (Hazony conceded, however, that the established Church of England did not much strengthen Christianity in the United Kingdom, which raises questions about his analysis of the causes of the decline of religion.) The failure to acknowledge God and cultivate a national religion was the flaw that allowed for the reemergence of Enlightenment liberalism in America. In this sense, the conditions for the 1947 *Everson* decision and those that followed had been laid at the outset. And so, because the religious, specifically Protestant, foundations of conservatism had not been properly constitutionalized, it had come to pass that "leading public figures had openly embraced a messianic vision of the 'end of history' and of the worldwide redemption that Enlightenment liberals would bring," suggesting that American liberals were really no different from the Jacobins of the French Revolution or the Marxists of the twentieth century, "promoting an atheistic religion to take the place of Christianity." And in doing so, they undermined not only the stability of public institutions but also the traditional family and the devotion of the people to the nation itself. "I believe the time has come to regard the encouragement of the traditional religion (or religions) of the nation as having a place of especial importance among the responsibilities of national government," Hazony announced. The regime needed to support the support that religion gave to the regime.[94]

For this to happen, Hazony proposed (re)installing Christianity as the "normative framework and standard determining public life," to be "strongly reflected in government and other institutions, wherever a majority of the public so desires." This would be less a restoration than a remaking of American church-state relations. Cognizant of the presence of non-Christians, he granted that "provision should be made for Jews and other minorities to ensure that their particular traditions and way of life are not encumbered" and that "the private life of dissenting individuals or communities should be protected within their own sphere." But such "provisions," grants of toleration, and the like ("to religious and social views that do not endanger the integrity and well-being of the nation as a whole") are not to be confused with juridically enforceable rights and the full equality of citizens. Hazony did not suggest that such a public Christianity would look like that of the mid-twentieth century, let alone the church establishments of the colonial era, but that new forms of public religion and state offers of toleration (at the discretion of the majority) would come to be in various states or regions as the diverse Christian groups and their non-Christian allies work together to negotiate the boundaries between "the Christian public sphere" and "spheres of legitimate non-compliance," a hodge-podge of experiments in governmentally endorsed and supported religion. The book did not entertain the idea of a public "Judeo-Christian tradition."[95]

This was, of course, a vision of Christian-dominated polity, yet with a curiously dogma-less Christianity resting at its center. For Hazony, religion is a constitutive part of national self-identity, cohesion, and solidarity and a source of moral authority. "God and Scripture" therefore needed to be publicly professed and respected. Yet, as I have noted, he eschewed any substantial discussion of Christianity itself, its doctrines and practices, and the long and complex history of theological reflection, controversy, and strife.[96] Indeed, as we have seen, the theological-political foundation of his conservatism was fundamentally Hebraic, emphasizing the paradigmatic example of ancient Israel as a national state. Nevertheless, it's notable, and somewhat unsettling, that those practicing Judaism in its various forms would appear to be relegated to second-class citizenship ("protected within their own sphere") in the scheme, even as Hazony argued that "orthodox Jews" and other conservative religious minorities ought to cooperate with conservative Protestants to impose a public Christianity that would do so. He could have, I suppose, offered up an argument (similar to the one John Courtney Murray made about the role of Roman Catholics schooled in the tradition of natural law) for a Jewish vocation to promote the Hebrew Bible's vision of nationalist politics. But this was a road not taken. One imagines Hazony (who identifies as a traditionally observant Jew and who decamped from the United States to reside and raise a family in Israel) seeing the nation of Israel (ancient and modern) as an adequate inspiration and model, and counseling Jewish Americans who don't fancy being accommodated as a tolerated minority in the United States to immigrate to a country where their traditions enjoy public support. That they currently enjoy greater liberty to practice their religion as they see fit in the United States than in the Jewish state is an irony well worth pondering. Then again, one gets the impression that Hazony might not consider non-orthodox expressions of Judaism traditions worthy of conservation.[97]

In June 2022, about a month after Hazony's *Conservativism* was published, the Edmund Burke Foundation released "National Conservatism: A Statement of Principles."[98] The text was drafted by Hazony and several NatCon collaborators, including Rod Dreher and R. R. Reno, and among its signatories were a number of people associated with Hillsdale College and the Claremont Institute, including Larry Arnn, chair of President Trump's "1776 Commission," and Michael Anton, author of the notorious 2016 pro-Trump essay "The Flight 93 Election"; such denizens of Trumpworld as former chief of staff Mark Meadows, Turning Point USA's Charlie Kirk, and tech entrepreneur and mega-donor Peter Thiel; and a smattering of old-guard and up-and-coming conservative American and European intellectuals and influencers. They identified themselves as "citizens of Western nations," Protestants, Catholics, and Jews, open to collaboration with similar non-Western movements in the postliberal counterrevolution. Conspicuous in their absence were past NatCon participants Patrick Deneen and Sohrab Ahmari, an indication of the breakdown of the nascent alliance between national conservative and Catholic integralist forces. That hoped-for new conservative fusion did not long endure, as the substantial strategic and policy differences took precedence over common purpose and shared hatreds. As Deneen put it in *Regime Change*, nationalism was "originally a key aspect of the liberal political project," reorienting citizens away from local, regional, and supranational identifications and attachments; "liberalism's architects deeply shared the aspiration to create and strengthen national sovereignty that would prove to be a new unifying force ... replacing the imperial structures of Christendom in the West."[99] Despite their shared anti-liberalism, their aspirations for a future regime are in the end irreconcilable.

The manifesto presented national conservatism as "the only genuine alternative to universalist ideologies now seeking to impose a homogenizing, locality-destroying imperium over the entire globe," and its language largely aligned with the description of "conservative democracy" Hazony had set out in his book. While the document paraphrased the Preamble to the Constitution ("The independent nation-state is instituted to establish a more perfect union among the diverse communities, parties, and regions of a given nation, to provide for their common defense and justice among them, and to secure the general welfare and the blessings of liberty for this time and for future generations"), there was no mention in it of the "liberal" principles of the Declaration of Independence— equality, natural rights, consent of the governed. The document endorsed the "federalist principle" of delegating power to the states, but only to a point: "In those states or subdivisions in which law and justice have been manifestly corrupted, or in which lawlessness, immorality, and dissolution reign, national government must intervene energetically to restore order." Despite the deployment of the language of constitutionalism, the details departed from America's actual and long-standing political traditions. It is not hard to perceive the desire to impose upon the country from above a religious and cultural uniformity that it never possessed.[100]

Nowhere did the statement of principles depart from the American tradition as blatantly as in the section "God and Public Religion":

> No nation can long endure without humility and gratitude before God and fear of his judgment that are found in authentic religious tradition. For millennia, the Bible has been our surest guide, nourishing a fitting orientation toward God, to the political traditions of the nation, to public morals, to the defense of the weak, and to the recognition of

things rightly regarded as sacred. The Bible should be read as the first among the sources of a shared Western civilization in schools and universities, and as the rightful inheritance of believers and non-believers alike. Where a Christian majority exists, public life should be rooted in Christianity and its moral vision, which should be honored by the state and other institutions both public and private. At the same time, Jews and other religious minorities are to be protected in the observance of their own traditions, in the free governance of their communal institutions, and in all matters pertaining to the rearing and education of their children. Adult individuals should be protected from religious or ideological coercion in their private lives and in their homes.[101]

Now, it's one thing to propose that "public life should be rooted in Christianity and its moral vision," that "the Bible should be read" in public schools, that the Sabbath be respected, that "authentic religious tradition" ought to shape morals, and so forth. But this throws us back to the particulars that have all been, and still are, deeply contested (for example, Which Bible is to be read, and who gets to interpret it? How exactly is Christianity to be "honored by the state"? In what manner is the Sabbath to be observed or worship to be conducted? Can protection from coercion in private coexist with public coercion? And what if Jews and other religious minorities attempted to observe and honor their traditions in the public realm? Would non-Christians be able to run for public office or serve in government? Or vote?) and more fundamentally to the question of who gets to decide whose religious tradition is "authentic" (or "orthodox") and whose are not. Some may concur that the Bible is "our surest guide" but will disagree about its "moral vision," what precisely the Bible actually commands and forbids, how the weak are to be defended, which things are sacred and how they are to be so recognized, whose marriages are authentic, whether abortion is permissible, whether slavery is sinful or ordained, whether subjects are to be obedient to rulers or ought to rise up against tyranny, and so forth. The devil is in the details, as they say, and the generalities and ambiguities of the NatCon proposal illuminate the ultimately quixotic nature of their advocacy of "public religion." American history records many such arguments between (and among) Anglicans and Congregationalists and Quakers and Presbyterians and Baptists and Methodists and Unitarians and Catholics and Mormons and so on, and modernists and fundamentalists, liberals and traditionalists, and Jews, Muslims, Hindus, Buddhists, and other non-Christian religious minorities, and those professing no religion at all, and of course those who prefer that religion be relegated to the sphere of private life or even dream of its eventual abolition. And this is not to mention the much more fierce and bloody clashes (between Catholic empires and Protestant-constructed national states, and also within them) that occurred on the other side of the Atlantic. There is no reason to believe that these arguments have been—or even could be—settled. And the proponents of public religion tend to be a disputatious bunch. Maybe the drafters and signatories of that manifesto simply didn't think things through. Given the inclination of some of them to appeal to Lincoln as a preeminent moral-political authority, NatCons and their allies would be well advised to read and reflect on his second inaugural address.

Be that as it may, the NatCons' call for the promotion and encouragement of "public" (apparently Anglo-Protestant) Christianity is a far cry from the robust protection of religious liberty (Christian and otherwise). To my ears, it sounds like a plan for the *establishment* of religion. In the American case, its full realization would effectively require the repeal of Article VI, Section 3, and the religion clauses of the First Amendment. (Indeed, the proposal itself stood in tension with the document's subsequent plank of the "rule of law" and its demand that all "[accept] and [live] in accordance with the Constitution of 1787 [and] the amendments to it.") The National Conservatives' appeal for public religion that would bind religious commitment to national belonging revealed their refusal to accept the nation's thoroughgoing pluralism (which goes far beyond the pan-Protestantism of yore) and failure to recognize how religions, even "traditional" ones, change over time, adapting to (or resisting) new ideas and circumstances; their unsupported confidence in the ability of public officials to promote religion; and their disregard for the corrupting influence of politics on religion and cavalier unconcern about reopening the sort of theological-political conflicts that Madison and Jefferson hoped to forestall.

The NatCon signatories would likely prefer not to admit publicly that they are really calling for a new, and to their minds better, founding. But they possibly recognize that their proposal stands in fundamental tension with the constitutional settlement of the relationship of church and state that came to be in the mid-twentieth century. Hazony, for his part, suggested that settlement was the first thing that needed to be brought to the chopping block: "The key to such a restoration would be overturning the postwar Supreme Court decisions that imposed the principle of 'separation of church and state' in America." It was the court's novel doctrine of separationism inaugurated with *Everson* that had "more than anything else . . . delegitimized Christianity as the basis for public life in America and other Western countries and initiated the ongoing cultural revolution with which we are familiar." Dismantling that obstacle would be the first step to a robust state promotion of "public religion" and the restoration of Christianity as the country's "normative framework."[102]

As it happened, the same month the NatCons released their statement of principles, the Supreme Court delivered what religious conservatives had for over fifty years longed for: the overturning of *Roe v. Wade* and the constitutional protection of a woman's reproductive rights. The conservative supermajority also decided two momentous religious liberty cases: *Carson v. Makin*, which required state funding for a sectarian school, and *Kennedy v. Bremerton School District*, affirming the right of a public school football coach to pray on the fifty-yard line after games. In doing so, the court furthered the dismantling of the postwar separationist settlement. Hazony believed his counterrevolution would be contingent on the justices demolishing the wall its predecessors had foolishly erected; it appears that these hopes may be on their way to being fulfilled. It remains to be seen whether or when those who demand religious liberty for themselves will succeed in restraining it for so many others.

Hazony had appealed to George Washington as an icon of national conservatism, noting his support for and deployment of a public Christianity from his time as the general of the Continental army through his tenure as president. Like Jonathan Boucher, he invoked the first president's Farewell Address and its stress on the importance of religion and morality as "indispensable supports" for "political prosperity."[103] But Washington had not called for the establishment of a national church or demanded that the Constitution of the United States acknowledge divine authority. And he was adamant that in America religious liberty was a fundamental right. After becoming president, Washington received numerous letters from religious groups around the nation—major Protestant denominations as well as minority faiths—bestowing their congratulations, praising his person, and offering prayers for his success. In many of his responses, Washington expressed his commitment to religious liberty and the rights of conscience.[104] The most famous and most eloquent of such statements came in his reply to a letter by Moses Seixas, the warden of the Congregation Yeshuat Israel of Newport, Rhode Island. Seixas was among the assemblage of clergymen who greeted and presented addresses to the president during his visit to that city on August 18, 1790. In their remarks, the Protestant clergy praised the president and called on God to endow him "with grace, wisdom, and understanding to go out and in before this numerous and free people" so that "all the families of these wide extended realms may enjoy under an equal and judicious administration of Government, peace and prosperity with all the blessings attendant on civil and religious liberty."[105] In his address, Seixas spoke directly of a new dispensation, marrying his praise of the regime with an explicit statement of the liberties he believed it afforded Jewish Americans: "Deprived as we heretofore have been of the invaluable rights of free Citizens, we now (with a deep sense of gratitude to the Almighty disposer of all events) behold a Government, erected by the Majesty of the People—a Government, which to bigotry gives no sanction, to persecution no assistance—but generously affording to All liberty of conscience, and immunities of Citizenship: deeming every one, of whatever Nation, tongue, or language, equal parts of the great governmental Machine." The federal union, Seixas went on to note, "we cannot but acknowledge to be the work of the Great God, who ruleth in the Armies Of Heaven and among the Inhabitants of the Earth, doing whatever seemeth him good."[106]

"The Citizens of the United States of America have a right to applaud themselves for having given to mankind examples of an enlarged and liberal policy: a policy worthy of imitation," Washington wrote in response. "All possess alike liberty of conscience and immunities of citizenship. It is now no more that toleration is spoken of, as if it was by the indulgence of one class of people, that another enjoyed the exercise of their inherent natural rights." The new government was not offering the Jews of Newport and other religious minorities an indulgence of toleration, for they had as much a right to religious liberty as their Protestant neighbors. And in his letter to that congregation—but really to the entire nation—the first president, echoing Seixas's celebration of the government, reaffirmed the guarantee of the nation's theological-political settlement: "For happily the Government of the United States, which gives to bigotry no sanction, to persecution no assistance requires only that they who live under its protection should demean themselves as good citizens, in giving it on all occasions their effectual support."[107]

Conclusion

Ideas, it has been said, have consequences, and theological ideas can indeed have political implications. It may well be that certain conceptions of God and his creation, the nature of human beings, the origin and purpose of civil government, and the plan of salvation sit well with liberal democratic ideas and institutions; others stand in some tension or outright opposition. Those ideas and institutions presuppose the displacement of religion from its prior dominant position in culture and the freeing up of so many of its domains from the churches' teachings, supervision, and discipline. (And they also informed and shaped religious beliefs and practices, rendering many of those religions in America, Christian and other, more "American," so to speak.) The US Constitution made that displacement explicit. Many religions have been able to accept the settlement, whether on principle or out of prudence, some joyfully, others grudgingly, and have taken their place in a free, bustling, and sometimes fiercely competitive marketplace of religions, organized and not. Others have resisted, wanting not to participate in the market but to have a monopoly over it, and have identified themselves and their witness in opposition to the nation and its pretentions.

The heretics and heresiarchs we've encountered in these pages did not recognize the happy symbiosis between religion and American democracy that Alexis de Tocqueville reported and so appreciated. As we have seen, they regarded the American political project as fundamentally—perhaps fatally—flawed. The lack of a proper religious foundation, they believed, was (and continues to be) the fount of present woes. They all opposed a political order dedicated to the preservation of individual rights, authorized by "we the people" and subject to their wisdom or folly. The *vox populi* was not to be confused with the *vox Dei*.

They wanted the United States to be not only a Christian nation but a Christian commonwealth through and through—a Christian government of a Christian people, by a Christian people, for a Christian people. A New World Christendom, one might say. Their religion would be properly constitutional-ized; political institutions would rest on sacred foundations and would culti-vate a religious people by supporting the church, maintaining ordained social hierarchies, and enforcing inherited moral norms and social practices. If you believe that the civil government is an ordinance of God, that the state ought to cultivate virtue, or that politics has a redemptive purpose, directing human beings to their highest good, you're unlikely to be satisfied with the ethos and procedures of liberal democracy and with a policy of religious liberty as the solution to the stubborn reality of religious pluralism. You may begin to dream of theocracy in America.

The heretics did not register a complaint merely against America's founding principles and constitutional provisions. As we have seen, theirs was a complaint about the very features of Western modernity: the displacement of religion from its long-standing dominant position in culture and the establish-ment of political orders under human rather than divine authority. The more maximalist the claims a religion makes—that is, the more its adherents strive to regulate human life and endeavors, private and public—the more difficult it may be for them to reconcile themselves to a pluralistic liberal democracy where most religious activities are relegated to the private sphere and rendered a matter of individual choice and where religion no longer serves as a unique stabilizing force anchoring society in the transcendent. The people we have considered all desired to reinstate religion's—their religion's—commanding place over culture. They dreamed of a politics suffused with deep spiritual meaning.[1]

We live, it appears, in increasingly—and dangerously—illiberal times. The much-anticipated "end of history"—the universal victory of liberal democracy over its ideological contenders—has not come to pass. On the contrary, the faults of that regime appear to have reopened the contest. Rather than having been vanquished, the forces of religion and nationalism have reemerged and are gaining strength; the hoary call for a unified religious-political community is resurgent. Perhaps some alternative modernity—some new-old theological-political possibility—waits just over the horizon.

Today's religious adversaries of American liberal democracy are many: so-called Christian nationalists who would reinstate conservative Protestant supremacy over public life; Catholic integralists calling for a confessional state; Charismatic Dominionists donning the "armor of God" for spiritual warfare to take control of the commanding heights of cultural, economic, and political power and bring about the "Kingdom Now"; among others. Their understandings of the nexus of religion and politics are quite different, yet these adversaries are only the latest of those striving for that perennial dream: to realize an intimate union of religion and the powers of the earth.

Behind all the clamor for some revolutionary refounding is the desire to utilize democratic processes and procedures to implement illiberal ends, to deploy civil power to promote religion, enforce morality, and suppress "heresy"—a program for authoritarianism. Despite whatever culture war cobelligerencies opponents of liberal democracy may be able to pull together at present, it ought to be evident that they hold very different and incompatible visions of what a redeemed nation would look like and what policies it would put into effect. In the event that any such effort were to be realized, the destruction of liberal democracy would not bring about a well-ordered state but rather usher in a terrible era of division and violence. Dreams of order can beget nightmares of chaos.

In the end, our consideration of these American heretics—in all their variety and complexity, their extremism and their brute incompatibility—brings us to reflect anew on why people came up with liberal ideas and why they were found compelling in the first place. The political project of liberalism, we should recall, provided an escape from the civil strife and outright violence instigated and exacerbated by religious disagreement—to solve, or at least stave off, our "theological-political problem." Liberal theorists strove to establish political institutions on secular foundations, to construct a polity on the basis of human reason rather than an appeal to revelation, by the people's consent rather than divine authority, and to seek ways to restrain the passions religion unleashed so that they would no longer trouble the civil order. A shifting of political horizons, they wagered, would return real dividends—not only in civil peace but also in the expansion of knowledge, economic growth, and human welfare. In short, they envisioned a politics that would work toward modest public goods, rather than seeking to impose a "highest good" that had been determined once and for all.

The architects of the American political project recognized the impossibility of coming to agreement on ultimate ends, and they planned accordingly.

The protection of religious liberty provided the solution to the reality of religious diversity and the attendant discord. By uncoupling a profession of faith from political belonging and protecting the liberty of conscience from government supervision or interference, liberating the churches from government favor and largess (and oversight and regulation), and leaving aside all the religious arguments that had so vexed earlier regimes, the American order established a heretical space, in the original Greek sense of the term—a space for choosing. In that space, a profusion of religious communities blossomed, as older denominations divided over differences in belief and practice, and new ones came into being; sometimes denominations merged, sometimes later splitting apart. Immigrants came and transplanted their traditions, which took root and grew in the fertile soil of religious liberty. Some of those religious communities flourished, others withered, and many changed, adapting to or fiercely resisting the dominant culture. In that space, individuals could choose to remain in the traditions of their birth or upbringing or to embark on their own journeys to find meaning, community, happiness, or solace and join another or several or none at all, or undertake new experiments in believing and belonging. This is admittedly not a satisfying state of affairs for those who believe they are in possession of the truth and would like to impose it on their compatriots, but for those who are committed to their own traditions and those willing to live in the uncertainties of the world, it is a great blessing—indeed, a policy worthy of imitation.[2]

Americans in the twenty-first century find themselves in a deeper and more radical situation of pluralism than did the revolutionaries of 1776 and the Framers of 1787. And the moral consensus that Tocqueville believed he had seen during his travels no longer pertains (if it ever had). Despite the hopes of the visionaries of future Christendoms, it is unrealistic—if not delusional—to imagine the American people coming to agree on the "highest good," or to envision a restoration of some imagined preliberal age of religious uniformity and social harmony. It may well be, too, that the time of an unofficial pan-Protestant establishment, a nonsectarian "Judeo-Christian" civil religion, whether animated by a biblical faith or grounded in natural law, or even some renewed "cultural Christianity," is long past. The nation's religious diversity continues to advance even as the numbers of Christians decrease (on account of disaffiliation or switching to another tradition). In 2022, a respected survey found that 64 percent of Americans identify as Christian, while 6 percent report being members of "other" religious traditions and 30 percent claim to be religiously unaffiliated (or "nones"). If present trends continue, the numbers of the unaffiliated and non-Christians will continue to rise, and those of Christians to shrink. The waning of "Christian America" may not be surprising to those who believe that America was never properly Christian to begin with. Nevertheless, this transformation may well intensify the sense of urgency felt by the adversaries of American liberalism, strengthening their determination to impose a comprehensive theological-political vision on a recalcitrant citizenry.[3]

If it is to endure, America's liberal democracy will have to be sustained in the absence of a moral consensus or clear-cut spiritual foundations. And its citizens and others who dwell and sojourn within its borders will have to manage to live together with all of their profound and intractable differences. This requires an ongoing exercise in democratic virtue and liberality—not without tensions and temptations, sometimes happily and sometimes with ambivalence, frustration, and conflict—within the admittedly not-entirely-neutral frame of our liberal democratic republic. That is, in its own way, a serious moral project. Our engagement with its theological-political heretics has the salutary effect of challenging us to reflect on the origins and limitations of our own commitments. Interpreting their dreams of order may help us more profoundly appreciate our own.

Notes

Introduction

1. Alexis de Tocqueville, *Democracy in America: Historical-Critical Edition of* De la Démocratie en Amérique, ed. Eduardo Nolla, trans. James T. Schleifer (Indianapolis: Liberty Fund, 2010), 2:479.

2. Ibid., 2:24, 488, 467–68, 471.

3. Ibid., 2:472–73, 475.

4. Ibid., 2:480; 3:746; 2:488.

5. John Locke, *A Letter Concerning Toleration*, ed. James H. Tully (Indianapolis: Hackett, 1983), 32.

6. For a general discussion of some of these movements and communities, see Stephen J. Stein, *Communities of Dissent: A History of Alternative Religions in America* (New York: Oxford University Press, 2000). See also R. Laurence Moore, *Religious Outsiders and the Making of Americans* (New York: Oxford University Press, 1986). For a wonderfully varied history of utopian experiments in nineteenth-century America, see Charles Nordoff, *The Communistic Societies of the United States* (1865).

The Church of Jesus Christ of Latter-day Saints (the Mormons) presents a fascinating, complex, and distinctly American case. Its founder and prophet, Joseph Smith Jr., told the world that it was his anxiety over the variety of sects that competed for souls in the "Burned-over district" of western New York that had brought about his spiritual vocation. With a new scripture—*The Book of Mormon* (published in 1830)—in hand, and new revelations flowing from his mouth, Smith preached a "restored" Christianity, along with a radical communitarianism appealing to those dissatisfied with American individualism and capitalism, and called the faithful to gather together to build a new Zion in America in preparation for the millennial reign of Christ. The Mormons' various attempts to put their vision into practice—in their early settlements, the Illinois city-state of Nauvoo, and later the Utah Territory—produced an enormous expanse of theological-political reflection about the political implications of their religious vision and the relationship of their community to the American government and nation. This body of thought includes Joseph

Smith's revelation that the US Constitution was a divinely inspired instrument and his proclamation of "theodemocracy"; church leaders' speculations on the authorized "kingdom of God" and condemnations of the illegitimacy and illegality of all human governments; appeals to the Constitution (to protect their religious liberty and practice of plural marriage) against corrupt federal and state governments and officials; and musings on the American republic as a provisional order, a stepping stone to a higher, perfected regime, or later as a partner in the spread of the restored gospel throughout the world. Often responding to specific circumstances and crises, these theological-political ruminations express the church's long struggle with and finally accommodation to—indeed embrace of—the United States.

See, for example, Thomas F. O'Dea, *The Mormons* (Chicago: University of Chicago Press, 1957); Leonard J. Arrington and Davis Bitton, *The Mormon Experience: A History of the Latter-day Saints*, 2nd ed. (Urbana: University of Illinois Press, 1992); Klaus J. Hansen, *Quest for Empire: The Political Kingdom of God and the Council of Fifty in Mormon History* (Lincoln: University of Nebraska Press, 1974); Spencer W. McBride, *Joseph Smith for President: The Prophet, the Assassins, and the Fight for American Religious Freedom* (Oxford: Oxford University Press, 2021); Benjamin E. Park, *Kingdom of Nauvoo: The Rise and Fall of a Religious Empire on the American Frontier* (New York: Liveright, 2020); Patrick Q. Mason, "God and the People: Theodemocracy in Nineteenth-Century Mormonism," *Journal of Church and State* 53, no. 3 (2011): 349–75; and Kathleen Flake, *The Politics of Religious Identity: The Seating of Reed Smoot, Mormon Apostle* (Chapel Hill: University of North Carolina Press, 2004).

7. There is a vast popular literature that claims the United States was established as a "Christian nation," imagines the Founding Fathers as pious Christians, and calls attention to the manifold ways in which Christianity has manifested itself in the life of the republic. See sources in chapter 6, note 9.

Considerations of the question by Christian scholars include Mark A. Noll, Nathan O. Hatch, and George M. Mardsen, *The Search for Christian America*, expanded ed. (Colorado Springs: Helmers & Howard, 1989); John Fea, *Was America Founded as a Christian Nation? A Historical Introduction*, rev. ed. (Louisville: Westminster John Knox, 2016); and Mark David Hall, *Did America Have a Christian Founding? Separating Modern Myth from Historical Truth* (Nashville: Thomas Nelson, 2019).

For a description of the various conceptions of America as a "Christian nation," critique of their methodologies, and an argument about how the myth first emerged during the early republic as part of the construction of a national identity, see Steven K. Green, *Inventing a Christian America: The Myth of the Religious Founding* (New York: Oxford University Press, 2015).

Ken I. Kersch, *Conservatives and the Constitution: Imagining Constitutional Restoration in the Heyday of American Liberalism* (Cambridge: Cambridge University Press, 2019), provides an analysis of conservative Protestant and Roman Catholic stories about the Constitution.

8. The classic presentation is Leo Pfeffer, *Church, State, and Freedom* (Boston: Beacon, 1953). See also Leonard W. Levy, *The Establishment Clause: Religion and the First Amendment* (New York: Macmillan, 1986); Frank Lambert, *The Founding Fathers and the Place of Religion in America* (Princeton: Princeton University Press, 2003); Geoffrey R. Stone, "The World of the Framers: A Christian Nation?," *University of California Law Review* 56 (October 2008): 1–26; and Isaac Kramnick and R. Laurence Moore, *The Godless Constitution: A Moral Defense of the Secular State*, 2nd ed. (New York: W. W. Norton, 2005).

For a critique of both the Christian and the secular "creation myths," see Noah Feldman, *Divided by God: America's Church-State Problem—and What We Should Do about It* (New York: Farrar, Straus and Giroux, 2006), especially 19–56.

For a provocative fleshing out of a vital via media between "radical secularism" and "religious nationalism," see Philip Gorski, *American Covenant: A History of Civil Religion from the Puritans to the Present* (Princeton: Princeton University Press, 2017).

9. The historian Sidney E. Mead argued that "the United States was never Protestant in the sense that its constitutional and legal structure was rooted in or legitimately by particularistic Protestant theology." It was rather the rationalist, inclusive, and "designedly antiparticularistic" "religion of the Republic" that lay "behind the legal structure of America, the theology on which the practice of religious freedom is based and its meaning interpreted. Under it, one might say, it is religious particularity that is heretical and schismatic—even un-American." *The Nation with the Soul of a Church* (New York: Harper & Row, 1975), 19, 22.

"There is an unresolved intellectual tension," Mead later noted, "between the theology professed and promulgated by the majority of the sects, and the theology that legitimates the institutional structures of the American democratic way and style of life." *The Old Religion in the Brave New World: Reflections on the Relation between Christendom and the Republic* (Berkeley: University of California Press, 1977), 3.

1. *Those Licentious Principles of the Times*

1. Myles Cooper, *National Humiliation and Repentance recommended, and the Causes of the present Rebellion in America assigned* (December 13, 1776), 22. The sermon was published the following month by the Clarendon Press in Oxford.

On Cooper, see Clarence Haydon Vance, "Myles Cooper," *Columbia University Quarterly* 22 (1930): 261–86; Robert McCluer Calhoon, *The Loyalists in Revolutionary America, 1760–1781* (New York: Harcourt Brace Jovanovich, 1973), 253–56.

2. David L. Holmes, "The Episcopal Church and the American Revolution," *Historical Magazine of the Protestant Episcopal Church* 47, no. 3 (1978): 263n5. Nancy L. Rhoden, *Revolutionary Anglicanism: The Colonial Church of England Clergy during the American Revolution* (New York: New York University Press, 1999), 11–12, 50, 64.

3. Calhoon, *Loyalists in Revolutionary America*, 253–56; John Frederick Woolverton, *Colonial Anglicanism in North America* (Detroit: Wayne State University Press, 1984), 215.

4. Cooper's "Stanzas written on the Eve of the 10th of May," in *Gentleman's Magazine*, July 1776, commemorated that experience.

5. Cooper, *National Humiliation and Repentance recommended*, 4, 2, 7.

6. Woolverton, *Colonial Anglicanism in North America*, 16–17; Rhoden, *Revolutionary Anglicanism*, 68; Glenn T. Miller, "Fear God and Honor the King: The Failure of Loyalist Civil Theology in the Revolutionary Crisis," *Historical Magazine of the Protestant Episcopal Church* 47, no. 2 (June 1978): 224.

7. Cooper, *National Humiliation and Repentance recommended*, 8, 10–11.

8. Peter William Walker, "The Church Militant: The American Loyalist Clergy and the Making of the British Counterrevolution, 1701–92" (PhD diss., Columbia University, 2016), 19–27.

  The Church of England may have been established in England (and there, too, the Toleration Act of 1689, granting dissenting Protestants freedom of worship, curtailed its truly national ambitions), but the Presbyterian Church remained established in Scotland. And the empire maintained multiple ecclesiastical establishments, as well as dissenters among them. So, while Great Britain could be considered a Protestant empire, the mother country and its colonial holdings were not united in a single Protestant establishment.

9. Woolverton, *Colonial Anglicanism in North America*, 17. Rhoden notes that England, too, fell short of the ideal model of establishment, as the Act of Toleration of 1689 conceded the reality of religious pluralism. *Revolutionary Anglicanism*, 12–13.

10. Jon Butler, *Awash in a Sea of Faith: Christianizing the American People* (Cambridge, MA: Harvard University Press, 1990), 102–3.

11. Holmes, "Episcopal Church," 261–68; Rhoden, *Revolutionary Anglicanism*, 10–36, 132.

12. Sidney E. Ahlstrom, *A Religious History of the American People* (New Haven: Yale University Press, 1972), 223–25.

13. Rhoden, *Revolutionary Anglicanism*, 50. See also Frederick V. Mills Sr., *Bishops by Ballot: An Eighteenth-Century Ecclesiastical Revolution* (New York: Oxford University Press, 1787), viii–ix, 137.

14. See Fredrick V. Mills, "Anglican Expansion in Colonial America 1761–1775," *Historical Magazine of the Protestant Episcopal Church* 39, no. 3 (September 1970): 315–24; Elizabeth H. Davidson, *The Establishment of the English Church in Continental America*

(Durham, NC: Duke University Press, 1936); Woolverton, *Colonial Anglicanism in North America*, 18–23, 136–72; Rhoden, *Revolutionary Anglicanism*, 14–17; Holmes, "Episcopal Church," 264.

15. Thomas Bradbury Chandler, *An Appeal to the Public in Behalf of the Church of England in America* (New York: James Parker, 1767), 79; Mills, *Bishops by Ballot*, 41–44.

On Chandler, see S. Scott Rohrer, *The Folly of Revolution: Thomas Bradbury Chandler and the Loyalist Mind in a Democratic Age* (University Park, PA: Penn State University Press, 2022).

16. Chandler, *Appeal to the Public*, 42, 58, 61–62, 117. Rhoden, *Revolutionary Anglicanism*, 56–58.

17. Chandler, *Appeal to the Public*, 115. Mills, *Bishops by Ballot*, 60, 143.

18. Patricia U. Bonomi, *Under the Cope of Heaven: Religion, Society, and Politics in Colonial America*, updated ed. (Oxford: Oxford University Press, 2003), 199–209; Butler, *Awash in a Sea of Faith*, 195–99; Carl Bridenbaugh, *Mitre and Sceptre: Transatlantic Faiths, Ideas, Personalities and Politics, 1689–1775* (New York: Oxford University Press, 1962), 260–87; Rhoden, *Revolutionary Anglicanism*, 37–63.

19. John Adams later claimed that "the apprehension of Episcopacy contributed . . . as much as any other cause, to arouse the attention not only of the inquiring mind, but of the common people, and urge them to close thinking on the constitutional authority of parliament over the colonies." Adams to Dr. J. Morse, Quincy (December 2, 1815), quoted in Bridenbaugh, *Mitre and Sceptre*, 233. For overviews of the bishop controversy and debates over its influence on the American Revolution, see Mills, *Bishops by Ballot*; Arthur L. Cross, *The Anglican Episcopate and the American Colonies* (New York: Longmans, Green, 1902); Rhoden, *Revolutionary Anglicanism*, 37–63; James B. Bell, *A War of Religion: Dissenters, Anglicans, and the American Revolution* (Houndmills, UK: Palgrave Macmillan, 2008), 3–120; William M. Hogue, "The Religious Conspiracy Theory of the American Revolution: Anglican Motive," *Church History* 45, no. 3 (September 1976): 277–92.

20. Butler, *Awash in a Sea of Faith*, 127–28.

21. Cooper, *National Humiliation and Repentance recommended*, 22.

22. [Thomas Bradley Chandler], *A Friendly Address to All Reasonable Americans, on the subject of our political confusions: in which the necessary consequences of violently opposing the King's troops, and of a general non-importation are fairly stated* (New York: James Rivington, 1774), 29–31.

23. Cooper, *National Humiliation and Repentance recommended*, 12–13, 15.

24. Ibid., 18.

25. While I use "Loyalist" throughout to denote opponents of colonial resistance to British authority throughout the era, Calhoon notes that the term "did not come into use until

late in the war, when exiles in England adopted it as a badge of honor." *Loyalists in Revolutionary America*, xi–xii.

26. "Were I a parson," Inglis wrote, "I should be better qualified to deal with him in this way. However, as I am a sincere believer in divine revelation, I sometimes read the Scripture for instruction—nor am I ashamed to own it—Boyle, Locke, and Newton, did the same." [Charles Inglis], *The True Interest of America Impartially Stated, in Certain Strictures on a Pamphlet intitled Common Sense. By an American.* (Philadelphia, 1776), 25.

27. [Inglis], *True Interest of America*, vi–vii, 10, 12, 31, 33. Bernard Bailyn, *The Ideological Origins of the American Revolution*, enlarged ed. (Cambridge, MA: The Belknap Press of Harvard University Press, 1992), 285–88.

28. [Seabury], "The Congress Canvassed: or, An Examination into the Conduct of the Delegates, at Their Grand Convention, Held in Philadelphia, Sept. 1, 1774. Addressed, to the Merchants of New-York" (New York, 1774), in *Letters of a Westchester Farmer, 1774–1775*, ed. Clarence H. Vance (White Plains, NY: Westchester County Historical Society, 1930), 97, 99.

29. On Chandler's historical researches, see Rohrer, *Folly of Revolution*.

30. [Chandler], *Friendly Address*, 46, 49, 52. On the argument that the political bond with England served to protect the religious liberty of smaller churches throughout the colonies, see Miller, "Fear God and Honor the King," 236–40.

31. [Chandler], *Friendly Address*, 49–51, 36.

32. On this number, see Mills (who adds that "six of these were either sons or grandsons of Anglican clergymen"), *Bishops by Ballot*, 152.

33. Mills, *Bishops by Ballot*, 134–35. As Holmes summarized the situation:

> Roughly speaking, *Anglican clergy were loyalists in direct proportion to the weakness of Anglicanism in their colony, to the degree of their earlier support of an episcopate for the American colonies, to the "highness" of their churchmanship, to the degree of their support by the S.P.G., and to the numbers of converts and recent immigrants from Britain and Scotland among them.* In lesser percentages, *Anglican laity tended to be loyalists for the same reasons.*
>
> Conversely, *with the exception of the clergy of Maryland, Anglican clergy were patriots in rough proportion to the strength of Anglicanism in their colony, to the degree of their earlier coolness towards an American episcopate, to the extent to which they were low or latitudinarian churchmen, and to the degree to which their parishes were self-supporting.* In greater percentages, *Anglican laity tended to be patriots for the same reasons.*

Holmes noted, too, that "over the issue of the Revolution itself, Anglicanism divided more than any of the major colonial denominations." "Episcopal Church," 264–65. See also

William Warren Sweet, "The Role of Anglicans in the American Revolution," *Huntington Library Quarterly* 11 (1947): 52–53.

34. Jonathan Boucher, "Preface," in *A View of the Causes and Consequences of the American Revolution; on Thirteen Discourses, Preached in North American between the Years 1863 and 1775: With an Historical Preface* (New York: Russell & Russell, 1967), lxxxiv.

35. Gregg L. Frazer, *God against the Revolution: The Loyalist Clergy's Case against the American Revolution* (Lawrence: University Press of Kansas, 2018), 38–45; Rhoden, *Revolutionary Anglicanism*, passim.

36. Cooper, *National Humiliation and Repentance recommended*, 22.

37. For biographic details, see Anne Y. Zimmer, *Jonathan Boucher: Loyalist in Exile* (Detroit: Wayne State University Press, 1978); Anne Young Zimmer and Alfred H. Kelly, "Jonathan Boucher: Constitutional Conservative," *Journal of American History* 58, no. 4 (March 1972): 897–922.

38. Boucher, "On Fundamental Principles," in *Causes and Consequences*, 303–4, 306–7.

39. [Chandler], *Friendly Address*, 5.

40. Boucher, "On Fundamental Principles," 310–14. To the published version, he affixed a note, saying, "In Christian States religion and government rest on the same basis; success in the latter being the necessary and constant result of sincerity on the former. The Church and the King do, as must, stand or fall together. . . . It is the peculiar boast of the Church of England, that, amidst all *the changes and chances* of our history, she never, either in her doctrine or her practice, has countenanced any principles tending to sedition, faction, or treason. Churchmen, as such, have often been sufferers for, but never the opposers of, lawful authority. This is so well known a fact, that, amidst all of the contumelies with which her enemies have so often loaded her, the resistance of just authority has never been objected to her" (311n). In a later sermon Boucher said, "There is a fashion in political, as well as in other, opinions: and it is in times of popular commotions, when revolutions are mediated, that the doctrines of natural rights and the natural *equality* of mankind are most countenanced." "On the Character of Ahitophel," in *Causes and Consequences*, 419.

41. Around the same time, Boucher preached a sermon titled "The Dispute between the Israelites and the Two Tribes and an Half, Respecting their Settlement beyond Jordan" in response to one by Reverend William Smith, the Provost of the College of Philadelphia. Boucher's texts were published twenty-two years later in *A View of the Causes and Consequences of the American Revolution*. In the preface to that volume, Boucher wrote that "the publication of two patriotic sermons in Philadelphia, by two clergymen of rank and weight in our Church, told the world but too plainly, that all our Clergy did not think unfavorably either of the insurgents or of their cause" ("Preface," xlix). As with other sermons in the collection, Boucher stated that "On Civil Liberty" was "professedly written with a view to

publication," but, as "the press was shut to every publication of the kind," circumstances in America rendered such hopes moot. "Preface," lxxxiv.

On Boucher's preaching with pistols, see his *Reminiscences of an American Loyalist, 1738–1789, being the autobiography of the Revd. Jonathan Boucher, Rector of Annapolis in Maryland and afterwards Vicar of Epsom, Surrey, England*, edited by his grandson Jonathan Bouchier (Port Washington, NY: Kennikat, 1967), 113, 118–24.

In his study on the ideological origins of the Revolution, Bernard Bailyn described Boucher's text as "a classic of its kind. It sums up, as no other essay of the period, the threat to the traditional ordering of human relations implicit in Revolutionary thought." *Ideological Origins of the American Revolution*, 314.

Despite Boucher's claim that his "opinions and principles have undergone no change" (*Causes and Consequences*, lxxxv), Zimmer and Kelly have suggested that he later "doctored" some of those texts "to fit the stance toward the revolutionary controversy which Boucher adopted after 1772," and "cannot be accepted simply as a literal reproduction of his American sermons." "Jonathan Boucher," 901–2.

42. On Jacob Duché, his prayer to the Continental Congress, and its reception, see Edward Duffield Neill, "Rev. Jacob Duché, the First Chaplain of Congress," *Pennsylvania Magazine of History and Biography* 2, no. 1 (1878): 58–73; Clarke Garrett, "The Spiritual Odyssey of Jacob Duché," *Proceedings of the American Philosophical Society* 119, no. 2 (April 1975): 143–55; Spencer W. McBride, *Pulpit and Nation: Clergymen and the Politics of Revolutionary America* (Charlottesville: University of Virginia Press, 2016), 54–60; and Kevin J. Dellape, *America's First Chaplain: The Life and Times of the Reverend Jacob Duché* (Bethlehem, PA: Lehigh University Press, 2013).

43. Jacob Duché, *The Duty of Standing Fast in our Spiritual and Temporal Liberties* (Philadelphia: James Humphreys Jr., 1775), 7, 9. For an assessment of the sermon and its reception, see Dellape, *America's First Chaplain*, 85–90. Dellape suggests Duché is best described as a "moderate revolutionary," who had supported armed resistance to Britain to restore rights but came to oppose independency (181–88).

44. Duché, *Duty of Standing Fast*, 11–13.

45. Ibid., 13–14, 17–22.

46. Boucher, "On Civil Liberty, &c.," in *Causes and Consequences*, 535; *Reminiscences*, 120.

47. Boucher, "On Civil Liberty, &c.," 496.

48. Ibid., 504–6.

49. Ibid., 498.

50. Ibid., 506–9.

51. Boucher, "On the Stride between Abram and Lot," in *Causes and Consequences*, 363.

52. Boucher, "On Civil Liberty, &c.," 514–16, 518.

53. Ibid., 520–21.

54. Ibid., 522.

55. In an earlier sermon, Boucher complained of those who would "rest our faith, not on the inspired and heaven-dictated dogmas of St. Paul, but on the subtle and uncertain deductions of Mr. Locke, and his numerous imitators." "The Israelites and the Two Tribes and an Half," 488–89.

56. Boucher, "On Civil Liberty, &c.," 523–27, 530, 532. In the published collection, Boucher amended to that sermon a long note on Filmer and Locke (526–33). While appealing to Filmer's account of patriarchal authority, he criticized Filmer for having "entertained some very extravagant notions of monarchy, and the sacredness of kings: and (what is perhaps still less pardonable) some disparaging and unjust opinions respecting the supremacy of law."

57. Ibid., 534.

58. Ibid., 534–38, 542.

59. Ibid., 544–45. Boucher had declared in another sermon that "the doctrine of 'non-resistance' is unquestionably 'a tenet of our Church.' It is the uniform doctrine of the Articles, the Liturgy, the injunctions, and Canons, and Homilies; in one of which I find the following strong words: 'Lucifer was the first author and founder of rebellion; which is the first, and the greatest, and the root of all other sins. Kings and princes, as well the evil as the good, do reign by God's ordinance; and subjects are bound to obey them, and for no cause to resist, or withstand, or rebel, or make any sedition against them, although they be wicked men. It were a perilous thing to commit unto subjects the judgment, which prince is wise, which government good; and which otherwise. A rebel is worse than the worse prince, and a rebellion worse than the worst government of the worst prince that hath hitherto been.' " "The Israelites and the Two Tribes and an Half," 485–86.

60. In a similar fashion, Seabury insisted that "passive obedience and non-resistance . . . is too much for *me*. I cannot swallow it; and if I could, I am sure my stomach would never digest it" ("Congress Canvassed," 90). So, too, Inglis did not want to appear to his readers as a promoter of a reactionary ideology. "I am none of your *passive obedience and non-resistance men*," he claimed. "The principles on which the glorious Revolution in 1688 was brought about, constitute the articles of my political creed; and were it necessary, I could clearly evince, that these are perfectly conformable to the doctrines of Scripture." *True Interest of America*, 31.

61. Boucher, "On Civil Liberty, &c.," 538, 546.

62. Ibid., 552–53.

63. *Declaration by the Representatives of the United Colonies of North-America, now met in General Congress at Philadelphia, setting forth the Causes and Necessity of their taking up Arms* (July 6, 1775).

64. Boucher, "On Civil Liberty, &c.," 553. Boucher slyly added, "That they have excited a very general panic, and many apprehensions of a real impending slavery, is no more than might have been expected in a country where there is literally 'absolute property in, and unbounded power over, human beings.' How far this was intended, I presume not to judge."

65. Ibid., 554–55.

66. Ibid., 558, 560.

67. Ibid., 543, 559–60.

68. Ibid., 560. Cooper, *National Humiliation and Repentance recommended*, 23.

69. Seabury delivered *St. Peter's Exhortation to Fear God and Honor the King, Explained and inculcated on Sunday, September 28, 1777 to His Majesty's Provincial Troops at King's-Bridge* (New York: H. Gaine, 1777); Charles Inglis (Rector of Trinity Church) delivered *The Duty of Honouring the King, explained and recommended in St. George's and St. Paul's Chapels in New York on January 30, 1780 being the anniversary of the martyrdom of King Charles I* (New York: Hugh Gaine, 1780). Inglis also preached *The Christian Soldier's Duty Briefly delineated before the American Corps at King's-Bridge on September 7, 1777*, three weeks prior to Seabury's sermon (New York: H. Gaine, 1777).

70. Inglis, *Duty of Honouring the King*, 5–6.

71. Seabury, *St. Peter's Exhortation*, 7–8.

72. Inglis, *Duty of Honouring the King*, 9.

73. Seabury, *St. Peter's Exhortation*, 8.

74. Inglis, *Duty of Honouring the King*, 10–11; cf. Seabury, *St. Peter's Exhortation*, 9–10.

75. Inglis, *Duty of Honouring the King*, 11.

76. Ibid., 15.

77. Inglis, *Christian Soldier's Duty*, 17.

78. Seabury, *St. Peter's Exhortation*, 10.

79. Inglis, *Duty of Honouring the King*, 11–12.

80. Ibid., 12.

81. Seabury, *St. Peter's Exhortation*, 11–12.

82. Inglis, *Duty of Honouring the King*, 11.

83. Ibid., 30.

84. Seabury, *St. Peter's Exhortation*, 15.

85. Ibid., 16–17.

86. Ibid., 18–20.

87. Inglis, *Christian Soldier's Duty*, 11, 18–19. He remarked on the advantages the Loyalist soldiers' commitment to order gave them over their opponents: "The Want of Subordination and Discipline among our infatuated Adversaries, afford you one great Advantage over them. Their wild Principles actually lead to these and other Disorders; and so far tend to defeat the Object they have in view" (11–12).

88. Cooper, *National Humiliation and Repentance recommended*, 18–19.

89. On this episode, see Bruce E. Steiner, *Samuel Seabury 1729–1796: A Study in the High Church Tradition* (Athens: Ohio University Press, 1971), 159–64.

90. E. Edwards Beardsley, *Life and Correspondence of the Right Reverend Samuel Seabury, D.D.: First Bishop of Connecticut, and of the Episcopal Church in the United States of America* (Boston: Houghton, Mifflin, 1881), 35–43, 46–47; Steiner, *Samuel Seabury*, 159–64.

91. Holmes, "Episcopal Church," 276–77; Rhoden, *Revolutionary Anglicanism*, 104–7.

92. Quoted in Bell, *A War of Religion*, 52.

93. Boucher, *Causes and Consequences*, xlviii. On the hardships endured by Loyalist clergy during the American Revolution, see Holmes, "Episcopal Church," 274–78; Charles Mampoteng, "The New England Anglican Clergy in the American Revolution," *Historical Magazine of the Protestant Episcopal Church* 9, no. 4 (1940): 267–303; Maud O'Neil, "A Struggle for Religious Liberty: An Analysis of the Work of the S. P. G.," *Historical Magazine of the Protestant Episcopal Church* 20, no. 2 (1951): 173–89; Rhoden, *Revolutionary Anglicanism*, 104–7; Walter Herbert Stowe, "A Study in Conscience: Some Aspects of the Relations of the Clergy to the State," *Historical Magazine of the Episcopal Church* 44, no. 5 (1975): 52–75; and Walker, "Church Militant," 153–61.

94. Rhoden, *Revolutionary Anglicanism*, 90, 88–115; Holmes, "Episcopal Church," 270–71.

95. Holmes, "Episcopal Church," 272–73.

96. Samuel A. Clark, *The Episcopal Church in the American Colonies: The History of St. John's Church, Elizabeth Town, New Jersey, from the Year 1703 to the Present Time. Compiled from Original Documents, the Manuscript Records and Letters of the Missionaries of the Society for Propagating the Gospel in Foreign Parts, and from Other Sources* (Philadelphia: J. B. Lippincott, 1857), 199. See also Stowe, "Study in Conscience," 69–70; Holmes, "Episcopal Church," 272–73.

97. Boucher, "On the Character of Ahitophel," 422–23.

98. Cooper, *National Humiliation and Repentance recommended*, 21.

99. Inglis, *Christian Soldier's Duty*, 17–18.

100. John F. Berens, " 'A God of Order and Not of Confusion': The American Loyalists and Divine Providence, 1774–1783," *Historical Magazine of the Protestant Episcopal Church* 47, no. 2 (June 1978): 219. For a broader study on this theme, see Berens, *Providence and Patriotism in Early America, 1640–1815* (Charlottesville: University Press of Virginia, 1978).

101. Cited in William Jones Seabury, *Memoir of Bishop Seabury* (New York: Edwin S. Gorham, 1908), 178.

102. Butler, *Awash in a Sea of Faith*, 257–68. On the process of disestablishment of the Church of England in the Southern states, see Mills, *Bishops by Ballot*, 168–77.

"Thomas Jefferson's Notes on Early Career (the so-called 'Autobiography'), [6 January–29 July 1821], with editorial note on the Notes on Early Career (the so-called 'Autobiography')," Founders Online, National Archives, https://founders.archives.gov/documents/Jefferson/03-17-02-0324-0002.

[Original source: *The Papers of Thomas Jefferson, Retirement Series*, vol. 17, *1 March to 30 November 1821*, ed. J. Jefferson Looney et al. Princeton: Princeton University Press, 2020, 309–80.]

On the process of disestablishment in the states, see Carl H. Esbeck and Jonathan J. Den Hartog, eds., *Disestablishment and Religious Dissent: Church-State Relations in the New American States, 1776–1833*, Studies in Constitutional Democracy (Columbia: University of Missouri Press, 2019).

103. That Convention also proposed "that the fourth of July shall be observed by this Church for ever as a day of thanksgiving to Almighty God, for the inestimable blessings of religious and civil liberty vouchsafed to the United States of America" and that a committee be formed to come up with appropriate prayers for the occasion. *Journal of a Convention of the Protestant Episcopal Church in the States of New-York, New-Jersey, Pennsylvania, Delaware, Maryland, Virginia, and South-Carolina, Held in Christ-Church in the City of Philadelphia, from September 27th to October 7th, 1785* (United States: Hall and Sellers, 1785), 5–6, 11. The suggestion proved too divisive to be accepted by the nascent organization. Rhoden, *Revolutionary Anglicanism*, 140.

104. Steiner, *Samuel Seabury*, 192–93.

105. Rhoden, *Revolutionary Anglicanism*, 145. For a discussion of the attitudes of American Anglican clergy over disestablishment, episcopacy, and modifications of the liturgy, see 116–43. Holmes, "Episcopal Church," 286. Garrett, "Spiritual Odyssey of Jacob Duché," 151, 153. Dellape, *America's First Chaplain*, 155–58.

106. Mills, *Bishops by Ballot*, vii, 307. On the process of reorganization of the Protestant Episcopal Church, see 157–307.

107. Quoted in Frederick Quinn, *A House of Prayer for All People: A History of Washington National Cathedral* (New York: Morehouse, 2014), 179; the entire document is reproduced in 177–83.

108. Elody R. Crimi, Diane Ney, and Ken Cobb (photographer), *Jewels of Light: The Stained Glass of Washington National Cathedral* (Washington National Cathedral, 2004), 41–44, 102–3. Jefferson had ordered these accomplishments to be inscribed on his gravestone. "Thomas Jefferson: Design for Tombstone and Inscription, before 4 July 1826, 4 July 1826," Founders Online, National Archives, https://founders.archives.gov/documents/Jefferson/98-01-02-6185.

109. Quoted in Neill, "Rev. Jacob Duché," 67.

110. "To George Washington from Jacob Duché, 8 October 1777," Founders Online, National Archives, https://founders.archives.gov/documents/Washington/03-11-02-0452.

On Duché's letter and its aftermath, see Dellape, *America's First Chaplain*, 123–33; McBride, *Pulpit and Nation*, 63–67.

111. "From George Washington to John Hancock, 16 October 1777," Founders Online, National Archives, https://founders.archives.gov/documents/Washington/03-11-02-0537.

In another letter, Washington confided, "I am still willing to suppose, that it was rather dictated by his fears, than by his real Sentiments."

"From George Washington to Francis Hopkinson, 21 November 1777," Founders Online, National Archives, https://founders.archives.gov/documents/Washington/03-12-02-0339.

112. Garrett, "Spiritual Odyssey of Jacob Duché," 154.

113. Boucher, "Preface," xxvi.

114. Ibid., liv. Regarding that volume, Moses Coit Tyler wrote, "Nowhere else, probably, can be found so comprehensive, so able, and so authentic a presentation of the deeper principles and motives of the American Loyalists, particularly from the standpoint of a high-church clergyman of great purity and steadiness of character, of great moral courage, of great learning, finally of great love for the country thus torn and distracted by fratricidal disagreements." *The Literary History of the American Revolution, 1763–1783* (New York: G. P. Putnam's Sons, 1897), 1:320–21.

115. Boucher, "Preface," xxv.

116. Ibid., xxvii. Inglis made the same point in *Duty of Honouring the King*, 24.

117. Boucher, "Preface," xxxi, l, xxiii.

118. Ibid., lvii, lxxi, lxx, lxxiii–lxxvi.

119. Boucher, "Dedica," in *Causes and Consequences*, n.p.

2. *We Cannot Yield Obedience, for Conscience Sake*

1. Steven K. Green notes that "while occasional religious imagery and metaphor can be found in the ratification debates, discussions about a religious purpose behind the national government were nonexistent during its drafting in Philadelphia." *Inventing a Christian America: The Myth of the Religious Founding* (New York: Oxford University Press, 2015), 179. There are few references to religion to be found in *The Federalist Papers*.

2. Isaac Kramnick and R. Laurence Moore, *The Godless Constitution: A Moral Defense of the Secular State*, 2nd ed. (New York: W. W. Norton, 2005).

3. On Hamilton's remark, see Catherine L. Albanese, *Sons of the Fathers: The Civil Religion of the American Revolution* (Philadelphia: Temple University Press, 1976), 202–3; Daniel L. Dreisbach, "In Search of a Christian Commonwealth: An Examination of Selected Nineteenth-Century Commentaries on References to God and the Christian Religion in the United States Constitution," *Baylor Law Review* 48, no. 4 (Fall 1996): 955–56, 994.

4. *Virginia Independent Chronicle*, October 31, 1787, in *The Complete Anti-Federalist*, ed. Herbert J. Storing (Chicago: University of Chicago Press, 1981), 5:126–27.

5. Storing, ed., *The Complete Anti-Federalist*, 1:22–23. Leonard W. Levy, *The Establishment Clause: Religion and the First Amendment* (New York: Macmillan, 1986). On the complaints of religious conservatives in the Anti-Federalist camp over the prohibition of a religious test and the failure to acknowledge the Deity, see Green, *Inventing a Christian America*, 178–88; Kramnick and Moore, *Godless Constitution,* 29–44; Derek H. Davis, *Religion and the Continental Congress, 1774–1789: Contributions to Original Intent* (New York: Oxford University Press, 2000), 204–9; and Spencer W. McBride, *Pulpit and Nation: Clergymen and the Politics of Revolutionary America* (Charlottesville: University of Virginia Press, 2016), 120–26. *The Sacred Rights of Conscience: Selected Readings on Religious Liberty and Church-State Relations in the American Founding*, ed. Daniel L. Dreisbach and Mark David Hall (Indianapolis: Liberty Fund, 2009), collects a representative sample of primary source documents (esp. 346–438, on the controversies surrounding religion and the Constitution).

6. "To John Adams from Benjamin Rush, 15 June 1789," Founders Online, National Archives, https://founders.archives.gov/documents/Adams/06-20-02-0019. (Original source: *The Adams Papers, Papers of John Adams*, vol. 20, June 1789–February 1791, ed. Sara Georgini, Sara Martin, R. M. Barlow, Gwen Fries, Amanda M. Norton, Neal E. Millikan, and Hobson Woodward [Cambridge, MA: Harvard University Press, 2020], 28–29.)

7. "From George Washington to the Presbyterian Ministers of Massachusetts and New Hampshire, 2 November 1789," in *The Papers of George Washington, Presidential Series*, vol. 4, *8 September 1789–15 January 1790*, ed. Dorothy Twohig (Charlottesville: University Press of Virginia, 1993), 274–77.

8. John Mitchell Mason, *Sermon, Preached September 20th, 1793; A Day Set Apart, in the City of New-York, for Public Fasting, Humiliation and Prayer, on Account of a Malignant and Mortal Fever Prevailing in the City of Philadelphia* (New York: Samuel Loudon & Son, 1793), 18–20.

9. John Mitchell Mason, *The Voice of Warning, to Christians, on the ensuing election of a president of the United States* (New York: G. F. Hopkins, 1800), 33–34. See also William Linn, *Serious Considerations on the Election of a President Addressed to the Citizens of the United States* (Trenton, NJ: Sherman, Mershon & Thomas, 1800).

10. "Thomas Jefferson to Danbury, Connecticut, Baptist Association, January 1, 1802, with Copy," Library of Congress, https://www.loc.gov/item/mtjbib010955/.

11. Samuel B. Wylie, *The Two Sons of Oil; or, The Faithful Witness for Magistracy and Ministry upon a Scriptural Basis*, 3rd ed. (Philadelphia: Wm. S. Young, 1850), Preface, 7, 47. Born in Northern Ireland and educated at the University of Glasgow, Wylie had been forced to immigrate to the United States on account of his revolutionary activities. He arrived in Philadelphia in 1797 and in June 1800 became the first minister of the denomination to be ordained in America. Three years later, he was installed pastor of the Reformed Presbyterian Congregation in Philadelphia. Wylie was appointed the first professor at the newly formed Reformed Theological Seminary in the same city and in 1828 took up the post of professor of humanities at the University of Pennsylvania, where he taught Hebrew, Greek, and Latin.

12. David Melville Carson, "A History of the Reformed Presbyterian Church in America to 1871" (PhD diss., University of Pennsylvania, 1964), 58–59; W. Melancthon Glasgow, *History of the Reformed Presbyterian Church in America: with Sketches of All Her Ministry, Congregations, Missions, Institutions, Publications, Etc., and Embellished with over Fifty Portraits and Engravings* (Baltimore: Hill and Harvey, 1888), 54, 78–79.

13. For the historical background, see Joseph S. Moore, *Founding Sins: How a Group of Antislavery Radicals Fought to Put Christ into the Constitution* (New York: Oxford University Press, 2015), 8–35; Robert Emery, "Church and State in the Early Republic: The Covenanters' Radical Critique," *Journal of Law and Religion* 25, no. 2 (2009): 487–501.

14. Moore, *Founding Sins*, 41, 43, 50.

15. Carson, "Reformed Presbyterian Church," 48–54; Moore, *Founding Sins*, 50–53.

16. James McKinney, "An Act of the Reformed Presbytery in America for a Day of Public Fasting, with the Causes thereof," reprinted in *Reformed Presbyterian and Covenanter* 2 (January 1864): 10–15 (quotation at 13–14).

17. Glasgow, *Reformed Presbyterian Church*, 69. See also Robert Baird's assessment of the denomination in *Religion in America; or, An account of the Origin, Relation to the State, and Present Condition of the Evangelical Churches in the United States. With Notices of the Unevangelical Denominations* (New York: Harper & Brothers, 1856), 511–14.

18. Glasgow, *Reformed Presbyterian Church*, 742.

19. Wylie, *Two Sons of Oil*, 7, 9–12. On Wylie's treatise (and William Findley's critique), see Steven Wedgeworth, " 'The Two Sons of Oil' and the Limits of American Religious Dissent," *Journal of Law and Religion* 27, no. 1 (2011): 141–61.

20. Wylie, *Two Sons of Oil*, 12–14, 16–17.

21. Ibid., 27, 29, 32–33.

22. Ibid., 37–38.

23. Ibid., 16, 21.

24. Ibid., 47.

25. Ibid., 44–49, 51–54.

26. Ibid., 55–57. Here again Wylie cited Isaiah 49:23.

27. Ibid., 57–58.

28. Ibid., 58–60.

29. Moore, *Founding Sins*, 32–34.

30. Alexander McLeod, *Negro Slavery Unjustifiable* (New York: T. & J. Swords, 1802). McLeod observed that "the Declaration of Independence has these words: 'We hold these truths to be self-evident—that all men are created equal—that they are endowed by their Creator with certain unalienable rights—that among these are life, liberty, and the pursuit of happiness—that to secure these rights governments are instituted among men.' The negroes are created equal with the whites according to this instrument. Their liberty is an unalienable right. But this nation has taken away this unalienable right from them. And although the nation declares that government is instituted to preserve this right, the government still continues to deprive them of it." *Negro Slavery Unjustifiable*, 19.

31. Wylie, *Two Sons of Oil*, 61.

32. Ibid., 62–63.

33. Ibid., 63, 65.

34. Ibid., 64–65, 69.

35. Ibid., 70–71.

36. Ibid., 72–73, 81.

37. Ibid., 94–95.

38. *Reformation Principles Exhibited, by the Reformed Presbyterian Church in the United States of America* (New York: Hopkins and Seymour, 1807), 2:102, 104, 108, 110; 1:136. The text condemned as errors the propositions "That it is lawful for civil rulers to authorize the purchase and sale of any part of the human family as slaves" and "That a constitution of government which deprives unoffending men of liberty and property a moral institution, to be recognized as God's ordinance" (1:108).

39. *Reformation Principles Exhibited*, 1:134. The Reformed Presbyterian Church was only a very small church, though its numbers were slowly growing, mostly because of emigration from Ireland in the late 1790s. Moore notes that by 1820 there were only about fifteen thousand across the Covenanter denominations (*Founding Sins*, 164). While the majority of its members were rural farmers, some of the church's influential pastors occupied pulpits in cities such as New York, Philadelphia, and Albany. Carson, "Reformed Presbyterian Church," 70–74.

40. William Findley, *Observations on "The Two Sons of Oil" Containing a Vindication of the American Constitutions, and Defending the Blessings of Religious Liberty and Toleration,*

against the Illiberal Strictures of the Rev. Samuel B. Wylie (Indianapolis: Liberty Fund, 2007), xix.

41. Ibid., xx–xxi, xxi, xxii, 142, 217. Some of this self-promotion may have been a bit of revisionist history on Findley's part. Moore notes that as an Anti-Federalist, Findley led the movement to stall ratification in Pennsylvania and even suggested that armed resistance might be necessary if the Constitution was passed (*Founding Sins*, 56–57, 69). Findley may have been particularly offended by Wylie's attacks on the Constitution of Pennsylvania, which he had helped draft.

42. Findley, *Observations*, xxvii.

43. Ibid., 15, 36, 112.

44. Findley misstated as "seven" the number of reasons Wylie detailed for why Reformed Presbyterians could not homologate with the government. Ibid., 142.

45. Ibid., 86, 88.

46. Ibid.,154–55, 161. Wylie, *Two Sons of Oil*, 61–62.

47. Findley, *Observations,* 164–65.

48. Ibid., 221–23, 137, 147–48; on this point, see Wedgeworth, " 'Two Sons of Oil,' " 155–56.

49. Glasgow, *Reformed Presbyterian Church*, 83.

50. Alexander McLeod, *A Scriptural view of the Character, Causes, and Ends of the Present War* (New York: Eastbury, Kirk, 1815), 54–57.

51. Ibid., 58–61, 99, 61. Moore, *Founding Sins,* 73–74.

52. Glasgow, *Reformed Presbyterian Church*, 725–26. Willson's earlier sermons on the topic included *The Subjection of Kings and Nations to Messiah* (1820) and *Sermon on Civil Government* (1821). On Willson's previous activities and writings, see James S. Kabala, " 'Theocrats' vs. 'Infidels': Marginalized Worldviews and Legislative Prayer in 1830s New York," *Journal of Church and State* 51, no. 1 (2009): 82–83. See also Kabala, *Church-State Relations in the Early Republic, 1787–1846* (London: Routledge, 2016).

53. James R. Willson, *Prince Messiah's Claims to Dominion Over All Governments and the Disregard of His Authority by the United States in the Federal Constitution* (Albany: Packard, Hoffman and White, 1832), 13–16.

54. Ibid., 17–18.

55. Ibid., 19, 21.

56. Willson was not moved by the mere allusion to the third commandment in the presidential oath and the concession to the Sabbath in Article I, Section 7 ("The fact demonstrates how very carefully the framers were to avoid every word, that might be construed into a declaration of respect to the statutes of Jehovah").

57. Willson noted that the Articles of Confederation acknowledged "the great Governor of the world," a locution which permitted the assent of deists, as there was no mention of the

Messiah. "It was a radical defect in that deed, that the Lord Jesus was not recognized as Sovereign of the United States." Ibid., 25.

58. Ibid., 21–30.

59. Ibid., 31.

60. On the promotion of the Washington hagiography in the early Republic, see Green, *Inventing a Christian America*, 202–11.

61. Willson, *Prince Messiah's Claims to Dominion*, 31–34, 42.

62. Ibid., 35–36.

63. Ibid., 36–38. On Sabbatarianism and the Post Office controversy, see Moore, *Founding Sins*, 79–82; Noah Feldman, *Divided by God: America's Church-State Problem—And What We Should Do About It* (New York: Farrar, Straus and Giroux, 2006), 54–56; Kramnick and Moore, *The Godless Constitution*, 132–44; Richard R. John, "Taking Sabbatarianism Seriously: The Postal System, the Sabbath, and the Transformation of American Political Culture," *Journal of the Early Republic* 10, no. 4 (Winter 1990): 516–67.

64. Willson, *Prince Messiah's Claims to Dominion*, 46.

65. J. B. Williams, "To American Politicians," in Willson, *Prince Messiah's Claims to Dominion Over All Governments: and the Disregard of His Authority by the United States, in the Federal Constitution* (Cincinnati: Smith and Chipman, 1848), 3.

66. The scandal over Willson's theological-political heresy had an interesting aftereffect of challenging the state's Protestant nonsectarian consensus. When a legislator proposed to renew the ban on Rev. Willson at the beginning of the New York State Assembly's 1833 session, a new debate on legislative prayer broke out. Although the Assembly reaffirmed the practice by an overwhelming 80–40 vote, a group of Albany's clergy—the list included James R. Willson—responded by announcing that they would decline further invitations. Legislative prayer was thus discontinued in the New York Assembly, until it was revived when the Whigs took the majority in 1838. See Kabala, " 'Theocrats' vs. 'Infidels,' " 85–101.

67. Willson, *Prince Messiah's Claims to Dominion* (1832), 40–43.

68. Those who longed for a reconsideration of the doctrine "wanted to breathe more freely," sneered a later Reformed Presbyterian historian. "Some of the learned doctors, who had grown weary of testimony-bearing, wrote articles to show how easily Covenanters, in consistency with their principles, could incorporate with the government and not be charged with complicity in the sins of the nation. This was 'new light' to those who had thought and held that the Constitution was defective and licensed immorality, and those who swore allegiance to it were justly implicated in the evil. Some of the leading men, who had spent their best days in upholding the principles of the Church and emitting publications in her defense, now 'changed their minds' and repudiated the sentiments held when they were 'beardless boys.' " Glasgow, *Reformed Presbyterian Church*, 88–89.

69. *The Original Draft of a Pastoral Address from the Eastern Subordinate Synod of the Reformed Presbyterian Church. To The People Under Their Immediate Inspection* (New York: W. Applegate, 1832), 8, 10.

70. Ibid., 10–12.

71. Ibid., 9, 19–26. The minority faction felt it was necessary to release the full draft of the Pastoral Address to protect the church "from the public odium which had arisen out of the attacks, made in certain notorious Albany pamphlets on General Washington, and other high functionaries of government, as well as from the misrepresentations contained in those caricatures of Reformation principles." Samuel Brown Wylie, *Memoir of Alexander McLeod, D.D.* (New York: Charles Scribner, 1855), 441–42.

72. Gilbert McMaster, *The Moral Character of Civil Government: Considered with Reference to the Political Institutions of the United States, in Four Letters* (Albany: W. C. Little; Schenectady: J. C. Magoffin, 1832), 2, 9.

73. Ibid., 10, 16, 19–20.

74. Ibid., 21–33, 39–42.

75. Ibid., 52, 55–56, 58, 63–64.

76. Ibid., 67.

77. Gilbert McMaster, *A Brief Inquiry into the Civil Relations of Reformed Presbyterians, in the United States, According to their Judicative Acts, Addressed to Those of that Communion* (Schenectady: S. S. Riggs, 1833), 9.

78. McMaster, *Moral Character of Civil Government*, 70.

79. Rev. David Scott, *Calm Examination of Dr. McMaster's Letters on Civil Government* (Newburgh, NY: Charles U. Cushman, 1832), 3; *Narrative of the Division of the Reformed Presbyterian Church, U.S., 1833* (Rochester, NY: Curtis, Burns, 1863), 22. Another exchange followed: McMaster, *Brief Inquiry into the Civil Relations*; David Scott, *An Exposure of Dr. McMaster's "Brief Inquiry"* (New York: H. Bunce, 1833).

80. *Sentiments of the Rev. Samuel B. Wylie, A.M. in 1803, Respecting Civil Magistracy and the Government of the United States Contrasted with Sentiments of the Rev. Samuel B. Wylie, D.D. in 1832, on the Same Subjects* (Montgomery, NY: Thomas & Edwards, 1832), 4, 8–9.

81. *The Original Draft of a Pastoral Address*, 26–29; Wylie, *Memoir of Alexander McLeod*, 256–57, 484–85.

82. See Moore, *Founding Sins*, 83–87. These events are narrated from the "Old Light" point of view in Glasgow, *Reformed Presbyterian Church*, 87–104, and from the "New Light" perspective in *Reformation Principles Exhibited; being the declaration and testimony of the Reformed Presbyterian Church in North America* (New York: Lee, Shepard and Dillingham, 1871), 187–203. See also Wylie, *Memoir of Alexander McLeod*, 428–68.

3. *An Excrescence on the Tree of Our Liberty*

1. B. M. Palmer, *National Responsibility before God* (New Orleans: Price Current Steam Book and Job Printing Office, 1861), 5–6, 11. Richard T. Hughes, "A Civic Theology for the South: The Case of Benjamin M. Palmer," *Journal of Church and State* 25, no. 3 (1983): 447–67.

   On Confederate fast days and fast day sermons, see Drew Gilpin Faust, *The Creation of Confederate Nationalism: Ideology and Identity in the Civil War South* (Baton Rouge: Louisiana State University, 1988), 25–34; Harry S. Stout, *Upon the Altar of the Nation: A Moral History of the Civil War* (New York: Penguin Books, 2006), 48–52.

2. Palmer, *National Responsibility before God*, 11–13. Palmer had been pondering this theme for some time. Back in 1853, he delivered a lecture in which he reflected on the ongoing saga of the Latter-day Saints with a mixture of wonder and scorn. "To a philosophic observer," Palmer remarked, "probably the most striking feature of Mormonism, is, *the attempt to realize the conception of a Theo-democratic government.*" The Mormon kingdom in the Mountain West was a manifestation of deep longing and, with its breaking down of boundaries between the ranks of rulers and subjects, was being performed in the fashion of the democratic age. The Mormon settlement contained a peculiar, and peculiarly American, paradox: "The democratic spirit thus pervades a Hierarchy, which, in its essential constitution, is an unlimited despotism. It is, however, an odd application of the democratic principle, which could not have been dreamed of, except in this democratic age and country, that by the vote of his peers a man should be designated to the office of a seer; and thenceforward obeyed with absolute submission, as the oracle by which the decrees of Heaven are infallibly conveyed." "It is very singular," Palmer reflected, "that governments the most absolute and despotic are often administered in the most democratic spirit." Palmer regarded the Mormon project of fusing civil and ecclesiastical power as a symptom of the deep malady pervading the American system. "It is the revival of theocracy in our country which excites the wonder of the curious. And who can say, but it may be the reaction of mind against the avowed and boasted atheism of our own government? In the effort to put an eternal divorce between church and state, we seem to have fallen upon the other extreme. There is in our constitution a studied silence as to the providence and government of God." The Mormons disclosed the natural desire for political recognition of the Deity. And Palmer forewarned, "If, at a future day, these theocratic pretensions of Mormonism should give trouble to our government, serious persons will scarcely be able to avoid the reflection that somewhat of rebuke, if not of retribution, is intended for practically ignoring the existence and control of Almighty God." "I do not mean to affirm," he hastened to add, "that Joseph Smith ever reasoned upon this singular defect in our political constitution, and that he brought forward his theocratic doctrine in formal rebuke and opposition to it." B. M. Palmer,

Mormonism: A Lecture Delivered before the Mercantile Library Association of Charleston, S.C. (Columbia, SC: I. C. Morgan, 1853), 23–25.

3. Gaines M. Foster provides some background to the wording: "The idea of acknowledging God in the Confederate Constitution originated with Thomas R. R. Cobb, a Georgian, a devout Presbyterian, and a temperance advocate. He convinced the committee drafting a provisional document to begin its proposed constitution, 'In the name of Almighty God.' After rejecting that wording and another offered by William P. Chilton, the provisional Congress voted four states to one to put 'Invoking the favor of Almighty God' in the provisional constitution. When the Confederate Congress adopted a permanent constitution, and with no record left of the reason, it invoked not only the favor but the 'guidance of Almighty God.'" *Moral Reconstruction: Christian Lobbyists and the Federal Legislation of Morality, 1865–1920* (Chapel Hill: University of North Carolina Press, 2002), 20. In 1863, the Confederacy took for its motto and seal the Latin phrase *Deo vindice*—God as our defender.

4. Palmer, *National Responsibility before God*, 13–14. See David B. Chesebrough, *"God Ordained This War": Sermons on the Sectional Crisis, 1830–1865* (Columbia: University of South Carolina Press, 1991), 197–200.

5. James Henley Thornwell, "The Relation of the State to Christ (A Memorial.)," in *The Collected Writings of James Henley Thornwell*, ed. John B. Adger and John L. Girardeau (Richmond: Presbyterian Committee of Publications, 1873), 4:549–50; "The Rev. Dr. Thornwell's Memorial on the Recognition of Christianity in the Constitution," *Southern Presbyterian Review* 16, no. 1 (July 1863): 77–86. For biographical details, see James Oscar Farmer Jr., *The Metaphysical Confederacy: James Henley Thornwell and the Synthesis of Southern Values* (Macon, GA: Mercer University Press, 1986).

6. Thornwell, "Relation of the State to Christ," 550.

7. Ibid. "Godless monster" in Thornwell, *Our Danger and Our Duty* (Columbia, SC: Southern Guardian Steam-Power, 1862), 4. In his fast day sermon, Thornwell bemoaned the nation's sin, the government's perversion of the representative principle into popular democracy: "We have deified the people, making their will, as will, and not as reasonable and right, the supreme law; and they, in turn, have deified themselves, by assuming all the attribute of government, and exercising unlimited domination.... What says the voice of the majority? *Vox populi, vox Dei.*" "Sermon on National Sins," in *Collected Writings of James Henley Thornwell*, 4:536.

8. Thornwell, "Relation of the State to Christ," 551–52.

9. Ibid., 553–54. On the Southern theologians' understanding of the reciprocal relationship between church and state, see Anne C. Loveland, *Southern Evangelicals and the Social Order 1800–1860* (Baton Rouge: Louisiana State University Press, 1980), 109–11.

10. Thornwell, "Relation of the State to Christ," 554–55.

11. Thornwell, "Sermon on National Sins," 514–15.

12. Thornwell, "Relation of the State to Christ," 551, 553.

13. Thornwell, "Sermon on National Sins," 528–30.

14. Ibid., 517–18.

15. Thornwell, "Relation of the State to Christ," 554.

16. Ibid., 550, 555–56. On Thornwell's earlier Unionist sentiments, see Farmer, *Metaphysical Confederacy*, 245–56.

17. B. M. Palmer, *The Life and Letters of James Henley Thornwell* (Richmond: Whittet & Shepperson, 1875), 507.

18. B. M. Palmer, *The rainbow round the throne; or, Judgment tempered with mercy; a discourse before the legislature of Georgia, delivered on the day of fasting, humiliation and prayer, appointed by the President of the Confederate States of America, March 27th, 1863* (Milledgeville, GA: Boughton, Nisbet & Barnes, 1863), 25. See also Hughes, "Civic Theology for the South," 459.

19. Robert L. Tsai, *American's Forgotten Constitution: Defiant Visions of Power and Community* (Cambridge, MA: Harvard University Press, 2014), 135. The Confederate Constitution's elements preserving and regulating slavery included Article I, Section 2 (2) retaining the three-fifths clause for apportionment purposes (which tipped the balance of representation to the larger slaveholding states); Section 9 (2) barring the importation of slaves and (2) granting Congress the power to prohibit introduction of slaves from outside the Confederacy, but (4) prohibiting laws "denying or impairing the right of property in negro slaves"; and Article IV, Sections 2 and 3 protecting slaveholders' property interests. Ibid., 141.

20. Farmer, *Metaphysical Confederacy*.

21. James W. Silver, *Confederate Morale and Church Propaganda* (New York: W. W. Norton, 1967).

22. On these divisions and their implications, see C. C. Goen, *Broken Churches, Broken Nation: Denominational Schisms and the Coming of the American Civil War* (Macon, GA: Mercer University Press, 1985). The Southern dioceses of the Episcopal Church formed the Protestant Episcopalian Church in the Confederate States of America in 1861.

23. The classic New Testament text for proslavery apologists was Paul's Letter to Philemon, in which the apostle seemed to instruct an escaped slave to return to his master. Proslavery apologists also appealed to 1 Corinthians 7:21; Colossians 3:22, 4:1; and Timothy 6:1–2.

24. Drew Gilpin Faust, *The Ideology of Slavery: Proslavery Thought in the Antebellum South, 1830–1860* (Baton Rouge: Louisiana State University Press, 1981), 15, 227.

25. Rev. J. H. Thornwell, *The Rights and the Duties of Masters: A Sermon Preached at the Dedication of a Church, Erected in Charleston, S.C., for the Benefit and Instruction of the Colored*

Population (Charleston, SC: Steam Power Press of Walker & James, 1850), 11. The word "brother" is italicized in the version (titled "The Christian Doctrine of Slavery) in *Collected Writings of James Henley Thornwell*, 4:403.

26. If the men and women working their plantations were the descendants of that accursed Canaan, masters had "a grand religio-scientific justification for white enslavement of blacks." Elizabeth Fox-Genovese and Eugene D. Genovese, *The Mind of the Master Class: History and Faith in the Southern Slaveholders' Worldview* (Cambridge: Cambridge University Press, 2005), 521, and the following discussion, 521–26. See also Stephen R. Haynes, *Noah's Curse: The Biblical Justification of American Slavery* (New York: Oxford University Press, 2002); Sylvester A. Johnson, *The Myth of Ham in Nineteenth-Century American Christianity: Race, Heathens, and the People of God* (New York: Palgrave Macmillan, 2004); and Stephen R. Haynes, "Race, National Destiny, and the Sons of Noah in the Thought of Benjamin M. Palmer," *Journal of Presbyterian History* 78, no. 2 (Summer 2000): 125–43.

27. Mark A. Noll argues that this strategy "contradicted democratic and republican intellectual instincts. In the culture of the United States, as that culture had been constructed by three generations of evangelical Bible believers, the nuanced biblical argument was doomed." *The Civil War as a Theological Crisis* (Chapel Hill: University of North Carolina Press, 2006), 49.

28. Albert Barnes, *The Church and Slavery* (Philadelphia: Parry & McMillan, 1857), 9–10, 197–204; Robert Baird, *Religion in America; or, An Account of the Origin, Relation to the State, and Present Condition of the Evangelical Churches in the United States* (New York: Harper & Brothers, 1856), 511–14. On the Covenanters' antislavery reading of Scripture, see Joseph S. Moore, *Founding Sins: How a Group of Antislavery Radicals Fought to Put Christ into the Constitution* (New York: Oxford University Press, 2015), 93–96.

29. See Noll, *Civil War as a Theological Crisis*, 46–47. See also Mark A. Noll, "The Bible and Slavery," in *Religion and the American Civil War*, ed. Randall M. Miller, Harry S. Stout, and Charles Reagan Wilson (New York: Oxford University Press, 1998), 43–73.

30. For general studies of proslavery social and religious thought, see Faust, *Ideology of Slavery*; Mitchell Snay, *The Gospel of Disunion: Religion and Separatism in the Antebellum South* (New York: Cambridge University Press, 1993); and Fox-Genovese and Genovese, *Mind of the Master Class*. On the importance of the religious press in the dissemination of proslavery materials in the South, see Fox-Genovese and Genovese, *Mind of the Master Class*, 435–36. After the war, the Presbyterian divine Robert L. Dabney, who had served as General Thomas "Stonewall" Jackson's secretary, wrote, "Our mere politicians . . . failed to meet the Abolitionists with sufficient persistence and force on the racial question—the righteousness of African servitude as existing among us. It is true that this fundamental point has received a discussion at the South, chiefly at the hands of

clergymen and literary men, which has evoked a number of works of the highest merit and power, constituting almost a literature on the subject. One valuable effect of this literature was to enlighten and satisfy the Southern mind, and to produce a settled unanimity of opinion, even greater than that which existed against us in other states." *A Defence of Virginia: And Through Her, of the South, in Recent and Pending Contests Against the Sectional Party* (New York: E. J. Hale & Son, 1867), 13–14.

31. Elizabeth Fox-Genovese and Eugene D. Genovese, "The Divine Sanction of the Social Order: Religious Foundations of the Southern Slaveholders' World View," *Journal of the American Academy of Religion* 55 (Summer 1987): 225–26.

32. Donald G. Mathews, *Religion in the Old South* (Chicago: University of Chicago Press, 1977), 167–70.

33. Drew Gilpin Faust observed that "although proslavery thought demonstrated remarkable consistency from the seventeenth century on, it became in the South of the 1830s, forties, and fifties more systematic and self-conscious; it took on the characteristics of a formal ideology with its resulting social movement. . . . The defenses of slavery of this period were . . . remarkably consistent with one another. While one advocate might specialize in religious arguments and another in the details of political economy, most acknowledged, accepted, and sometimes repeated the conclusions of their fellow apologists. The high level of conformity within proslavery thought was not accidental. Consistency was seen as the mark of strength and the emblem of truth" (*Ideology of Slavery*, 4, 10). Mathews, however, notes the difference between the "proslavery ideology" and the minister's "slaveholding ethic": the former "took no account at all of the moral character of black people and whatever rights they might be expected to have," and the latter, a religious discourse, "emphasized the moral responsibilities of both master and slave and was concerned with securing benefits to both." *Religion in the Old South*, 172–74.

On denominational conflicts over doctrine and ecclesiology and differences in style and decorum, see Fox-Genovese and Genovese, *Mind of the Master Class*, 444–72. On the role of the Southern clergy in the slavery debate, see Farmer, *Metaphysical Confederacy*, 195–233.

34. Though they made up but a small percentage of churchgoers in the antebellum South (the vast majority being Methodists or Baptists), Southern Presbyterians wielded considerable religious and cultural clout. Their clergy were the best educated in the region and presided over the seats of higher learning, entrusted with training its social and political elite. Members of the church were some of the largest slaveholders in the South. They also tended to be politically conservative Whigs, and up to the election of Lincoln, Unionists. Farmer, *Metaphysical Confederacy*, 6, 201, 245–46.

35. Thornwell, *Rights and the Duties of Masters*. Farmer suggests that Thornwell's "treatment of the issue so epitomized the views of the Southern pulpit that he became virtually the

spokesman for the Southern church on this crucial sectional issue." *Metaphysical Confederacy*, 216; on "The Rights and the Duties of Masters," see 220–26.

36. Thornwell, *Rights and the Duties of Masters*, 14.

37. Ibid., 19, 24–25.

38. Ibid., 28–30.

39. Ibid., 31–33. On the clergy's interest in the "amelioration" of slavery, see Loveland, *Southern Evangelicals*, 209–11.

40. Thornwell, *Rights and the Duties of Masters*, 38, 43–44, 48.

41. Ibid., 49, 51.

42. Ibid., 40.

43. Ibid., 9, 14–15, 13.

44. Ibid., 12.

45. E. N. Elliott, ed., *Cotton Is King, and Pro-slavery Arguments: Comprising the Writings of Hammond, Harper, Christy, Stringfellow, Hodge, Bledsoe, and Cartwright, on This Important Subject* (Augusta, GA: Pritchard, Abbott & Loomis, 1860), x.

46. Benjamin M. Palmer, *Thanksgiving Sermon, Delivered at the First Presbyterian Church, New Orleans on Thursday, November 29, 1860* (New York: George F. Nesbitt, 1861); reprinted as "Slavery a Divine Trust: Duty of the South to Preserve and Perpetuate It," in *Fast day sermons: or, The pulpit on the state of the country* (New York: Rudd & Carleton, 1861), 57–80. On this sermon and its reception, see Thomas Cary Johnson, *The Life and Letters of Benjamin Morgan Palmer* (Richmond, VA: Presbyterian Committee of Publication, 1906), 205–23; Hughes, "Civic Theology for the South," 451–52; Conrad Cherry, ed., *God's New Israel: Religious Interpretations of American Destiny*, revised and updated ed. (Chapel Hill: University of North Carolina Press, 1998), 164–66.

47. Palmer, *Thanksgiving Sermon*, 7–8.

48. Ibid., 8–12. This argument was echoed after the war by Dabney: "It will in the end become apparent to the world, not only that the conviction of the wickedness of slaveholding was drawn wholly from sources foreign to the Bible, but that it is a legitimate corollary from that fantastic, atheistic, and radical theory of human rights, which made the Reign of Terror in France, which has threatened that country, and which now threatens the United States, with the horrors of Red-Republicanism. Because we believe that God intends to vindicate His Divine Word, and to make all nations honour it; because we confidently rely in the force of truth to explode all dangerous error; therefore we confidently expect that the world will yet do justice to Southern slaveholders." *A Defence of Virginia*, 9.

49. Palmer, *Thanksgiving Sermon*, 16.

50. Ibid., 17.

51. Ibid.

52. Ibid., 19. See Jack P. Maddex, "Proslavery Millennialism: Social Eschatology in Ante-bellum Southern Calvinism," *American Quarterly* 31, no. 1 (1979): 46–62.

53. Thornwell, "Sermon on National Sins," 529.

54. James Henley Thornwell, *Our Danger and Our Duty* (Columbia, SC: Southern Guardian Steam-Power Press, 1862), 5, 14.

55. Palmer, *Thanksgiving Sermon*, 14.

56. On these statements, see Tsai, *American's Forgotten Constitution*, 128–32.

57. Davis, "First Inaugural Address," in *The Papers of Jefferson Davis*, vol. 7, *1861*, ed. Lynda Lasswell Crist and Mary Seaton Dix (Baton Rouge: Louisiana State University Press, 1992), 45–51.

58. Palmer, *National Responsibility before God*, 24–26.

59. Carl L. Becker, *The Declaration of Independence: A Study in the History of Political Ideas* (New York: Vintage Books, 1942), 240–43; Pauline Maier, *American Scripture: Making the Declaration of Independence* (New York: Vintage Books, 1998), 189–208. William H. Seward, " 'Higher Law' speech on the Compromise of 1850," delivered on the US Senate floor on March 11, 1850.

It's worth recalling that Jefferson's original draft included what John Adams called a "vehement philippic against negro slavery." In promoting the slave trade, King George, Jefferson wrote, "has waged a cruel war against human nature itself, violating its most sacred rights of life and liberty in the persons of a distant people who never offended him. . . . This piratical warfare, the opprobrium of *infidel* powers, is the warfare of the *Christian* king of Great Britain." Congress struck the passage from the final version. Becker, *Declaration of Independence*, 212–13.

60. Abraham Lincoln, "Speech at Peoria, Illinois" (October 16, 1854), in *The Collected Works of Abraham Lincoln*, ed. Roy P. Basler (New Brunswick, NJ: Rutgers University Press, 1953–1955), 2:276. Abraham Lincoln, "Speech at Springfield, Illinois" (June 26, 1857), in Basler, *Collected Works*, 2:405–6. In another speech, Lincoln proclaimed that "I have never had a feeling politically that did not spring from the sentiments embodied in the Declaration of Independence." "Speech in Independence Hall, Philadelphia, Pennsylvania" (February 22, 1861), in Basler, *Collected Works*, 4:240.

61. Frederick Douglass, "What to the Slave Is the Fourth of July?" (1852), in *Oration, Delivered in Corinthian Hall, Rochester, July 5th, 1852* (Rochester: Lee, Man, 1852), 18–19, 9, 14, 28–29, 34, 36–37.

62. "William Lloyd Garrison to Rev. Samuel J. May, July 17, 1845," in *The Letters of William Lloyd Garrison*, ed. Walter M. Merrill (Cambridge, MA: Harvard University Press, 1973), 3:303; *The Liberator*, May 6, 1842. On this problem, see William M. Wiecek, *The Sources of Antislavery Constitutionalism in America, 1760–1848* (Ithaca, NY: Cornell University Press, 1977), and Robert M. Cover, *Justice Accused: Antislavery and the Judicial Process* (New Haven: Yale University Press, 1975).

63. *Declaration of Sentiments of the American Anti-Slavery Society: adopted at the formation of said Society in Philadelphia on the 4th day of December, 1833* (New York: American Anti-Slavery Society, 1833), 1–2.

64. Quoted in Noll, *Civil War as a Theological Crisis*, 41.

65. Barnes, *Church and Slavery*, 37–38.

66. Frederick A. Ross, *Slavery Ordained of God* (Philadelphia: J. B. Lippincott, 1857), 97.

67. John C. Calhoun, "Speech on the Oregon Bill" (June 27, 1848), in *Union and Liberty: The Political Philosophy of John C. Calhoun*, ed. Ross M. Lence (Indianapolis: Liberty Fund, 1992), 570.

68. Dred Scott v. Sandford, 60 U.S. 407 (1857).

69. Chancellor Harper, "Slavery in the Light of Social Ethics," in Elliott, *Cotton Is King*, 553.

70. Albert Taylor Bledsoe, *An Essay on Liberty and Slavery* (Philadelphia: J. B. Lippincott, 1856), 124; the text was republished as *Liberty and slavery: or, Slavery in the light of moral and political philosophy* in the popular proslavery anthology *Cotton Is King, and Pro-slavery Arguments*.

71. Ross, *Slavery Ordained of God*, 5. On Ross, see Tommy W. Rogers, "Dr. F. A. Ross and the Presbyterian Defense of Slavery," *Journal of Presbyterian History* 45, no. 2 (June 1967): 112–24.

72. Ross, *Slavery Ordained of God*, 93, 97.

73. Ibid., 116.

74. Ibid., 104–5.

75. Ibid., 118–19.

76. Ibid., 121, 123.

77. Ibid., 124–26. While Ross believed women to be "the weaker vessel" (1 Peter 3:7), he saw them dangerously influencing the antislavery position in his denomination.

78. Ibid., 128.

79. Ibid., 133, 135, 138–39.

Prior to his election, Abraham Lincoln had occasion to peruse Frederick A. Ross's book and confided his thoughts about it to his journal. "The sum of pro-slavery theology," he observed, "seems to be this: 'Slavery is not universally *right*, nor yet universally *wrong*; it is better for *some* people to be slaves; and, in such cases, it is the Will of God that they be such.'" Lincoln was not impressed with such calm confidence in the decrees of Providence. "Certainly there is no contending against the Will of God; but still there is some difficulty in ascertaining, and applying it, to particular cases," he remarked.

"For instance," he reasoned, "we will suppose the Rev. Dr. Ross has a slave named Sambo, and the question is 'Is it the Will of God that Sambo shall remain a slave, or be set free?' The Almighty gives no audable [*sic*] answer to the question, and his revelation—the Bible—gives none—or, at most, none but such as admits of a squabble, as to it's meaning. No one thinks of asking Sambo's opinion on it. So, at last, it comes to this, that *Dr. Ross* is to decide the question. And while he consider[s] it, he sits in the shade, with gloves on his hands, and subsists on the bread that Sambo is earning in the burning sun. If he decides that God Wills Sambo to continue a slave, he thereby retains his own comfortable position; but if he decides that God will's Sambo to be free, he thereby has to walk out of the shade, throw off his gloves, and delve for his own bread. Will Dr. Ross be actuated by that perfect impartiality, which has ever been considered most favorable to correct decisions?"

He continued, "But, slavery is good for some people!!! As a good thing, slavery is strikingly perculiar [*sic*], in this, that it is the only good thing which no man ever seeks the good of, for himself." Lincoln clearly understood the interest behind such pious appeals to Providence. "Nonsense! Wolves devouring lambs, not because it is good for their own greedy maws, but because it [is] good for the lambs!!!" Abraham Lincoln, "Fragment on Proslavery Theology," in Basler, *Collected Works*, 3:204–5.

80. Thomas Smyth, *The Sin and the Curse; or, the Union, The True Source of Disunion, and our Duty in the Present Crisis, a discourse preached on the occasion of the Day of Humiliation and Prayer appointed by the Governor of South Carolina, November 21, 1860* (Charleston, SC: Steam Power Presses of Evans and Cogswell, 1860), 5.

81. Ibid., 13–15.

82. Ibid., 15–16, 18.

83. "Speech known as 'THE CORNER STONE,' delivered at the Athenaeum, Savannah, Georgia, March 21, 1861," in Henry Cleveland, *Alexander H. Stephens in Public and Private. With Letters and Speeches, Before, During, and Since the War* (Philadelphia: National Publishing Company, 1866), 721.

84. Ibid., 721–23.

85. Mark 12:10; Matthew 21:42; Luke 20:17. See also Isaiah 28:16: "Therefore thus saith the Lord God, Behold, I lay in Zion for a foundation a stone, a tried stone, a precious corner stone, a sure foundation: he that believeth shall not make haste."

86. Abraham Lincoln, "Address Delivered at the Dedication of the Cemetery at Gettysburg" (November 19, 1863), in Basler, *Collected Works*, 7:17–23. Stephen Prothero, *The American Bible: How Our Words Unite, Divide, and Define a Nation* (New York: HarperOne, 2012), 330–34. Garry Wills, *Lincoln at Gettysburg: The Words That Remade America* (New York: Simon & Schuster, 1992).

4. *The Crowning, Original Sin of the Nation*

1. "Interview with the President," *Reformed Presbyterian and Covenanter* 1, no. 1 (January 1863): 16–18, which provides the text of the ministers' presentation; Milligan's account of their mission to Washington and the conversation with Lincoln was published in the

subsequent issues as "Interview with the President," *Reformed Presbyterian and Covenanter* 1, no. 2 (February 1863): 48–52. Joseph S. Moore, *Founding Sins: How a Group of Antislavery Radicals Fought to Put Christ into the Constitution* (New York: Oxford University Press, 2015), 120–25; on the Reformed Presbyterians' antislavery activities, see 88–118.

2. "Interview with the President," 18.

3. "Interview with the President," 50–51.

4. W. Melancthon Glasgow, *History of the Reformed Presbyterian Church in America: with Sketches of All Her Ministry, Congregations, Missions, Institutions, Publications, Etc., and Embellished with over Fifty Portraits and Engravings* (Baltimore: Hill and Harvey, 1888), 125–26.

5. Stewart Olin Jacoby, "The Religious Amendment Movement: God, People and Nation in the Gilded Age" (PhD diss., University of Michigan, 1984), 47–48.

6. Ibid., 55–65.

7. Horace Bushnell, *Reverses Needed* (Hartford: L. E. Hunt, 1861), 9.

8. Ibid., 9, 11, 13, 20–22.

9. Ibid., 25–26.

10. Harry S. Stout, *Upon the Altar of the Nation: A Moral History of the Civil War* (New York: Penguin Books, 2006), 70–71. On Northern ministers' call for a "Christian Constitution," see 77, 373.

11. Ibid., 48, 475n5.

12. On the Civil War conferences in general and the Xenia meeting in particular, see Jacoby, "Religious Amendment Movement," 113–28.

13. See Jacoby, "Religious Amendment Movement," 153n15.

14. Quoted in T. P. Stevenson, "Origin and Progress of the Movement to Secure the Religious Amendment of the Constitution of the United States," in *Proceedings of the National Convention to Secure the Religious Amendment of the Constitution of the United States [Held in Cincinnati Jan. 31 & Feb. 1, 1872]* (Philadelphia: James B. Rogers, 1872), iv–v; Jacoby, "Religious Amendment Movement," 121–22. Alexander later wrote that "the great original sin of our nation consisted in adopting our National Constitution without any distinct recognition of God, Christ or the Divine law—in setting up our national government in the name of the new deity 'we the people.' " John Alexander, *History of the National Reform Movement* (Pittsburgh: Shaw Brothers, 1893), 5–6.

15. Stevenson, "Origin and Progress," v; Jacoby, "Religious Amendment Movement," 122–24.

16. David McAllister, "The Origin and Progress of the Movement for the Religious Amendment of the Constitution of the United States," in *Proceedings of the National Convention to Secure the Religious Amendment of the Constitution of the United States: Held in Pittsburg,*

February 4, 5, 1874. With an Account of the Origin and Progress of the Movement (United States: Christian Statesman Association, 1874), 6.

17. Stevenson, "Origin and Progress," vii. On the National Reform Association, see Morton Borden, *Jews, Turks, and Infidels* (Chapel Hill: University of North Carolina Press, 1984), 58–74, and Isaac Kramnick and R. Laurence Moore, *The Godless Constitution: A Moral Defense of the Secular State,* 2nd ed. (New York: W. W. Norton, 2005), 144–49.

18. Jacoby, "Religious Amendment Movement," 167–75.

"Addresses to the President," *Reformed Presbyterian and Covenanter* 2 (March 1864): 88–92. The article includes reports of both delegations' addresses to Lincoln. The Reformed Presbyterian representatives told Lincoln that "it is our profound conviction that the only hope for our country's abiding pacification and tranquility, and for its future greatness and prosperity, lies in such a reconstruction of the national edifice as will make the stone rejected of our builders the head-stone of the corner."

19. Joshua Hall McIlvaine, *"A Nation's Right to Worship God.": An Address before the American Whig and Cliosophic Societies of the College of New Jersey. Delivered June 28th, 1859* (Trenton, NJ: Murphy & Bechtel, 1859).

20. Stevenson, "Origin and Progress," vii–viii. They also petitioned that "such changes with respect to the oath of office, slavery, and all other matters, should be introduced into the body of the Constitution as may be necessary to give effect to these amendments in the preamble." Jacoby, "Religious Amendment Movement," 141.

21. Stevenson, "Origin and Progress," ix. As Alexander remarked in a later lecture on the movement, "We do not advocate union of Church and State, an error into which man ignorant of the subject have fallen. On the contrary we are uncompromisingly opposed to such a system; as it has been well put, 'we desire to divorce Church and State that the State may marry Religion.'" Alexander, *History of the National Reform Movement*, 20.

22. Stevenson, "Origin and Progress," x. A story later circulated that Lincoln had informed the ministers that he intended to work for the amendment in his second term. The first report of the anecdote was by Thomas Spoull, "Reminiscence of President Lincoln," *Reformed Presbyterian and Covenanter* 3 (November 1865): 347. John Alexander repeated this story in a lecture on the NRA and recalled Lincoln's "failure to recognize his own obligation as well as that of the nation which he represented to obey the law of God as higher than all human laws." Perhaps, Alexander mused, this was why Lincoln, like Moses, died before accomplishing his goal. *History of the National Reform Movement*, 22–24. David McAllister, *Christian Civil Government in America: The National Reform Movement. Its History and Principles*, revised by T. H. Acheson and Wm. Parsons, 6th ed. (Pittsburgh: National Reform Association, 1926), 24. Jacoby, "Religious Amendment Movement," 171–72, 222n12.

23. *Constitution and Addresses of the National Association for the Amendment of the Constitution of the United States* (Philadelphia: Jas. B. Rogers, 1864), 5–7.

24. Ibid., 8–12.

25. Ibid., 6–7.

26. Ibid., 13–15.

27. Ibid., 15–17. Jacoby, "Religious Amendment Movement," 184–85, 190–97.

28. Jacoby, "Religious Amendment Movement," 203–17.

29. Morton Borden, "The Christian Amendment," *Civil War History* 25, no. 2 (June 1979): 162.

30. The Congressional Globe, 38th Congress, 2nd Session, March 2, 1865; quoted in Stevenson, "Origin and Progress," xiii. See also Steven K. Green, *The Bible, the School, and the Constitution: The Clash That Shaped Modern Church-State Doctrine* (Oxford: Oxford University Press, 2012), 142–43.

31. Jacoby, "Religious Amendment Movement," 231–32, 260–73. McAllister also published the *National Reform Manual* in 1871.

32. Jacoby, "Religious Amendment Movement," 292–308; Green, *The Bible, the School, and the Constitution.*

33. National conventions were held in Pittsburgh (1870, 1874), Philadelphia (1871, 1876), Cincinnati (1872), and New York City (1873).

34. Most notably, in 1868 the Association elected William Strong, then sitting on the Pennsylvania Supreme Court and soon to be US Supreme Court justice (he was appointed in 1870), as its president. He was succeeded in 1873 by Felix Brunot, chairman of the federal government's Board of Indian Commissioners.

35. Jacoby, "Religious Amendment Movement," 327–38, 346–55.

36. McAllister, "The Aims and Methods of the Movement," in *Proceedings of the National Convention* (1872), 7.

37. Stevenson, "The Legal Effect and Practical Value of the Proposed Amendment," in *Proceedings of the National Convention* (1872), 56–66. In 1874, Stevenson added the usefulness for the international reputation of the American republic: "Christian men in Europe fear republican ideas because they are connected in their minds with the abandonment of national religion. We owe it to God and the Christian faith, we owe it to the cause of popular government, to disabuse their minds of this." Stevenson, "The Ends We Seek," in *Proceedings of the National Convention* (1874), 30. In a similar manner, A. M. Milligan worried that European nations "struggling up toward republican liberty" might "point to us as an infidel nation, prove their assertion by the Constitution, and attribute our liberty and prosperity to our infidelity. What a mistake!" Milligan, "Address before the Convention," in *Proceedings of the National Convention to Secure the Religious Amendment of the Constitution of the United States. Held in New York Feb 26 & 27, 1873* (New York: John Polhemus, 1873), 74.

38. Stevenson, "Ends We Seek," 26, 29.

39. Milligan, "Address before the Convention," 71–75.

40. McAllister, "On the Origins and Progress of the Movement for the Religious Amendment of the Constitution of the United States," in *Proceedings of the National Convention* (1874), 1–2.

41. McAllister, "The Religious Amendment Movement Just, Seasonable, and Necessary," in *Proceedings of the National Convention* (1873), 5–6. In his address, McAllister name-dropped a host of European theorists—De Maistre, Rothe, and Stahl—and the Americans Orestes Brownson, John C. Hurd, Judge John Alexander Jameson, and Elisha Mulford. He quoted from these writers at some length in the *National Reform Manual*.

42. McAllister, "Religious Amendment Movement," 6–8, 10. One of the sources for the argument about the nation's twofold constitution was the Catholic convert Orestes Brownson's work, *The American Republic* (1865). A passage from that work was quoted (without attribution) in *Christian Civil Government*, 141.

43. Proponents of the Religious Amendment groused that the Mormons had been cynically exploiting the flaw in the Constitution. It was true that nearly from the time they appeared on the scene as an odd new religious movement, restorationist in claim but ablaze with millennial anticipation, the Mormons appealed to the Constitution for protection. First, they called on the federal government to defend them from anti-Mormon state governments and mobs, and then, years later, they appealed to the Constitution—the rights of local majorities under federalism and its First Amendment guarantees of religious liberty—to defend themselves from an encroaching federal government. In their eyes, they were the true believers in and defenders of the nation's governing instrument, which they understood as part of providential design. Perhaps the Mormons' deeper heresy was incorporating the Constitution into their own sacred history—believing that it was an inspired document, providing the opening for their religious dispensation and a stepping stone for the building up of the truly legitimate regime—their political Kingdom of God.

44. McAllister, "Aims and Methods of the Movement," 5–7.

45. McAllister, "Religious Amendment Movement," 10.

46. McAllister, "Testimonies to the Religious Defect of the Constitution" (1874), 40–59. On this point, Jacoby writes, "It is a striking and unavoidable conclusion that McAllister, himself a minister of the Reformed Presbyterian Church, consciously obscured the pivotal involvement of his denomination in carrying over a period of seventy years the opposition to the godless Constitution. His research made clear that only the Covenanters had carried the testimony against the godlessness of the Constitution continuously from 1789, a record that McAllister could well have cited with pride. Both his choices and his

commentary too clearly bypass the Reformed Presbyterian Church for the neglect to have been unconscious." "Religious Amendment Movement," 453.

47. Jacoby, "Religious Amendment Movement," 361–63.

48. Sydney E. Ahlstrom and Robert Bruce Mullin, *The Scientific Theist: A Life of Francis Ellingwood Abbot* (Macon, GA: Mercer University Press, 1987), 50–51.

49. "Prospectus," *The Index* 1, no. 1 (January 1, 1870): 5.

50. Green notes that *"The Index* and *The Christian Statesman* engaged in their own private war, with each journal criticizing the other organization while justifying its own existence by the presence of the other." *The Bible, the School, and the Constitution*, 150–51.

51. "Church and State," *The Index* 1, no. 11 (March 12, 1870): 4–5.

52. "The Conflict Coming," *The Index* 2, no. 3 (January 21, 1871): 20.

53. "The Proposed Christian Amendment to the United States Constitution," *The Index* 3, no. 106 (January 6, 1872): 1–2.

54. "Act Promptly!," *The Index* 3, no. 106 (January 6, 1872): 5; Green, *The Bible, the School, and the Constitution*, 154.

55. Green, *The Bible, the School, and the Constitution*, 154, 158.

56. Philip Hamburger, *Separation of Church and State* (Cambridge, MA: Harvard University Press, 2002), 293.

57. "Protest of Mr. Abbot," in *Proceedings of the National Convention* (1872), 33–35. In a response to Abbot's address, Rev. A. D. Mayo, one of the organization's vice presidents and a Unitarian minister, denied that the proposed amendment would have the repressive consequence that Abbot feared. "The trouble with him and this class of thinkers," he said, "is that they do not understand the practical character of the American people. . . . The glory of the great Anglo-Saxon peoples is that they are not ridden by this petty, logical mania for pushing an abstraction out to anarchy that curses the Red Republican party of Europe and America" (35–36). A few years later, Abbot reciprocated the offer, inviting the Association's corresponding secretary, T. P. Stevenson, to address a meeting of his Liberal League. Green, *The Bible, the School, and the Constitution*, 167.

58. "The Demands of Liberalism," *The Index* 3, no. 119 (April 6, 1872): 108–9.

59. *The Index* 4, no. 158 (January 4, 1873): 1. The National Reformers saw the "Demands of Liberalism" as a boon to their own efforts: "Every canvasser for signatures should carry with him a copy of the 'Demands of Liberalism.' Few who see them refuse to give their names." *National Reform Manual: Suggestions and Data for District Secretaries and Others* (Philadelphia: Christian Statesman Office, 1877), 25.

60. "First Session: Adoption of the Constitution," in *Equal Rights in Religion: Report of the Centennial Congress of Liberals, and Organization of the National Liberal League, at Philadelphia, on the Fourth of July, 1876* (Boston: National Liberal League, 1876), 42.

61. F. E. Abbot, "The Liberal League Movement. Its Principles, Objects, and Scope," in *Equal Rights in Religion*, 69–70.

62. "Patriotic Address," in *Equal Rights in Religion*, 163.

63. Ibid., 164.

64. Ibid., 167–68.

65. Francis E. Abbot, "Church and State: A Lecture Before the Music Hall Society, in Boston, Oct. 5, 1873," *The Index* 5, no. 210 (January 1, 1874): 2–3.

66. Ibid., 2.

67. Ibid., 2–3.

68. Ibid., 2–3.

69. Ahlstrom and Mullin, *Scientific Theist*, 126.

70. "Wanted: A Religious Freedom Amendment to the United States Constitution," *The Index* 5, no. 210 (January 1, 1874): 6–7. According to Green, "In 1875, eight of thirty-seven state constitutions required religious tests for public office holding, tests that disqualified non-Christians from office holding. Most states still imposed a requirement of a belief in God to take an oath as a witness or juror in a court proceeding. Furthermore, all of the states, with the single exception of Louisiana, had laws enforcing Sabbath practices or observances. Laws governing profane swearing and maintaining Christian features of marriage and divorce were also common." *The Bible, the School, and the Constitution*, 163.

71. "The Unfinished Window," *The Index* 7, no. 315 (January 6, 1876): 7. Green, *The Bible, the School, and the Constitution*, 164.

72. "The Unfinished Window," 6–7.

73. F. E. Abbot, "Address of Welcome," in *Equal Rights in Religion*, 37.

74. F. E. Abbot, "The Liberal League Movement. Its Principles, Objects, and Scope," in *Equal Rights in Religion*, 71.

75. "Patriotic Address," 167–69.

76. Quoted in Hamburger, *Separation of Church and State*, 322.

77. *Congressional Record*, 4(1): 205 (H.R., Dec. 14, 1875).

78. "Patriotic Address," 168.

79. "Mr. Blaine's Amendment," *Christian Statesman* 9, no. 18 (December 18, 1875): 124; "The Outlook" and "An Open Letter to Members of Congress," *Christian Statesman* 9, no. 50 (August 12, 1876): 403, 406; "The Defeated Constitutional Amendment," *The Index* 7, no. 348 (August 24, 1876): 402; Moore, *Founding Sins*, 139–42; Steven K. Green, "The Blaine Amendment Reconsidered," *American Journal of Legal History* 36, no. 1 (1992): 61.

80. Green, "Blaine Amendment Reconsidered," 67–69. Green argues that Blaine had introduced the amendment as a vehicle to advance his chances at the Republican nomination for president. When Ohio governor Rutherford B. Hayes was selected at the party's National Convention in June, Blaine lost interest in his proposal. By 1890, Blaine-style

amendments or statutes prohibiting public funding to sectarian schools were adopted by twenty-nine states. See Noah Feldman, *Divided by God: America's Church-State Problem—and What We Should Do about It* (New York: Farrar, Straus and Giroux, 2006), 86.

81. "The Defeated Constitutional Amendment," *The Index* 7, no. 348 (August 24, 1876): 402–3.

82. House Miscellaneous Reports Vol. 1623, 43rd Congress, 1st Session, 1873–1874; Green, *The Bible, the School, and the Constitution*, 159; Jacoby, "Religious Amendment Movement," 455–57.

83. The proponents of the Christian amendment also lobbied to have Christ acknowledged in state constitutions. To this end, Alexander and Stevenson appeared before the convention in Philadelphia in March 1873. The document ratified in December did not use the Association's formula, in its stead thanking God "for the blessings of civil and religious liberty, and humbly invoking His guidance." Green, *The Bible, the School, and the Constitution*, 156–58.

84. Ahlstrom and Mullin, *Scientific Theist*, 109–10.

85. Green, *The Bible, the School, and the Constitution*, 172–74; Hamburger, *Separation of Church and State*, 328–34.

86. Jacoby, "Religious Amendment Movement," 462.

87. Gaines M. Foster, *Moral Reconstruction: Christian Lobbyists and the Federal Legislation of Morality, 1865–1920* (Chapel Hill: University of North Carolina Press, 2002), 73–117; Jacoby, "Religious Amendment Movement," 485.

88. Church of the Holy Trinity v. United States, 143 U.S. 457 (1892); Green, *The Bible, the School, and the Constitution*, 176; Moore, *Founding Sins*, 134–35.

89. Alexander, *History of the National Reform Movement*, 22.

90. Ibid., 17.

91. George M. Docherty, "Under God," sermon at New York Avenue Presbyterian Church, February 7, 1954, https://www.nyapc.org/wp-content/uploads/2014/01/Under_God_Sermon.pdf. For Docherty's account of the origins of the sermon and its reception by Eisenhower and on Capitol Hill, see George M. Docherty, *I've Seen the Day* (Grand Rapids: Eerdmans, 1984), 158–60.

92. It is one of the ironies of America's civil religion that school performance of the earlier version of the Pledge triggered the Supreme Court's consideration of the meaning and extent of the First Amendment provisions, when Jehovah's Witnesses refused to participate in a secular patriotic ritual that they considered to be an idolatrous act forbidden by the Ten Commandments (Exodus 20:3–5). Minersville School District v. Gobitis, 310 U.S. 586 (1940) and West Virginia State Board of Education v. Barnette, 319 U.S. 624 (1943). In Cantwell v. Connecticut, 310 U.S. 296 (1940), which came down two weeks before *Gobitis*, the Supreme Court incorporated the Free Exercise Clause of the First Amendment.

93. "Text of Eisenhower Speech," *New York Times*, December 23, 1952. Quoted in Mark Silk, "Notes on the Judeo-Christian Tradition in America," *American Quarterly* 36, no. 1 (Spring 1984): 65. The Eisenhower quote has a fascinating reception history. See Patrick Henry, " 'And I Don't Care What It Is': The Tradition-History of a Civil Religion Proof-Text," *Journal of the American Academy of Religion* 49 (1981): 35–49. Deployed earlier in opposition to fascism (and fascist appropriation of "Christian"), the term "Judeo-Christian tradition" was easily repurposed for the Cold War to express the religious basis of American democracy against its atheistic challengers. It became, as Mark Silk noticed, an "anticommunist shibboleth." But it was a lower lowest common denominator than what had been proposed by the "nonsectarians" of the National Reform Association and its allies. Silk, "Notes on the Judeo-Christian Tradition in America," 66, 84. See also K. Healan Gaston, *Imagining Judeo-Christian America: Religion, Secularization, and the Redefinition of Democracy* (Chicago: University of Chicago Press, 2019), 72–96.

94. Raymond Haberski Jr., *God and War: American Civil Religion since 1945* (New Brunswick, NJ: Rutgers University Press, 2012).

95. Mark Silk, *Spiritual Politics: Religion and America Since World War II* (New York: Simon & Schuster, 1988), 96–100; Martin E. Marty, *Modern American Religion*, vol. 3, *Under God, Indivisible, 1941–1960* (Chicago: University of Chicago Press, 1996), 298–301; Kevin M. Kruse, *One Nation Under God: How Corporate America Invented Christian America* (New York: Basic Books, 2015), 100–111; Dwight D. Eisenhower, "Statement by the President upon Signing Bill to Include the Words 'Under God' in the Pledge to the Flag," The American Presidency Project, https://www.presidency.ucsb.edu/node/232153.

   See William Lee Miller, *Piety along the Potomac: Notes on Politics and Morals in the '50s* (Boston: Houghton Mifflin, 1964), 45–46; Richard J. Ellis, *To the Flag: The Unlikely History of the Pledge of Allegiance* (Lawrence: University Press of Kansas, 2005), 121–39.

96. Quoted in Marty, *Modern American Religion*, 3:296. Kruse, *One Nation Under God*, 111–25.

   This Cold War great awakening was not without its spiritual detractors. In his popular 1955 book *Protestant-Catholic-Jew*, Will Herberg lamented that "the new religiosity pervading America seems to be very largely the religious validation of the social patterns and cultural values associated with the American Way of Life," a religiosity that "comes to serve the spiritual reinforcement of national self-righteousness and a spiritual authentication of national self-will." Such appeals to God served "primarily as sanction and underpinning for the supreme values of the faith embodied in the American Way of Life," and the "Americanization" of religion by which "the authentic character of Jewish-Christian faith is falsified, and the faith itself reduced to the status of an American culture-religion."

What was shared could be regarded as "the civic religion of the American people." But such civic religion ought not to be confused with true faith. Herberg warned that "civic religion has always meant the sanctification of the society and culture of which it is the reflection, and that is one of the reasons why Jewish-Christian faith has always regarded such religion as incurably idolatrous. Civic religion is a religion which validates culture and society, without in any sense bringing them under judgment. It lends ultimate sanction to culture and society by assuring them that they constitute an unequivocal expression of 'spiritual ideals' and 'religious values.' Religion becomes, in effect, the cult of culture and society, in which the 'right' social order and the received cultural values are divinized by being identified with the divine purpose."

Will Herberg, *Protestant-Catholic-Jew: An Essay in American Religious Sociology*, rev. ed. (Chicago: University of Chicago Press, 1983), 263, 82–83, 262, 263.

As it turned out, Reverend Docherty in time came to regret that "the new Pledge" he had helped bring about "unfortunately served as one more prop supporting the civil religion that characterized the institutionalized Christianity of the fifties." Docherty, *I've Seen the Day*, 160.

97. Everson v. Board of Education of Ewing Township 330 U.S. 9–11, 15–16, 18 (1947); Feldman, *Divided by God*, 173–76 (quotation at 175–76).

98. Zorach v. Clauson, 343 U.S. 312 (1952). Justice William O. Douglas may have declared in *Zorach v. Clauson* that "we are a religious people whose institutions presuppose a Supreme Being," but he went on to say, "We guarantee the freedom to worship as one chooses. We make room for as wide a variety of beliefs and creeds as the spiritual needs of man deem necessary. We sponsor an attitude on the part of government that shows no partiality to any one group and that lets each flourish according to the zeal of its adherents and the appeal of its dogma." This marked a significant departure from those earlier court declarations that the United States was a "Christian nation." *Zorach*, 343 U.S. 313. It is also worthwhile to recall Justice Hugo Black's words in his dissent to *Zorach*: "It was precisely because Eighteenth Century Americans were a religious people divided into many fighting sects that we were given the constitutional mandate to keep Church and State completely separate." *Zorach*, 343 U.S. 318–19.

99. Engle v. Vitale, 370 U.S. 430–31 (1962).

100. School District of Abington Township, Pennsylvania v. Schempp, 374 U.S. 222, 226 (1963). Unsurprisingly, in the wake of those decisions, numerous constitutional amendments to permit prayer and Bible reading in public schools have been proposed. None have been ratified.

101. "Statement on Church and State" (June 17, 1948), *First Things*, October 1992, https://www.firstthings.com/article/1992/10/statement-on-church-and-state#print; Gaston, *Imagining Judeo-Christian America*, 148–49.

102. Will Herberg, "The Biblical Basis of American Democracy," *Thought: Fordham University Quarterly* 30, no. 1 (Spring 1955): 37–50 (quotation at 50), 38, 41, 42.

103. Will Herberg, "Secularism in Church and Synagogue," *Christianity and Crisis* 10, no. 8 (May 15, 1950): 58.

104. Will Herberg, "Faith and Politics: Some Reflections on Whittaker Chamber's *Witness*," *Christianity and Crisis* 12, no. 16 (September 29, 1952): 122–23.

105. Will Herberg, "Communism, Democracy, and the Churches: Problems of 'Mobilizing the Religious Front,'" *Commentary* 19, no. 4 (April 1955): 391.

106. Herberg, "Biblical Basis of American Democracy," 48–50. See also Herberg, *Judaism and Modern Man: An Interpretation of Jewish Religion* (New York: Farrar, Straus and Young, 1951), esp. 168–92. Herberg nonetheless believed that some secularists could indeed participate in the democratic religious front against Communism. Referencing King Cyrus of Persia, he said that "men—thank God—are often better than their religious philosophies, and many a secular liberal who brashly proclaims himself without God may well be doing God's work." Herberg, "Communism, Democracy, and the Churches," 393.

107. Foster records that "between 1894 and 1919, twelve resolutions with various wordings designed to put God in the Constitution were introduced. None ever made it out of committee." *Moral Reconstruction*, 109.

108. Moore, *Founding Sins*, 154–55; Anthony A. Cowley, "From Whence We Came: A Background of the National Reform Association," in *Explicitly Christian Politics: The Vision of the National Reform Association*, ed. William Einwechter (Pittsburgh: Christian Statesman Press, 1997), 10–12.

109. *Senate Committee on the Judiciary, Hearings before a Subcommittee of the Judiciary, United States Senate, Eighty-Third Congress, Second Session on S.J. Res. 87 Proposing an Amendment to the Constitution of the United States Recognizing the Authority and Law of Jesus Christ* (Washington, DC: Government Printing Office, 1954), 1.

110. For an analysis of the hearings, see Katharine Batlan, "One Nation Under Christ: US Christian Amendment Attempts and Competing Visions for America in the 1940s and 1950s," *Journal of Church and State* 61, no. 4 (Autumn 2019): 658–79.

111. In his sermon, Rev. Marshall averred that "the source of democracy is Christianity, and liberty comes from God. . . . It is strange, and I believe tragic, that the Constitution makes no reference to God. It was not a perfect document, as all the amendments prove." "New Glory for Old Glory" (June 29, 1947). *Eighty-Third Congress, Second Session on S.J. Res. 87*, 55–56. Moore notes that Graham's sermon, titled "The Faith of George Washington," rooted its message in an Old Testament verse championed by the American Right for the next half-century: "If my people, which are called by my name, shall humble themselves, and pray, and seek my face, and turn from their wicked ways, then will I hear from heaven,

and will forgive their sin, and will heal their land [2 Chronicles 7:14]." *Founding Sins*, 153–54.

112. *Eighty-Third Congress, Second Session on S.J. Res. 87*, 16–18, 20–21, 46.

113. Ibid., 26.

114. Ibid., 82, 84, 85.

115. The Synagogue Council of America and the National Community Relations Advisory Council represented the major branches of American Judaism and a wide swath of Jewish communal and civic organizations. The American Jewish Committee entered a separate letter; a counsel from the Anti-Defamation League attended the hearing and made a brief comment. Batlan notes that other prominent opponents of the amendment were not in attendance, suggesting that this was on account of the little advance notice of the hearing. "One Nation Under Christ," 673.

116. Pfeffer had drafted an amicus brief for the American Jewish Committee and the Anti-Defamation League backing McCollum. The National Community Relations Advisory Council sponsored the suit against New York state's release-time program; Pfeffer recounted that the American Jewish Committee, fearing the case might stoke antisemitism, agreed to go along with the suit only so long as the lead attorney (Kenneth Greenawalt) and the lead plaintiff (Tessim Zorach) were not Jewish themselves. Pfeffer was nonetheless responsible for drafting the legal briefs. He dryly noted that both Greenawalt and Zorach had "names that to many would sound Jewish." In the complaint and briefs they stressed that, unlike the atheistic McCollum, the plaintiffs attended religious instruction outside public school hours. Leo Pfeffer, "An Autobiographical Sketch," in *Religion and the State: Essays in Honor of Leo Pfeffer*, ed. James E. Wood Jr. (Waco: Baylor University Press, 1985), 487–533, esp. 498–99. Gregg Ivers, *To Build a Wall: American Jews and the Separation of Church and State* (Charlottesville: University of Virginia Press, 1995).

117. Leo Pfeffer, *Church, State, and Freedom* (Boston: Beacon, 1953), 605.

118. *Eighty-Third Congress, Second Session on S.J. Res. 87*, 71–78, 80–81.

119. Ibid., 87–88, 91–92.

120. Pfeffer, *Church, State and Freedom*, 209–10.

121. *Eighty-Third Congress, Second Session on S.J. Res. 87*, 90. Pfeffer drew the reference to "the group of Presbyterians" from Philip Schaff, *Church and State in the United States; or, The American Idea of Religious Liberty and Its Practical Effects* (New York: G. P. Putnam's Sons, 1888), 51.

122. *Eighty-Third Congress, Second Session on S.J. Res. 87*, 8–9. The women stated that the Christian Patriotic Rally had been working with the NRA to support the measure in Southern California. All three were members of far-right outfits. The president of the California League of Christian Parents, Paquita de Shishmareff, was a far-right author

and activist and promoter of the antisemitic *Protocols of the Elders of Zion*. Nancy D. Applewhite was acting chairman of the Militant Christian Patriots. A third woman, Nagene Bethune, appeared on the first day of the hearings but did not return to submit testimony the following Monday. Batlan, "One Nation Under Christ," 670-71.

123. *Eighty-Third Congress, Second Session on S.J. Res. 87*, 10-12. In his *McCollum* brief, Pfeffer noted "the stigmatizing effect of teaching Jewish participation in the crucifixion" ("Autobiographical Sketch," 493). He quoted the trial testimony in *Church, State and Freedom*, 345-46.

124. Quoting C. J. Schreiber, Christian Patriotic Rally, Reseda, California. *Eighty-Third Congress, Second Session on S.J. Res. 87*, 11-12.

5. *A Derailment of the Christian Political Tradition*

1. Robert N. Bellah, "Civil Religion in America," from the issue titled "Religion in America," *Dædalus, Journal of the American Academy of Arts and Sciences* 96, no. 1 (Winter 1967): 97, 100, 116.

2. John F. Kennedy, "Inaugural Address" (January 20, 1961), John F. Kennedy Presidential Library and Museum, https://www.jfklibrary.org/archives/other-resources/john-f-kennedy-speeches/inaugural-address-19610120.

   Bellah, "Civil Religion in America," 98, 100-101, 105. Kennedy's inaugural speech was drafted by the self-described "Danish Russian Jewish Unitarian" Theodore Sorensen. In his memoir, Sorensen recalled that en route to the Houston address, Kennedy playfully asked, " 'Is any of my Catholicism rubbing off on you?' 'No,' I replied, 'but I think some of my Unitarianism is rubbing off on you.' Many of the speeches I drafted reflect Unitarian principles." Sorensen, *Counselor: A Life at the Edge of History* (New York: Harper, 2008), 75. It's interesting, too, that the Houston address included the line "For while this year it may be a Catholic against whom the finger of suspicion is pointed, in other years it has been, and may someday be again, a Jew—or a Quaker— or a Unitarian—or a Baptist." Sorensen's father was brought up Baptist, his mother Jewish. He told an interviewer that "in the inaugural address, [Kennedy] concludes saying, 'With history the final judge of our deeds . . .' That's not what other churches would say. That's Unitarianism." Jane Greer, "Ted Sorensen, JFK's Unitarian Speechwriter," *UUWorld*, Winter 2008, https://www.uuworld.org/articles/ted-sorensen-jfks-unitarian-speechwrit.

3. Bellah, "Civil Religion in America," 99, 101.

4. Kennedy had not always presented himself as such a "strict separationist." As a congressman, he had supported legislation to provide funding to Catholic schools in the wake of the *Everson* decision. As senator, he had originally endorsed establishing diplomatic relations with the Vatican but turned against the idea as his political ambitions

began to mature. See John F. Quinn, "John Courtney Murray, SJ: The Man JFK Didn't Understand," *Crisis Magazine*, October 1, 1999.

5. John F. Kennedy, "Address to the Houston Ministers Conference" (September 12, 1960), John F. Kennedy Presidential Library and Museum, https://www.jfklibrary.org/learn/about-jfk/historic-speeches/address-to-the-greater-houston-ministerial-association.

For a detailed discussion of the background of this speech and its immediate reception, see Shaun A. Casey, *The Making of a Catholic President: Kennedy vs. Nixon 1960* (Oxford: Oxford University Press, 2009). See especially his treatment of the speech and of Kennedy's discussion with the ministers that followed his remarks (164–76). Lest we think that Kennedy was endorsing politics as a purely secular field of endeavor, the candidate concluded the question-and-answer session by saying, "I think religion is basic in the establishment of the American system, and, therefore, any candidate for office, I think, should submit himself to the questions of any reasonable man."

6. In 1958, the Kennedy team reached out to Murray to get his thoughts on "the perennially troublesome question: Can a Catholic support, in principle, the religion clauses of the Constitution?" Quoted in John T. McGreevy, *Catholicism and American Freedom: A History* (New York: W. W. Norton, 2003), 213.

7. See the address Murray delivered May 3, 1948, in Wilmington, Delaware, in response to the *McCollum* decision. John Courtney Murray, "A Common Enemy, a Common Cause," published in *First Things*, October 1992, https://www.firstthings.com/article/1992/10/a-common-enemy-a-common-cause.

Joseph A. Komonchak, John Courtney Murray, Samuel Cardinal Stritch, and Francis J. Connell, " 'The Crisis in Church-State Relationships in the U.S.A.' A Recently Discovered Text by John Courtney Murray," *Review of Politics* 61, no. 4 (1999): 687–88.

8. Murray quoted in McGreevy, *Catholicism and American Freedom*, 206.

9. Pius IX, *The Syllabus of Errors* (1864), §§55, 77, 78, 80.

10. Casey notes that "the Syllabus was the most frequently cited source in the anti-Catholic literature of the entire campaign. These citations were the backbone of the theological case against Kennedy." *Making of a Catholic President*, 174.

11. See John Courtney Murray, *The Problem of Religious Freedom*, Woodstock Papers 7 (Westminster, MD: Newman, 1965), in J. Leon Hooper, S.J., ed., *Religious Liberty: Catholic Struggles with Pluralism* (Louisville: Westminster John Knox, 1993), 136.

12. José Casanova, *Public Religions in the Modern World* (Chicago: University of Chicago Press, 1994), 183.

13. *Longinqua Oceani: Encyclical of Pope Leo XIII on Catholicism in the United States* (January 6, 1895).

14. *Testem Benevolentiae Nostrae: Concerning New Opinions, Virtue, Nature and Grace, With Regard to Americanism* (January 22, 1899). *Pascendi Dominici gregis: On the Doctrines of the Modernists* (September 8, 1907).

    See Robert D. Cross, *The Emergence of Liberal Catholicism in America* (Cambridge, MA: Harvard University Press, 1958); Bernard M. Reardon, *Roman Catholic Modernism* (Stanford, CA: Stanford University Press, 1970). On the controversy itself, see Thomas Timothy McAvoy, *The Americanist Heresy in Roman Catholicism, 1895–1900* (Notre Dame, IN: University of Notre Dame Press, 1963).

    That strategy has been succinctly described by José Casanova as developing "Catholic counterculture and countersociety built around the neighborhood ethnic parish with its distinct form of 'devotional Catholicism,' the Catholic school system (from elementary school to college), a distinct Catholic world view based on a refurbished 'Neo-Thomism' and a mythical view of the Catholic Middle Ages, separate Catholic mass media, and myriad Catholic voluntary associations (religious, professional and recreational)." *Public Religions in the Modern World*, 174.

15. Will Herberg, *Protestant-Catholic-Jew: An Essay in American Religious Sociology*, rev. ed. (Chicago: University of Chicago Press, 1983), 136. See McGreevy, *Catholicism and American Freedom*, 166–88.

16. Rev. John A. Ryan, D.D., "Comments on the 'Christian Constitution of States,'" in *The State and the Church*, ed. John A. Ryan and Moorehouse F. X. Millar (New York: Macmillan, 1922), 38–39. This passage was retained in John A. Ryan and Francis J. Boland, *Catholic Principles of Politics*, revised edition of *The State and the Church* (New York: Macmillan, 1940), 320–21.

17. "The Church teaches that the American practice of treating all religions on an equal plane is temporarily acceptable but ultimately wrong, since the state should give a preferred position to the Catholic faith. Accordingly, Catholics are taught to offer no resistance to the American policy of freedom at the present time but to take advantage of this freedom while working to destroy it—through the setting up of a state which will prevent the dissemination of non-Catholic views and limit the public activities of non-Catholic sects." *American Freedom and Catholic Power*, 2nd ed. (Boston: Beacon, 1958), 71. McGreevy, *Catholicism and American Freedom*, 166–68.

18. Komonchak et al., " 'Crisis in Church-State Relationships,' " 687.

19. Ibid., 687–90, 700–701. K. Healan Gaston, *Imagining Judeo-Christian America: Religion, Secularization, and the Redefinition of Democracy* (Chicago: University of Chicago Press, 2019), 135–36, 138–39.

20. Komonchak et al., " 'Crisis in Church-State Relationships,' " 694, 699, 702–3.

21. McGreevy, *Catholicism and American Freedom*, 207–8.

22. John Courtney Murray, S.J., *We Hold These Truths: Catholic Reflections on the American Proposition* (New York: Sheed and Ward, 1960), vii–ix.

23. Ibid., x, 16, 28.

24. Ibid., 28, 30–32.

25. Ibid., 33–35.

26. Ibid., 45–46, 23–24.

27. Ibid., 48–49

28. Ibid., 51–52.

29. Ibid., 54, 60, 63.

30. Ibid., 63–64, 70, 68. In an earlier article, Murray wrote, "It is indeed a curious paradox that, at a time when the Roman curia was intensely preoccupied with problems of political realizations and the philosophy behind them, they had apparently no interest in the most striking and successful political realization of modern times, despite the fact that the philosophy behind it was of linear descent from the central political tradition of the West, which the Church herself had helped fashion out of Greek, Roman, and Germanic elements." John Courtney Murray, "The Church and Totalitarian Democracy," *Theological Studies* 14 (December 1952): 551.

31. Murray, *We Hold These Truths*, 72.

32. At this point, Murray added (oddly) that the Civil War was "not an ideological conflict but simply, in the more descriptive Southern phrase, a war between the states, a conflict of interests." Ibid., 73.

33. Ibid., 77.

34. Ibid., 75.

35. Ibid., 30, 66.

36. Ibid., 41.

37. The book also received positive notices from such conservative luminaries as William F. Buckley Jr. in *National Review* (who later included an excerpt in his anthology of contemporary conservative writing) and by Yale professor Willmoore Kendall in *Modern Age*. On the book's reception, see John F. Quinn, "*We Hold These Truths* at Fifty: John Courtney Murray's Contested Legacy," *American Catholic Studies* 122, no. 3 (Fall 2011): 31–51.

38. McGreevy, *Catholicism and American Freedom*, 212; Douglas Auchincloss, "The City of God and Man," *Time*, December 12, 1960, cover and 64–70.

39. Murray, *We Hold These Truths*, 40, 42–43.

40. Komonchak et al., " 'Crisis in Church-State Relationships,' " 689–90.

41. Editorial, "The Silent Church," *Triumph* 5, no. 1 (January 1970): 42.

42. On *Triumph*, see Patrick Allitt, *Catholic Intellectuals and Conservative Politics in America, 1950–1985* (Ithaca, NY: Cornell University Press, 1993), 141–60; George H. Nash, *The Conservative Intellectual Movement in America, since 1945* (New York: Basic Books, 1976),

310–13, 317–18; Mark D. Popowski, *The Rise and Fall of* Triumph*: The History of a Radical Roman Catholic Magazine, 1966–1976* (Lanham, MD: Lexington Books, 2012); Daniel Kelly, *Living on Fire: The Life of L. Brent Bozell Jr.* (Wilmington, DE: ISI Books, 2014).

43. On this project, see Nash, *Conservative Intellectual Movement*, 154–85.

44. F. Clinton White, quoted in Kelly, *Living on Fire*, 51. On Bozell and Goldwater, see D. G. Hart, *American Catholic: The Politics of Faith during the Cold War* (Ithaca, NY: Cornell University Press, 2020), 115–21.

45. Kelly, *Living on Fire*, 66.

46. On that brouhaha, see Nash, *Conservative Intellectual Movement*, 310–11; Kelly, *Living on Fire*, 43–44; Garry Wills, *Politics and Catholic Freedom* (Chicago: Henry Regnery, 1964), 1–20. See *National Review* 11, no. 6 (August 12, 1961): 81–85; quip at 77.

47. Frank S. Meyer, "The Twisted Tree of Liberty," *National Review* 12 (January 16, 1962), 25–26.

48. L. Brent Bozell, "Freedom or Virtue?," *National Review* 13 (September 11, 1962): 181–87, 206, https://www.nationalreview.com/2017/01/freedom-virtue-conservatism-goal-society-freedom-or-virtue/. On the exchange, see Kelly, *Living on Fire*, 70–73; Nash, *Conservative Intellectual Movement*, 171–77.

49. However, Kelly notes Bozell and Wilhelmsen had been toying with the idea for a magazine to counter the liberal oligarchy in Catholic journalism during their time together in Spain. It was to be called *La Inquisición.* Kelly, *Living on Fire*, 103.

50. John B. Judis, *William F. Buckley, Jr.: Patron Saint of the Conservatives* (New York: Simon & Schuster, 1988), 318–19.

51. Kelly, *Living on Fire*, 117.

52. Michael Lawrence, ed., *The Best of* Triumph (Front Royal, VA: Christendom, 2001), xix.

53. The editors explained that "as Christians we bear the happy duty of trying to hasten Christ's final Triumph over the world, and we rejoice in a turn of events that has bidden us to inscribe that goal on our banner." "Future's Triumph," *Triumph* 1, no. 1 (September 1966): 6.

54. The first issue included some of the responses to the fundraising appeal, including the following unfavorable notice from a well-known former nun: "I hope your magazine will either never appear or very soon be forbidden to appear. How can grown-up intelligent Catholics be such an obstacle to the working of the Holy Ghost?—Maria Augusta Trapp, Stowe Vermont." "Reactions," *Triumph* 1, no. 1 (September 1966): 3.

55. Lawrence, *Best of* Triumph, xxvii.

56. Ibid., xvii.

57. The Editors, "Soul, Brother," *Triumph* 2, no. 9 (September 1967), in Lawrence, *Best of* Triumph, 338. Michael Lawrence wrote that the article was a turning point in the

magazine's political analysis and posture: "A new politics must be fashioned to lead America (and the world) back to the rule of God." "Our First Three Years," *Triumph* 4, no. 9 (September 1969): 12–13.

58. Editors, "Soul, Brother," 341–42, 346–47.

59. Ibid., 347–49, 352, 355. Popowski, *Rise and Fall of Triumph*, 133–34.

60. Editors, "Soul, Brother," 350, 355.

61. "The Negro Revolution," *Triumph* 2, no. 8 (August 1967): 38.

62. Editors, "Soul, Brother," 352, 355.

63. "Past Imperfect: Black Power," *Triumph* 2, no. 1 (January 1967): 8.

64. Editors, "Soul, Brother," 351, 355–56.

65. "The Autumn of the Country," *Triumph* 3, no. 6 (June 1968), in Lawrence, *Best of* Triumph, 412, 415.

66. Ibid., 416–17.

67. The Editors, "The Land of the Sacred," *Triumph* 2, no. 6 (June 1967): 46.

68. "Autumn of the Church," 93, 95–100.

69. Bozell, "Freedom or Virtue?"

70. L. Brent Bozell, *The Warren Revolution: Reflections on the Consensus Society* (New York: Arlington House, 1966), 25, 34–35.

71. L. Brent Bozell, "The Death of the Constitution," *Triumph* 3, no. 2 (February 1968), in Lawrence, *Best of* Triumph, 387.

72. Ibid., 387–88.

73. Ibid., 388–89.

74. Ibid., 389–90.

75. Ibid., 390–91. William F. Buckley Jr. was not impressed by his brother-in-law's volte-face. In a letter to *Triumph*, the *National Review* editor appealed to Father Murray's assertion that the Bill of Rights was "a product of Christian history" but went on to write: "All of history concerts to render Mr. Bozell's essay nothing more than an act of piety, history having shown us that great constitutions larded with religious sycophancy have failed in and of themselves to promulgate a free society, let alone a noble society. If we can have bad popes and corrupt Vaticans, surely we can have bad civil societies even if God is cited in their constitutions. There are no ties to God that any constitution-makers can establish which last an instant longer than the hold that God has upon the people and their governors. . . . I for one prefer the profanation of our Founding Fathers to the (inevitable) profanation of God, which would have resulted if our ancestors had swaggered about Philadelphia prompting a God-ordained America which, weeks later, would, as other societies have, be racked with the conventional, secular anxieties."

In an accompanying letter, Professor Charles E. Rice sided with Bozell and added that "maybe the time has come to reject explicitly the implications here of Father John

Courtney Murray's accommodation. Instead of paying homage to the pluralistic society maybe we should emphasize more strongly the ultimate degeneracy of such a society when it lacks, as ours does, a theologically-grounded set of limitations." "Reactions: Death of the Constitution," *Triumph* 3, no. 4 (April 1968): 3–4.

76. L. Brent Bozell, "Letter to Yourselves I," *Triumph* 4, no. 3 (March 1969), in Lawrence, *Best of Triumph*, 4–10. In a later essay, Bozell pondered why the Christian civilization of the Middle Ages did not hold. "The suspicion is that in this era Christians tended to concentrate on the Creator at the expense of His Creation. And by doing that they set up a gap between God and man. . . . The Middle Ages were intellectually and spiritually—though not in practice—Manichaean." This produced a "cultural guilt complex" and led to the breakup of the Christian lifestyle. "What Went Wrong in the Middle Ages?," *Triumph* 5, no. 10 (November 1970): 26.

77. Bozell, "Letter to Yourselves I," 10–11.

78. W. H. Marshner, "Politique d'Abord," *Triumph* 7, no. 9 (November 1972), in Lawrence, *Best of Triumph*, 544. The title of the essay, the slogan of the French reactionary and founder of the Action Française, Charles Maurras, was no doubt a provocation.

79. Michael Lawrence, "What's Wrong with the American Myth?," *Triumph* 5, no. 10 (December 1970): 16–19. Lawrence's article was a review of Willmoore Kendall and George W. Carey's *The Basic Symbols of the American Political Tradition* (1970), excerpts of which appeared in the same issue of *Triumph*.

80. Jean Danielou, *Prayer as a Political Problem*, trans. J. R. Kirwan (New York: Sheed and Ward, 1967).

81. L. Brent Bozell, "Letter to Yourselves II: Politics of the Poor," *Triumph* 4, no. 4 (April 1969), in Lawrence, *Best of Triumph*, 13–17.

82. Marshner, "Politique d'Abord," 545.

83. Frederick D. Wilhelmsen, "Hallowed Be Thy World," *Triumph* 3, no. 6 (June 1968), in Lawrence, *Best of Triumph*, 421–23.

84. Wilhelmsen, "Hallowed Be Thy World," 423–24. On the Augustinian tactic of "occupying" pagan institutions, see Wilhelmsen, "Toward an Incarnational Politics: Against Despair," *Triumph* 8, no. 2 (February 1973), in Lawrence, *Best of Triumph*, 560–69.

85. Wilhelmsen, "Hallowed Be Thy World," 424–26.

86. Ibid., 426.

87. Ibid., 427.

88. Ibid., 428–29.

89. Ibid., 429.

90. On Wilhelmsen's arguments on the virtues of dynastic monarchy, see Mark D. Popowski, "The Political Thought of Frederick D. Wilhelmsen," *Catholic Social Science Review* 20 (2015): 21–38.

91. The term is multivocal (used in somewhat different ways in the Brazilian, Portuguese, and Spanish contexts), but here Wilhelmsen deployed it in what he regarded as its French philosophical and theological usage. "It does not designate a specific political commitment," he suggested, "but rather a way of looking at the world, a tactic of survival elaborated since the French Revolution by men and women whose lives are often splendid witnesses to the truth of the Faith. An Integralist is a kind of 150 percent Catholic, at least in his own reading of himself." Wilhelmsen, "Toward an Incarnational Politics: Against Despair," 561.

92. Wilhelmsen, "Toward an Incarnational Politics: Against Despair," 566, 568–69.

93. Frederick D. Wilhelmsen, "Toward an Incarnational Politics II: The Hour Is Short; The Hour Is Now," *Triumph* 8, no. 4 (April 1973), in Lawrence, *Best of* Triumph, 573–75, 578. Bozell remarked too that "it is possible that the state's rank in the public life will be taken over by television." "Letter to Yourselves II," 17.

94. L. Brent Bozell, "The Confessional Tribe," *Triumph* 5, no. 7 (July 1970), in Lawrence, *Best of* Triumph, 32–33.

95. Wilhelmsen, "Toward an Incarnational Politics II," 576.

96. Popowski, *Rise and Fall of Triumph*, 123–28.

97. Bozell, "Confessional Tribe," 34,

98. Ibid., 34–37.

99. Ibid., 37.

100. Ibid., 38.

101. Ibid., 37.

102. Ibid., 40–42.

103. "Yes. Or No," *Triumph* 5, no. 10 (October 1970): 41.

104. Stephen J. Tonsor in "The Confessional Tribe under Fire," *Triumph* 5, no. 10 (October 1970): 23.

105. Will Herberg in "The Confessional Tribe under Fire," 23.

106. See also the description of the Society for the Christian Commonwealth initiatives in "The SCC Guild Program: Building the Christian Commonwealth," *Triumph* 7, no. 3 (March 1972): 11–18. "Four hundred years of secularization and materialism are drawing to a close," Wilhelmsen told a group at the close of one of those programs. "The time has come to plant and water a new tree of civilization amidst the barbarism surrounding us. . . . We will make America Catholic as the conquistadores made half the world Catholic, and if we do not do so we will have had the satisfaction of having served the King, of having attempted to save his innocents, in sacralizing the vast expanse of our own nation, of setting down the Cross in our front-rooms and on our plains." Frederick D. Wilhelmsen, "A Parting of Friends," *Triumph* 7, no. 10 (October 1972), in Lawrence, *Best of* Triumph, 58.

107. Kelly, *Living on Fire*, 160–66; Popowski, *Rise and Fall of Triumph*, xi–xii, 208–10. See also Carol Mason, *Killing for Life: The Apocalyptic Narrative of Pro-Life Politics* (Ithaca, NY: Cornell University Press, 2002), 130–57.

108. On the parallels, see Allitt, *Catholic Intellectuals and Conservative Politics*, 160.

109. Michael Lawrence, "Up from Americanism," *Triumph* 3, no. 9 (September 1968), in Lawrence, *Best of* Triumph, 444, 450–52.

110. Ibid., 452.

111. Ibid., 450–51, 454.

112. Ibid., 453.

113. Other *Triumph* articles on Murray offered more balanced assessments of his work and legacy. Martin F. Larrey contended that Murray's position was based on two pillars—a moral consensus and a self-limited state. By then, both of these preconditions had collapsed. "John Courtney Murray: A Reappraisal," *Triumph* 7, no. 10 (December 1972): 22.

114. Wilhelmsen concurred that Murray had switched the terms of Catholic political thinking: "Full confessionality, the *thesis* of older theologians, became the *hypothesis* of the now fading school of John Courtney Murray." "Toward an Incarnational Politics: Against Despair," 566.

115. William F. Buckley Jr., *Cruising Speed—A Documentary* (New York: G. P. Putnam's Sons, 1971), 236. Buckley's correspondent reported of his grim experiences at the summer institute, where, upon offering modest praise of John Courtney Murray, "I quite expected an auto-da-fé in the courtyard followed by interment in the Escorial cellar." *Cruising Speed*, 236–37.

116. Bozell, "The Church and the Republic," *Triumph* 8, no. 9 (November 1973): 9–10.

117. *Testem Benevolentiae* (1899).

118. "Up from Pluralism," *Triumph* 9, no. 2 (February 1974): 45.

6. The Constitution Cannot Save This Country

1. Jerry Falwell, *Listen, America!* (Garden City, NY: Doubleday, 1980), 20.

2. Ibid., 20–22. A few pages later, Falwell correctly attributed the statement to the Declaration of Independence (30) but then repeated the confusion of the two documents (69). The error remained uncorrected in subsequent editions of the book. Michael Lienesch notes that similar mix-ups can be found throughout the writings of the New Christian Right, suggesting that "the statement is not merely a mistake, for these political thinkers wish to make it clear that Constitution and Declaration are intimately related, almost interchangeable." *Redeeming America: Piety and Politics in the New Christian Right* (Chapel Hill: University of North Carolina Press, 1993), 147–48.

3. Falwell, *Listen, America!*, 29–30.

4. Jerry Falwell, *Ministers and Marchers* (Lynchburg, VA: Liberty House, 1965), 7. The sermon was delivered in response to the civil rights marches in Selma, Alabama. "I do question the sincerity and non-violent intentions of some civil rights leaders such as Dr. Martin Luther King Jr., Mr. James Farmer, and others, who are known to have left-wing associations," he stated at the beginning of his address (2).

Frances FitzGerald, "A Disciplined, Charging Army," *New Yorker*, May 18, 1981. Daniel K. Williams, *God's Own Party: The Making of the Christian Right* (Oxford: Oxford University Press, 2010), 6. Williams notes that "despite the claims of some evangelical leaders, the 'New Christian Right' that Falwell, Robertson, and others formed did not actually represent a majority of Americans, and their coalition was never as broadly based as they had hoped it would be" (160).

5. On the varying reactions among evangelicals and fundamentalists to *Engel* and *Schempp*, see Williams, *God's Own Party*, 62–67.

6. On conservative Christian opposition to government pressure to desegregate Christian academies as the leading impetus for the formation of the New Christian Right, see Randall Balmer, *Thy Kingdom Come: An Evangelical's Lament* (New York: Basic Books, 2006), 13–15.

7. FitzGerald, "Disciplined, Charging Army."

8. George Marsden noted that "Francis Shaffer was the key person in articulating this new comprehensive yet simple paradigm." The term was popularized by Tim LaHaye in *The Battle for the Mind* (1980), which argued that "secular humanism was not so much a cultural trend as an organized conspiracy." For conservative Protestants, secular humanism became "the code word for enemy forces in the dichotomized world of the emerging mentality of culture wars." *Fundamentalism and American Culture*, 3rd ed. (Oxford: Oxford University Press, 2022), 303–7.

For an influential definition of "secular humanism" as a religion and analysis of its major tenets (in contrast to "traditional theism") that circulated widely in the religious right, see John W. Whitehead and John Conlan, "The Establishment of the Religion of Secular Humanism and Its First Amendment Implications," *Texas Tech Law Review* 10, no. 1 (1978): 1–66. See also Whitehead's *Second American Revolution* (Elgin, IL: David C. Cook, 1982). Whitehead, who founded the Rutherford Institute in 1982, was a key player in the New Christian Right.

For a discussion on how Justice Black's use of the term was exploited "by champions of fundamentalism as justification for either censorship of public school instruction or introduction of religious instruction or both," see Leo Pfeffer, "The 'Religion' of Secular Humanism," *Journal of Church and State* 29, no. 3 (Autumn 1987): 495–508.

9. Peter Marshall and David Manuel, *The Light and the Glory* (Old Tappan, NJ: Fleming H. Revell, 1977), 169. The book was a classic of the genre of providential history. Marshall was

the son of Peter Marshall, a Scottish-born minister who was pastor of the New York Avenue Presbyterian Church in Washington, DC, and then served as Senate chaplain until his death in 1947.

There is a massive popular literature that claims the United States was established as a "Christian nation," imagines the Founding Fathers as pious Christians, sees the American Revolution and the Founding as providentially guided events, and calls attention to the manifold ways in which Christianity has manifested itself throughout the history of the republic, in the actions of its leaders, and in the public lives of its citizens. Some of the modern classics promoting these positions are Marshall and Manuel, *The Light and the Glory*; Tim LaHaye, *Faith of Our Founding Fathers* (Brentwood, TN: Wolgemuth & Hyatt, 1978); Falwell, *Listen, America!*; W. Cleon Skousen, *The Five Thousand Year Leap: Twenty-Eight Great Ideas That Are Changing the World* (Salt Lake City: Freemen Institute, 1981), later: *The Five Thousand Year Leap: Twenty-Eight Great Ideas That Changed the World* (Washington, DC: National Center for Constitutional Studies, 1991, 2006); John Eidsmoe, *Christianity and the Constitution: The Faith of Our Founding Fathers* (Grand Rapids: Baker Book House, 1988); Gary DeMar, *God and Government*, 3 vols. (Atlanta: American Vision, 1982; Brentwood, TN: Wolgemuth & Hyatt, 1986); and the many books of David Barton, especially *The Myth of Separation* (Aledo, TX: WallBuilder, 1992), *America's Godly Heritage* (Aledo, TX: WallBuilder, 1993), and *Separation of Church and State: What the Founders Meant* (Aledo, TX: WallBuilder, 2007).

10. Falwell, *Listen, America!*, 29.

11. "Today we find that America is more a democracy than a republic. Sometimes there is mob rule. In some instances a vocal minority prevails. Our Founding Fathers would not accept the tyranny of a democracy because they recognized that the only sovereign over men and nations was Almighty God." Falwell, *Listen, America!*, 52.

12. Ibid., 53–54.

13. While the general lines are similar, careful perusal of their works reveals some differing understandings of these principles. Lienesch, *Redeeming America*, 139–94.

14. "The greatest legal minds of two centuries have continued to marvel at it as being almost beyond the scope and dimension of human wisdom. When one stops to consider the enormous problems the Constitution somehow anticipated and the challenges and testings it foresaw, that statement appears more understated than exaggerated. For not even the collective genius of the fledgling United States of America could claim credit for the fantastic strength, resilience, balance, and timelessness of the Constitution.... *Why* does it work so well? Aside from the divine origin of its inspiration, the Constitution was the culmination of nearly two hundred years of Puritan political thought." Marshall and Manuel, *The Light and the Glory*, 343–44.

On how this rhetoric of "miracle" produced fundamentalist "Constitution worship," see John E. Finn, *Fracturing the Constitution: How the Alt-Right Corrupts the Constitution* (Lanham, MD: Rowman & Littlefield, 2019), 35–74.

15. Falwell, *Listen, America!*, 251–52.

16. Ibid., 50, 81, 265. For an analysis of *Listen, America!* as articulating "the core set of beliefs, grievances, and goals" of the New Christian Right, see José Casanova, *Public Religions in the Modern World* (Chicago: University of Chicago Press, 1994), 150–57, 282n57.

17. The newly engaged leaders, conservative Protestant television evangelists such as Falwell, Pat Robertson, and James Robinson, built up the movement with considerable organizational and financial support from such "New Right" activists as Paul Weyrich, Richard Viguerie, and Howard Phillips. Lienesch, *Redeeming America*, 8. Williams, *God's Own Party*, 167–71.

On Christian Zionism, see Samuel Goldman, *God's Country: Christian Zionism in America* (Philadelphia: University of Pennsylvania Press, 2018).

18. Falwell, *Listen, America!*, 107–13 (quotation at 113); Lienesch, *Redeeming America*, 229–37; on Christian Zionism, see Samuel Goldman, *God's Country: Christian Zionism in America* (Philadelphia: University of Pennsylvania Press, 2018).

19. Mark Silk, *Spiritual Politics: Religion and America Since World War II* (New York: Simon & Schuster, 1988), 164.

20. Raymond Haberski Jr., *God and War: American Civil Religion since 1945* (New Brunswick, NJ: Rutgers University Press, 2012), 98–142.

As it happened, the matter of America as a Christian nation was brought to the fore when it was reported that as a young congressman, independent candidate John Anderson, encouraged by a member of the Christian Amendment Movement, had sponsored a Christian amendment in 1961, 1963, and 1965. Although Anderson had come to disavow the Christian Amendment, as well as to oppose amendments to prohibit abortion and restore prayer in public schools, the questions raised by his previous support for the measure proved a major obstacle to the campaign. Joseph S. Moore, *Founding Sins: How a Group of Antislavery Radicals Fought to Put Christ into the Constitution* (New York: Oxford University Press, 2015), 154–55; Jim Mason, *No Holding Back: The 1980 John B. Anderson Presidential Campaign* (Lanham, MD: University Press of America, 2011), 22–23, 240.

21. Kenneth Woodward, "Guru of Fundamentalism," *Newsweek*, November 1, 1982.

22. Francis A. Schaeffer, *A Christian Manifesto* (Westchester, IL: Crossway Books, 1981), 10.

23. Williams, *God's Own Party*, 208–9; Lienesch, *Redeeming America*, 177.

24. Schaeffer, *Christian Manifesto*, 18, 23–24, 55, 29.

25. Ibid., 31–32, 105–6, 55.

26. Ibid., 39, 46, 49, 34–36, 54. See also John W. Whitehead's contention that the First Amendment's religion clauses protected only "denominational pluralism" (Judeo-Christian theism), which is not to be confused with "the new concept of pluralism, which commands compete acceptance of all views, even secular humanism." Whitehead distinguished his Christian nation from a theocracy (which he described as both "the government of a state by immediate divine guidance" and "the government of a state by officials who are regarded as divinely guided"). *Second American Revolution*, 74, 96–7.

27. Schaeffer, *Christian Manifesto*, 73–79, 82–83, 86, 61. On Schaeffer's reservations over Falwell and his movement's style and flag-wrapped-cross piety, see Barry Hankins, *Francis Schaeffer and the Shaping of Evangelical America* (Grand Rapids: Eerdmans, 2008), 201–4. See also Frank Schaeffer, *Crazy for God: How I Grew Up as One of the Elect, Helped Found the Religious Right, and Lived to Take All (or Almost All) of It Back* (New York: Carroll & Graf, 2007).

28. Schaeffer, *Christian Manifesto*, 91–93.

29. Ibid., 101–2.

30. Ibid., 126–27, 117.

31. Ibid., 128.

32. Schaeffer backpedaled at the beginning of the next chapter: "What does all this mean in practice to us today? I must say, I really am not sure all that it means to us in practice at this moment." Ibid., 130–31.

33. In their 1983 book, *The Search for Christian America*, Mark A. Noll, Nathan O. Hatch, and George M. Marsden sifted through the historical evidence and found little to support that story. While they acknowledged that a Judeo-Christian heritage was an important influence on the ideology of the Revolution and the Constitution, they found "little *direct link* between explicitly Christian thinking and the founding documents." And they gently pushed back at Schaeffer's conflation of the intellectual outlook of the Reformation with that of the founding era in general and his claims regarding the expansive influence of Rutherford and his *Lex, Rex* on the thinking of John Witherspoon and the other Founding Fathers in particular. *The Search for Christian America* (Westchester, IL: Crossway Books, 1983), 130, 141–43. For a discussion of the back and forth between the academics and Schaeffer, see Hankins, *Francis Schaeffer*, 209–27.

34. Schaeffer, *Christian Manifesto*, 46, 136–37.

35. Gary North and David Chilton, "Apologetics and Strategy," in *Tactics of Christian Resistance*, ed. Gary North, Christianity and Civilization 3 (Tyler, TX: Geneva Divinity School Press, 1983), 116–31. For a friendlier review from someone within the Reconstructionist camp, see Howard Ahmanson, review of *A Christian Manifesto*, by Francis A. Schaeffer, *Journal of Christian Reconstruction* 9, nos. 1 and 2 (1982–1983): 506–7.

36. Schaeffer, *Christian Manifesto*, 136–37.

37. North and Chilton, "Apologetics and Strategy," 122, 127–28.

38. Ibid., 136–37, 139.

39. Gary North and Gary DeMar, *Christian Reconstruction: What It Is, What It Isn't* (Tyler, TX: Institute for Christian Economics, 1991), 52.

40. Sara Diamond, *Spiritual Warfare: The Politics of the Christian Right* (Montreal: Black Rose Books, 1990), 136.

41. Quoted in Michael J. McVicar, *Christian Reconstruction: R. J. Rushdoony and American Religious Conservatism* (Chapel Hill: University of North Carolina Press, 2015), 5.

42. McVicar, *Christian Reconstruction*, 5.

43. Molly Worthen, "The Chalcedon Problem: Rousas John Rushdoony and the Origins of Christian Reconstructionism," *Church History* 77, no. 2 (June 2008): 401.

44. Julie J. Ingersoll, *Building God's Kingdom: Inside the World of Christian Reconstruction* (Oxford: Oxford University Press, 2015), 1.

45. North and Chilton, "Apologetics and Strategy," 126. They had good reason to quibble. *A Christian Manifesto* was actually researched and drafted by John W. Whitehead, a formerly hard-partying civil rights lawyer who, inspired by a reading of Hal Lindsey's apocalyptic *The Late Great Planet Earth,* turned to Christ and moved out to California to join Lindsey's Jesus Christ Light and Power Company. There the young lawyer came under the tutelage of an idiosyncratic scholar named R. J. Rushdoony, who was preaching what he called Christian Reconstructionism, and soon turned his talents to Christian legal advocacy. It was this legal work that drew the attention of Franky Schaeffer, with whose assistance he put together a legal foundation that would in the end be named the Rutherford Institute. In a later book, North accused Schaeffer of outright plagiarism. Gary North, *Political Polytheism: The Myth of Pluralism* (Tyler, TX: Institute for Christian Economics, 1989). See also North, "The Intellectual Schizophrenia of the New Christian Right," in *The Failure of the American Baptist Culture*, ed. James B. Jordan, Christianity and Civilization 1 (Tyler, TX: Geneva Divinity School Press, 1983), 1–40.

William Edgar recalled that Schaeffer led a seminar at L'Abri in 1964 on Rushdoony's book *This Independent Republic.* "On the Passing of R. J. Rushdoony," *First Things*, August 2001, https://www.firstthings.com/article/2001/08/the-passing-of-r-j-rushdoony. See also McVicar, *Christian Reconstruction*, 211–13.

46. Mark R. Rushdoony, "Rousas John Rushdoony: A Brief History, Part II 'You Are Going to Be a Writer,' " Chalcedon Foundation, April 21, 2016, https://chalcedon.edu/magazine/rousas-john-rushdoony-a-brief-history-part-ii-you-are-going-to-be-a-writer.

47. McVicar, *Christian Reconstruction*, 38. The Dutch-born Van Til was himself influenced by the nineteenth-century Dutch theologian and politician Abraham Kuyper, who posited a comprehensive Calvinist worldview to stand in opposition to the teachings of the Enlightenment.

48. Cornelius Van Til, *The Defense of the Faith: A Survey of Christian Epistemology* (Phillipsburg, NJ: P&R, 1977), 298; quoted in Worthen, "Chalcedon Problem," 405.

49. Worthen, "Chalcedon Problem," 421.

50. Michael McVicar, "Christian Reconstruction and the Austrian School of Economics," in *Hayek a Collaborative Biography, Part IX: The Divine Right of the "Free" Market*, ed. Robert Leeson, Archival Insights into the Evolution of Economics (New York: Palgrave Macmillan, 2017), 191–247.

51. R. J. Rushdoony, "Foundation of Western Liberty," *Triumph* 2, no. 3 (March 1967): 26–29.
   An editorial comment described Rushdoony simply as "a noted Protestant theologian." The placement of his essay in the radical Catholic magazine is curious. In one of his Bible study groups, Rushdoony referred to *Triumph* as "a very well-written and able Catholic monthly put out by some friends of mine." He specifically regarded them in alignment on the issue of abortion. I thank Michael McVicar for alerting me to this reference. R. J. Rushdoony, "Salvation and Godly Rule: Repentance," accessed at Pocket College, https://pocket-college.com/transcript/RR136W42.html.

52. For a discussion of the theological issues at stake, see Jaroslav Pelikan, *The Emergence of the Catholic Tradition (100–600)* (Chicago: University of Chicago Press, 1971), 226–77.

53. Rousas John Rushdoony, *The Foundations of Social Order: Studies in the Creeds and Councils of the Early Church*, 3rd ed. (Vallecito, CA: Ross House Books, 1998), 53–54.

54. Ibid., 56.

55. Ibid., 65.

56. Rushdoony, *This Independent Republic* (Vallecito, CA: Ross House Books, 2001), 10.

57. McVicar, "Christian Reconstruction," 216; Rushdoony, *Foundations of Social Order*, 53.
   Rushdoony's books are available as PDFs on the Chalcedon Foundation website. All quotations from these texts and from the *Journal of Christian Reconstruction* are keyed to those editions. There are literally hundreds of Reconstructionist books, articles, and other media, much of it accessible online on the Chalcedon Foundation's and Gary North's websites in PDF format.

58. Rushdoony, *Foundations of Social Order*, 58.

59. Rushdoony, *This Independent Republic*, 136.

60. Ibid., 14.

61. Rushdoony, *Foundations of Social Order*, 62, 66.

62. Ibid., 182, 186. Mark R. Rushdoony, "Rousas John Rushdoony: A Brief History, Part VI 'The Lord Will Perfect That Which Concerneth Me,'" Chalcedon Foundation, December 17, 2016, https://chalcedon.edu/magazine/rousas-john-rushdoony-a-brief-history-part-vi-the-lord-will-perfect-that-which-concerneth-me.

63. Rushdoony, *The Nature of the American System* (Vallecito, CA: Ross House Books, 2001), 3. On Chalcedon, see Rushdoony, *This Independent Republic*, 10, 35, 37.

64. Rushdoony, *This Independent Republic*, xiii.

65. Ibid., 20. See also his discussion in "The Myth of an American Enlightenment," *Journal of Christian Reconstruction* 3, no. 1 (1976): 91–96.

66. Rushdoony, *This Independent Republic*, 14–15, 20.

67. Rushdoony, *This Independent Republic*, 127, 31; *Nature of the American System*, 82–86.

68. Rushdoony, *This Independent Republic*, 31–37. Rushdoony also noted John Courtney Murray's claim that "the term 'legal sovereignty' makes no sense in America, where sovereignty (if the alien term must be used) is purely political." Murray, *We Hold These Truths*, 70; Rushdoony, *This Independent Republic*, 33.

69. Rushdoony, *Nature of the American System*, 55–56, 7.

70. Rushdoony, *This Independent Republic*, xiv.

71. Rushdoony, *This Independent Republic*, xiv; *Nature of the American System*, 6–7. The Supreme Court's claim to jurisdiction by means of the Fourteenth Amendment was, in Rushdoony's view, "a violation of the First Amendment." *Nature of the American System*, 9.

72. Rushdoony, *This Independent Republic*, 96.

73. Rushdoony, *Nature of the American System*, 25–26; *This Independent Republic*, 131.

74. Rushdoony, *Nature of the American System*, 58–61.

75. Ibid., 58–59. Rushdoony went so far as to suggest that "an important aspect of the Civil War was the Unitarian statist drive for an assault on its Calvinistic enemy, the South" (58).

76. Rushdoony took the term from an 1873 book of that title by Octavius Brooks Frothingham, president of the Free Religion Association and coeditor of *The Index*. He spent several pages discussing his thought in *Nature of the American System*, 97–108.

    On Rushdoony's promotion of the "theological war thesis," see Edward H. Sebesta and Euan Hague, "The US Civil War as a Theological War: Confederate Christian Nationalism and the League of the South," *Canadian Review of American Studies* 32, no. 3 (2002): 253–84. On the influence of Southern proslavery theology on the Reconstructionists, see Ingersoll, *Building God's Kingdom*, 16–19.

77. According to Rushdoony, the ("illegally ratified") Fourteenth Amendment broke with this tradition and "began the [Supreme] court's recession from its conception of America as a Christian country and its development of the thesis of unitary state." Rushdoony, *This Independent Republic*, 34.

78. Rushdoony, *Nature of the American System*, 61.

79. "The term 'Judeo-Christian' is most commonly used by the adherents of the religion of humanity, who are insistent on reading their religion into both Judaism and Christianity. No doubt, if Buddhism were a factor on the American scene, we would hear references to our Buddho-Judeo-Christian heritage." The term is "an offence to true believers." Ibid., 80.

80. Ibid., 107.

81. Rushdoony, *Independent Republic*, 113.

82. Rushdoony, *The Nature of the American System*, 122–23.

83. Rushdoony, *Independent Republic*, 112–13; John Dewey, *A Common Faith* (New Haven: Yale University Press, 1934), 84. In a later work, Rushdoony wrote, "In early America, there was no question, whatever the *form* for the civil government, that all legitimate authority is derived from God. The influence of the classical tradition revived the authority of the people, which historically is equally compatible with monarchy, oligarchy dictatorship, or democracy, but it is not compatible with the doctrine of God's authority. As a result, the authority of God has been progressively displaced in America by the authority of the new god, the people. When God is invoked, He is seen as someone who bows to the people, as a God who longs for democracy." *Institutes of Biblical Law*, vol. 1 (Vallecito, CA: Ross House Books, 2020), 217.

84. Rushdoony, *This Independent Republic*, 65.

85. Rushdoony, *Nature of the American System*, 13.

86. Rushdoony, *Institutes of Biblical Law*, 101–2, 520.

87. Rushdoony, *This Independent Republic*, 120–22.

88. Rushdoony, *This Independent Republic*, xv.

89. Rushdoony, *Nature of the American System*, 29–30; *This Independent Republic*, xv, 109.

90. Quoted in McVicar, *Christian Reconstruction*, 127.

91. R. J. Rushdoony, *Biblical Faith and American History* (Vallecito, CA: Chalcedon Foundation, 2002).

92. North and DeMar, *Christian Reconstruction*, xi–xii.

93. Rushdoony, *Institutes of Biblical Law*, 102.

94. Ibid., 3–5.

95. "Calvin wanted the establishment of the Christian religion; he could not have it, nor could it last long in Geneva, without Biblical law" (Rushdoony, *Institutes of Biblical Law*, 10). Rushdoony argued that the Reformation was "stillborn" on account of its failure to recognize theonomy: "The Reformation as a whole moved from victory to defeat, from relevance to irrelevance, from a challenge to the world to a surrender to the world or a meaningless withdrawal from it." Ibid., 678.

96. The term itself is believed to have been coined by the first-century Jewish writer Josephus in his *Against Apion*. Josephus stressed the wisdom of Moses as a legislator for "placing all sovereignty and authority in the hands of God." *The Life, Against Apion*, trans. H. St. J. Thackeray (Cambridge, MA: Harvard University Press, 1956), 359.

97. Rushdoony, "The Meaning of Theocracy," *Chalcedon Position Paper* no. 15 (1980). McVicar notes a tendency of critics to "Islamize" Christian Reconstructionism, dubbing Rushdoony as "the Ayatollah of Holy Rollers" or a "Christian Jihadi" (*Christian Reconstruction*,

215). The comparisons of Rushdoony to the supreme leader of Iran and the radical Islamic movement that had taken over Afghanistan, at a time of heightened fears of "political Islam" and its ambition to implement sharia, were meant to be disparaging and inflammatory. Yet there are comparisons to be made between the Reconstructionist case for theonomy and the arguments presented by some Muslim and Jewish thinkers on the necessity of living in accordance with a divinely revealed law as opposed to law legislated by fallible human beings. Even "divine" laws, however, are neither self-interpreting nor self-enforcing, of course.

98. Rushdoony, *Institutes of Biblical Law*, 13, 243; Rushdoony, "Meaning of Theocracy." As Gary North put it, "The Reconstructionists' version of theocracy is a decentralized system of multiple competing governments in which the modern messianic State and its economic subsidies would be dismantled." *Political Polytheism*, 585.

99. Rushdoony, *Institutes of Biblical Law*, 238. (Rushdoony considered homosexuality to be "an expression of apostasy." Ibid., 180.)

100. Ibid., 240, 525. Reconstructionists regarded such a proposal as consistent with the Thirteenth Amendment, which prohibited slavery "except as a punishment for a crime whereof the party shall have been duly convicted." North and DeMar, *Christian Reconstruction*, 10. For North's take on biblical slavery, see Gary North, *Tools of Dominion: The Case Laws of Exodus* (Tyler, TX: Institute for Christian Economics, 1990), 111–206.

101. For a description of the guidelines for political action necessary for "reconstituting civil government," see Gary DeMar, *Ruler of the Nations: Biblical Blueprints for Government* (Fort Worth: Dominion, 1987), 203–24. DeMar suggested that Christians withdraw from the public ("government") schools, serve on juries (to convict evildoers and refuse to convict people of crimes that are not "biblical"), use the democratic process to elect representatives to vote for biblically based laws (such as bans on abortion), abolish past legislation, and scale back the administrative state.

For an analysis of the "Biblical Blueprint" series, see Ingersoll, *Building God's Kingdom*, 54–78. On North's "theocratic interpretation of the Austrian School" and his work in disseminating these ideas to a broader conservative Christian audience, see McVicar, "Christian Reconstruction," 217–35.

102. North, *Christian Reconstruction*, xxi.

103. "The Debate over Christian Reconstruction" (Dominion Press, 1988), posted October 9, 2020, Esperanza en lo Invisible, YouTube, https://www.youtube.com/watch?v=pz6y TXGekHo.

104. North, *Tactics of Christian Resistance*, xxvii–xl. The question of the relationship between Christian Reconstructionism and violence came to the fore with the radical antiabortion activism of Paul Jennings Hill, a former student of Bahnsen, who used theonomist writings and ideas to justify violent action, which culminated in his murder of Dr. John

Britton and his bodyguard in 1994. North responded to Hill's attempted correspondence to him with a book-length missive, *Lone Gunners for Jesus: Letters to Paul J. Hill* (Tyler, TX: Institute for Christian Economics, 1994). Ingersoll, *Building God's Kingdom*, 227–35; McVicar, *Christian Reconstruction*, 160–61.

105. On the tensions between Rushdoony and North, the events leading to the split between the two men, and the differences between the Vallecito and Tyler branches of Christian Reconstruction, see McVicar, *Christian Reconstruction*, 182–94. North documents his side of the affair in "Honest Reporting as Heresy," in *Westminster's Confession: The Abandonment of Van Til's Legacy* (Tyler, TX: Institute for Christian Economics, 1991), 317–41.

106. For accounts of these influences, see McVicar, *Christian Reconstruction*, 195–201; Ingersoll, *Building God's Kingdom*, 189–212. See also Frederick Clarkson, "Dominionism Rising: A Theocratic Movement Hiding in Plain Sight," *The Public Eye*, Summer 2016.

107. North, "Intellectual Schizophrenia," 12.

108. Rushdoony himself was known to grouse about the lack of recognition of his influence. In his journals, he wrote, "Read Francis A. Schaeffer: *A Christian Manifesto*, Another book using some of my material, with phone calls for citations, with no mention of me; for most writers, I am useful but unmentionable! Not faith but timidity is the march of too many Christians today, including able men like Francis." Mark R. Rushdoony, "Rousas John Rushdoony: A Brief History, Part VII 'He's on the Lord's Side,'" Chalcedon Foundation, February 21, 2017, https://chalcedon.edu/magazine/rousas-john-rushdoony-a-brief-history-part-vii-hes-on-the-lords-side.

Rodney Clapp, "Democracy as Heresy," *Christianity Today*, February 20, 1987, 17–23.

109. An editorial note explained the rationale for the piece: "Stimulated and spurred on by inquisitive readers and friends asking such questions as: 'Do reconstructionists really want to trade the freedoms of American democracy for the strictures of Old Testament theocracy?' and the more basic 'Who are these people and should I be concerned?' we finally turned the idea (and the writing of the article) over to associate editor Rodney Clapp." In doing so, the *Christianity Today* article set the tone for subsequent assessments of the movement in both the Christian and secular media. There followed many breathless articles and books exposing the Reconstructionists as religious deviants posing a clear and present danger to the American republic and way of life. McVicar, *Christian Reconstruction*, 203.

In a long critique of the *Christianity Today* article, North complained that Clapp had composed "a hatchet job . . . the latest in a long line of frivolous attacks on those Christians who believe that it is the Bible, rather than the latest essay on the Op Ed page of the *New York Times*, that should be the authoritative guideline for Christian activism" ("Honest Reporting as Heresy," 340). Reviewing McVicar's book, North alleged that Clapp was "a closet disciple" of theological ethicist Stanley Hauerwas and therefore had "a hidden agenda" against Christian Reconstruction and indeed to *Christianity Today's* more modest calls for a Christian reform of American politics. "McVicar on Rushdoony: A Review Article," Gary North's Specific Answers, October 10, 2020, https://www.garynorth.com/public/21423.cfm.

110. Ken I. Kersch, *Conservatives and the Constitution: Imagining Constitutional Restoration in the Heyday of American Liberalism* (Cambridge: Cambridge University Press, 2019), 96–102.

111. Edwin Meese III, "Speech by Attorney General Edwin Meese III before the American Bar Association on July 9, 1985," The Federalist Society, https://fedsoc.org/commentary/publications/the-great-debate-attorney-general-ed-meese-iii-july-9-1985.

112. Edwin Meese III, "Speech by Attorney General Edwin Meese III before the DC Chapter of the Federalist Society Lawyers Division, November 15, 1985," The Federalist Society, https://fedsoc.org/commentary/publications/the-great-debate-attorney-general-ed-meese-iii-november-15-1985.

For a classic statement of the "constitutional vision of human dignity," see Justice William J. Brennan Jr., "The Constitution of the United States: Contemporary Ratification," in *Interpreting the Constitution: The Debate over Original Intent*, ed. Jack N. Rakove (Boston: Northeastern University Press, 1990), 23–34.

113. Meese, "American Bar Association."

114. Yet there were limits to this approach. The nomination of the arch-originalist Robert H. Bork generated enough opposition to be defeated in a bipartisan Senate vote. The man who ultimately took the seat, Anthony Kennedy, would later infuriate religious conservatives by upholding abortion rights in *Planned Parenthood v. Casey* (1992) and authoring the majority opinions in a number of gay rights cases, including *Lawrence v. Texas* (2003), which found that criminal laws against sodomy are unconstitutional, and *Obergefell v. Hodges* (2015), which guaranteed the right of same-sex couples to marry.

115. R. J. Rushdoony, "The United States Constitution," *Journal of Christian Reconstruction* 12, no. 1 (1988) (electronic version, 2012): 42–43. "The Constitution gives us procedural law, not a substantive morality, so anyone can use the Constitution for good or for ill," Rushdoony told Bill Moyers in a 1987 PBS interview. Bill Moyers, *God and Politics: On Earth as It Is in Heaven* (New York: Public Affairs Television, 1987).

Meese himself may have believed that "the source of authority for the highest leaders and the source to guide the lowest citizen remains the same: the word of God, as expressed in the Bible" (as he told Moyers on that same program), but most of those who stood within the originalist tent did not speak of the Constitution as "inspired" or argue it was to be interpreted by means of a higher law or principle outside the text (whether that be the Bible or natural law).

116. Rushdoony, "United States Constitution," 26, 44.

117. Ibid., 24, 28, 29.

118. Ibid., 34, 28, 46, 45.

119. North, *Political Polytheism*, 677, 681, 690, 694. North actually misrepresented Rushdoony's position when he asserted that "Rushdoony still believes that a restoration of Constitutional order is the best strategy for Christian Reconstruction in the United States." North, *Political Polytheism*, 683. Frustrated that his thesis did not receive the attention and critical engagement that he believed it deserved, North reiterated and updated his argument in *Conspiracy in Philadelphia: Origins of the United States Constitution* (Harrisonburg, VA: Dominion Educational Ministries, 2004).

120. North, *Political Polytheism*, 534–35.

121. Ibid., 315, 311, 691.

122. Ibid., 699. See also North's earlier reading of the Declaration of Independence as a "fusionist document": "The Declaration of Independence as a Conservative Document," *Journal of Christian Reconstruction* 3, no. 1 (1976): 123–49.

123. North, *Political Polytheism*, 311, 391–93, 410–11, 511, 529.

124. Ibid., 696, 427.

125. A review of *Political Polytheism* in Rushdoony's journal argued that the dating was a recognition of Christ's lordship and the covenantal relation of the state to him, thus authorizing the Constitution as an explicitly Christian charter. Religious oaths were therefore unnecessary as the oath to the Constitution implied the commitment to its Christian nature. Archie P. Jones, "*The Myth of Political Polytheism*: A Review Article," *Journal of Christian Reconstruction* 14, no. 1 (1988): 315–34.

126. North, *Political Polytheism*, 371, 655, 702, 691.

127. Ibid., 565, 411, 653. He added, "It is not sufficient to call for an amendment that names Jesus Christ as Lord of the national covenant. There are cults that proclaim Jesus Christ as Lord. They are anti-Trinitarian, however, and the inclusion of a statement identifying God as a Trinity is necessary."

128. Ibid., 572, 657.

129. Ibid., 647, 649–50. North also endorsed a strategy of elite replacement. In a book published a year earlier, he stated that "Christians must begin to organize politically within the present party structure, and they must begin to infiltrate the existing institutional order," and learn how to manipulate government bureaucracies in order "*to gum up the existing humanistic social order through its own red tape*" but also to "smooth the transition to Christian political leadership." Gary North, *Is the World Running Down? Crisis in the Christian Worldview* (Tyler, TX: Institute for Christian Economics, 1988), 250–51.

130. North, *Political Polytheism*, 578, 650.

131. In *Conspiracy in Philadelphia*, North commented on Rushdoony's failure to respond to his critique of his position on the Constitution. "I think the reason for silence is that he could not reconcile his conflicting positions: his biblical presuppositionalism vs. his defense of the Constitution. He never wavered in this defense of the Constitution, from *This Independent Republic* until the end of his life. He sacrificed the basics of his philosophy—Van Til's presuppositionalism, Calvin's covenant theology, biblical law, and the idea that neutrality is always a myth—on the altar of this false deity: the U.S. Constitution. It was a high price to pay" (385).

132. See, for example, George Grant, *The Changing of the Guard: Biblical Blueprints for Political Action* (Fort Worth: Dominion, 1987), 39–40. DeMar, *Ruler of the Nations*, 225–40.

133. Gary DeMar, "The Theonomic Response to National Confessionalism," in *God and Politics: Four Views on the Reformation of Civil Government: Theonomy, Principled Pluralism, Christian America, National Confessionalism*, ed. Gary Scott Smith (Phillipsburg, NJ: Presbyterian and Reformed, 1989), 205, 208–9.

134. William Edgar, "The National Confessional Major Response," in Smith, *God and Politics*, 259.

135. Anthony Cowley, "From Whence We Came: A Background of the National Reform Association," in *Explicitly Christian Politics: The Vision of the National Reform Association*, ed. William Einwechter (Pittsburgh: Christian Statesman Press, 1997), accessed at https://web.archive.org/web/20050206211616/http://www.natreformassn.org/ecp/chap1.html.

136. Andrew Sandlin, "Biblionomic National Confessionalism," *Christian Statesman* 141, no. 2 (March/April 1998), accessed at https://web.archive.org/web/20050214064821/http://www.natreformassn.org/statesman/98/natcon.html.

137. William Einwechter, "Evangelical Political Compromise," *Christian Statesman* 141, no. 6 (November–December 1998), accessed at https://web.archive.org/web/20050213160343/http://www.natreformassn.org/statesman/98/polcompr.html; Andrew Sandlin, "Biblionomic National Confessionalism," *Christian Statesman* 141, no. 2 (March/April 1998); William Einwechter, "The Christian Statesman: A Unique Publication," *Christian Statesman* 139, no. 5 (September–October 1996), accessed at https://web.archive.org/web/20050210180400/http://www.natreformassn.org/statesman/96/unique.html.

138. Richard John Neuhaus, "Why Wait for the Kingdom? The Theonomist Temptation," *First Things*, May 1990, 13–21. On Neuhaus's theological-political journey and *First Things*, see Damon Linker, *The Theocons: Secular America Under Siege* (New York: Doubleday, 2006).

7. A Mistake with Lasting Consequences

1. Obergefell v. Hodges, 576 U.S. 644 at 651–52, 681 (2015).

2. *Obergefell*, at 718, 713–14, 717, 721, 735, 721 (2015). As Thomas is regarded as an originalist and a textualist, it's interesting that the word "dignity" does not appear anywhere in the Declaration of Independence.

3. Robert P. George, Peter J. Leithart, and Rod Dreher in "After Obergefell: A First Things Symposium," *First Things*, June 27, 2015, https://www.firstthings.com/web-exclusives/2015/06/after-obergefell-a-first-things-symposium.

4. Robert P. Jones, *The End of White Christian America* (New York: Simon & Schuster, 2017), 142, 144.

5. Dreher in "After Obergefell." Rod Dreher, "Benedict Option: A Medieval Model Inspires Christian Communities Today," *American Conservative*, December 12, 2013, https://www.theamericanconservative.com/articles/benedict-option/.

6. Rod Dreher, *The Benedict Option: A Strategy for Christians in a Post-Christian Nation* (New York: Sentinel, 2018), 3, 9.

7. Ibid., 25.

8. Ibid., 25, 21–47. Brad S. Gregory, *The Unintended Reformation: How a Religious Revolution Secularized Society* (Cambridge, MA: Belknap Press of Harvard University Press, 2012). For a critique of this kind of "World We Have Lost theological-political mythmaking," see Mark Lilla, *The Shipwrecked Mind: On Political Reaction* (New York: New York Review of Books, 2016), especially 67–85.

9. Dreher, "Christian and Counter-Cultural."

10. Dreher, *Benedict Option*, 35–36, 96. A study guide included with the book confronts the reader with a set of provocative questions: "Do you think that Americans are a 'moral and religious people'? If not, when did things go wrong? And how would you justify the judgment that Americans were ever moral and religious given grave sins of past eras, such as slavery and Jim Crow?" (247).

11. Dreher, *Benedict Option*, 43–44. Planned Parenthood v. Casey 505 U.S. 851 (1992).

12. Dreher, *Benedict Option*, 10–12. Christian Smith and Melinda Linquist Denton, *Soul Searching: The Religious and Spiritual Lives of American Teenagers* (New York: Oxford University Press, 2005). The Catholic conservative *New York Times* columnist Ross Douthat advanced a similar complaint in his book *Bad Religion: How We Became a Nation of Heretics* (New York: Free Press, 2012).

13. Rod Dreher, "Christian and Countercultural," *First Things*, February 2015, https://www.firstthings.com/article/2015/02/christian-and-countercultural.

14. Dreher, *Benedict Option*, xvii, 10–11. See also Dreher, "Christian and Countercultural."

15. Dreher cited the passage from MacIntyre and raised the idea of domestic, secular "monasteries" in his earlier *Crunchy Cons: How Birkenstocked Burkeans, Gun-Loving Organic Gardeners, Evangelical Free-Range Farmers, Hip Homeschooling Mamas, Right-Wing Nature Lovers, and Their Diverse Tribe of Countercultural Conservatives Plan to Save America (or at Least the Republican Party)* (New York: Crown Forum, 2006), 241–47.

16. Alasdair MacIntyre, *After Virtue: A Study in Moral Theory*, 2nd ed. (Notre Dame, IN: University of Notre Dame Press, 1984), 263. MacIntyre himself was critical of Dreher's

appropriation of his most famous sentence and the politically conservative purposes it had been put to support. In a 2017 address, he said, "So, when I said we need a new St. Benedict, I was suggesting we need a new kind of engagement with the social order, not any kind of withdrawal from it." I am indebted to Max Bodach for pointing me to this statement. " 'A New Set of Social Forms': Alasdair MacIntyre on the 'Benedict Option,' " Tradistae, April 21, 2020, https://tradistae.com/2020/04/21/macintyre-benop/.

17. Rod Dreher, "Benedict Option: A Medieval Model Inspires Christian Communities Today," *American Conservative*, December 12, 2013; Dreher, *Benedict Option*, 120–21, 192–94.

Crawford Gribben describes the "internal migration" of a younger generation of theonomists, influenced by the work of R. J. Rushdoony and Gary North, who have migrated to the Pacific Northwest to establish intentional communities from which "they plan to construct a radically conservative and authentically Christian America," the basis of "a global hegemony of Christian faith." Gribben notes that Dreher had originally planned to profile one of these communities in *The Benedict Option* but removed the material when a pastoral scandal came to light. *Survival and Resistance in Evangelical America: Christian Reconstruction in the Pacific Northwest* (New York: Oxford University Press, 2021), 6, 3, 8. See also Rod Dreher, "Scandal in Moscow," *American Conservative*, September 29, 2015, https://www.theamericanconservative.com/dreher/scandal-in-moscow/.

For an ethnographic study of American converts to the Russian Orthodox Church and resistance to American democratic ideals, see Sarah Riccardi-Swartz, *Between Heaven and Russia: Religious Conversion and Political Apostasy in Appalachia* (New York: Fordham University Press, 2022).

18. Patrick J. Deneen, *Why Liberalism Failed* (New Haven: Yale University Press, 2018), 1.

19. Clare Foran, "Here's What's on Barack Obama's Reading List," June 16, 2018, https://www.cnn.com/2018/06/16/politics/barack-obama-reading-list-mitch-landrieu/index.html. Barack Obama, Facebook, June 16, 2018, https://www.facebook.com/barackobama/posts/10155941960536749.

20. Deneen, *Why Liberalism Failed*, 24, 1, 19, 31, 36, 17, 27, 38, 3, 154.

21. Ibid., 5, 101, 164–65, 18.

22. Ibid., 180–81.

23. Ibid., 191–92, 196–97.

24. Jon Baskin, "Academia's Holy Warriors: How a Group of Catholic Intellectuals Is Making the Case against Liberalism," *Chronicle of Higher Education*, September 12, 2019, https://www.chronicle.com/article/academias-holy-warriors/.

25. For a trenchant analysis and critique of Deneen's *Why Liberalism Failed* that raises some of these issues, see Laura K. Field, "Revisiting Why Liberalism Failed Part 1: The

Intellectual and Political Stakes," Niskanen Center, December 21, 2020, https://www
.niskanencenter.org/revisiting-why-liberalism-failed-part-1-the-intellectual-and-political-
stakes/.

See also Samuel Goldman, "The Inevitability of Liberal Failure?," Kirk Center, January
15, 2018, https://kirkcenter.org/reviews/the-inevitability-of-liberal-failure/.

26. Dreher, *Benedict Option*, 84. He eventually decamped to Budapest in 2022. Rod Dreher,
"Goodbye, Louisiana. I Tried," October 2, 2022, https://www.theamericanconservative
.com/goodbye-louisiana-i-tried/.

27. Adrian Vermeule, "Integration from Within," *American Affairs* 2, no. 1 (Spring 2018),
https://americanaffairsjournal.org/2018/02/integration-from-within/. Vermeule, "All
Human Conflict Is Ultimately Theological," *Church Life Journal*, July 26, 2019, https://
churchlifejournal.nd.edu/articles/all-human-conflict-is-ultimately-theological/.
Vermeule's account of "sacramental liberalism" appears indebted to the work of the
Polish philosopher Ryszard Legutko. See Vermeule, "Liturgy of Liberalism," *First Things*,
January 2017. On Vermeule's background in administrative law and its influence on
his integralism, see James Chappel, "Nudging Toward Theocracy: Adrian Vermeule's War
on Liberalism," *Dissent*, Spring 2020, https://www.dissentmagazine.org/article/nudging-
towards-theocracy.

28. Vermeule, "Integration from Within."

29. Adrian Vermeule, "Beyond Originalism," *The Atlantic*, March 2020, https://www.theatlantic
.com/ideas/archive/2020/03/common-good-constitutionalism/609037/. Vermeule,
Common Good Constitutionalism: Recovering the Classical Legal Tradition (Cambridge: Polity
Press, 2022).

30. Vermeule, "Beyond Originalism."

31. Ibid.; *Common Good Constitutionalism*, 37.

32. "The general-welfare clause . . . is an obvious place to ground principles of common-good
constitutionalism (despite a liberal tradition of reading the clause in a cramped fashion),
as is the Constitution's preamble, with its references to general welfare and domestic tranquility, to the perfection of the union, and to justice" (Vermeule, "Beyond Originalism").
"Only when we read the Preamble against the backdrop of the classical tradition can we
see that, properly understood, it aims to constitute a political authority for the purpose of
promoting justice, peace ('tranquility'), and the flourishing of the res publica (the 'general
welfare'). . . . The fundamental teleological aims of government identified by the classical
tradition are also the aims of our constitutional order," Vermeule claims in *Common Good
Constitutionalism*, 38–39.

33. William J. Brennan Jr., "The Constitution of the United States: Contemporary Ratification," in *Interpreting the Constitution: The Debate over Original Intent*, ed. Jack N. Rakove
(Boston: Northeastern University Press, 1990), 23.

34. Vermeule, *Common Good Constitutionalism*, 37; Vermeule, "Beyond Originalism."

35. Vermeule, "Beyond Originalism." It is worth noting that Vermeule claimed that his "common-good constitutionalism draws inspiration from the early modern theory of *ragion di stato*" set forth by the Catholic writer Giovanni Botero.

36. Vermeule, *Common Good Constitutionalism*, 4, 2.

37. Ibid., 182.

38. It may be that here Vermeule was following the prudential advice of Botero. "Nothing is more hateful in governments than to change things which have acquired esteem through their antiquity," he quotes Botero as saying, recommending a ruler make incremental changes while respecting and maintaining forms and names. As Vermeule notes, "Botero sees the avoidance of flagrant disruption of tradition as important in the founding of new regimes as well as in their steady-state preservation." Vermeule, "All Human Conflict Is Ultimately Theological."

39. Ibid., 47, 52.

40. Vermeule, "Beyond Originalism." A hyperlink embedded in his passage takes the reader to a translation of Augustine's Letter 185 (his justification for the coercion of heretics).

41. Jason Blakely, "The Integralism of Adrian Vermeule," *Commonweal*, October 5, 2020, https://www.commonwealmagazine.org/not-catholic-enough.

42. Vermeule, "Beyond Originalism."

43. Vermeule, "Liberalism's Good and Faithful Servants," *Compact*, February 28, 2003, https://compactmag.com/article/liberalism-s-good-and-faithful-servants.

44. Adrian Vermeule, "Ralliement: Two Distinctions," The Josias, March 16, 2018, https://thejosias.com/2018/03/16/ralliement-two-distinctions/.

45. The journal *Compact* and the *Postliberal Order* Substack are prominent outlets for their work. The website The Josias, edited by Cistercian monk Father Edmund Waldstein, is a leading forum for the discussion of integralist arguments. As he described the theory, "Catholic Integralism is a tradition of thought that, rejecting the liberal separation of politics from concern with the end of human life, holds that pollical rule must order man to his final goal. Since, however, man has both a temporal and an eternal end, integralism holds that there are two powers that rule him: a temporal power and a spiritual power. And since man's temporal end is subordinated to his eternal end, the temporal power must be subordinated to the spiritual power." "Integralism in Three Sentences," The Josias, October 17, 2016, http://thejosias.com/2016/10/17/integralism-in-three-sentences/.

See also Thomas Crean and Adam Fimister, *Integralism: A Manual of Political Philosophy* (Neunkirchen-Seelschied: Editiones Scholasticae, 2020). For a critical analysis of integralism, see Kevin Vallier, *All the Kingdoms of the World: On Radical Religious Alternatives to Liberalism* (New York: Oxford University Press, 2023).

46. Michael Hanby, "For and Against Integralism," *First Things*, March 2020, https://www .firstthings.com/article/2020/03/for-and-against-integralism.

47. Gladdin Pappin, "From Conservatism to Postliberalism: The Right after 2020," *American Affairs* 4, no. 3 (Fall 2020): 174–90, https://americanaffairsjournal.org/2020/08/ from-conservatism-to-postliberalism-the-right-after-2020/.

48. Deneen, "Preface to the Paperback Edition," in *Why Liberalism Failed* (New Haven: Yale University Press, 2019), xxii–xxiv.

49. Deneen, *Why Liberalism Failed* (2018), xv. Patrick J. Deneen, *Regime Change: Toward a Post-liberal Future* (New York: Sentinel, 2023), xiii.

50. Deneen, *Regime Change*, xiv, 160, 95, 147.

51. Ibid., 59–60, 164–65, 168–84 (quotations at 180, 182–84).

52. Ibid., 184, 187, 225, 192–97, 228.

53. Ibid., 231–37 (quotation at 237).

54. Ahmari, "New American Right."

55. Patrick J. Deneen, "A Catholic Showdown Worth Watching," *American Conservative*, February 6, 2014, https://www.theamericanconservative.com/a-catholic-showdown-worth-watching/. Baskin, "Academia's Holy Warriors." Park MacDougald, "A Catholic Debate over Liberalism," *City Journal*, Winter 2000, https://www.city-journal.org/ catholic-debate-over-liberalism.

56. Adrian Vermeule, "A Principle of Immigration Priority," *Mirror of Justice* (blog), July 20, 2019, https://mirrorofjustice.blogs.com/mirrorofjustice/2019/07/a-principle-of-immigra-tion-priority-.html.

57. Rod Dreher, "What Do Integralists Want," *American Conservative*, October 27, 2021, https://www.theamericanconservative.com/dreher/what-do-integralists-want-reactionary-catholicism/.

58. James M. Patterson, "After Republican Virtue," *Law and Liberty*, April 22, 2020, https:// lawliberty.org/after-republican-virtue/.

59. Deneen, *Why Liberalism Failed* (2018), xiv, 178.

60. On evangelicals' engagement with and enduring commitment to Trump, see John Fea, *Believe Me: The Evangelical Road to Donald Trump* (Grand Rapids: Eerdmans, 2020); Katherine Stewart, *The Power Worshippers: Inside the Dangerous Rise of Religious Nationalism* (New York: Bloomsbury, 2019), 51–52; Sarah Posner, *Unholy: Why White Evangelicals Worship at the Altar of Donald Trump* (New York: Random House, 2020), 29–36; Anthea Butler, *White Evangelical Racism: The Politics of Morality in America* (Chapel Hill: University of North Carolina Press, 2021). On the "health and wealth gospel" and its "admiration of success," see George M. Marsden, *Fundamentalism and American Culture*, 3rd ed. (Oxford: Oxford University Press, 2022), 333–35.

61. Elizabeth Dias, "Christianity Will Have Power," *New York Times*, September 8, 2020, https://www.nytimes.com/2020/08/09/us/evangelicals-trump-christianity.html.

62. Lance Wallnau, "Why I Believe Trump Is the Prophesied President," Charisma News, October 5, 2016, https://www.charismanews.com/politics/opinion/60378-why-i-believe-trump-is-the-prophesied-president.

63. Steven E. Strang, *God and Donald Trump* (Lake Mary, FL: FrontLine, 2017). Hanne Amanda Trangerud, "The Trump Prophecies and the Mobilization of Evangelical Voters," *Studies in Religion / Sciences Religieuses* 51, no. 2 (June 2022): 202–22.

64. Peter Montgomery, "POTUS Shield: Trump's Dominionist Prayer Warriors and the 'Prophetic Order of the United States,'" Right Wing Watch, August 2017, https://www.rightwingwatch.org/report/potus-shield-trumps-dominionist-prayer-warriors-and-the-prophetic-order-of-the-united-states/. Brad Christerson and Richard Flory, *The Rise of Network Christianity: How Independent Leaders Are Changing the Religious Landscape* (New York: Oxford University Press, 2017). John Weaver, *The New Apostolic Reformation: History of a Modern Charismatic Movement* (Jefferson, NC: McFarland, 2016). Matthew D. Taylor, "Charismatic Revival Fury," Straight White American Jesus (podcast), https://www.straightwhiteamericanjesus.com/series/charismatic-revival-fury/. Matthew D. Taylor, *The Violent Take It by Force: Spiritual Warfare, Charismatic Evangelicals, and the Making of the Capitol Riot* (Minneapolis: Broadleaf Books, 2024).

65. Fea, *Believe Me*, 134–37.

66. "Executive Order on the Establishment of a White House Faith and Opportunity Initiative," The White House, May 3, 2018, https://trumpwhitehouse.archives.gov/presidential-actions/executive-order-establishment-white-house-faith-opportunity-initiative/.

67. David Brody, "On Air Force One with President Trump: 'Nobody's Done More for Christians or Evangelicals,'" CBN, November 1, 2018, https://www1.cbn.com/cbnnews/politics/2018/november/on-air-force-one-with-president-trump-nobodys-done-more-for-christians-or-evangelicals; Alia Shoaib, "Donald Trump Told a Christian TV Network That Nobody Had Done More for 'Christianity or for Evangelicals or for Religion Itself' Than Him," *Business Insider*, October 3, 2021, https://www.businessinsider.com/donald-trump-said-that-nobody-has-done-more-for-religion-than-him-2021-10.

On the religious dimension of January 6, 2021, see the collaborative digital project Uncivil Religion, https://uncivilreligion.org.

68. Sohrab Ahmari, "Against David French-ism," *First Things*, May 29, 2019, https://www.firstthings.com/web-exclusives/2019/05/against-david-french-ism. See also "Against the Dead Consensus," *First Things*, March 21, 2019, https://www.firstthings.com/web-exclusives/2019/03/against-the-dead-consensus; Sohrab Ahmari, "The New American Right: An Outline for a Post-Fusionist Conservatism," *First Things*, October 2019, https://www.firstthings.com/article/2019/10/the-new-american-right.

Dreher, by contrast, insisted that "the idea that someone as robustly vulgar, fiercely combative, and morally compromised as Trump will be an avatar for the restoration of Christian morality and social unity is beyond delusional. He is not the solution to the problem of America's cultural decline, but a symptom of it." He fretted, too, about the repercussions to the church of "the scandal of purported men of God appearing to be supporting an ungodly leader in exchange for power." *Benedict Option*, 79, 91, xvi.

69. Emma Green, "The Nationalists Take Washington," *The Atlantic*, July 17, 2019, https://www.theatlantic.com/politics/archive/2019/07/national-conservatism-conference/594202/. As it happened, both of those leading minds of contemporary anti-liberalism, Hazony and Deneen, were graduate students in political science around the same time at Rutgers University.

70. On the project of (re)instating the Hebrew Bible to its rightful place in Western philosophical tradition, see Yoram Hazony, *The Philosophy of Hebrew Scripture* (Cambridge: Cambridge University Press, 2012); quotes from 4, 41.

71. Yoram Hazony, *The Virtue of Nationalism* (New York: Basic Books, 2018), 19, 100, 76–79, 3, 94.

72. Hazony, *Virtue of Nationalism*, 240n9, though see the discussions of the time of the judges and the institution of the monarchy where Hazony expands on the Israelite theory of a limited state seeking "the good and the right," which distinguishes it from those of "all the nations" (*Philosophy of Hebrew Scripture*, 144–54). The Hebrew Bible contains five descriptions of the boundaries of the land promised to Abraham and to be conquered by the Israelites. Hazony would note that they all nevertheless describe a delimited territory and did not provide a warrant for an expansionist empire.

73. Hazony, *Virtue of Nationalism*, 21, 229.

74. Ibid., 220.

75. Ibid., 7, 23–28. Hazony conceded the British, Dutch, and later American empires "were all too ready to devise reasons for maintaining colonial empires based on the conquest and subjection of foreign peoples," a historical reality that effectively disturbs his national state / universal empire dichotomy.

76. Ibid., 3, 27–28.

77. Ibid., 30–31, 33, 233, 49. Hazony suggested Locke's treatise could be read "as a commentary on the Hebrew Bible," but not "an especially sound interpretation of the biblical teaching" (245n35).

78. Ibid., 167–76.

79. Ibid., 156–57.

80. In addition to "right-liberalism," Hazony dismissed as "plausible alternatives" the "neo-Catholic" theory of the Integralists, on account of its dependence on universal reason, ambivalence over the national state, and internationalist vision of a "new Christendom,"

thus inclining toward imperialism, as well as "neo-nationalist (or statist)" movements that, as descendants of the ideology of the French Revolution, unmoored from religion and cultural tradition, seek to bind the people to the state as "man's highest end," and thus incline toward authoritarianism. Ibid., 52–54.

81. Yoram Hazony, *Conservatism: A Rediscovery* (Washington, DC: Regnery Gateway, 2022), xx.

82. Ibid., 82–83, 33–34.

83. Hazony minimalized the reality of pluralism in the period, citing as the Constitution's "nationalist framework" John Jay's claim of a more or less homogeneous society in *Federalist* No. 2 ("Providence has been pleased to give this one connected country to one united people—a people descended from the same ancestors, speaking the same language, professing the same religion, attached to the same principles of government, very similar in their manners and customs"), rather than Madison's argument in *Federalist* No. 10 about how a republic could work in a large and diverse society by playing faction against faction. In any event, whatever John Jay might have said about the populace in 1787, by the mid-nineteenth century it was certainly no longer the case that the American people remained as he had described them. Ibid., 44–45.

84. In *The Virtue of Nationalism*, Hazony suggested that "American independence" was justified less by "the relatively mild forms of abuse" that the colonists suffered under British rule than by the geographical distance that separated them (171).

85. Hazony, *Conservatism*, xx, 82–83, 341; see also his discussion in *Virtue of Nationalism*, 160–61.

86. Hazony, *Conservatism*, 333–35.

87. Ibid., 262.

88. Hazony, *Conservatism*, 263–64, 267–69.

89. Ibid., 272–73, 296–310. Hazony contended that William F. Buckley Jr. redefined "conservatism" by bringing anti-Communist liberals (now calling themselves "libertarians") into an alliance with true conservatives. A prudent coalition builder, Buckley retained nationalists and traditionalists while barring such libertarian "radicals" as Ayn Rand and Murray Rothbard. (Hazony did not mention Buckley's handling of the John Birch Society or his break with L. Brent Bozell.) For his condemnation of post–Cold War neoconservatism, see Hazony's 2019 address to the National Conservatism Conference in Washington, DC, available at "A Conference in Washington, DC, July 14–16, 2019: Yoram Hazony," National Conservatism, https://nationalconservatism.org/natcon-dc-2019/presenters/yoram-hazony/.

90. Hazony, *Conservatism*, 307. In his NatCon 2019 address, Hazony complained about the catastrophe brought about by the privatization (and uprooting) of religion: "It turns out it was God and Scripture that was holding in place the entire set of structures. Not

reason; tradition. You throw out Christianity and the Jewish contribution to it . . . and within two generations people can't tell the difference between a man and a woman. They can't tell the difference between a foreigner and a citizen. They can't tell the difference between this side of the border and the other side of the border." "A Conference in Washington."

91. Hazony, *Conservatism*, 208–10, 340–44, 251.

92. Ibid., 191, 194–96, 200, 203, 205–6.

93. Ibid., xx, 250–51; on repentance (*teshuva*) as a return to religious tradition, see 382.

94. Hazony, *Conservatism*, 75, 249, 252–53.

95. Ibid., 341–42, 337, 345–46.

96. Others in the broader National Conservative camp would develop and advance more Christ-centric, or Christian nationalist, proposals. For a particularly controversial example of theorizing from a Reformed Protestant perspective, see Stephen Wolfe, *The Case for Christian Nationalism* (Moscow, ID: Canon Press, 2022). "A pioneering work . . . relentlessly innovative," reads the front-cover endorsement from Hazony. The book, which has also been promoted on the National Conservatism website, recommends that Westerners turn from universalism and the current "gynocracy" and instead "become more exclusive and ethnic-focused" (459) under the rule of a "Christian prince" who would support the church and suppress and punish heresy. For a Christian critique of such efforts, see Paul D. Miller, *The Religion of American Greatness: What's Wrong with Christian Nationalism* (Downers Grove, IL: InterVarsity Press, 2022).

97. Hazony, *Conservatism*, 346. In a note in the autobiographical section of *Conservatism*, Hazony recalled, curiously without commentary, a private conversation in which Irving Kristol suggested "as a matter of political theory" that voting rights in Christian-majority countries ought to be restricted to Christians, and in a Jewish-majority country to Jews. Becoming part of the political community could be achieved by adopting its public religion (435). Interestingly in this regard, in *The Virtue of Nationalism* Hazony lamented that the Christian national states of the past (including the United States) had "placed a variety of barriers before the participation of Jews in national life," practices that Hazony said "we would and should find objectionable" (28).

98. "National Conservatism: A Statement of Principles," Edmund Burke Foundation, June 15, 2022, https://nationalconservatism.org/wp-content/uploads/mailings/2022/statement/.

99. Deneen, *Regime Change*, 220–21.

100. Cf. Hazony, *Conservatism*, 340–44. Cathy Young, "About that 'National Conservatism' Statement," *The Bulwark*, June 22, 2022, https://www.thebulwark.com/about-that-national-conservatism-statement-of-principles/. Kathryn Joyce, " 'National Conservative' Manifesto: A Road Map for Autocracy—and It's Not Just Theoretical," *Salon*, June 24,

2022, https://www.salon.com/2022/06/24/national-conservative-manifesto-a-plan-for-fascism--but-its-not-hypothetical/.

101. "National Conservatism: A Statement of Principles."

102. Hazony, *Conservatism*, 344–47. Hazony did not explain how those US Supreme Court decisions affected church-state relations in those "other Western nations."

103. George Washington, "Farewell Address, 19 September 1796," Founders Online, National Archives, https://founders.archives.gov/documents/Washington/05-20-02-0440-0002. (Original source: *The Papers of George Washington, Presidential Series*, vol. 20, *1 April–21 September 1796*, ed. David R. Hoth and William M. Ferraro [Charlottesville: University of Virginia Press, 2019], 703–22.)

104. See, for example, the correspondences collected at "George Washington to Religious Organizations," George Washington's Mount Vernon, accessed January 9, 2024, https://www.mountvernon.org/george-washington/religion/george-washington-to-religious-organizations/.

105. "From George Washington to the Clergy of Newport, Rhode Island, 18 August 1790," Founders Online, National Archives, https://founders.archives.gov/documents/Washington/05-06-02-0132. (Original source: *The Papers of George Washington, Presidential Series*, vol. 6, *1 July 1790–30 November 1790*, ed. Mark A. Mastromarino [Charlottesville: University Press of Virginia, 1996], 279–82.)

106. "From George Washington to the Hebrew Congregation in Newport, Rhode Island, 18 August 1790," Founders Online, National Archives, https://founders.archives.gov/documents/Washington/05-06-02-0135. (Original source: *Papers of George Washington, Presidential Series*, 6:284–86.)

107. "From George Washington to the Hebrew Congregation in Newport, Rhode Island, 18 August 1790."

Moses Seixas also prepared a letter to Washington on behalf of King David's Lodge of Free and Accepted Masons, to which the president also sent a reply in August. "From George Washington to the Masons of King David's Lodge, Newport, Rhode Island, 18 August 1790," Founders Online, National Archives, https://founders.archives.gov/documents/Washington/05-06-02-0136. (Original source: *Papers of George Washington, Presidential Series*, 6:287–88.)

Conclusion

1. Bruce Lincoln, *Holy Terrors: Thinking about Religion after September 11* (Chicago: University of Chicago Press, 2003), 51–61.

2. Peter L. Berger, *The Heretical Imperative: Contemporary Possibilities of Religious Affirmation* (Garden City, NY: Anchor, 1979), 28–29.

"One way of describing a liberal democracy is as an order in which heresy is just another opinion." Leon Wieseltier, "Christianism," *Liberties* 2, no. 3 (Spring 2022): 351. The article is a particularly spirited critique of the neo-integralist vision: 326–63.

3. "Modeling the Future of Religion in America," Pew Research Center, September 13, 2022, https://www.pewresearch.org/religion/2022/09/13/modeling-the-future-of-religion-in-america/.

And yet, another 2022 Pew survey found that 45 percent of Americans believed that the United States ought to be a "Christian Nation" today—but they held varying opinions about what the term actually meant. Of those, 28 percent agreed that "the federal government should declare the U.S. a Christian nation," and 31 percent that "the federal government should stop enforcing the separation of church and state." (Of all those surveyed, only 15 percent said that "the federal government should declare the U.S. a Christian nation," and 19 percent that it "should stop enforcing the separation of church and state.") Gregory A. Smith, Michael Rotolo, and Patricia Tevington, "45% of Americans Say U.S. Should Be a 'Christian Nation,'" Pew Research Center, October 2022, https://www.pewresearch.org/religion/2022/10/27/45-of-americans-say-u-s-should-be-a-christian-nation/.

For a study of the "nones" (atheists, agnostics, and those who report their religion is "nothing in particular"), including their beliefs, attitudes toward traditional religions, and level of civil engagement, see Gregory A. Smith et al., "Religious 'Nones' in America: Who They Are and What They Believe," Pew Research Center, January 2024, https://www.pewresearch.org/religion/2024/01/24/religious-nones-in-america-who-they-are-and-what-they-believe/.

Acknowledgments

This book is the result of some five years of research and many more of reflection. It is, in many respects, a study of complaints. It is a pleasure to express my appreciation for the individuals and institutions who made it possible.

The Berkley Center for Religion, Peace, and World Affairs at Georgetown University provided an institutional home base as I set off on this journey. I thank its staff and particularly its executive director, Michael J. Kessler. In 2019, I was privileged to have been awarded a Jefferson Fellowship at the Smithsonian Institution's National Museum of American History to support my research. I am indebted to the librarians at the Library of Congress, Geneva College, and the University of Virginia who replied to my queries without delay and located, scanned, and dispatched articles, book chapters, and some largely forgotten nineteenth-century pamphlets.

My thinking on religion, politics, and America has been profoundly shaped through my engagement with an array of intellectual confidants and sparring partners. Many thanks to Peter Manseau, a faithful fellow traveler on the winding road of religion in America. Philip Gorski has been a fabulous conversation partner on American civil religion and its discontents. John E. Finn, who first introduced me as a college sophomore at Wesleyan University to some of the problems of political theory that this book engages, read draft upon draft and provided insights, trenchant comments, and much enthusiasm. Laura K. Field, Ger FitzGerald, Samuel Goldman, Benjamin Leff, Martyn Oliver, and Ariel Sabar offered themselves as sounding boards, bestowing valuable suggestions and helping me clarify my thoughts. Their contributions reverberate throughout these pages. I have been fortunate to have an exceptional group of interlocutors—Anthea Butler, Julie Ingersoll, Kathryn Joyce, Peter Montgomery, Sarah Posner, and Adele Stan. Our conversations on difficult books and the contemporary situation (often complemented by Doug Wolfe's beautifully crafted cocktails) have challenged my presuppositions and often pointed me in new and unexpected directions.

During the course of my research, I consulted with a number of scholars who generously took the time to speak with me about their areas of expertise; several kindly read drafts of chapters and offered helpful suggestions. I'd like to extend my thanks to Seth Cotlar, Daniel L. Dreisbach, Massimo Faggioli, Nathan Lassen Jones, Michael J. McVicar, Patrick Q. Mason, Benjamin E. Park, James Patterson, Gregory Prince, S. Scott Rohrer, Matthew Rose, Robert Cady Saler, and Matthew D. Taylor. I have also profited tremendously from conversations with Michael J. Altman, Steven Beller, Jacques Berlinerblau, Evan Berry, Max Bodach, Brian Britt, Sam Brody, David Buckley, Shaun Casey, E. J. Dionne, Kevin Eckstrom, Brian Epstein, Tom Ferguson, Cass Fisher, Grace Y. Kao, Shaul Magid, Charles Matthews, Andrew R. Murphy, Erik Owens, Elizabeth Palmer, Benjamin E. Sax, Mark Silk, Sarah Skwire, Sarah Riccardi-Swartz, Nelson Tebbe, Julian G. Waller, and Robert Yelle.

My agent, Amanda Annis, encouraged me to take on this project and has been a constant advocate through its joys and challenges. I am deeply grateful to Jennifer Banks, my editor at Yale University Press, for her judgment, patience, and support of this project at every stage, to her editorial team for helping pull it all together, and to Ryan Davis for his sensitive and meticulous work copyediting the manuscript.

Many friends have supported and sustained me as I labored on this book—with advice, encouragement, and camaraderie. I am grateful to all those who have indulged me as I described the project, rehearsed its arguments, and sometimes breathlessly reported what I had recently learned. I would like especially to thank Sidney Blumenthal, Ada Brunstein, Marland Buckner, Peter Calafiura, Renée Carl, Whitney Fisler, Ira N. Forman, Zac Hill, Holly and Jason Huffnagel, Karen and Nik Kaludov, Amy Lillis, Marz and Bruce McNamer, Kareema Mitchell-Allen, Martha Norton, Jeremy Sacks, and James E. Young.

And to Mom, Andrew, Nadine and Jeremy, Aaron and Jenna—who I know continually wondered how this book was coming along (and only on occasion asked out loud)—my love and gratitude is simply beyond expression.

Index